EUROPEAN BANKING LAW: THE BANKER–CUSTOMER RELATIONSHIP

Series Consultant Editor
Prof. Joseph J. Norton, S.J.D, D.Phil.

ALSO IN THIS SERIES:

EUROPEAN BANKING LAW: THE BANKER–CUSTOMER RELATIONSHIP

EDITED BY

ROSS CRANSTON

Visiting Professor of Commercial Law, London School of Economics and Political Science
Formerly Director of the Centre for Commercial Law Studies
Queen Mary and Westfield College, University of London

SECOND EDITION

PUBLISHED JOINTLY WITH
THE CENTRE FOR COMMERCIAL LAW STUDIES
AND THE LONDON INSTITUTE OF INTERNATIONAL
BANKING, FINANCE AND DEVELOPMENT LAW

LONDON   HONG KONG
1999

LLP Reference Publishing
69–77 Paul Street
London EC2A 4LQ
Great Britain

EAST ASIA
LLP Asia
Sixth Floor, Hollywood Centre
233 Hollywood Road
Hong Kong

First published in Great Britain 1993

Second edition 1999

British Library Cataloguing in Publication Data

A catalogue record
for this book is available
from the British Library

ISBN 1–85978–691–X

Text set 10 on 12 pt Linotron 202 Sabon by
Mendip Communications Ltd.
Frome, Somerset
Printed in Great Britain by
WBC Ltd.
Bridgend, Mid-Glamorgan

CONTENTS

CONTENTS

CHAPTER 8. SWEDEN *Krister Moberg*

CHAPTER 10. EUROPEAN AND GLOBAL HARMONISATION OF THE LAW OF BANKING TRANSACTIONS *Uwe H. Schneider*

CONTRIBUTORS

LODEWIJK J. HIJMANS VAN DEN BERGH, Advocaat, De Brauw Blackstone Westbroek, Amsterdam.

WILLIAM BLAIR QC, 3, Verulam Buildings, Gray's Inn, London; Visiting Professorial Fellow, Centre for Commercial Law Studies; Visiting Professor, London School of Economics and Political Science.

PASCALE BLOCH, Professor of Law, University of Paris XIII; Director, Institut de recherche de droit des affaires (IRDA), Villetaneuse, France.

FERNANDO SANCHEZ CALERO, Chaired Professor of Law, Universidad Complutense, Madrid; Estudio Juridico Sánchez Calero, Madrid, Spain.

SIMONETTA COTTERLI PhD, EUI-FIESOLE.

ROSS CRANSTON QC, Visiting Professor of Commercial Law, London School of Economics and Political Science; formerly Director, Centre for Commercial Law Studies.

NORBERT HORN, Professor of Law and Director, The Banking Law Institute and The Law Centre for European and International Cooperation (RIZ), University of Cologne, Germany.

KRISTER MOBERG, Associate Professor, Faculty of Law, University of Lund, Sweden.

†CHRISTIAN MOULY, Late Professor of Law, University of Montpellier; Member of the Bar, Narbonne, France.

JOSEPH J. NORTON, Sir John Lubbock Professor of Banking Law, Centre for Commercial Law Studies; Professor of Banking Law, Southern Methodist University, Dallas, Texas.

UWE H. SCHNEIDER, Professor of Law, University of Darmstadt; Director of the Center for German and International Law of Financial Services at the Johannes Gutenberg University of Mainz, Germany.

GEOFFREY YEOWART, Partner, Lovell White Durrant, London.

TABLE OF CASES

TABLE OF LEGISLATION

Figures in **bold** *indicate where the text of the Legislation has been set out*

xxiii

CHAPTER 1

INTRODUCTION[1]

European banking law is a broad subject. European banking regulation has received some attention,[2] but little has been written about the European private law of banking transactions. One aspect of the latter is the law governing the banker–customer relationship. Rooted in contract, the relationship is overlaid with a range of rights and obligations having their derivation in tort (delict), notions of equity and good faith, and statute.

THE BASIC BANKER–CUSTOMER RELATIONSHIP

Central to the banker–customer relationship in all European jurisdictions is contract. The banker–customer relationship is rarely reduced to the one document, however, but instead comprises a variety of written forms, supplemented by terms implied by law. Typically, a standard form contract will govern specific aspects of the banker–customer relationship, whether it be the general account, electronic funds transfers or security (including guarantees). In places like Germany, the Netherlands and Switzerland there are general banking conditions, drawn up by associations of banks.[3] Exceptionally in Britain banks have not had a standard form contract for the general account and the parameters of the relationship have been set by a series of terms which the courts have implied over the years. British banks have adopted a code of practice for banks dealing with personal customers;[4] it is not of itself legally binding but the courts may well use it as a base for implying terms into the banker–customer relationship.

There is more scope with the standard form contracts, general banking conditions, and British code for incorporation of the customer viewpoint in their

1. Since commissioning the subsequent chapters, I have moved from the academic to the political world. I should make clear that the views expressed by the contributing authors whose chapters follow do not necessarily reflect my own views as editor.
2. e.g. R. Cranston (ed.), *The Single Market and the Law of Banking*, 2nd edn (1995); J. Norton (ed.), *Bank Regulation and Supervision in the 1990s* (1991). See also the series Legislazioni Bancarie Dei Paesi Della Comunità Europea published under the auspices of the Associazione Bancaria Italiana.
3. The German General Business Conditions are reproduced in Appendix 1.
4. See Appendix 2.

drafting. One approach is that adopted in the Netherlands: there representatives of customers negotiate directly with the banks.[5] Another approach—at the other end of the spectrum—is regulation: the state acts as a surrogate for the customer and compels banks to meet standards purportedly in the customer interest. By contrast with Europe, the banker–customer relationship in the United States is more heavily infected with regulation.[6] This is not to say that regulation is unknown in Europe; in Sweden, for example, the Finance Inspection Board has made important rulings relevant to aspects of the basic relationship.[7] In various jurisdictions regulation of unfair contract terms, now reinforced in the European Community by the Unfair Terms in Consumer Contracts Directive, has a more general impact on the banker–customer relationship.

Perhaps unsurprisingly, stress has arisen over the same sort of issues in the banker–customer relationship in the different European jurisdictions. Is a bank statement binding on customers if they do not object to its contents within a specified period? May a bank vary the terms of the relationship without agreement and/or without notice to customers? What services is a bank obliged to provide and, generally, what can it charge for its services? How enforceable is a guarantee or security given by a person for the business debts of a spouse or other close relation? The answers to these questions are not uniform across jurisdictions, and in any one jurisdiction subtle rephrasing of the issue may produce a different response.

Banks in many countries adhere to one or more interbank agreements which have implications for the banker–customer relationship. These may not be incorporated directly in the banker–customer contract; indeed, customers may not even be aware of their existence. Typical are the interbank agreements on payment. Of wider import is the Italian interbank agreement, and related codes, which are designed to ensure transparency in the price of banking services and the content of bank statements.[8] The recent British Banking Code falls into the same category, although it is more ambitious, covering a range of matters from information to be provided to customers to standards of service. Interbank agreements are often binding between the banks themselves, as a matter of contract. But to what extent do they confer or subtract from the rights of customers? In Italy, for example, the interbank agreement is regarded as binding on banks in their relationship with customers because it gives content to the principle of good faith in article 1375 of the Civil Code. There can be no objection to this result when advantages are being conferred on customers, but surely there must be limits on the extent to which interbank arrangements can bind customers to their detriment. Unfortunately, this issue has been given little attention.

5. Below, p. 110.
6. Below, Ch. 9.
7. Below, Ch. 8.
8. Below, p. 89.

CONFIDENTIALITY[9]

All European jurisdictions recognise a form of bank confidentiality, in which banks are legally compelled to keep the financial affairs of their customers secret. Although as a matter of policy bank confidentiality is based on the customer's right of privacy, conceptually it tends to have other derivations. This discrepancy can lead to privacy being breached with the law's sanction. An example is the so-called status opinion, where a trader will obtain information about the financial standing of another trader through the banking system. In France this breach of confidentiality is legally acceptable because the banker is said to be giving simply *"l'opinion de la place"*.[10]

Multifunctional banking is one reason why confidentiality is under attack at present: banks distribute information throughout the corporate group so that the whole range of bank services can be marketed to customers, albeit that this may be in breach of the principle. The other, and more defensible, reason that bank confidentiality is currently being undermined is because the banking system has been used for fraudulent and criminal activity. Money laundering is at the top of regulators' agenda, but other concerns include tax evasion, securities violations and insolvency offences.[11] Disclosure of information to regulators from other jurisdictions has given rise to a considerable number of problems, many of which have still to be resolved.

THE MULTIFUNCTIONAL BANK

No European country has yet adequately addressed all the conflicts of interest thrown up by the multifunctional bank, even those countries such as Germany that have long had universal banking. Yet the potential conflicts are legion. For example: a bank recommends to or effects for a customer a purchase of securities, the issue of which is being underwritten by the bank; similarly, where the transaction relates to an issue of securities of a company and the bank is a substantial creditor of the company, or is a financial adviser to the company, or is advising someone who is contemplating a substantial acquisition of securities in the company. The assumption seems to have been that competition will act as the regulator, driving customers from banks abusing their position. Reliance may also have been placed on agency law: an agent must not use his or her position to acquire benefits for himself at the expense of his principal (conflict of interest and duty). Therefore a bank instructed to buy a certain quantity of securities cannot buy on its own account. If it does, it must account for the profits. But agency law is not easily applied to the multifunctional bank. One

9. See also D. Campbell (ed.), *International Bank Secrecy* (1992); F. Neate and R. McCormick (eds), *Bank Confidentiality* (1990), both of which survey the law of various jurisdictions.
10. Below, p. 42.
11. See e.g., F. Baldwin and R. Munro, *International and Domestic Money Laundering*, looseleaf.

theoretical problem is knowledge: can the knowledge of its different parts be attributed to the business as a whole, even if one part does not know in fact what another part knows, and especially if there are barriers such as Chinese Walls which have prevented the free flow of information? And there are also problems at the level of practice; for example, it is not always very easy to distinguish the case where a bank acts as agent for its customer from the case where the bank buys securities in its own name and subsequently resells them to the customer.

The ordinary law has sometimes treated disclosure as a solution to the problem of conflicts of interest. Make full disclosure of the conflict to the customer, and the bank is absolved of any wrongdoing. Yet disclosure of a conflict of interest may be in breach of a duty to another customer. The bank advising customer A to invest in the securities of customer B, whose financial health is dubious, should disclose that fact to A—but to do that would be in breach of the duty of confidentiality to B. If, as in this case, disclosure is a breach of duty to another, it may be that the bank must desist completely from acting. In the situation referred to, therefore, the bank would have to inform the client or customer that it was unable to advise or assist. The difficulty arises, of course, if one department of a multifunctional bank does not know that there is a conflict of interest as a result of what another department is doing. A Chinese Wall may be in operation, designed to achieve ignorance on the part of particular parts of a bank as to what the other parts are doing. A strict application of the rule "disclose or desist", however, means that the existence of a Chinese Wall is not sufficient. The bank must take positive steps to ensure that there is disclosure, where this is permissible, or desist from acting. Such positive steps would include the American restricted list procedure, where the bank would make no recommendations about, and would not deal in, the securities of a company, either on its own account or on a discretionary basis, as soon as it enters into a close business relationship with that company.

Only recently has regulatory law in Europe grappled with conflict of interest problems.[12] The criminalisation of insider dealing is an example, although it misses a great deal of the informational and positional advantages which can give rise to conflicts of interest. Obligations in company legislation on insiders to disclose share holdings and criminal prohibitions on concealing information and creating a false market are also relevant. European countries are now developing an elaborate system of investor protection, in broad outline inspired by the US system of securities regulation. Detailed rules may prescribe acceptable behaviour for a bank engaged in securities activity; breach can be a disciplinary offence and can ultimately lead to a bank's having its authorisation to engage in such activity withdrawn. Objections may legitimately be raised, however, about the ambit and force of such rules. Generally speaking, Chinese

---

12. See generally K. Hopt, "Inside Information and Conflicts of Interests of Banks and other Financial Intermediaries in European Law", in K. Hopt and E. Wymeersch (eds), *European Insider Dealing* (1991).

Walls are, for example, treated as an absolute defence when "disclose or desist" may be the better response.

LIABILITY FOR ADVICE

Advice can be given to customers or to third parties. At one time, liability to third parties—such as those seeking credit assessments of another through their own bank—foundered on the absence of contract. Now tortious (or delictual) liability enables third parties to sue banks for negligent advice, as well as for fraudulent advice. A contractual nexus may still be necessary, however, in the case of innocent misrepresentation.

Conceptually, liability of banks for advice arises in at least three ways— advice *mala fide*, negligent advice, and the failure to advise when there is a duty to do so. (The failure to advise of a conflict of interest where there is a duty to do so has already been addressed.) The first is uncommon but not unknown. Little need be said about fraud except that in Europe (by contrast with the United States) there seems to be some reluctance to allege fraud against banks and a difficulty in proving it. Omissions, so that advice is really a misrepresentation, may also give rise to liability.

At one time it was said in some jurisdictions that a bank could not be liable for negligent advice given by its officers, since it was not a banking function to give advice. But even before banks began to promote themselves as financial advisers it was unrealistic to divorce advice from banking; advice has always been intimately linked with the taking and lending of money. In any event, the reasoning was surely flawed if grounded on the law of agency: a principal must be liable for the wrongs of an agent if the agent does what can be expected even if (unbeknown to the third party) it is prohibited from doing it. A more serious legal obstacle has been the reluctance in some jurisdictions to impose non-contractual liability for economic loss disassociated from physical injury. The potential enormity of recoverable damages is perceived as the major obstacle. Whatever the general problem with "pure" economic loss, however, the extent of the liability consequent on negligent advice is bounded—the money itself and the profit which may have been generated through its employment elsewhere. It is not surprising, therefore, that in these jurisdictions negligent advice has been carved out as an exception to the rule that there is no liability for pure economic loss.

Liability for negligent advice is imposed irrespective of whether it is given gratuitously. Clearly this is right in principle if the aim is compensating for loss, although it is fair to add that until recently economic exchange has generally been a prerequisite to civil liability; thus the defective gift did not lead to the donor having to pay damages whereas if a good was sold, sales law would have imposed that result. Of course, the reality is that, while a bank may not make a specific charge for advice, it is not done without benefit to the bank; the bank may provide one of its services as a result or, at the other end of the spectrum, simply retain a satisfied customer.

Some jurisdictions draw a distinction between a bank passing on information about, say, a potential investment and a bank actually giving advice on that investment. Liability is not imposed in the case of the former, albeit that it may be in the case of the latter, the justification being that a conduit should not be made responsible for what is transmitted through it. The reasoning is fallacious: the retailer has long been held liable in contract for defective mass produced goods, even though it does not have the opportunity of examining them as they pass along the distribution chain started by the manufacturer. Moreover, the bank passing on information is not analogous to a telephone line; there can be no strict dichotomy between passing on information and giving advice. At the least, a bank passing on information is giving some imprimatur to the contents, unless this is expressly disclaimed. How else is its act to be construed? This does not mean that the bank's negligence is necessarily equated to the negligence (if there be any) of the person preparing the information. Depending on the circumstances, its responsibility may arise in law only in its choice of the source.

It would seem right as a matter of policy for a bank to be able to avoid the consequences of giving negligent advice by suitable notice to those receiving it. Whether this is regarded conceptually as aborting liability or as exempting from liability already begotten is beside the point. The central issue in practice should be whether the disclaimer of, or exemption from, liability has been made clear to those being advised so they are in no doubt that the bank is washing its hands of the consequences of the advice proving inappropriate or wrong. Thus a small print clause in a document given to those being advised is unlikely to satisfy this test.

In what circumstances do banks have a duty to advise, so that if they do not do so liability is imposed on them? There is some reluctance in common and civil law systems to impose liability for omissions; in the present context the liberal assumption that dealings are between equal and equally knowledgeable parties dies hard, whatever the reality. Circumstances must be special before a failure to act becomes culpable. In the context of advice, there are examples of a manifestly unequal relationship, or one of fidelity and trust, triggering a duty to act. The differing conceptual bases need not concern us. More interesting is a series of cases, not yet a stream, but sufficient for the banks to be concerned about staunching their source, where courts have held them to have failed their customers in not advising them adequately, or at all, about high risk transactions involving foreign currency, derivatives and the like. The US jurisprudence is, as ever, in the forefront, but on particular occasions other jurisdictions have been as creative.[13]

---

13. Below, Ch. 9. See also R. Cranston (ed.), *Banks, Liability and Risk*, 2nd edn (1995), *passim*.

CONSUMER PROTECTION

Specific consumer protection for bank customers is a rarity. However, both Britain and Spain have banking ombudsmen, although ombudsmen in other jurisdictions handle banking complaints. Several EC initiatives on funds transfers have led to consumer protection measures in the Member States. At the regulatory level it can be argued that prudential supervision ensures a sound banking system and thus protection for customers. In particular, deposit guarantee and protection schemes give some comfort to customers in the event—thankfully, not as frequent as in the United States and elsewhere—that banks fail. Competition law may also be said to have a role in furthering the consumer interest, although the entry of foreign competitors may be a more effective stimulus to price and service competition. Usury laws, which limit interest charged on loans, have gone by the board in Europe, although disclosure of interest and charges features prominently in the consumer credit laws of the different countries (which in some respects have been brought into line in the EC as a result of Directives). The counterpart of consumer credit disclosure— disclosure by the bank of interest and charges payable to depositors—is less developed in most jurisdictions.

As we have seen, general banking conditions, drawn up by associations of banks, have long been a feature of some European countries. Elsewhere, contracts such as guarantees have by their nature always been in writing. The introduction of electronic funds transfers has led banks across Europe to prepare standard terms for their customers. Judicial and legislative control of standard form contracts apply in theory to banks. Judicial control has operated by construing ambiguities in the banks' contracts against them and by invoking doctrines which in broad terms attack inequality of bargaining power. Legislative control has largely replaced judicial control, although the courts are the instruments by which the legislative goal is achieved. In some European countries the solution to standard clauses is in part administrative.[14]

Control of standard term banking contracts has been given impetus by the EC Directive on Unfair Terms in Consumer Contracts.[15] Potentially this strikes at a number of standard clauses in banking contracts which could be said to violate the reasonable expectations of customers. One example is the clause which renders a bank statement conclusive if a customer fails to object within a set period, say 30 days, despite the notorious inability of many customers (at least if the experience of the present writer is anything to go by) so to organise their lives that bank statements are diligently and regularly checked. Another example is the clause which enables the bank to vary the contract at will: it may be that

---

14. See, e.g., N. Reich and H. Micklitz, *Consumer Legislation in the EC Countries* (1980), pp. 161–184; H. Beale, "Unfair Contracts in Britain and Europe" [1989] *Current Legal Problems* 197.

15. Directive 93/13, [1993] OJ L95/29. See M. Tenreiro, "The Community Directive on Unfair Terms and National Legal Systems" (1995) 3 *Eur. R. Priv. L.* 273.

customers reasonably expect their bank to have a right to vary the interest rate, but not the entire contract without adequate notice.

Consumer protection measures need to be concerned as much with raising standards of banking service as with resolving individual complaints. Administrative machinery is the essential twin of the judicial and legislative process; the Swedish example is instructive in this respect. Cross-border banking transactions are becoming more common among ordinary consumers. EC measures in areas of consumer credit, electronic funds transfer and unfair contract terms are a step in the right direction (as well as raising standards in most jurisdictions). There still remain problems for consumers that are not always satisfactorily resolvable by principles of private international law.

SECURITY

Security is one area of the law where the variation between European countries is considerable, yet banks typically wish to take security, even if only personal security, by way of guarantee. There are exceptions, such as international banking, where security is unusual either because banks have been confident (in the event, wrongly) of repayment and of their assessment of creditworthiness, or were prevented by the nature of the borrower from taking it (much lending to governments).

Banks feel safest when they have security over land and buildings. All European legal systems recognise this type of security, as well as pledge, although pledge is sometimes confined to actual or constructive possession of goods. Legal inventiveness in some jurisdictions has enabled forms of security over tangible movables not in the possession of a bank.[16] Moreover, security may also be possible over intangible movables—documents of title to goods and company securities (i.e. their stocks and shares).[17] Security over bank accounts is possible in some jurisdictions; contractual set-off may produce the same result.[18]

Because of the differences between European countries' law on security, it is an area where harmonisation is likely to proceed at a snail's pace. The European Community made one attempt at harmonising retention of title clauses, at the time when they burst upon the Europe-wide stage (although they had been quietly used in some countries before that), but that attempt soon lost steam.[19] Law reformers occasionally invoke Article 9 of the Uniform Commercial Code of the United States as a guidepost for rationalising security interests and

16. As well as below, see M. Dickson, W. Rosener, P. Storm, *Security on Movable Property and Receivables in Europe* (1988).

17. The possible confusion between security and securities in the English language recalls the message sent by General Sir Charles Napier in 1843 to announce his conquest of the Sind, in north-west India—the one word, in Latin, *peccavi*—I have sinned (Sind).

18. F. Neate (ed.), *Using Set-Off as Security* (1990) surveys the law in eleven jurisdictions.

19. Draft Proposal for a Council Directive on the legal consequences of agreements creating simply reservation of title to goods, Commission of the EC, Directorate-General for Internal Market and Industrial Affairs, III/872/79–EN.

providing a model for how they ought to be registered. Unlike Canada, Europe is unlikely to tread this path in the near future.

ENVIRONMENTAL LIABILITY

Lawyers hoping to generate work from banks these days may well use the phrase "environmental liability of banks" rather liberally. For good measure, an atrocity story from the United States may be related of how banks have been held liable for environmental clean-up. In the absence of statutory intervention, however, bank liability for the environmental damage caused by their customers or borrowers is only a remote possibility in Europe. The clearest situation where banks might be held liable is if they take possession of land when exercising their rights to security. In the worst case, unbeknown to them the land may contain nuclear or other hazardous waste. Consideration of whether liability may also arise for a bank because of its membership of the borrower's board or its interference in its management will also be found in the following pages.

THE FUTURE?

Certainly there is some convergence in Europe in the law relating to the banker–customer relationship. That convergence is nothing like what has been achieved in bank regulation as a result of the work of the Basle Committee on banking regulations and of the directives of the European Community. Moreover, it is a convergence in outcome rather than in the means to that outcome; the different statutory and judicial methods remain as divergent as ever.

The pressures to convergence will continue. In all countries banks face similar demands for more accountability and better service. European Community initiatives in consumer credit, unfair contract terms and electronic funds transfers are bearing fruit. Legal transplanting will continue, often unnoticed and unacknowledged, both within Europe and from outside (US developments are sometimes the important stimulus). International regulatory efforts will remain as a catalyst for change in domestic law—the drive against money-laundering and its impact on opening accounts and bank confidentiality are illustrative.[20] In all, it has never been a livelier time for banking lawyers.

ROSS CRANSTON

20. See generally A. Hirsch, "Worldwide Legal Harmonization of Banking Law and Securities Regulation", in R. Buxbaum, G. Hertig, A. Hirsch, K. Hopt (eds), *European Business Law* (1991).

CHAPTER 2

ENGLAND

INTRODUCTION

From the point of view of the English banker, the salient reality of the early 1990s was economic recession. This, in turn, placed strains on the relationship between banker and customer. But there have been other pressures of a more specific kind that have contributed to a redefining of the legal nature of the relationship: consumer rights have been taken up by politicians of all persuasions; environmentalists have focused on the liability of lenders for the polluting activities of their borrowers; banks have been expected to police the financial system to avoid money-laundering and the like. At the same time, the business of banks themselves has changed, with the sale of ancillary financial services such as insurance and investment services heavily promoted through the branch network.

This chapter considers aspects of the banker–customer relationship under English law.[1] The legal content of the relationship was the subject of unprecedented scrutiny in the form of a Review Committee on Banking Law and Practice set up by the Government in 1987 in response to the political pressures generated by a bank collapse. The Committee, under the chairmanship of Professor R.B. Jack, reported in 1989,[2] and its recommendations resulted in significant changes in practice and a few statutory changes in the law. In particular, codes of practice have sought to spell out specifically the duties of banks towards their customers, not merely in terms of legal obligation, but in terms of best banking practice. This may be seen as part of a trend towards a recognition of the social responsibilities inherent in the conduct of banking in a modern economy. The challenge for the banker is to reconcile these responsibilities with the commercial imperative of maintaining a financially sound and competitive business.

---

1. For a modern treatment of the broader aspects of international banking, see Ross Cranston, *Principles of Banking Law*, Clarendon Press, Oxford, 1998.
2. Cm. 622, HMSO, London.

11

THE BASIC BANKER–CUSTOMER RELATIONSHIP

The basic relationship

The banking relationship between a bank and its customer is likely to include a range of separate contracts, depending on the nature of the business transacted between them. Loan agreements, security transactions, applications to open letters of credit, safe custody agreements and the like will constitute separate, and separately documented, contracts. The term "banker–customer relationship" is generally taken to refer to the specific legal relationship generated by the opening and operation of a bank account. A feature of English banking practice is that the legal content of this relationship is usually not spelt out in a comprehensive written contract between the parties entered into when the account is opened; rather it has been defined over the years in the case law.

The basic principle is that the relationship created by the deposit of money with a bank by a customer is that of debtor and creditor. Money, when paid into a bank, ceases to be the money of the depositor; it is the bank's money to deal with as its own.[3] One consequence of this is that on the bank's insolvency the depositor's rights are generally those of an unsecured creditor, even in the case of a "trust" account.[4]

But there are complexities inherent in the banker–customer relationship which distinguish it from the ordinary relationship of debtor and creditor. In the leading case of *Joachimson* v. *Swiss Bank Corpn*[5] the Court of Appeal analysed the nature of the contract made between a bank and its customer when a current account is opened. Atkin LJ rejected the view that the contract consists of a simple contract of loan by customer to bank, with added obligations on the bank's part. He said that the relationship consists of one contract involving obligations on both sides. The bank's promise to repay is treated as localised at the branch where the account is kept, because it is only there that the precise liabilities are known (he was of course speaking before the time of central computerised accounting systems). It is a promise to pay on demand during banking hours. It is a term of the contract that the bank will not cease to do business with the customer except upon reasonable notice. The customer on his part undertakes to exercise reasonable care in executing his payment orders so as not to mislead the bank or to facilitate forgery. The bank is not liable to repay the customer until he demands payment from the bank at the branch at which the account is kept.[6]

This statement of the parties' rights and obligations still summarises the basic position in English law, and has been applied by the courts in various different

3. *Foley* v. *Hill* (1848) 2 HL Cas 28, HL.
4. *Space Investments Ltd* v. *Canadian Imperial Bank of Commerce Trust Co (Bahamas) Ltd* [1986] 1 WLR 1072, PC.
5. [1921] 3 KB 110, CA.
6. *Ibid.*, p. 127. The demand must be one which the bank is obliged to comply with; *Libyan Arab Foreign Bank* v. *Bankers Trust Co* [1989] QB 728 at 749, Staughton J.

contexts.[7] In subsequent cases, obligations additional to those stated have been recognised, such as the bank's duty to keep its customers' affairs confidential (which is described below), and the paying bank's duty of care when making payments on its customers' behalf.[8]

Recently banks have issued codes of practice applicable to certain classes of customer, which seek to restate or supplement these principles. The most important of these, "Good Banking",[9] contains a code of practice to be observed by banks, building societies and card issuers when dealing with personal customers. One of the aims of the code is to provide greater transparency in the relationship, so that a customer may have a clear explanation of the terms upon which services are offered, and proper information as to charges and interest. The effect, if any, of the code on the legal content of the banker–customer relationship has yet to be determined.[10] There is also a Mortgage Code providing a code of good lending practice.

Governing law

The *Joachimson* case concerned a single bank account. An analysis of the relationship can be difficult when more than one account is held by the same customer, as was the case in the *Libyan Arab Foreign Bank* litigation. This arose out of the sanctions imposed on Libya by the United States in January 1986, freezing Libyan assets within the United States and also dollar deposits held for Libyans by US banks outside the United States. The plaintiffs maintained a dollar current account in New York, and a dollar deposit account in London, with the balance over a "peg" being transferred daily to London. Repayment was lawful under English law, but not under New York law. It was essential therefore to identify which law governed the bank's repayment obligations.

In the first of the cases (*Libyan Arab Foreign Bank* v. *Bankers Trust Co*[11]) the court rejected an argument that there were two separate contracts, one in respect of the London account and one in respect of the New York account. It was held that there was only one contract, but that the rights and obligations of the parties in respect of the London account were governed by English law, and in respect of the New York account by New York law (i.e. that the contract had a "split" proper law). In *Libyan Arab Foreign Bank* v. *Manufacturers Hanover Trust Co (No 2)*[12] on the other hand, it was held on similar facts that there was a separate contract in respect of each account, the London account contract being

---

7. E.g. *Arab Bank Ltd* v. *Barclays Bank (DCO)* [1954] AC 495, HL (the effect of war on a bank's duty to repay), and *Hart* v. *Sangster* [1957] Ch 329 CA (liability to tax on deposit account interest).

8. *Westminster Bank Ltd* v. *Hilton* (1926) 135 LT 358 at 362, Atkin LJ (reversed on appeal without affecting this point, (1926) 136 LT 315, HL), *Barclays Bank plc* v. *Quincecare Ltd* [1992] 4 All ER 363.

9. Revised edition effective from 31 March 1999. See Appendix 2.

10. Compare the Cabinet Office Guidance on statutory codes of practice issued in December 1987; the "Good Banking" code is, of course, non-statutory.

11. [1989] 1 QB 728, Staughton J.

12. [1989] 1 Lloyd's Rep 608, Hirst J.

governed by English law, and the New York account contract being governed by New York law.

Although the precise legal analysis differed, it was held in both cases that it is the general rule that the law governing a bank account is the law of the place where the account is kept (in the absence of agreement to the contrary). It was recognised that under modern conditions it may not be strictly accurate to speak of the branch where the account is "kept", in that banks no longer depend on books in which they write entries; they have terminals by which they give instructions; and the computer itself with its magnetic tape, disk or some other device may physically be located elsewhere. Nevertheless, it should not be difficult to decide where an account is kept for the purposes of ascertaining the governing law.[13] It was pointed out that there are good practical reasons for such a rule, and that solid grounds are needed for holding that it does not apply.[14]

This approach (which it is submitted is a sensible and workable one) must be reconsidered in the light of the Rome Convention on the law applicable to contractual obligations. This was given the force of law in the United Kingdom on 1 April 1991 by the Contracts (Applicable Law) Act 1990. The basic rule under the Convention is that in the absence of a choice of law, a contract is governed by the law of the country with which it is most closely connected.

The basic rule is qualified by a number of (rebuttable) presumptions. It is presumed that the contract is most closely connected with the country where the party who is to effect "characteristic performance" has its central administration. (In respect of a bank account, the bank should probably be regarded as such party.) However, if the contract is entered into in the course of that party's trade (which will be the case as regards a bank opening an account), the governing law will be that of the country in which the party's principal place of business is situated or, where performance is to be effected through a place of business other than the principal place of business, the country in which that other place of business is situated.

These presumptions do not readily lend themselves to the obligations created by bank accounts. However, it is believed that characteristic performance in respect of a bank account should be regarded as "to be effected through" the branch where the account is kept. That being so, it is the law of the country where that place is situated which should govern the contract, as it did under pre-Rome Convention English law. This view appears to be consistent with that expressed in the Giuliano-Lagarde Report—*travaux préparatoires* to the Convention—which states (admittedly somewhat elliptically) that "in a banking contract the law of the country of the banking establishment with which a transaction is made will normally govern the contract".

---

13. [1989] QB 728 at 746.
14. *Libyan Arab Foreign Bank* v. *Manufacturers Hanover Trust Co* [1988] 2 Lloyd's Rep 494 at 502, Hirst J.

Confidentiality

English law holds that certain "confidential" relationships, such as those between lawyer and client and doctor and patient, give rise to a duty not to disclose information acquired in confidence. In the leading case of *Tournier* v. *National Provincial & Union Bank of England*[15] it was held by the court of Appeal that a similar prohibition applies to the banker–customer relationship. It is an implied term of the contract between them that the bank is under a duty to abstain from disclosing information as to its customer's affairs without his consent.[16] This is generally known as the bank's duty of confidentiality, or secrecy. It applies to prevent disclosure between one separate juridical entity in a group and another.[17]

In the *Tournier* case the Court was unanimous in holding that the duty is not an absolute but a qualified one. The qualifications were classifed under four heads, namely:

1. Where disclosure is under compulsion by law.
2. Where there is a duty to the public to disclose.
3. Where the interests of the bank require disclosure.
4. Where the disclosure is made by the express or implied consent of the customer.[18]

There are a growing number of instances in which the "compulsion by law" qualification applies. Thus, a bank must provide information pursuant to an inspection order by the court under the Bankers' Books Evidence Act 1879. However "law" appears to refer to English law, so that a foreign subpoena to produce documents in a foreign court will not fall within it.[19] More recent examples of legislation under which information must be provided include the Police and Criminal Evidence Act 1984 and the Drug Trafficking Act 1994 which, together with the Money Laundering Regulations 1993, place substantial duties on banks in respect of both the opening and operation of accounts to prevent money laundering. And the effect of s. 98 of the Criminal Justice Act 1988 is that a bank *may* disclose to the police its suspicion or belief that property has been obtained in connection with the commission of an indictable offence without breach of its duty of confidentiality.

There is little authority concerning "duty to the public to disclose"; one case indicates that this qualification might include disclosure by a bank of sensitive information to the central bank.[20] The interest of the bank will require disclosure when, for example, it states the details of the account in legal proceedings to recover a customer's indebtedness.

15. [1924] 1 KB 461, CA.
16. *Ibid.*, p. 484, Atkin LJ.
17. *Bank of Tokyo* v. *Karoon* [1987] AC 45 at 53–54, CA.
18. *Ibid.*, p. 473, Bankes LJ.
19. *X AG and others* v. *A bank* [1983] 2 All ER 464, Leggatt J.
20. *Libyan Arab Foreign Bank* v. *Bankers Trust Co.* [1989] QB 728 at 770–771, Staughton J.

The fourth qualification concerns disclosure made with the express or implied consent of the customer. Implied consent may justify the well-established practice whereby banks give credit references concerning customers at the request of other banks without asking on each occasion for the customer's express consent.[21] Reporting in 1989, the Review Committee on Banking Services Law and Practice recommended that a bank should be able to rely on implied consent only if it could show that the customer was aware of the purpose for which the consent was required, and advised that he was free to withhold his consent.[22] This recommendation has not been adopted.

The Review Committee regarded the duty of confidentiality as at the heart of the banker–customer relationship,[23] and was concerned that it was being gradually eroded.[24] The Government's response was that broader public policy issues often overrode the need to preserve confidentiality.[25] It is submitted that although there are plainly many instances in which the duty must be treated as subordinate to the public interest, the Committee was right to stress the desirability of preserving it where possible.

The Review Committee's report has not been entirely without practical results. It appears that banks routinely circulated information about their customers within the group for the purpose of marketing non-banking services. The "Good Banking" code of practice now states that banks will observe a strict duty of confidentiality about their customers' (and former customers') personal financial affairs and, in the absence of express consent, will not disclose details of customers' accounts or their names and addresses to any third party, including other companies in the same group, other than in the four exceptional cases permitted by the law.[26]

THE MULTIFUNCTIONAL BANK

English law does not prescribe or limit the activities that banks may conduct, nor is there a Glass-Steagall type barrier between banking and securities business. Nevertheless, until the mid 1980s banks did circumscribe their activities, and their exclusion from the securities business was reinforced by a Stock Exchange

21. In *Tournier* Atkin LJ mentioned, without deciding, that if the practice was justified it must be on the basis of the customer's implied consent; *ibid.*, p. 486. It is submitted that the giving of bankers' references can be justified on this basis.

22. Cm. 622, paras 6.26 *et seq.* An earlier committee recommended that "banks should give [customers] the opportunity either to seek a standing authority for the provision of references or to require the bank to seek their consent on every occasion"; *Report of the Committee on Privacy*, 1972, Cmnd 5012 at para. 307. As regards personal customers, the "Good Banking" code states that banks will on request explain how the system of bankers' references works.

23. *Ibid.* para. 5.26.

24. *Ibid.* para. 5.08.

25. Cm. 1026, March 1990, para. 2.13.

26. This is in accordance with the views expressed by the Government in response to the report of the Review Committee; Cm. 1026 para. 2.16, March 1990.

rule book that prevented outsiders from taking a controlling interest in member firms.[27]

This and other restrictions were abolished in the series of reforms which culminated in "Big Bang" in 1986. The reforms in part reflected, and in part contributed to, the movement towards the "financial conglomerate" that aimed to provide its customers with an extended range of banking and financial services within the one group. These moves have not been uniformly successful, with some entrants having to withdraw from the securities business after incurring colossal losses. There are signs that some banks are now focusing on their core banking activities.

However, the financial conglomerate is firmly established on the banking scene. Its emergence has had considerable regulatory implications, because the regulation of financial institutions as it has developed in the United Kingdom over the past few years has been on a functional rather than on an institutional basis. Thus, a bank's deposit-taking business was until recently regulated by the Bank of England under the Banking Act 1987. But a bank carrying on investment business within the United Kingdom is also within the regulatory regime established by the Financial Services Act 1986. Separate authorisations are required. Most banks that need it have obtained authorisation by joining one of the self-regulatory organisations (SROs) set up under the Act to regulate the investment services industry.[28]

The inconvenience of this dual system[29] is mitigated to some extent by the "lead regulation" principle under which the Bank of England has responsibility for the financial supervision of banks. This is formalised by memoranda of understanding between the Bank of England and the SROs which stipulate that the SROs financial resources rules do not apply to its member banks, the financial health of which continues to be monitored in accordance with the Bank of England's normal risk asset ratio and gearing requirements. Furthermore, the wholesale money markets remained until recently under the supervision of the Bank of England on a non-statutory basis (by virtue of an exemption in FSA, s. 43).

At the banker–customer level, the conduct of a bank's investment business is the subject of conduct of business rules. There are ten principles of good business conduct expressed at a very general level. There are also "core" conduct of business rules which spell out in more detail the essence of the obligations of a firm in the conduct of its investment business.[30] They cover such matters as

27. R. Dale, *International Banking Deregulation*, Blackwell, Oxford, 1992, p. 6.

28. Primarily the Securities and Futures Authority (SFA) and the Investment Management Regulatory Organisation (IMRO).

29. The banks lobbied Professor Gower (whose reports on investor protection inspired the FSA) on this point without success. He took the view that the Bank of England's regulatory role was primarily to ensure that banks maintained their overall solvency; L.C.B. Gower, *Review of Investor Protection, A Discussion Document*, HMSO, London, 1982, p. 125.

30. M. Blair, *Financial Services, The New Core Rules*, Blackstone Press, London, 1991.

advertising and marketing, standards of advice, best execution, churning,[31] complaints procedure and the like. Finally, there are rules promulgated by the SROs applicable to their own members. A contravention of the conduct of business rules (though not the principles) is actionable at the suit of a "private investor" who suffers loss as a result.[32]

This cumbrous system is in the process of being fundamentally reformed. A single financial regulator (the Financial Services Authority) has been formed, and powers of banking supervision have been vested in it under the Bank of England Act 1998. Further legislation (the Financial Services and Markets Bill) will complete the process of unification, and a much improved regulatory system should emerge as a result.

Although conflicts of interest[33] are nothing new in the financial field, the conglomerate combining banking and securities businesses in the same group has an increased risk of generating them. The policy issue is to achieve a reasonable balance between the interests of clients, who rightly expect that a firm acting for them will not have a conflict with either its own or another client's interests, and what is (apparently) the operational reality that the conduct of a modern financial services business will inevitably give rise to some conflicts of interest. Difficult legal questions arise as to whether such conflicts must be avoided, or whether, and if so how, they can be "managed". These issues are presently far from resolved.[34]

One quite long-established means of "managing" conflicts of interest is the so-called Chinese Wall. This is in essence an arrangement by which different parts of a business are compartmentalised to avoid the leakage of sensitive information from one part to the other.

The effectiveness of the Chinese Wall must be judged against the law relating to "fiduciaries". A fiduciary is one who owes special duties because of the nature of his position.[35] An agent is a fiduciary with regard to his principal. Thus a fiduciary relationship is capable of arising between corporate financier and client, stockbroker and client, insurance broker and client and investment adviser and client. Other examples of fiduciary relationships are those between trustee and beneficiary, solicitor and client, director and company and partner and fellow partner. A fiduciary relationship can also arise by virtue of the nature of special circumstances, for example because a relationship of "confidence" exists between the parties.[36]

---

31. The term used to describe the practice of excessive share dealing to generate commission.
32. FSA 1986, ss. 62 and 62A.
33. See generally Blair, Allison, Palmer, Richards-Carpenter, and Walker, *Banking and Financial Services Regulation*, 2nd edn, Butterworths, London, 1998.
34. For a good discussion of the issues see the Law Commission, Consultation Paper No. 124, *Fiduciary Duties and Regulatory Rules* (HMSO 1992).
35. *Re Coomber* [1911] 1 Ch 723 at 728–729, CA, *Reading* v. *Attorney-General* [1949] 2 KB 232 at 236, CA, and see [1951] AC 507, HL.
36. *Lloyds Bank Limited* v. *Bundy* [1975] QB 326, CA.

The duties which the law generally imposes on a fiduciary may be summarised as follows. He must not place himself in a position where his own interest conflicts with that of his customer. He must not profit from his position at the expense of his customer. He owes undivided loyalty to his customer, and therefore must not place himself in a position where this duty owed towards one customer conflicts with the duty that he owes to another customer. A consequence is that a fiduciary must make available to a customer all the information in his possession that is relevant to the customer's affairs. A fiduciary must use information obtained in confidence from his customer for the benefit of the customer, and not for his own advantage or for the benefit of any other person.[37]

The following is a summary of the techniques which have been developed in the United States and the United Kingdom to prevent or "manage" conflicts:

Among the preventive procedures commonly used are Chinese Walls, restricted lists and watch lists. A Chinese Wall isolates the trading side of the firm from the investment banking side. A restricted list prohibits recommendations to customers relating to, or solicitation of customer orders to purchase or sell, a particular security, and prohibits trading for the firm's own account in the security. Another type of restricted list enables the firm to prevent such activities as the issuance of a research recommendation concerning a security. Firms frequently use a watch list to monitor trading activity to determine whether any leaks in the Chinese Wall have occurred.[38]

An alternative or additional technique is the disclosure to the client of an actual or potential conflict of interest, and the obtaining of consent to the firm continuing to act.

The theory is that the "mischief" caused by a conflict of interest is that it prevents a firm from acting single-mindedly in the best interests of the client. That mischief can be avoided, so the theory goes, if those who are handling a transaction are wholly unaware that a conflicting interest or duty exists.[39] Whether a Chinese Wall is effective in law to prevent a conflict of interest arising, or at least to relieve a firm of the consequences of such a conflict where one has arisen, has been much debated. There is little modern English case law. But in two recent cases concerning solicitors, some scepticism was expressed by the courts as to the effectiveness of Chinese Walls, one judge doubting whether an impregnable wall can ever be created.[40]

However, it is possible to argue that rules that apply to solicitors should not necessarily apply in the financial field. Indeed, in the financial services field there is statutory recognition of the practice. Financial Services Act, s. 48(2)(h) (which provides for the making of conduct of business rules) enacts that such rules may

37. See the summary in The Law Commission Consultation Paper No. 124, at p. 32.

38. This passage is contained in a letter dated 12 May 1988 written by the SEC in connection with the litigation resulting from the hostile tender offer made by the Beazer plc joint venture partnership to acquire Koppers Co. It is quoted in a paper given by J.W. Mayo on 18 November 1991, "Conflicts of Interest—the Theory and Practice of Chinese Walls".

39. *Ibid.*

40. *Re a firm of solicitors* [1992] 1 All ER 353 at 363, Parker LJ; see also *Lee (David) & Co (Lincoln)* v. *Coward Chance* [1991] Ch 259, Browne-Wilkinson V-C.

make provision enabling or requiring information obtained by an authorised person in the course of carrying on one part of his business to be withheld by him from persons with whom he deals in the course of carrying on another part, and for that purpose enabling or requiring persons employed in one part of that business to withhold information from those employed in another part. Rules to this effect have been promulgated (for example Core Conduct of Business Rules, rule 36[41]).

The effect of the above provisions of the Financial Services Act and the Core Rules on the general law relating to fiduciaries as it applies in the financial context is unclear. The Law Commission "inclines to the view" that the Financial Services Act, s. 48(2)(h), authorises modification of the private law rights and duties of those dealing with persons authorised under the Act, albeit within its limited sphere.[42] Its provisional view is that fiduciary law should take account of rules made by regulatory bodies which operate in the public law sphere, either because there is statutory authority to make rules to modify common law and equitable obligations (i.e. Financial Services Act, s. 48(2)(h)) or because the court should take account of reasonable regulatory rules in ascertaining the precise content of the common law or equitable duty.[43] It is believed that such an approach would commend itself to the courts. If that is correct, then it may be predicted that a properly implemented Chinese Wall may be effective in certain circumstances to prevent what would otherwise be a conflict of interest arising, or at least may relieve a firm of what would otherwise be the legal consequences of such a conflict.

LIABILITY OF BANKS FOR ADVICE

When a bank advises a customer as to financial matters it must, of course, do so with reasonable skill and care.[44] However, the English courts have tended against recognising any general duty on banks to advise their customers. Thus, it has been held that in general a bank does not owe a customer a duty to advise on the prudence of borrowing,[45] and that a bank's duty of care does not extend to requiring it to advise the customer of the risks involved in the collection of cheques.[46]

Much of the recent case law has concerned the nature of a bank's duty to advise in the case of third party security, particularly where the security is to be

41. Core Rule 36 appears reproduced in the SRO Rules, for example IMRO Rules, Chapter 1.4, r.4.2(1).

42. Consultation Paper No. 124, p. 238.

43. *Ibid.* p. 242.

44. *Woods* v. *Martins Bank Ltd* [1959] 1 QB 55, Salmon J.

45. *Williams & Glyn's Bank Ltd* v. *Barnes* [1981] Com LR 205; it has been pointed out that the decision was dependent on the facts of the case; R. Salter, *Banks—Liability and Risk*, Lloyd's of London Press, 1990, p. 80 (ed. R. Cranston).

46. *Redmond* v. *Allied Irish Banks plc* [1987] 2 FTLR 264, Saville J.

given by the principal debtor's wife, or some other person closely related to him. It is clear that a creditor does not in general owe any legal duty to a proposed surety to explain to the surety the effect of the proposed suretyship transaction or the effect of any security proposed to be given.[47] This applies notwithstanding that the internal rules of many (or most) banks have for a long time contained instructions to the effect that a proposed surety should receive such an explanation, or be told to obtain independent legal advice.

And there are good reasons for this course, because unless a bank has advised the proposed surety to take independent legal advice as to the nature of the transaction, it risks finding itself fixed with any undue influence that has been exerted by the debtor to obtain the security, or with any misrepresentation that has been made by the debtor to the surety. It has been held that a bank is so affected where the debtor acted as its agent in obtaining the security, and where it was on notice of the undue influence or misrepresentation.[48]

Thus, it was held that if a creditor, or potential creditor, of a husband desires to obtain, by way of security for the husband's indebtedness, a guarantee from his wife or a charge on property of his wife, and if the creditor entrusts to the husband himself the task of obtaining the execution of the relevant document by the wife, then the creditor can be in no better position than the husband himself, and the creditor cannot enforce the guarantee or the security against the wife if it is established that the execution of the document by the wife was procured by undue influence by the husband and the wife had no independent advice.[49] The same principle applies in the case of a husband who in similar circumstances procures the execution of the document by giving his wife a deliberately false explanation.[50]

In the leading acase of *Barclays Bank plc* v. *O'Brien*,[51] much of the old law was swept away. The House of Lords held that the applicable principle under which a lender incurs liability for the wrongdoing of a third party (thereby preventing the enforcement of a security) is that of notice. The court held that in certain situations, such as that which arises when a couple live together, notice will exist unless the bank has taken certain steps to see that the proposed surety was fairly apprised of his or her legal position. There have been a large number of decisions by the Court of Appeal since then, and it is clear that a bank will normally avoid difficulties in enforcing its security by recommending the

---

47. See, e.g., *Barclays Bank plc* v. *Khaira* [1992] 1 WLR 623, Mr Thomas Morison QC. It has been said, *obiter*, that such a duty may be owed by a bank where the surety is the bank's customer; *Cornish* v. *Midland Bank plc* [1985] 3 All ER 513, 522–523, Kerr LJ, CA; *sed quaere*.

48. *Bank of Credit and Commerce International SA* v. *Aboody* [1990] 1 QB 923 at 979, CA, per Slade LJ. In English law, victimisation of one party by the other is the principle that justifies the setting aside of a transaction on the ground of undue influence; before a transaction can be set aside therefore, it has to be shown that it constituted a manifest disadvantage to the person seeking to avoid it: *National Westminster Bank plc* v. *Morgan* [1985] AC 686, HL.

49. *Kingsnorth Trust Limited* v. *Bell* [1986] 1 WLR 119 at 123, CA, per Dillon LJ.

50. *Ibid.*, per Dillon LJ, at 123–124.

51. [1994] 1 AC 180 (not followed in Australia—see *Garcia* v. *National Australia Bank Ltd*, HCA, 6 August 1998).

proposed surety to take independent legal advice. It is not responsible for the quality of that advice.

As regards personal customers, the Mortgage Code of Practice states that banks will advise private individuals proposing to give them a guarantee or other security for another person's liabilities that by giving the guarantee or third party security he or she might become liable instead of or as well as that other person, and should take independent legal advice. Guarantees and other third party security forms will contain a clear and prominent notice to this effect. Unlimited guarantees are no longer taken.

CONSUMER PROTECTION

English law has been slow to recognise that the customer of a bank needs any protection over and above established rules as to misrepresentation, undue influence and the like. In this as in other fields, freedom of contract has been the order of the day. But in recent times recession and unprecedented levels of problem domestic debts[52] have contributed to growing political pressure for greater sensitivity to the position, not just of the consumer, but also of the small business. As one leading banker has put it, the 1990s will be a caring decade, where the power of the consumer will require banks to be more responsive to the needs of their customers.[53] Its response to these pressures is one of the major challenges presently facing the banking industry.

The main heads of consumer protection as they now exist are summarised below, under six heads. It should also be mentioned that a number of existing and proposed EC Directives are having an increasing impact.

Case law

English law has not so far recognised an overriding principle of good faith in the making and carrying out of contracts, such as that existing in many civil law systems, or that enshrined in the Uniform Commercial Code as enacted in the United States.[54] Judicial attempts to limit the effect of exclusion clauses by developing the "fundamental breach" doctrine came to nothing.[55] The courts did develop rules strongly protective of the position of a surety, but these rules are largely ineffective as providing real protection because they are subject to contrary agreement between the parties,[56] and are inevitably excluded in

---

52. Bank of England, *Banking Act Report for 1991/92*, p. 10.

53. Lord Alexander of Weedon QC, Chairman of National Westminster Bank plc, Chartered Institute of Bankers Bristol Lecture, 26 November 1991.

54. § 1–203 of which provides that every contract or duty within the Code imposes an obligation of good faith in its performance or enforcement (reflecting existing case law to the effect that every contract implies good faith and fair dealing between the parties).

55. *Suisse Atlantique Société d'Armement Maritime SA* v. *MV Rotterdamsche Kolen Centrale* [1967] 1 AC 361.

56. E.g. *Perry* v. *National Provincial Bank of England* [1910] 1 Ch 464 at 473, CA.

standard bank guarantee forms. However, in some circumstances the courts will intervene to strike down onerous contractual terms. In *Interfoto Picture Library Ltd* v. *Stiletto Visual Programmes Ltd*[57] it was held that where clauses incorporated into a contract contain a particularly onerous or unusual condition, the party seeking to enforce that condition must show that it was brought fairly and reasonably to the attention of the other party.

Statute law

Two statutes will be mentioned here. The first is the Consumer Credit Act 1974, which provides detailed protection for individuals in relation to small credit transactions; the limit is currently £15,000. The Act provides for the licensing of consumer credit businesses, and regulates such matters as advertising, canvassing, the form and content of agreements, cooling-off periods, the liability of creditors for breaches by the supplier, and default and termination. There are also provisions relating to credit cards.[58]

Current account overdrafts granted by banks are exempt from Part V of the Act (which provides for the form and content of agreements and cooling-off periods) by virtue of a determination by the Director General of Fair Trading made on 21 December 1989 under s. 74(1)(b) of the Act. To take advantage of the exemption, a bank must inform the Office of Fair Trading in writing of its general intention to grant such overdrafts, and comply with certain conditions as to the provision of information to the borrower concerning the credit limit, interest and charges.

The second is the Unfair Contract Terms Act 1977, which provides that a person cannot unreasonably exclude liability for negligence. It also provides that where one party deals as consumer, or on the other's written standard terms, the other party cannot unreasonably exclude or restrict his liability for breach of contract.[59] The possible impact of the 1977 Act on exclusion clauses routinely adopted by banks in standard form documentation has been little explored in the authorities. In one case it was suggested that a clause in a guarantee making the guarantor liable for a larger sum than the principal debtor would be unenforceable by virtue of the Act.[60]

In some respects, the Unfair Terms in Consumer Contracts Regulations 1994 (which implement the EC Council Directive 93/13/EEC of 5 April 1993) are wider in that they apply more generally than just to exclusion clauses. However, they are restricted to consumer contracts. The Regulations also seek to promote the use of plain, intelligible language in standard contract provisions.[61]

---

57. [1989] QB 433, CA.
58. For a full analysis, see R.M. Goode, *Consumer Credit Legislation*, London, Butterworths, looseleaf.
59. A proposed EC Directive on unfair terms in consumer contracts is presently being discussed.
60. *Standard Chartered Bank Limited* v. *Walker* [1982] 1 WLR 1410 at 1416, Lord Denning MR, CA.
61. For a full discussion, see Cranston, *op. cit.*, pp. 159–168.

Extortionate credit bargains[62]

The Consumer Credit Act 1974, s. 137, empowers the court to reopen a credit agreement so as to do justice between the parties if it finds the credit bargain extortionate. This provision applies to credit agreements generally, not just those regulated under the Act. A credit bargain is extortionate if it requires the debtor to make payments which are grossly exorbitant, or otherwise grossly contravenes ordinary principles of fair dealing (s. 138). The provision omits the useful presumption that was contained in the moneylenders' legislation to the effect that interest exceeding 48 per cent per annum is deemed to be excessive unless the contrary is shown. In the relatively few reported cases, the courts have used their powers sparingly.[63] The Director of Fair Trading has criticised the provision, and recommended the replacement of the concept of "extortionate credit bargain" with that of "unjust credit transaction".[64]

Office of Fair Trading

The OFT was set up under the Fair Trading Act 1973, and has important licensing and administration functions under the Consumer Credit Act 1974. It also has a "watchdog" role in relation to consumer affairs generally, and from time to time pronounces on questions of banking practice.

Alternative disputes resolution

Rights are, of course, of limited value unless they can be enforced. The courts of law are often an unsuitable forum for settling consumer type disputes between banks and customers, not only because the amounts concerned are comparatively small, but also because a degree of expertise in the arbiter can be helpful in resolving the dispute fairly. The financial services industry generally has taken considerable strides in the setting up of alternative disputes resolution schemes. These include the Banking Ombudsman, Investment Ombudsman, Insurance Ombudsman and Building Society Ombudsman schemes. A common feature of such schemes is that there is a limit of £100,000 on what can be awarded; this covers the vast majority of consumer claims. From the complainant's perspective there is the great advantage that using the service normally costs nothing. It is of course essential to the credibility of the schemes that the Ombudsmen are seen to be independent.

The Banking Ombudsman's function is to receive complaints relating to the provision of banking services by any member bank (the main UK retail banks are all members) to any individual, and to facilitate the settlement of such complaints by agreement or by the making of recommendations or awards. In

---

62. R.M. Goode, *op. cit.*, Chapter 32.
63. E.g., *Woodstead Finance Limited* v. *Petrou* [1986] FLR 158, CA.
64. *Unjust Credit Transactions*, September 1991.

making any recommendation or award, the Ombudsman is to have reference to what is fair in all the circumstances, and is to have regard to general principles of good banking practice and any relevant code of practice; the latter now includes the "Good Banking" code of practice.

Codes of practice

Arguably the most significant recent development has been the adoption of a banking code of practice. The Jack Committee recommended that banks should promulgate an agreed code of banking practice to achieve the improvements in banking practice which the Committee recommended should be introduced.[65] After considerable consultation, the British Bankers' Association, the Building Societies Association and the Association for Payment Clearing Services have produced the "Good Banking" code of practice. It will be reviewed at least once every two years and monitored on an annual basis. The code sets out the standards of good banking practice to be observed by banks, building societies and card issuers when dealing with personal customers in the United Kingdom. A sister code is the Mortgage Code issued by the Council of Mortgage Lenders, which seeks to promote best practice in this area.

Some of the provisions of the code relating to transparency, confidentiality and third party security have already been commented on. There are also important provisions relating to cards (i.e. credit and debit cards). A subject of particular contention is the incidence of liability for unauthorised use. The code limits customers' liability for unauthorised transactions to a maximum of £50 save in cases of the customer's fraud or "gross negligence".[66] In cases of disputed transactions the burden of proving fraud or gross negligence lies with the card issuer.

It is one of the governing principles of the code that banks will act fairly and reasonably in all their dealings with their customers. It is however non-statutory and not in itself legally binding. The extent to which its provisions may translate into legal rights and liabilities is an open question. It seems unlikely that the courts will ignore it in determining the legal content of the banker–customer relationship. An analogy may perhaps be drawn with s. 63C of the Financial Services Act 1986 which empowers the issue of codes of practice in that field. It provides that, whilst a contravention of such code does not in itself give rise to liability or invalidate a transaction, in determining whether a person's conduct amounts to a breach of the law, contravention of the code may be relied on as tending to establish liability, and compliance relied on as tending to negative liability.

---

65. *Banking Services: Law and Practice, Report by the Review Committee*, Cm. 622, Chapter 16.

66. It is unclear how far the exception so far as it refers to "gross negligence" is compatible with sections 83 and 84 of the Consumer Credit Act 1974, which provide (in respect of credit cards) that the cardholder is only liable for misuse of the card up to £50 unless the loss results from use by a person who acquired the card with his consent.

SECURITY

As in other countries, secured lending is prevalent in English banking practice. The law governing the taking of security is a vast and complex subject. Complexity is multiplied by the old division between common law and equity. These once separate legal systems have been administered jointly since 1873, but English law still distinguishes between the "legal" and the "equitable" mortgage, an example of the latter being an informal mortgage; traditionally, equity looks to the substance of a transaction, whereas the common law looks to the form. There have been proposals for reform, most recently in 1989 in respect of security interests in property other than land,[67] and in 1991 in respect of land mortgages.[68] There seems little immediate prospect of such proposals being implemented.

Security is created where one person (the creditor) to whom an obligation is owed by another (the debtor) obtains (in addition to the personal promise of the debtor to discharge the obligation) rights exercisable against some property in which the debtor has an interest in order to enforce the discharge of the debtor's obligation.[69] It may be distinguished from a guarantee or bond, which consists of the personal promise of the guarantor to discharge the debtor's obligation, but does not give any proprietary claim over the guarantor's assets.

The consensual security interests recognised by English law are the pledge, the mortgage and the charge.[70] A pledge is created by the actual or constructive delivery of possession of the thing pledged to the pledgee.[71] Only assets capable of physical delivery such as goods, documents of title to goods and negotiable securities[72] may be pledged. A mortgage is created by the transfer of ownership in an asset to the mortgagee by way of security upon the express or implied condition that ownership will be retransferred to the mortgagor on discharge of the secured obligation. The form of the mortgage has been modified since 1925 in the case of mortgages of land; legal mortgages over land are effected not by transfer of ownership of the land but by a charge by deed expressed to be by way of legal mortgage.[73] Unlike the pledge, a mortgage is a non-possessory security.

---

67. Professor A.L. Diamond, *A Review of Security Interests in Property*, London, HMSO, 1989 (commissioned by the DTI). Professor Diamond proposed a new law on security interests other than those over land based on US and Canadian models. A new "security interest" to include mortgages, charges and other security interests would be created, together with a new register of security interests. Possessory security interests, as now, would not require registration. Registration would go to priority (for example in a liquidation) rather than to the validity of the security as between the parties. The secured party would have the remedies currently available to a mortgagee.

68. The Law Commission, *Transfer of Land—Land Mortgages*, London, HMSO, 1991 (Law Com. No. 204).

69. *Bristol Airport plc* v. *Powdrill* [1990] Ch 744 at 760, Browne-Wilkinson V-C.

70. The contractual lien may also be included in the classification.

71. *Official Assignee of Madras* v. *Mercantile Bank of India* [1935] AC 53 at 58, PC.

72. E.g. *The London Joint Stock Bank* v. *Simmons* [1892] AC 201, HL.

73. Law of Property Act 1925, s. 85 (freeholds), s. 86 (leaseholds). The other available method of creating a legal mortgage is by demise, or sub-demise, for a term of years absolute, subject to a provision for cesser on redemption. Equitable mortgages arise where there is an enforceable agreement to mortgage but insufficient formalities to create a legal mortgage.

The term "charge" is often used in the cases and in the statutes interchangeably with the term "mortgage". In strict analysis however, a mortgage involves the transfer of property subject to a right of redemption, whereas a charge does not affect a transfer of property, merely giving the chargee certain rights over the property as security for the loan.[74] The term "hypothecation" is sometimes used in banking security documentation; it generally refers to a security by way of charge.

A document by which a company creates or acknowledges the existence of indebtedness, and secures repayment of that indebtedness on all or part of its property, is commonly described as a "debenture". This term has no fixed technical meaning,[75] and is used to describe security documents of this type as well as debt securities such as instruments in a series ranking *pari passu* and creating permanent loan capital.[76] Typically, an "all monies" debenture granted by a company to a bank will comprise a mortgage over the company's land, a fixed charge over book debts and other named classes of assets such as goodwill, and a floating charge over the company's assets not the subject of fixed security (particularly its stock in trade).

Taking security over fluctuating assets such as stock in trade gives rise to special problems. English law has tackled these by developing the "floating" charge, by which companies can create security over such assets whilst remaining free to deal with them in the ordinary course of business. The floating charge is an equitable charge over the assets of a company or a class of those assets as subsisting from time to time; it does not attach to a particular asset until an event occurs which "crystallises" the charge (such as the appointment by the creditor of a receiver in the event of default). When that happens, the charge becomes in equity a fixed charge on all the assets of the relevant class which then belong to the company; but until that time, the company has power to deal with the assets in the ordinary course of its business without reference to the creditor.[77]

Where possible, banks seek to include a company's book debts within the ambit of a fixed charge. According to a leading textbook, a charge over book debts present and future will generally be construed as a floating charge, even if described as fixed charge in the deed creating the charge.[78] On the other hand it has been held[79] that a debenture in terms creating a fixed charge over all existing and future book debts owing to a company, requiring the company to pay the

---

74. *Re Bond Worth Ltd* [1980] Ch 228 at 250, Slade J. The artificiality inherent in distinguishing a charge from a mortgage created by an assignment, and also the difficulty of locating precisely where the distinction lies, is well stated in F. Oditah, *Legal Aspects of Receivables Financing*, London, Sweet & Maxwell, 1991, pp. 95–96.

75. *Lemon* v. *Austin Friars Investment Trust Ltd* [1926] Ch 1, CA.

76. *Encyclopaedia of Banking Law*, para. E(1031).

77. *Encyclopaedia of Banking Law op. cit.*, para. E(1051). Except under special statutory provisions (such as the Agricultural Credits Act 1928, s. 5) an individual cannot create a floating charge.

78. *Gore-Browne on Companies*, 44th edn, para. 18.1.

79. *Siebe Gorman & Co Ltd* v. *Barclays Bank Ltd* [1979] 2 Lloyd's Rep 142 at 159, Slade J.

proceeds of those debts to the credit of its account with the debenture holder and
to execute a legal assignment of them on demand, and prohibiting any charge or
assignment of them to a third party without the debenture holder's consent, is
apt to create a fixed equitable charge on the debts as soon as they came into
existence, and on their proceeds when received. Subsequent decisions have
emphasised that a charge over book debts whether or not described as a fixed
charge will be construed as a floating charge if in substance the company is
entitled, without reference to the debenture holder, to get in the debts and use
the proceeds in its business.[80] It has been held in Australia that where a company
is allowed freedom to deal with debts when realised (even if this is only by leave
and licence of the debenture-holder), such debts will be treated as part of the
assets which are intended to be dealt with by the company in the ordinary course
of its business, and subject to a floating rather than a fixed charge.[81] It would
seem therefore that if a bank is to maintain the validity of a charge over book
debts as fixed rather than floating, it must impose restrictions on its corporate
customer's freedom to deal with its debts and their proceeds, and see that those
restrictions are observed in practice.

The registration of security is frequently essential to protect its validity.
Security over land is registrable under the Land Registration Act 1925. Security
created by companies over specified types of assets must be registered under the
Companies Act 1985. Documentary non-possessory security over goods created
by individuals is registrable under the Bills of Sale Acts 1878 and 1882. Security
by way of pledge is not registrable.[82]

Where a company raises finance and secures it by creating a charge on all or
some of its assets, and the charge requires registration but is not registered, it will
be void against a liquidator or, in effect, any secured creditor of the company.
However, there are techniques by which a company can raise finance without
charging its assets and which therefore do not attract registration requirements,
but which give the creditor the economic equivalent of security. Two well-tried
routes are the factoring of book debts and the block discounting of hire-
purchase or credit sale agreements. It is well established that factoring or block
discounting amounts to a sale of book debts, rather than a charge on book debts,
even though under the relevant agreement the purchaser is given recourse
against the vendor in the event of default of payment of the debt by the debtor.[83]

The following describes in outline the assets commonly taken by banks as
security, and the legal techniques used to do so. A number of sub-classes of assets
(such as ships and aircraft) attract special rules and are not considered here.

80. *Re Armagh Shoes Ltd* [1984] BCLC 405; *Re Keenan Bros Ltd* [1986] BCLC 242; *Re Brightlife Ltd* [1987] Ch 200, Hoffmann J.
81. *Waters* v. *Widows* [1984] VR 503.
82. *Re David Allester Ltd* [1922] 2 Ch 211, Astbury J.
83. *Welsh Development Agency* v. *Export Finance Co. Ltd.* [1992] BCLC 148 at 154, Dillon LJ, CA. Another such technique is the finance lease; see generally R.M. Goode, *Commercial Law*, Penguin, London 1982, Chapter 31.

Land

Mention has already been made of the methods of obtaining a legal mortgage over land. Equitable mortgages of land are also possible.[84] The Law Commission has proposed new forms of land mortgage to replace existing methods of consensually mortgaging and charging interests in land.[85] A number of far-reaching proposals are also made for the protection of the mortgagor some of which potentially affect banks. For example, it is proposed that the rights, remedies and powers of a mortgagee under a land mortgage would be exercisable only in good faith and for the purpose of protecting or enforcing the security. The court would have power to set aside or vary any terms of a mortgage with a view to doing justice between the parties if principles of fair dealing were contravened when the mortgage was granted, or the mortgage required payments to be made which were exorbitant. There is no sign of these proposals being implemented.

Goods

It is, of course, unusual for banks to take physical possession of goods (i.e. tangible movables) by way of pledge. There are also legal impediments to using goods as security in that the creation of non-possessory security over goods by individuals is inhibited by the technicalities of the Bills of Sale Acts. The two methods by which banks habitually take security over goods are:

1. By way of the floating charge over stock in trade contained in company debentures which has been described above.
2. In connection with trade financing, where a bank makes an advance against the security of imported goods.

A bank may obtain security over the goods (including the proceeds of sale of the goods) by obtaining possession of the bill of lading in respect of the shipment concerned, and thereby "constructive" possession of the goods. As the law presently stands, it seems that a bill of lading is the only document to title sufficient to give constructive possession for these purposes.[86] Alternatively, constructive possession of the goods may be obtained by a third party having possession of them (such as warehouseman) "attorning" to the bank (i.e. acknowledging on the instructions of the pledgor that the goods are being held for the pledgee). A valid pledge has the attraction that it is generally not registrable under the Companies Acts.[87]

Security may also be obtained by what are variously called letters of

84. For a description of risks to banks in lending secured on land, see G.J.S. Hill, *Banks—Liability and Risk*, Lloyd's of London Press, 1990, Chapter 4 (ed. R. Cranston).

85. See footnote 68 above.

86. *Official Assignee of Madras* v. *Mercantile Bank of India Ltd* [1935] AC 53 at 59, PC. Anomalously, under the Factors Acts, "mercantile agents" can pledge goods by pledge of various other documents.

87. *Re David Allester Ltd* [1922] 2 Ch 211, Astbury J.

hypothecation, pledge or lien in respect of goods and transport documents delivered into the bank's possession. Such security is normally taken on a general basis rather than in respect of individual shipments. The limited case law[88] suggests that these documents are best regarded as creating charges; such charges may be registrable under the Companies Acts. A mortgage of goods is also possible, but avoided by banks because of the risk of becoming liable under the contract of carriage.[89]

In practice, lending secured on goods is normally accomplished by leasing. The finance company acquires the item concerned, which is then leased to the user. The English courts to not characterise this transaction as creating security.

Negotiable bearer securities

An instrument which is payable to bearer, is proved to be treated in the market as negotiable and is not on its face non-negotiable, is likely to be treated in law as a negotiable instrument. Examples include bonds, certificates of deposit, bearer notes (such as floating rate notes), share warrants and the like. Security may be taken over such securities by pledge (by way of delivery of possession of the instrument concerned to the pledgee). A mortgage or charge over the instrument is also possible.[90]

A pledgee of a negotiable bearer security may obtain good title provided that it was taken in good faith and for value. For example, in *The London Joint Stock Bank* v. *Simmons*[91] a broker fraudulently deposited by way of pledge bearer negotiable securities belonging to a client with a bank as security for lending. There was nothing to put the bank on inquiry that the pledge was fraudulent. The broker defaulted and the bank realised the securities. It was held that because the securities were negotiable, the bank having taken for value and in good faith obtained a valid title.

Debts

In general, any debt (except perhaps a debt non-assignable by its terms[92]) may be taken as security. Security may be by way of legal or equitable mortgage over the debt, or by way of equitable charge. A mortgage of a debt is achieved by assigning the debt to the mortgagee subject to the mortgagor's equity of redemption. A charge gives the chargee a right to payment out of the debt, without transferring it.[93] Charges created by a company over book debts owing to the company have already been mentioned.

---

88. *Official Assignee of Madras* v. *Mercantile Bank of India, op. cit.,* at 64–65.
89. *Sewell* v. *Burdick* (1884) 10 App Cas 74, HL.
90. Compare M. Holden, *The Law and Practice of Banking*, Volume 2, Pitman, London 1986, p. 185; and Penn, Shea and Arora, *The Law Relating to Domestic Banking*, London, Sweet & Maxwell, 1987, p. 431.
91. [1892] AC 201, HL.
92. *Helstan Securities Limited* v. *Hertfordshire County Council* [1978] 3 All ER 262.
93. See Sykes, *The Law of Securities*, 4th edn, p. 704. But see footnote 74 above.

Priority is generally governed by the rule in *Dearle* v. *Hall*,[94] which is to the effect that as between competing assignments, the first in respect of which notice is given to the debtor prevails. In the case of mortgages, the rule is subject to the qualification that the party giving the notice must not have known of the prior interest when lending the money.

Shares

A share is treated in English law as a chose in action (i.e. a debt)[95] and not, as for example under the Uniform Commercial Code,[96] as a negotiable security.[97] It is, of course, a chose in action with special characteristics carrying with it a bundle of rights and obligations.[98]

To obtain a legal mortgage over shares, title to the shares must be transferred to the mortgagee (in the case of a bank, normally a nominee company of the bank). An equitable mortgage over shares may be created by an agreement to transfer the shares to the mortgagee or, more commonly, by the deposit of the share certificates as security. It has been held that such a transaction creates an equitable mortgage over the shares rather than a pledge.[99] In practice, a bank mortgagee will also take a memorandum of deposit setting out its powers in relation to the shares, and often a blank transfer as well so as to facilitate realisation in the event of default.

There is not believed to be any English authority as to the effect of taking security over a portfolio of shares the content of which changes with greater or lesser frequency. The Singapore courts, however, have considered the legal effect of "letters of hypothecation" by which stockbrokers charged to various banks tranches of shares identified daily in certificates provided to the banks concerned. It was held that the unascertainability of the shares charged and the liberty accorded to the charging company to substitute shares (which meant that the company had the right to trade in the shares) had the result that the letters of hypothecation created floating charges, and required registration as such. The arrangements set out in the letters of hypothecation and the daily certificates showed that there was no final and irrevocable appropriation of the shares listed in the daily certificates so as to create a fixed equitable charge as the banks had argued.[100]

Specific provision is made for charging shares held in the CREST system in dematerialised form. Mention should also be made of the issues which arise when securities are held through custodians. Security should be available over

---

94. (1823) 3 Russ 1.
95. *Re VGM Holdings Ltd* [1942] Ch 235 at 241, CA.
96. See Article 8-105(1).
97. *London and Country Bank* v. *London and River Plate Bank* (1887) 20 QBD 232, at 239.
98. See the analysis in *Gower's Principles of Modern Company Law*, 6th edn, London, Sweet & Maxwell, 1997, pp. 299–302.
99. *Harrold* v. *Plenty* [1901] 2 Ch 314.
100. *Re Lin Securities Pte* [1988] 2 MLJ 137; *Re City Securities Pte* [1990] 2 MLJ 257; *Dresdner Bank* v. *Ho Mun-Tuke Don* [1993] SLR 114; see also *Re London Wine Company* [1986] PCC 121.

the account, as is provided for specifically by rules applicable to clearing houses such as Euroclear and Cedel.[101]

Life assurance policies

Life assurance policies (though not other types of insurance policy) may be taken as security by legal mortgage (by way of assignment under the Policies of Assurance Act 1867) or by equitable mortgage or charge (by way of agreement or by the deposit of the policy with the intent that it should be security).

Money deposits

English law recognises the banker's right of set-off, that is, the right to combine or consolidate a customer's debit balance with his credit balance so that only the balance is payable.[102] The right is available where the accounts are of the same customer, held in the same name and in the same right.[103] Thus, personal indebtedness cannot be set off against money held by the customer in a trust capacity. The banker's right of set-off has its limitations, in that it is subject to contrary agreement express or implied, and contingent or unmatured liabilities of the customer cannot be set off against a deposit presently repayable.

There are a number of situations in which a bank may stipulate for a specific deposit against a specific liability, for example when issuing a performance guarantee at a customer's request, and in these circumstances security over the deposit is required. Security documentation is taken in the form of a contractual set-off right, or an agreement by the customer that the deposit is not to be repayable until the relevant obligations are repaid to the bank or a charge over the deposit (or a combination of all three). There was controversy over the question whether a bank can, strictly speaking, take a charge over a deposit held with itself (as opposed to a deposit held with another bank), it being argued that there are conceptual difficulties in a debtor (i.e. the bank holding the deposit) taking a charge over its own indebtedness to the chargor.[104] Recent authority, however, has established that such a charge is legally effective.[105]

ENVIRONMENTAL LIABILITY

There has been intense recent debate in England as to the circumstances, if any, in which a bank as lender may incur liability under new environmental

101. As to governing law, see *Macmillan Inc* v. *Bishopsgate Investment Trust plc (No. 3)* [1996] 1 WLR 387, CA.

102. See, further, P.R. Wood, *English and International Set-Off*, London, Sweet & Maxwell, 1989, Chapter 3.

103. *Bhogal* v. *Punjab National Bank* [1988] 2 All ER 296, CA; *Uttamchandami* v. *Central Bank of India*, NLJ, 17 February 1989, CA.

104. *Re Charge Card Services* [1987] Ch 150 at 175, Millett J.

105. *Re Bank of Credit and Commerce International SA (No. 8)* [1997] 4 All ER 568, HL.

protection legislation for the polluting activity of its borrowers. Comparisons have been drawn with the position in the United States, where the Comprehensive Environmental Response Compensation and Liability Act of 1980 (CERCLA) as amended in 1986 by the Superfund Amendments and Reauthorisation Act 1986 (Superfund) permits the Federal Government to clean up sites at which hazardous substances have been released or deposited. Liability for the cost of the cleaning up operation rests upon the "owner or operator" of the site concerned. The definition of "owner or operator" excludes a person who "without participating in the management of the facility, holds indicia of ownership primarily to protect his security interest in the . . . facility" (the secured lender exemption). Despite its apparently plain purpose, some court decisions appeared to give a restricted interpretation to the secured lender exemption;[106] there have been recent moves both in Congress and by the Environmental Protection Agency to strengthen the exemption (a new rule was introduced by the agency in April 1992).

The European Union has been considering its own rules, the most recent being the Amended Proposal for a Council Directive on civil liability for damage caused by waste,[107] which, however, is unlikely to be adopted. The Commission produced a Green Paper on "Remedying Environmental Damage" in 1993.

In the United Kingdom, the Environmental Protection Act 1990 introduced a new system of integrated pollution control for industry "for the purpose of minimising pollution of the environment due to the release of substances into any environmental medium" (s. 4(2)). Section 61 imposes certain duties on local authorities to clean up polluted land, and gives the authority the right to recover the cost incurred in doing so from the person who is for the time being the owner of the land. It seems clear that a bank could not be an owner for these purposes merely by virtue of a mortgage over the land, except (perhaps) if it has taken possession of the land following the borrower's default and possibly in other circumstances in which it exercises a degree of control. There are other potentially relevant provisions under this and other statutes (such as the Water Resources Act 1991 in respect of water pollution) but in general it is believed that the circumstances in which a bank will incur liability for its borrower's pollution will be comparatively rare.[108]

TERMINATION OF THE RELATIONSHIP

A number of events such as the customer's death, mental incapacity or insolvency, terminate the banker–customer relationship by operation of law.

---

106. E.g., *United States* v. *Fleet Factors* 901 F. 2d 1550 (11th Cir. 1990), cert. denied 112 L. Ed 2d 772 (1991).

107. OJ No. C192/6 of 23.7.91.

108. A number of articles contain helpful analyses of the potential risks for lenders, e.g. Beringer and Thomas, "Lenders and Environmental Liability", *Practical Law for Companies*, November 1991, p. 3.

The relationship is also terminated by the winding up or dissolution of the bank.[109] The outbreak of war between the customer's country and that of his bank does not terminate the relationship, though the account cannot be operated for the duration of the war. It follows that the customer's right to demand payment of his credit balance is only suspended by the outbreak of war.[110] A similar principle has been applied to economic sanctions freezing deposits in a particular currency; the bank's repayment obligation is suspended not discharged.[111]

The customer may generally terminate the relationship at any time. The balance on his account is repayable on demand made at the branch where the account is kept, though no demand is necessary in the event of the bank's repudiation of the customer's right to be paid.[112] The bank is also entitled to terminate the relationship, but (in the absence of any unlawful operation of the account by the customer) must do so on reasonable notice. This principle is now enshrined in the "Good Banking" code of practice, which states that banks and building societies will not close personal customers' accounts without first giving reasonable notice (para. 3.5).

The banker's duty of confidentiality in respect of its customer's account extends beyond the period when the account is closed.[113] It seems unlikely that a demand for repayment by the bank in itself brings to an end the relationship of banker and customer. In any event, the bank is entitled to continue to charge compound interest on the contractual basis until repayment or judgment.[114]

WILLIAM BLAIR QC*

---

109. *Re Russian Commercial and Industrial Bank* [1955] Ch 148, Wynn-Parry J.
110. *Arab Bank Limited* v. *Barclays Bank (DCO)* [1954] AC 495, HL.
111. *Libyan Arab Foreign Bank* v. *Bankers Trust Co.* [1989] QB 728 at 772, Staughton J.
112. *Joachimson* v. *Swiss Bank Corpn* [1921] 3 KB 110 at 132, Atkin LJ, CA; *Re Russian Commercial and Industrial Bank* [1955] Ch 148 at 156–157.
113. *Tournier* v. *National Provincial and Union Bank of England* [1924] 1 KB 461 at 473, Bankes LJ, CA.
114. *National Bank of Greece SA* v. *Pinios Shipping Co.* [1990] 1 AC 637, HL.
* I am grateful to Mr A. M. Rutherford-Warren for commenting on this chapter in draft.

CHAPTER 3

FRANCE

INTRODUCTION

The French law on the banker–customer relationship is one of contract. This contract is largely implied, as for current accounts or for some credit facilities, or is drafted by the banker on printed sheets that are seldom read in detail, as for credit cards or credit forms.

The economic role of the banks influences the solutions used to settle conflicts between banks and their customers. In France the intervention of the government is one important feature of the banking environment. It has some effect on most of the topics under study, namely: the basic banker–customer relationship, confidentiality, consumer protection and security. This intervention is less effective as regards the multifunction bank, liability for advice and environmental liability.

THE BASIC BANKER–CUSTOMER RELATIONSHIP

Courts have played a part in the solution of banker–customer disagreements, but regulation by statute seems predominant.

A large part of the banker–customer relationship derives from the general law of contract and tort. It is mostly dealt with through every type of contract agreed upon by the parties: current account, credit and loan, safe custody, collection of cheques etc. There is no chapter in the textbooks devoted to the banker–customer relationship as such. However, it is true that the banker–customer relationship is strongly influenced by the control of the state over the banks. The rules on information to be provided to the customer, on the right to have an account or on the decisions pronounced by the banker in the name of the state are applications of the influence of statute.

The role of the courts

French courts do not have a tendency to discover implied terms in any kind of contract. They achieve the same result by other means, using statutory provisions in unusual interpretations to impose their own view of the solution. In banking matters, three examples can be given.

Interest rate

During the twentieth century, courts did not interfere so much until the second half of the 1980s, but then they changed their minds on the crucial problem of the interest rate paid on the debit balance of a current account.

In France, a large part of the short-term credits to business firms and a small portion of consumer credits are given through an authorised overdraft. Until the 1980s, this kind of contract was seldom put in writing, nor were other banking contracts, except for loans and collateral. Contracts for current accounts, discounting or overdrafts were oral. The interests and costs of the banks were decided through oral negotiation at the first application, and through customary calculation afterwards.

French courts have recently increased the duty of banks to inform their customers of the rate of interest charged for a debit balance on their account. Usually, banks charged their current rate of interest at the time of the bank statement. Under the Civil Code, it was admitted that bank accounts were not covered by article 1907 al. 2 which provides:

The rate of the contractual interest should be specified in writing.

Accepted as a rule of evidence and not as going to the validity of the contract,[1] this article was not applied to current accounts by the courts on the basis of an opposite custom, followed by all the banks. This caused no problem because usually current account contracts were not in writing; therefore it could be said that article 1907 al. 2, designed only for contracts in writing, should not apply to them.

The Cour de cassation suddenly changed the rule in 1988. In the first case, named *Toulon*, from the name of the plaintiff, decided on 9 February 1988,[2] the civil chamber of France's highest court, without any explanation or apparent motive, held (a) that Article 1907 should apply to a current account, and (b) that if there was no written statement of the rate of interest, only the legal rate should apply. During the first half of the 1980s, the contractual rate of interest for a debit balance was between 18 and 22 per cent, whilst the legal rate was at 9.5 per cent. Banks were shocked, and argued that they could be liable for more than 50 billion francs (£5 billion), as none of them issued written statements for the contractual rate of interest. As the effect of a change in law decided by a French court applies to the past, as well as to the present and the future, banks could not change past and present contracts, and would have to repay the excess previously collected.

Through the ministry of finance, these explanations came to the Cour de

1. Like the provision of art. 1905 C. civ. which imposes a document for the existence of an interest: Com. 26 June 1963, D. 1963, 521, note R. Rodière.
2. *Banque* 1988, 590 obs. J.-L. Rives-Lange; *JCP* 1988, II, 21026 note C. Gavalda and J. Stoufflet.

cassation, which slightly modified its solution. A second case decided by the commercial chamber of the same Cour de cassation, on 12 April 1988,[3] took its justification from a decree promulgated on 4 September 1985, made under an Act on usury issued 20 years earlier.[4] This decree states briefly the method of calculating the effective rate of interest.[5] The court, citing Article 1907 of the Civil Code, the 1966 Act on usury and the decree, decided that its new interpretation of Article 1907 promulgated in 1988 did not go back beyond the date of the decree, 4 September 1985.

Although these decisions were badly grounded in law, they were applied by the banks to future relationships. Nowadays, any account statement showing debit items for a previous debit balance shows at the same time the rate of interest to be paid. It can be said that the previous solution, well suited for nineteenth-century businessmen in their relationships with their banks, did not suit private customers. In addition, in order to protect bank customers, the courts tend to control variations of interest rates by the banks.

First, the intrusion of the courts in the bank contracts concerned the validity of the provision whereby the contractual interest rate would vary with the current bank interest rate. As from 1990 and until 1996, the Cour de cassation cancelled this provision when the bank had retained the right to change the rate of interest on the ground of Article 1129 of the Civil Code, which requires the agreement of both parties for the determination of a contractual obligation.[6]

But the courts were aware that the cancellation of such provision could have an unfair impact on the customers if the whole contract was cancelled. Consequently, the Cour de cassation limited the nullity to the clause providing for interest rate variations and therefore maintained the contract with the bank at the previous rate of interest.

However, in a second stage, the Cour de cassation changed its position and displaced the control rather on the execution of the contract and of the variations of the rates of interest by the bank. On 1 December 1995, the Assemblée plénière of the Cour de cassation denied the application of Article 1129 of the Civil Code to the validity of the determination of prices in contracts for services.[7] Consequently thereafter, the Cour de cassation regarded as valid the reference to the variation of the bank rate of interest. However, the Cour de cassation emphasised the control of the judges on the changes of interest rates in order to avoid abuses against bank customers who might claim for compensation in case they proved damages.[8]

Apart from interest matters, court interference in bank contracts is quite

3. Reported in reviews cited at footnote 2; reported alone in *D*. 1988, 309, concl. Av. gal Jéol.
4. Loi 28 December 1966, still in force.
5. TEG, Taux Effectif Global, close to the rate described by the EEC Directives 87/102 of 22 December 1986 and 90/88 of 22 February 1990, on consumer credit.
6. Cass. Civ. 1, 2 May 1990, *Banque* nov. 1990, no 510, obs. J.-L. Rives-Lange, *Rev. trim. dr. com.* 1991, 76, obs. Cabrillac et Teyssié.
7. Ass. Plén. 1 December 1995, *Bull. civ. Ass. plén.* no 7, 8 et 9.
8. Com. 9 July 1996, *Bull. civ.* I, no 205.

small. For instance, in the 1960s, French courts decided not to reduce excessive penalty clauses, which are valid under French law, even though some were deemed unfair and too onerous, especially in hire-purchase contracts. The solution was rooted in the principle that a judge cannot modify a contract. A 1975 statute expressly gave judges the right to modify the penalty clause, and they now readily do this in bank credits and loans.

Bank statements

The value of a bank statement was discussed in France in the mid 1970s, and quickly settled by a clear solution given by the Cour de cassation: silence of the customer at reception of a monthly statement showing payment of interest is a valid acceptance of that payment.[9] The issue was reopened in the late 1980s, as a related issue to the previous question of customer knowledge of the interest rate. Some bank customers sued their bank to set off their debt with the bank with the amount of excess interest the bank owed them. Banks contended that these customers were informed of the interest rate through the amount of interest written on the monthly statement, and that the absence of reaction by the customer on receipt of the statement proved his acceptance of that amount. That argument was based on Article 1906 of the Civil Code which provides that when a debtor pays undisclosed interest, he cannot be reimbursed, nor claim a set-off with the remainder of capital. The Cour de cassation accepted this argument and applied Article 1906 C. civ., but it did so only for the period before the decree of 4 September 1985. Moreover, the contractual and the legal rates of interest came closer to each other after 1985, so the discussion is less relevant.

This issue is limited to the contractual rate of interest inasmuch as it is valid and accepted in writing between the parties.[10] However, consumer credits are subject to other legal requirements and the Cour de cassation stipulates that the TEG (global effective rate) be mentioned not only in the contract proposal and in the agreement but, in addition, in the periodical bank statements.[11] In the absence of such requirement, the bank is prevented from claiming the interest.

Banking customs and interbank agreements

French bankers readily quote a Cour de cassation case which decided on 16 May 1984 that the interbank agreement on clearing houses has effect only between

9. Cass. 14 April 1975, D. 1975, 596, Rev. trim. dr. com. 1975, 881 obs. M. Cabrillac and J.-L. Rives-Lange; M. Cabrillac and J.-L. Rives-Lange, "Les problèmes juridiques et règlementaires posés par les intérêts dans les crédits bancaires", in C. Gavalda (ed.), Responsabilité professionnelle du banquier, Economica, Paris, 1978, at p. 16.
10. Com. 10 May 1994, Bull. civ. IV, no 174; D. 1994, 550, note D. Martin; Civ. 1, 17 January 1995, Bull. civ. I, no 36; D. 1995, 213, note D. Martin.
11. Com. 4 May 1993, Bull. civ. IV, no 170; JCP ed E, 1993, I, 302, no 5, obs. Gavalda et Stoufflet; Rev. jur. com. 1993, 335, obs. Grua.

banks and cannot be invoked by nor used against customers. Therefore rejection of cheques after the allowed period of three days would be valid as against customers whilst contrary to the interbank agreement. However, a few months later, on 9 October 1984, the same court decided that a third party could rely on the interbank agreement.[12] These solutions rely on the effect of banking usages, which can be invoked by customers as well as used against them. However, this practice is an unclear form of remuneration for bank services and the courts tend to criticise it when it is not justified. They found a ground for control in the requirement of a *cause* under Article 1131 of the Civil Code for the validity of debts. Consequently, on 6 April 1993, the Cour de cassation decided that some value dates have no consideration (*cause*) on the ground of Article 1131 of the Civil Code for bank deposits or withdrawals since those operations can be realised immediately.[13] Therefore, the banking practice of value date is only valid when it applies to the performance of transactions which imply some delays, such as cheque recovery. For instance, the practice of the value date, largely used amongst the French banking community and applied to individual as well as to business accounts, is accepted by the courts independently of the terms of the contract. This case strengthened the argument that banking customs and practice are mandatory for the banks, and for the customer, even when they are not explained or written in the documents delivered to the customer.

The statutory regulation of the relationship

In four matters, statutes give protection to a bank customer to facilitate his basic relationship with his bank.

Information

Customer information is a fashion which developed during the 1970s among French politicians and lawyers. It is based on the assumption that information given by the professional party to the customer would improve the customer's situation and diminish his risk of making a mistake. This trend was first developed in insurance matters. Now, and especially since the 1980s, banking matters are under pressure. It goes with the mass society; banking became a mass phenomenon only during the 1960s.

By statute, banks have the obligation to give to their customers their *conditions générales de banque*.[14] They are generally shorter than the German ones, and consist only in the fee or rate due for the various services and credits

12. Com. 9 October 1984, *Bull.* IV no 255; *R.T.D.Co.* 1984, 388, obs. M. Cabrillac and J.-L. Rives-Lange. Also Com. 2 October 1978, *D.* 1979, 349 note M. Vasseur.
13. Com. 6 April 1993, *Bull. civ.* IV, no 138; *JCP* 1993, II, 22062, note Stoufflet; *D.* 1993, 310 note Gavalda; *Rev. dr. bancaire et bourse* no 37, May/June 1993, 126, obs. Crédot et Gérard; Com. 29 March 1994, *Bull. civ.* IV, no 134; 7 June 1994, *Bull. civ.* IV, no 201; 10 January 1995, *Bull. civ.* IV, no 8.
14. Article 7 of the application decree of the Banking Act 1984.

offered by the bank. Most of the banks deliver a sheet of paper nicely printed with a list of the services and their cost.[15] Such information should be available not only to bank customers but also to the public.[16] This list gives only general information, subject to negotiation by each client. However, it is useful to get an idea of what is offered and at what price.

According to the same statute,[17] banks should also deliver information to their customers *on the terms and conditions of use of the current account* on the opening of the account. This information should also cover the price of the various services attached to it, and the reciprocal duties of the bank and the customer. As in England, French banks now deliver small booklets or tiny printed contract forms containing this information. This is recent, because before 1984 it was usual to get nothing when you opened a bank account, the bank keeping a few signed documents and delivering no document for the use of the customer except a small card with the account number. The current account relationship was more customary than explicit at that time. Courts and legislation have changed this.

The right to basic services

The Banking Act 1984 provides for a special solution when a customer has such a bad credit record that no bank will accept him as a customer. Since payment of wages to the customer and payment for consumer goods must, according to French regulations, be made by cheque, everybody needs a bank account. Article 58 of the Banking Act 1984 provides:

Any person who has been refused the possibility of opening an account by several banks, and who therefore has no bank account, can ask the Banque de France to designate a bank . . . with which he may open an account.
    The bank may limit its services to cash transactions.

The Banque de France controls the administrative process. The customer must send a written request to and get a written refusal from at least two banks. He then goes to the local branch of the Banque de France to get his right. The Banque de France indicates the bank which is obliged to open an account. Between 200 and 300 customers get this service every year. To avoid such a solution, the Banque de France issues recommendations to the banks not to close accounts of bad debtors and not to refuse to open accounts to customers who have been rejected by competitors![18]

In parallel to this, in June 1992 the CNC[19] published an agreement between banks and consumer associations to help people having financial difficulties,

---

15. The "Association Française des Banques", a compulsory association for clearing banks, issued a standard form with 20 items grouped in six chapters, the whole thing on a single sheet of paper. This form is not legally mandatory, but would be considered as a minimum by the courts.
    16. Precision given by the decree.
    17. Article 7, para. 2.
    18. Avis de la Banque de France of 1 August 1984.
    19. The official Conseil National du Credit, run by the Banque de France.

and defining the minimum banking service: bank account and printed account references,[20] cheque collection, automatic withdrawal card, and a limited number of cheques. The account can only be closed after a period of a month's notice.

The "sentencing" banker

When a customer issues a dud cheque, he is liable to a penalty applied by his bank. The Act of 30 December 1991 provides for a ban on issuing cheques and a fine which is decided by the bank, increasing the punishment previously stated. The process is as follows:

1. The bank which has insufficient funds to pay a cheque sends a letter to its customer with the injunction to return immediately all the cheque-books issued by all banks and prohibiting any drawing of cheques on any account held by the customer, in any bank.
2. The bank also sends the information to the Banque de France, which runs an electronic record of those prohibited from issuing cheques. It is now connected with the secret record used for a long time by the taxman, listing the various banks and bank accounts of any citizen. This record is open to all banks which can enquire about any person. It will also give the red light or the green light to any person asking to know whether or not a given cheque is illegal. When the Banque de France receives notice of the default of payment of a cheque and of the connected prohibition to issue cheques, it circulates the information through the various banks having accounts for the customer. The drawer can avoid the prohibition by paying the cheque, and a fine of £12. As long as he does not do so, the prohibition length is 10 years. Moreover, the drawer who issues a cheque in spite of the prohibition can be fined and imprisoned by a court.

The prohibition applies to every owner of a collective account except when they appointed one of them as the only responsible customer.[21]

About a million customers were previously prohibited, under the 1975 Act.[22] It is feared that the figure will reach several million under the new Act, based as it is on the same idea applied with more severity. It has been in force since 1 June 1992.

Obligation to continue the credit in case of bankruptcy

When a bank customer goes bankrupt, the traditional solution was to close his bank account and all his bank credits. The Bankruptcy Act 1985, as construed

---

20. Named RIB (*Relevé d'identité bancaire*), it is requested by some debtors, such as employers and the state, to be by direct transfer.
21. Act of 16 July 1992.
22. They caused every year an estimated loss of £300 million.

by the Cour de cassation in 1987,[23] changed this. Now the receiver, or even the customer himself when there is no receiver appointed, can force the bank to continue the previous relationship. The current account continues to run, and credits, especially revolving credits, must continue for the customer. This situation will last as long as the so called "observation period", which usually lasts from two months in 75 per cent of the cases to one or two years in the other cases.

CONFIDENTIALITY

Two opposing solutions are accepted in France. Banks have the duty to conceal precise information from private bodies and to disclose all kinds of information to the taxman. The recent regulations on money-laundering broaden this last duty.

Confidentiality towards private bodies

Confidentiality is accepted as a professional duty of banks. The Banking Act 1984 restates in Article 57 the rule commonly accepted previously. Any violation of professional secrecy that is not authorised is a criminal offence.[24] Convictions are rare. The banks take the precaution not to write about these matters. Information is given orally, most often by telephone.

Banks succeed in performing their conflicting duties to give advice or information to their clients on other clients or through the banking profession, and not to infringe the confidentiality of the information they can collect on their clients in the course of their business. This conflict is settled through the distinction between precise facts, and general appraisal. Precise facts, such as figures or individual events, are strictly confidential. A banker cannot give the balance of a current account, the amount of debt or of loans, not even the balance sheet which is filed in the public registry of business.

By contrast a general appraisal on a client is accepted as not confidential. When a banker is asked by a colleague or by somebody who is not his client to give information on one of his clients, he is most often evasive. He gives what is called *l'opinion de la place*, meaning that of the local financial community. For instance, he will speak of perfect honour and great seriousness, or irregular payments, temporary difficulties and garnishee proceedings.

Exceptions to the duty of confidentiality are set by statute.[25] The bank must disclose the required information to:

1. the Banque de France, which is the agent of the government, as provided in Article 20 of the Banque de France Act dated 4 August 1993;

---

23. Com. 8 December 1987, *Banque* 1988, p. 96 obs. J.-L. Rives-Lange; *JCP* 1988, II, 20927, note M. Jeantin.
24. Article 378 Code pénal.
25. Mainly Art. 57 of the Banking Act 1984, and other specific provisions.

2. the *Commission bancaire*, the official governmental agency in charge of the control of banks and banking activities in France;
3. the *Commission des Opérations de Bourse* (COB, sister agency of the American SEC or the British Securities and Investments Board);[26]
4. a court or any judicial body in criminal matters, such as the government prosecutor or the *juge d'instruction*; but there is no way of compelling a bank to disclose the bank account in civil or commercial matters, except in the following cases:
    (a) a customer's creditor acting under a garnishee order. Courts impose on the bank, on the basis of a text which is quite general, an obligation to disclose the balance of all the accounts belonging to its customer;[27]
    (b) the family court, with restrictions, in divorce proceedings;[28]
    (c) the bankruptcy court (*Tribunal de commerce*).[29]

Disclosure to the taxman

Even before the nationalisation of the whole French banking system in 1982, the taxman gained from the government, without serious control by the parliament and no protection from the courts, rights to many kinds of information. Article L. 83 of a special code called *Livre des procédures fiscales* provides that any body under the control of the state must disclose all information required by the taxman. The administrative tribunals decided without scruple that since World War II the banks have been under the control of the state for the sake of the application of this Article.[30] The same tribunals also decided that a bank is not obliged to inform its customer of the disclosure.

During the period of the complete nationalisation of French banks, confidentiality was threatened. Since privatisation, the situation has not greatly improved. Banks, like insurance companies, are eager to satisfy the taxman's requests, and open all their books, records and knowledge. They know that any lack of cooperation could bring retaliation against themselves personally. The same right, called "right to communication", is given to the Customs.[31]

Moreover banks have the duty to transfer spontaneously to the taxman, without request, information on:

1. the opening of any account to anybody, anywhere;[32]
2. the payment of any interest or sum, by an employer or any payer, once a year.

26. Art. 5, Ordonnance 28 September 1967 on the COB.
27. Art. 559 Code de procédure civile, which could have been discarded by the duty of professional secrecy.
28. Art. 259–3 (2) C. civ.
29. Bankruptcy Act 1985, Art. 19; and Art. 36 Loi, 1 March 1984 on a contractual procedure managed by courts.
30. *C.E.* 22 December 1982, D.F. 1983, c. 1988; *D.* 1983, IR 407 obs. M. Vasseur.
31. Art. 455 C. douanes.
32. CGI, annex IV, Art. 164 FB sq.

Disclosure for money-laundering

The Money Laundering Act 1990[33] created a special division of the Customs, called TRACFIN, with enlarged powers to investigate banks. It also compels the banks to reveal "any sum written into their books" which is suspect.[34] Banks are protected against any liability, criminal or civil, for this disclosure.[35] They are incited to disclose by a protection from criminal proceedings,[36] and are prevented by a criminal fine[37] from informing the suspected customer.

By the Act of 13 May 1996, the customs officers have been allowed to enquire and extend their control on any professional document in relation to offices dealing in currency exchange (*changeurs manuels*). The change officers are incited to disclose the documents by criminal and disciplinary sanctions.[38]

THE MULTIFUNCTIONAL BANK

Some French banks are extremely big, offer a wide range of services and have always offered services related to securities, such as portfolio management and advice in financial matters. In the 1980s, the move toward "Allfinanz" was greater than before, but did not cause too many difficulties. The questions raised by this activity, considered here, relate only to confidentiality and liability for insufficient cover.

Securities management

Confidentiality and conflict of interest are the topics under discussion in France. The COB[39] published in 1974 a recommendation[40] stating that:

financial agents should keep confidential privileged information they may know through their financial or commercial operations, not only with regard to third parties but also inside their company, with regard to departments and people that are not directly concerned, and with regard to SICAV (Unit trusts) with which they have relationships.

The European code of good conduct, attached to the EEC Commission recommendation of 25 July 1977, states in the same way[41] that "financial agents must endeavour to keep secret, even between the various departments of their companies, information they get through their activity . . .". Article 57 of the Banking Act 1984[42] reminds the banks of their duty under professional secrecy.

33. Loi 90–614 12 July 1990 "relative à la participation des organismes financiers à la lutte contre le blanchiment des capitaux provenant du trafic des stupéfiants". This Act was adopted before the European Directive, and is more severe.
34. Art. 3.
35. Art. 8.
36. Art. 9.
37. From £1,500 to £15,000, Art. 10.
38. Art. 25 bis introduced by the Act 96–392 of 13 May 1996.
39. See the text referred to by footnote 26.
40. Recommendation of 19 March 1974. See on secrecy the short account given by J.-L. Rives-Lange, obs. in *Banque* 1990, 192.
41. Arts. 8 and 9 of the code.
42. See above, p. 42.

Concern about the conflict of interest grew in the 1980s with the increase in banks' involvement in financial operations, due both to the move towards universal banking and to the spread of unit trusts, named *OPCVM* in French.[43] During the 1980s any French bank of respectable size could create a variety of unit funds called in France *SICAV* for the largest, and *Fonds Communs de Placement* (FCP) for the others. The promotion of these in-house products may conflict with the customer interest. The governmental authorities controlling the banking profession and the COB appointed a commission chaired by M. Brac de la Perrière to write a report on that problem. It drafted rules of ethics[44] which were included in two recommendations issued by the COB in 1988.[45] The basic idea is to build "Chinese walls" between the various departments of the same bank, namely customer representatives, portfolio managers, brokers, back officers, etc. Apart from the action of the COB and the Brac de la Perrière report, there is no case law, and little doctrinal debate on that problem.

The Act of 2 July 1996 relating to investment services prevents conflicts of interests between the companies and the members of the Conseil des marchés financiers who hold an interest or a position in said companies.[46] In addition, the law stipulates that employees of the investment service companies must deal in compliance with the rules of conduct developed by the Conseil des marchés financiers and the COB.[47]

Specific problem of insufficient cover

Even when a customer manages his own portfolio, he nevertheless has frequent contact with his bank. He sometimes asks for advice, and the bank can be liable, as shown below. Even without giving any advice, the bank can be liable for negligence. When the customer speculates in operations on the futures markets, the broker, and the bank which transfers the order, must demand cover from the customer.[48] Sometimes they forget, and if the deal goes wrong, the customer sues the bank, contending that the absence of cover facilitated the loss in encouraging him in the investment. Most of the judgments are in favour of the bank, stating without explanation that the lack of demand for cover cannot be a case of negligence but is only a professional offence.[49] However, more recent cases have held that the bank has a duty to inform the customer of the existence, the

43. Organismes de Placement Collectif de Valeurs Mobilières.

44. The report is printed as an annex to the *Bulletin mensuel de la COB*, no 212, March 1988: Rapport général du groupe de déontologie des activités financières.

45. Recommendations of 24 March and 24 June 1988. On the action of French authorities in that matter, see P. Bezard, "Des problèmes de gestion de portefeuille", *Banque & droit* 1990, p. 37.

46. Loi 96–597 2 July 1996, Art. 30.

47. Act 96–597 of 2 July 1996, Art. 58 and réglement COB 96–03 relatif aux règles de bonne conduite applicables aux services de gestion de portefeuille pour le compte de tiers, JO 22 January 1997, Hovasse, *Dr. sociétés*, 1997, no. 35.

48. Art. 4.6.2 and 4.6.4 of the Règlement Général du Conseil des Bourses de Valeurs.

49. That was the solution of the 1890 decree on the matter, repealed in 1988.

meaning and the importance of the cover,[50] especially on futures markets, which are highly speculative.[51] When the bank omits to give such information, it can be liable. This is nearly a liability for advice,[52] which is therefore related to the capacity of the customer. Damages for the wrong suffered are difficult to assess, and the courts are sometimes arbitrary.[53]

BANK'S LIABILITY FOR ADVICE

Two kinds of liability for advice provide evidence for the saying that "advisers are not payers". They apply to the creditworthiness of a customer and to investments.

Advice on the creditworthiness of a bank customer

The conduct of banks in this regard has been described under the heading of confidentiality; they rarely put any advice in writing. Therefore evidence of any discrepancy between the advice and the reality, or any negligence in the collection of information, cannot be brought to court. There is no discussion about the question of whether answering enquiries from another bank or from a third person is within the scope of banking business. It is an accepted practice, and is even encouraged by the obligation imposed on banks to indicate their phone number on the cheque forms they issue.

Liability to the enquirer

With the enquirer, the bank enters into a contract. Banks do not charge for this service either when they enquire on behalf of their customer, or when they answer an enquiry. However, it is not gratuitous, since it is part of the services commonly provided by banks to attract and to keep their customers. Therefore a liability could occur more easily for simple negligence; there is no requirement for this to be a specific or very serious fault. The banker should have checked the information delivered to the enquirer, with fairness and efficiency.[54] If the bank

50. The earliest case from the Cour de cassation was Com. 28 October 1974, *Bull.* IV, n. 264; D. 1976, 373 note J. Decamme; *JCP* 1976, II, 18251 note M. Boitard; at the same time, various Courts of Appeal decided in the same way. Then, the Cour de cassation reversed its solution. Eventually, it held again that the bank can be liable: Civ.1, 22 May 1985, *Bull. civ.* I, n. 160; *Gaz. Pal.* 1986, 1, 24 note A. Piedelievre; Com. 23 October 1990, *Bull. civ.* V, n. 243.
51. Com. 5 November 1991, *Bull. civ.* IV, n. 327; *Gaz. Pal.* 1992, pan. 20.
52. It was also said that the absence of cover gives evidence of an implied credit that the banker should not interrupt without notice, but this kind of implied term is not really convincing. On the argument, see M. Storck, "La responsabilité encourue pour le défaut d'exigence de couverture d'opérations à terme", D. 1992, chr., p. 71.
53. *Ibid.*, p. 74.
54. The principle that the bank only carries an "obligation de moyens" has been recalled by the Cour de cassation, Com. 10 October 1988, *Rev. droit bancaire et bourse* 1989, n. 12, p. 66 obs. Crédot et Gérard. That means that the bank should take the precautions available to a reasonable man with a view to delivering fast information.

asks a corresponding bank to deliver the information it is liable only if the chosen correspondent is not trustworthy.[55]

There is another specific aspect of the liability, which is the causal link between the false information and the prejudice suffered by the enquirer. It is sometimes difficult to prove this link, and the bank cannot be held liable in this case.

Liability to customer about whom information is given

The bank can be liable for wrong or fraudulent information given to its customer. It can even be liable for correct information given with the intention to cause prejudice to him. The bank can also be liable for the breach of the obligation to maintain secrecy, but only when it exists. There are no cases on such a situation.[56]

Advising on investment

In one situation, the bank openly accepts the duty to give advice on the best investment or on the credit and standing of companies offering stocks and shares on the stock exchange. Some banks specialise in this field, and a large national clearing bank has been active in trying to acquire a reputation in this area. This is the case when the bank manages the finance and investment department of a company or an investor. Since 1988, most of the banks have acquired control of a stockbroking company; prior to this, they had direct connections with the stock exchange to follow the value of stocks and securities. Banks are therefore liable for negligence or wrong advice.

In another situation, the bank agrees on a contract for the management of the stocks and bonds. It acts as an agent of the customer, with a certain amount of independence in the choice of investments.[57] The customer is supposed to have ratified the operations when he remains silent on reception of the advice of execution (*avis d'opéré*). The bank can refuse to follow the choice expressed by the customer, when it deems this choice inconsistent with the global policy adopted for the management of the portfolio.[58] The liability of the bank is assessed not on the result reached, but on the conduct adopted. The bank should manage the portfolio as a "bon père de famille", a reasonable man with some expertise. Often, banks include in the contract a limitation of their liability for very serious fault; however, courts are ready to classify any fault in the advice or choice as a very serious one.

In a third situation, the bank receives stocks or bonds belonging to the

---

55. See P. Delebecque, "Contrat de renseignement", *J. Cl. Contrats-Distribution*, Fasc. 795, 1991, n. 98.

56. P. Delebecque, *op. cit.*, n. 103.

57. F. J. Crédot and P. Bouteiller, "La responsabilité des banques en matière de conservation, de gestion et de placement de valeurs mobilières", *Banque* 1988, 615.

58. Com. 12 July 1971, D. 1972, 153 note C. Gavalda; *Rev. trim. dr. com.* 1972, 144 obs. M. Cabrillac and J.-L. Rives-Lange.

customer under a contract for deposit. Since the 1983 Act on dematerialisation of stocks and shares, all of them are represented only by a line in an account. There is no longer a duty to keep, to watch over and to return the stocks and shares. But there is a duty to keep track of the operations made, and to repay their price whenever the customer sells them. The bank is often asked for advice, or even offers advice in such situations. It can be liable for wrongful advice,[59] or for inducing the customer to pursue an unsuitable choice.[60] It can also be liable for advising a risky investment to a customer without expertise.[61] Courts take into consideration the age, the wealth and the expertise of the customer to assess the quality of the advice given. Courts might tend to consider that a bank is liable for negligence and lack of information of the customer when it omitted to give advice to an ignorant customer on risky investments and to alert him to losses so that the customer was not aware of the damages he suffered and had no advice for reducing or limiting his investments.[62]

The question has arisen whether a bank is liable for negligence in omitting to give information on a company in a bad financial situation to its customer investing in bonds offered by this company. In spite of the absence of a management duty, the Paris Court of Appeal held the bank liable.[63] The Cour de cassation reversed the decision, rapidly by French procedural standards, on the grounds that the bank has no specific duty to give advice, and that information was widely available from newspapers.[64] Banks have recovered their composure.

CONSUMER PROTECTION

In banking matters, protection of the consumer arises largely from the intervention of the courts and the state. However, three specific developments must be referred to.

The state control of banks

The bulk of legal solutions in banker–customer relationships arise out of the action of lawyers, namely legal authors and the courts. The government

59. For instance in tax matters, Aix 17 September 1985, *Bull. Aix* 1985, no 3–4, p. 73, no 144.
60. Civ. 24 February 1987, *Gaz. Pal.* 1987, pan., p. 109.
61. F. J. Crédot and P. Bouteiller, *op. cit.*, at pp. 622 *et seq.*
62. Com. 27 January 1998, *JCP ed. G*, 1998, IV, 1577 upholding a claim for damages against a bank when the customer had a solid experience of the stock market for two years and could not prove that the losses which he suffered for the last four months were caused by a fault of the bank which omitted to give information in risky investments; Com. 26 November 1996, *Rev. droit bancaire et bourse* 1997, no 59, p. 24, no 4 partly denying a customer's claim for damages against a bank for lack of information on highly speculative investment and negligence in asking the customer to cover the margins on the ground that the customer investor was aware of the hazardous transactions on the MATIF and that the ignorance of his losses was not sufficient to prove that the negligence of the bank was related to his losses.
63. Paris 13 July 1988, *Banque* 1988, 929 obs. J.-L. Rives-Lange. The company was Creusot-Loire, whose bonds were then deprived of any value.
64. Com. 9 January 1990, *D.* 1990, 173 note J.-P. Brill; *Banque* 1990, 192, obs. J.-L. Rives-Lange.

interferes with the banker–customer relationship less than it does with general banking matters, which is why the regulations on consumer protection in relation to banks appear only in specific matters.

Such a phenomenon can partly be explained by the specific organisation of the French banking system, heavily controlled by the government, both technically and legally. In 1982, the whole banking system was nationalised. Long before, the government had been in a position to dictate any rule of special conduct to banks, through various channels, amongst which was legislation issued in 1941 during World War II, for a war economy, and fully continued afterwards. In 1986–87, during a more liberal period, 19 major banks were successfully privatised, but the majority remain state-controlled. The Banking Act 1984[65] remained unchanged, and was characterised by a bias in favour of a central and planned economy, with strong powers in the hands of the government.

The French bank customer can therefore be compared, at least partly, with the French user of electricity or gas, governed by a state monopoly. The government, which controls the whole law-making system, is not prepared to consider that there is a need for customer protection. When customers show some desire for protection the solution is not legal, but political. For instance, when in 1988 and 1989 some banks tried to increase the cost of credit cards, the finance minister decided that it was contrary to his views, and the banks gave up. No statute or decree was issued. The retaliation that the government was able to take against a private bank which disobeyed would have been too severe. For instance, banks do not want to lose privileges they receive from the state, like the prohibition on paying interest on current accounts. And the regulatory agencies, the tax controllers, the authorities delivering numerous authorisations, or the state-controlled banks in a position to ban another bank can all be used to punish banks which disobey. This may seem strange in comparison with the development of consumer law in the sales or services areas; however, the various agencies set up to deal with consumer protection do not emphasise a need for legislation in this area.

Courts have recently developed consumer protection, using the basic articles of the Civil Code in a strange manner. We have seen above the cases stating the obligation to write down expressly the interest rate on the debit balance of the current account. In the same way, a curious case[66] held that the banks could no longer change their base rate of interest without informing the customer. This was based in the old and general Article 1129 of the Civil Code requiring that what one party undertakes should be known by both parties.[67] This bold construction was already used in retailers' contracts for sale of petrol or beer. However, the Cour de cassation recently abandoned the application of this article which impaired the validity of contracts; the court preferred to replace this ground by requiring good faith of the bank in the execution of its rights and

65. Statute No 84–46 issued on 24 January 1984, on the activity and the control of credit institutions.
66. Civ.1, 2 May 1990, *Banque* 1990, 1097 obs. J.-L. Rives-Lange; D. 1991, 41 note C. Gavalda.
67. B. Nicholas, *French Law of Contract*, Butterworths, 1982, p. 108.

obligations and recognising a customer's right to compensation for damages due to the bank's bad faith.[68]

Consumer Credit Acts

The Banking Act 1984 contains only two articles dealing with consumer protection. Article 58 created the right to an account, explained above. Article 59 set up the "users committee", described below. The bulk of legislation on consumer protection comes from three specific statutes.

The 1978 and 1979 Acts

On 10 January 1978, two statutes were published on consumer protection. One is general,[69] and deals with sales and services contracts, and especially with frauds. It does not concern banks as such. The other[70] deals with consumer credit, by a supplier or a bank, for personal property. Before that time only specialised banks were engaged in credit for home equipment and cars. During the 1980s, all the banks engaged in this activity had to apply the regulation. On 13 July 1979, an Act was voted to apply the same kind of protection to housing credits.

The major features of the protection are the following:

1. A cooling-off period of 7 days, including a weekend, allows the consumer to cancel his acceptance of the credit, or of the credit sale.
2. During this cooling-off period, the supplier of goods or services has no obligation to deliver the goods. To obtain immediate delivery, consumers are prepared to indicate a false date 7 days earlier, and thus to give up the protection. This is not so usual in banking credits, except for credits by banks which specialise in consumer sales credit, when the credit is in fact negotiated by the salesman.
3. The bank must prepare an offer on a form, the content of which is set by decree. This offer indicates the interest rate,[71] the total cost of the credit, the amount and schedule of repayments, the cost of insurance if any, and other minor provisions.
4. The agreements for sale and credit are connected in such a way that a claim for nullity of the contract for sale is a like claim against the banker.
5. Advertisements should contain some of the information listed at point three.
6. Only credits longer than 3 months and smaller than 140,000 FF (£14,000) are covered.
7. Payment by bills or notes is prohibited.

68. Assemblée Plénière Cour de cassation, 1 December 1995, *Bull. civ.*, no 9; D. 1996, 13, concl. Jéol, note Aynès.
69. Loi no 78–23.
70. Loi no 78–22.
71. Named Global Effective Rate, something close to the British APR, and to the Annual Global Interest Rate described in the EEC Directive on Consumer Credit of 22 December 1986.

8. All claims come within the jurisdiction of the civil small claims court (*tribunal d'instance*), with a limitation period of 2 years.

The 1979 Act on housing credit prescribes similar rules, supplemented with provisions specific to property:

1. The value of the credit must be equal to or greater than 140,000 FF (£14,000).
2. The 10 day cooling-off period prevents the consumer from accepting the credit, with a severe fine for the creditor who obtains a signature within this period.
3. The connection between sale and credit is improved: the sale cannot be concluded if the consumer does not obtain the credit, and the credit is cancelled if the consumer does not buy the house within four months.
4. If there are several credits for the same purchase, each of them becomes final only when the others are agreed upon.

These two Acts were introduced in the Consumer Code under Articles L. 311–1 to L. 313–16.[72] The banks are incited to comply with the legal requirements and to give information to consumers through civil sanctions which discharge customers from paying interest and through criminal proceedings.[73] In addition, French courts have a tendency to prohibit any bank practice which could destroy the legal protection of the customer, since legal provisions are imperative. For instance, the Cour de cassation decided that the absence of the global interest rate in the credit documents may not be replaced by the acceptance of the customer in another document which refers to new terms of payments.[74] This issue is sufficient to deter banks from such failure in the contracting documents with the threat of losing the right to claim for interest, as provided in the consumer credit laws.

Furthermore, the courts allow consumers claims for reimbursement of the interest paid when the 1978 and the 1979 Acts are violated.[75] In addition to the sanctions provided by the Acts, the courts decide that a loan is void when the prior offer for credit does not provide for each term the information on the amortisation of the principal and of the interest.[76]

The 1989 Act

A specific Act of 31 December 1989, named loi Neiertz from the name of a former secretary of state, has a specific procedure for bankruptcy for consumers. It was reformed and introduced in the Articles L. 331–1 to L. 331–8 of the Consumer Code by the Act 95–125 dated 8 February 1995. The protection has

72. Loi 93–949 26 July 1993.
73. Articles L. 311–33 to L. 311–36 of the Consumer Code for consumer credit and Arts. L. 312–32 to L. 312–35 of the Consumer Code for housing credit.
74. Civ. 1, 3 March 1993, *Bull. civ.* I, no. 95; idem Civ. 1, 30 March 1994, *Bull. civ.* I, no 130.
75. Arts. L. 311–33 and L. 312–33 of the Consumer Code, Civ. 1, 18 February 1997, *Bull. civ.* I, no 66; Civ. 1, 21 January 1992, *Bull. civ.* I, no 22.
76. Civ. 1, 20 July 1994, *Bull. civ.* I, no 262; *RTD civ.* 1995, 883 obs. J. Mestre.

been extended to French debtors domiciled out of France who contracted debts in France. This is not a winding-up but a moratorium. This moratorium is set up first by a specific local commission run by the county branch of the Banque de France, and secondly, if necessary, by the civil small claims court. Banks are represented in the local commission by one representative, together with a number of civil servants representing the taxman, the ministry of finance and other departments. The major features of these proceedings are:

1. Only consumers overcome by their debts are concerned. The Banque de France considers that repayments reaching two-thirds of earnings give rise to the right to a moratorium.
2. The case is initiated by the Banque de France, based only on the consumer's declaration!
3. Debts and credits for professional matters are excluded.
4. The commission elaborates a moratorium with a long repayment period, with or without interest. The moratorium, called a "plan", should be agreed upon by each creditor and by the debtor. Banks are under pressure to agree, but 90 per cent of the agreed moratoria are not carried out by the debtors.
5. The consumer can go to the small claims court to get the same kind of moratorium either when an agreement cannot be reached through the commission or as an alternative to going to the commission. The consumer gains additional protection. All proceedings against him are stopped. No agreement is required from creditors, but the maximum length of the moratorium is five years, with a very low interest rate.
6. Bankers and creditors who are suspected of having increased the indebtedness of a consumer could be treated more severely by a judge.

Today, after a few years of this statute being in force, it is difficult to say that it is a success except in threatening bankers. As between 31 July 1995 and 31 January 1998, an issue was given in 70 per cent of the files. At the end of 1997, more than 600,000 borrowers had filed an application for a moratorium due to unemployment difficulties. Almost 300,000 obtained a longer repayment period (beyond 10 years).

Some reforms have been enacted on 29 July 1998 in order to consider the situation of debtors who have no economic support, providing for a longer moratorium (eight years instead of the present five years) and even for a discharge of the debtor in the event of persistent insolvency.[77]

The Consumer Code

In 1990 a commission of lawyers and civil servants drafted a complete code of consumer law, with extensive protection for consumers. These protections integrate the existing ones, and new ones which range from the nullity of a long

77. Loi 98–675 29 July 1998, J.O. 31 July 1998.

list of "unfair clauses" to a mandatory fund for insurance and legal aid. Bankers are concerned by these provisions. There is currently no official plan to enforce the code as such, but some provisions or ideas from it are incorporated in various statutes.

The Act 93–949 dated 26 July 1993 enacted the consumer protection. These rules integrate the existing ones and new ones which range from the nullity of a long list of "unfair clauses" to a mandatory fund for insurance and legal aid.

In 1994, the Commission des clauses abusives recommended the elimination of some clauses used in credit card agreements, for instance those providing for changes in the obligations imposed by the bank without obtaining prior and express consent of the debtor, or those preventing the customer from proving against a payment made with a credit card in the absence of authentification.[78]

In addition, the Act 95–96 dated 1 February 1995 was adopted in order to introduce in France the European directive on abusive clauses. Like the directive, this Act lists a number of clauses which may be considered by the judges as abusive. The Act provides for some exceptions regarding the banks, such as the right to decide to terminate an agreement without prior notice with sufficient reason and under the condition that the bank gives immediate information to the other parties.

According to this text, abusive clauses are disregarded by the courts inasmuch as they give banks superior rights than those given to consumers. Absent any legal definition, some variations have been noticed in determining customers to be protected. In 1987, the Cour de cassation granted the protection to parties contracting outside their professional competence.[79] Thereafter, the scope for protection seemed limited when the Cour de cassation denied protection to parties who contracted for business purposes.[80] This tendency was confirmed in 1996, when the Cour de cassation reconsidered the protection from abusive clauses and excluded the services directly related to the professional activity of the debtor.[81]

It should be noticed that the scope of the protection from abusive clauses may be different depending on the proceedings. Either protection is claimed by a contracting party and the abusive clause may be dismissed from the agreement according to Article L 132–1 of the Consumer Code, or the protection is sought by consumer associations and the abusive clause is deleted from all the agreements signed by the bank with its customers.

Consumer agencies

Three agencies are operating in banking matters.

1. The "Users Committee" at the Banque de France is the only one totally

---

78. Recommendation de la commission des clauses abusives No 94–02 relative aux contrats porteurs de cartes de paiements assorties ou non d'un credit, BOCC 27 September 1994.
79. Civ. 1, 28 April 1987, *Bull. civ.* I, no 134.
80. Civ. 1, 21 February 1995, *JCP* 1995, II, 22502, note G. Paisant.
81. Civ. 1, 3 January 1996 and 30 January 1996, *Bull. civ.* I, no 9 and no 55.

devoted to banking problems. It was set up by the Banking Act 1984, as an advisory committee. It conducts studies on credit cards, means of payment, bankers costs and fees, etc.

2. The Unfair Contract Terms Agency (*Commission des clauses abusives*) has jurisdiction over every kind of contract. It has jurisdiction only for putting forward reforms or solutions in troublesome contracts. Every year it publishes a report containing its studies and proposals, which has few consequences.

3. The Competition Council (*Conseil de la concurrence*) dealt with banking matters when it decided to impose a modification of the fee of a partnership set up by the banks to organise the credit card settlements, called the *GIE Cartes Bancaires*.[82] This problem was then examined in a Users Committee report.[83]

There is no special mechanism to handle complaints in banking matters, and no kind of ombudsman.

EFT (electronic funds transfers)

Nothing special has been done about EFT. French lawyers have a long expertise in bank transfers, called "virements". Since World War II, these transfers have been encouraged by the government for tax reasons. There are few disputes, no specific legislation, and few legal articles. The basic solutions derive from the analysis of the electronic transfer as a transfer of money, like banknotes or gold:

1. the payment is final when the transfer is credited to the creditor's account, and when it has been accepted by him;
2. the transfer cannot be stopped or reversed when it is debited from the payer's account, or from the intermediary bank if any.

In 1990, the "Users Committee" drafted a report on payment systems, with a view to protecting the consumer using a credit card against excessive cost.[84]

SECURITY

French banks rely heavily on security, and are criticised for that. However, their conduct is perfectly logical. First, the consumer society encourages banks to give credit to unknown customers; secondly, bankruptcy law reduces the effects of security. Therefore, banks are encouraged to multiply securities and search for new forms of security.

---

82. Décisions 88–D–37 of 11 October 1988 and 89–D–15 of 3 May 1989, partly annulled by the Paris Court of Appeal 16 November 1989 and 26 April 1990.
83. *Nouveaux travaux sur les cartes de paiement*, Oct. 1990.
84. *Ibid.*

The securities most used by banks, apart from the discount of bills, are the guarantee and the new simplified security over book debts. Security over shares is traditional. There is no efficient security over a company's general fund of assets like the floating charge; the *nantissement du fonds de commerce* is a pale equivalent. It covers only non-corporeal assets such as the name or the location; these assets have a low value when a business goes bankrupt.

Insolvency law

The French Insolvency Act 1985[85] relies on the idea that a bad business can be saved by stopping all the claims from creditors, and by management by a professional receiver appointed by the court. In pursuit of this mirage, the Act dismisses the creditors by various means, some of which are unfair. Banks suffer from bankruptcies, named *redressement judiciaire*, even when they lead to the winding-up of the business, named *liquidation judiciaire*. Legal fees, the lien for wages, and tax liens have priority and they frequently absorb the few remaining assets. During the first part of the proceedings, the debtor runs his business without paying his creditors, but with a credit that he can impose on his bank.

This Act respects only two forms of security: the possession of goods and ownership. So hire-purchase, the retention of title and the ownership over book debts developed steadily, along with guarantees which permit a claim against somebody who is not bankrupt. Hire-purchase, named *crédit-bail*, is proposed by specialised banks, often subsidiaries of bank holding companies. Retention of title benefits mainly the suppliers, and not the banks.

Banks use more and more possessory securities, like the traditional pledge. Five years ago, the two companies offering field warehousing were boosted by the Insolvency Act 1985, which gives first rank to a possessory security while depriving other securities of their force. They act as a receiver of the pledged goods, kept in the pledgor's own warehouse rented to the receiver. One specific security, named *warrant agricole*, offers the advantages of both a legal possession to the creditor and a real possession to the debtor. It is used to pledge future crops, existing crops, cattle, machines and other farming equipment. It works well with wine stocks, thanks to the control imposed by the taxman over the movement of wine.

Banks have also developed a pledge over bank balances and marketable securities. Under French law, there is no problem comparable to the British "Chargecard" case: any pledge on a bank account or a sum of money (*gage-espèces*) is fully valid and very efficient as long as the debtor's account is blocked by the bank. Enforcement of the pledge on a bank account was recently enhanced by a decision *contra legem* of the Cour de cassation. The supreme court upheld that the creditor could retain the pledged sums when the debtor defaulted in payment on due date on the ground that no transfer of property

85. Loi 25 January 1985.

was involved.[86] It was noticed that in such circumstances the execution of the security was simply a compensation between the sums held by the bank as a pledge and the amount due by the debtor.

As for choses in action such as the claims arising from a contract, French lawyers deem that the assignee has possession as soon as he has the control of the claim by preventing the assignor from being paid by the paying debtor; such prevention is effected by notice given to the paying debtor. For stocks and bonds which are dematerialised, i.e. existing only as a line in an account, possession results in blocking this account (see below).

Insolvency proceedings may have consequences on the enforcement of securities, especially on the mortgagees when debtors are married. The Cour de cassation decided on 14 May 1996 that the bank creditor may only enforce its mortgage and obtain the sale price of a mortgaged common property if the bank filed a declaration for the insolvency proceedings in order to obtain first the debtor's share in the amount resulting from the liquidation of the property and secondly the share belonging to the *in bonis* spouse.[87]

Guarantee

The widespread use of guarantees by banks started in the 1960s. The legal solutions were based on the freedom of contract, so the banks imposed unlimited guarantees on the directors of any company. They also asked all borrowers for guarantees from their relatives; even these guarantees, limited to the amount of the loan, were onerous in case of default, when penalty clauses and a high rate of interest were applied.

In the 1970s, courts began to reduce the creditor's advantages. This intervention peaked in the 1980s when they decided that most of the guarantees should bear a special clause above the signature, written by hand, with a wording such that the agreement could be easily annulled. In 1989,[88] the Cour de cassation reversed its position, but continued to control guarantees to avoid unfair situations.[89]

Even though the law of guarantee is complicated, this security remains very useful for the banks. It provides a way of putting pressure on the directors, which induces them to make the company pay the bank first. In the same way, borrowers are persuaded not to go bankrupt, to avoid their relatives' assets being seized. In case of bankruptcy, courts give guarantors some protection, and put some of the burden on the creditor, but the guarantee remains valid and the bank can sue the guarantor, often successfully.

86. Com. 9 April 1996, *RTD civ.* 1996, 669; *D.* 1996, 399, obs. Ch. Larroumet; *Rev. droit bancaire et bouse* 1996, 117, obs. J. F. Crédot et Y. Gérard.
87. Com. 17 June 1997, *RTD civ.* 1997, 711, obs. P. Crocq; Com. 14 May 1996, *RTD civ.* 1996, 666, no 4; Assemblée Plénière 23 December 1994, *Bull. Inf. C. Cass.* no 402, 1 February 1995, p. 1, concl. Ch. Roerich et rapport Y. Chartier; *D.* 1995, 145, note F. Derrida.
88. Civ.1, 15 November 1989, *Bull. civ.* 1989, IV, n. 348; *D.* 1990, J., p. 177, note C. Mouly.
89. M. Cabrillac and C. Mouly, *Droit des Sûretés*, Litec, 2nd ed., 1992, n. 103s.

Simplified security over book debts

Book debts were traditionally offered as a security to French banks through the discounting of bills of exchange. From the 1950s to the mid 1980s, discounting was the major method of bank credit. Circuits were well fuelled, from the small business to the Banque de France, through the channel of private banks and state-owned banks who encouraged the process. Indeed, they were so well fuelled that the cost of managing the mountain of paper made from bills, and false economic ideas about inflation, gave rise to attacks against discounting in the 1970s. The government tried several times to come up with a good alternative. Until the 1981 Act, it was unsuccessful. This short statute, enacted on 2 January 1981, allows businessmen to transfer the title to payment by their own debtors to the banks. Banks were not at ease with such a security, which looks like a discount but does not offer the same protection. They sometimes used it in the wrong way, as a discount, while it is designed as a global security over a bulk of receivables providing a yield at realisation.

The basic idea underlying this security is to operate with a minimum of documents and costs.

1. The security is completed by the writing of a list of debtors, signed by the customer and dated by the bank. Even future receivables can be listed, but banks are still reluctant to accept them.
2. The civil law rule of perfection of the assignment of debts through a sheriff's notice to the debtor is suppressed. Nothing replaces it.
3. The bank is not obliged to give notice of the transfer to the debtor. The legislator assumed that in 90 per cent of cases the security would not be realised, because of the repayment of the credit by the customer. In such circumstances the bank is allowed to let the customer receive the payment as an agent or, if it prefers, it can notify the debtor that the debt has been transferred to the bank. This notification is as costly as the discount, but less systematic. From that point on, the debtor must pay the bank, but the debtor can still argue against the bank all the claims he has against the bank's customer. The Act allows an acceptance, similar to the drawee signature; but banks cannot obtain such acceptance in practice. In spite of some drawbacks, this security over book debts is highly praised by banks.

Security over shares

Two kinds of shares can be offered as security. The first kind is the shares of the small company, *société à responsabilité limité* (SARL) or *société anonyme* (SA), which is the bank's customer—they are offered by the director, as a pledge, and their value disappears at the time of realisation. The same can be said for the shares of a company bought under a LBO. The other type is the marketable shares or securities owned as an investment by the customer, whoever he is. These stocks and shares have been dematerialised, as are the shares of any small

SA. Only partnership shares were excepted (SARL, *sociétés civiles*, commercial partnerships with unlimited risk). The shares of a *société civile immobilière* are often pledged because such partnerships are used for tax reasons to hold property. This pledge is less onerous than a mortgage.

Three ways now exist to create a security over shares, depending on the nature of the shares:

1. Specific statutory provisions for security over dematerialised stocks and shares. Dematerialisation was decided upon by a 1981 statute, and carried out by the Act 83-1 of 3 January 1983. Article 29 provides for security, which is a pledge. Dematerialised stocks and shares are represented by a credit in a specific account, in the books of the issuing company, of a bank or of a stockbroker. All are registered in the name of the stockholder; bearer shares were suppressed, for tax policy reasons, because they are anonymous. It is therefore easy to create a pledge. The stockholder signs a declaration creating the pledge. A notice is sent to the account holder (bank or company), which should deliver a receipt and transfer the "shares" to a special account. The process is similar to an EFT, except that the special account is still in the stockholder's name, but it complies with the special regime of the pledge.

2. Other specific statutory provisions provide a solution for shares of sociétés civiles,[90] and shares of SARL.[91] Security requires a document in writing, notified by a sheriff to the company. For the sociétés civiles, the creditor must in addition file the document with the registry of companies.

3. For the remainder of commercial companies, namely the rare partnerships with unlimited risk, there are no specific provisions. A pledge is obtained through the normal process for assignment of debts—a document in writing, notified by a sheriff to the company.

The Act 96-597 dated 2 July 1996 introduced a new provision in Article 29 of the Act of 3 January 1983 whereby the signed declaration of the stockholder to the account holder is the only requirement for the validity of the pledge. Therefore, the Act dismissed the courts, which decided that the statutory required declaration was not a condition for the validity of the pledge.[92]

The Act of 1996 gave additional protection to the pledgor by allowing provisions in the pledge covering the existing stocks or shares or its extension to the shares held in the stock account. This pledge may therefore include new shares or new stocks registered in the account as a result of any change in the capital of the company. This legal issue tends to dismiss the prior court decisions which declared that the pledgor rights could not be extended to new shares or

90. Art. 1866 C. civ.
91. Art. 46 Companies Act 1966.
92. Com. 7 March 1995, *Bull. civ.* IV, no 73; *JCP* 1995, ed. G, I, 3889, no 19, obs. Ph. Delebecque; *Rev. Sociétés* 1995, 743, note M. Jeantin; *Bull. Joly* 1995, 674, obs. P. Le Cannu; Decree 97–509 dated 21 May 1997, J.O. 23 May 1997.

new stocks subscribed by the debtor after an increase of capital of a company when the pledged shares had disappeared further to a prior reduction of the said capital (*coup d'accordéon*).[93] This issue gives protection to the pledgee since the creditor does not need another agreement with his debtor for including the new shares or stocks into the pledge.

Moreover, the Act of 1996 improved the rights of the creditor by allowing the pledgee to retain the sums produced either by the pledged shares or stocks or by the sale of those shares or stocks. However, the application of the reform has been postponed until the adoption of the decree 97–509 dated 21 May 1997, ten months later, and it has been limited in scope to dematerialised stocks as an exception to the general rules applying to the enforcement of the pledge.

Consequently, pledges on other shares are still subject to the Civil Code, which prohibits the "pacte commissoire" and forbids the creditor to keep the pledged shares in the absence of payment on due date. According to Article 2078 alinea 1 of the Civil Code and to Article 93 alinea 1 of the Commercial Code, the creditor must obtain a judicial order for a public auction sale of the shares in order to obtain payment of the due amount.

Liability for excess credit

Business credit

When a business goes bankrupt, creditors, guarantors or the receiver sometimes sue the banker on the basis of the tort he committed in giving credit to the business. They argue successfully that the credit permitted the customer to pursue an unprofitable business, and that he would otherwise have been unable to proceed to his downfall. Such a credit is named *soutien abusif*. They argue that, during this period, the customer was in a position to contract new debts with them, which will remain unpaid, so there is harm caused by the bank. They also argue that during this period, the bank was repaid from previous credit, by receivables transferred to the current account, and that the credit was only justified by the bank's desire to reduce the debit balance. If this is proved, the liability of the banker is fair, but it is not often the case, and sometimes liability occurs for credit given which was only imprudent.

Consumer credit

The Neiertz Act of 31 December 1989, described above, sets up bankruptcy proceedings for the case of "overindebtedness" (*surendettement*). According to ministry officers, overindebtedness occurs when a consumer is liable to pay credit repayments amounting to more than two-thirds of his gross income. Also according to them, 200,000 families were in such a situation at that time. Banks,

93. Com. 10 January 1995, D. 1995, 203, note A. Couret; *JCP* 1995, ed. G, I, 3851, note Delebecque; *Rev. Sociétés* 1995, note P. Le Cannu.

consumer credit institutions, and profit oriented companies were designated as the major causes of this overindebtedness. Since then, more than 100,000 proceedings have been filed, and the number keeps growing, showing that the appraisal of the problem was inaccurate, and that people are abusing the proceedings.

Liability for termination of the credit

Banks are sometimes rude to a customer, suddenly deciding one morning to reject cheques and bills without informing the customer that they cannot tolerate an accrued overdraft. Often, such a termination of the credit leads the customer to bankruptcy. Courts have declared banks liable for abusive termination of credit, with large damages being paid to the creditors of the bankrupt. Article 60 of the Banking Act 1984 approved this solution.

ENVIRONMENTAL LIABILITY

There is no case in France of the environmental liability of banks, neither is there any example of a bank's liability for any kind of tort caused by the client through use of a bank credit.

The fact that a creditor holds security over land or premises which can be the source of hazardous waste does not give rise to a claim against him for damages. There is still no specific statute on hazardous waste disposal. The French common law of mortgage contains a sharp analysis of the security, which prevents liability for damage. This security gives the creditor a right to the value of the property, but no right to its utility. Even when the secured creditor is in possession he has no right to the utility, which remains with the debtor. Therefore, the creditor cannot be liable since he cannot be the tortfeasor. The same reasoning should apply to the transfer of title used as security, avoiding liability on the secured creditor.

Bank liability under French law is different, and sometimes strange anyway. As stated above, banks can be liable for having given too much credit to a client. They are also liable for having suppressed credit too quickly. The activity of banking becomes increasingly difficult! The idea is close to that which led to environmental liability. Maybe one day a common law oriented judge could decide to impose bank liability for environmental damage.

CONCLUSION

The modern banker–customer relationship is full of traps, more for the banker than for the customer. The last report on bank profits shows that they were slightly profitable. Bank customers are not dissatisfied with their banks, especially since European law introduced some freedom and more active competition to the French banking community.

THE LATE CHRISTIAN MOULY, AND PASCALE BLOCH

CHAPTER 4

GERMANY

INTRODUCTION: THE MAIN LEGAL SOURCES

The banker–customer relationship is typically based on one or more contracts concluded between a bank and its customer. Accordingly, the legal regime of this relationship is constituted by the principles of general contract law as found in the German Civil Code (*Bürgerliches Gesetzbuch*; BGB) and Commercial Code (*Handelsgesetzbuch*; HGB). These codes do not contain special provisions on banking transactions. Instead, the general provisions on contracts, e.g. on credit contracts (Arts 607 *et seq.* BGB), agency contracts (Arts 675, 662 *et seq.* BGB), purchase contracts (Arts 433 *et seq.* BGB, Arts 373 *et seq.* HGB), commission contracts (Arts 383 *et seq.* HGB) and others as well as the general principles of good faith (Art. 242 BGB) and on the interpretation of contracts (Art. 157 BGB, Art. 346 HGB) are applicable. In addition, the rules and principles on precontractual duties and on tort liability under the German Civil Code come into play. Courts and legal doctrine have adapted the general provisions and principles of private and commercial law to the special needs and problems of banking transactions and have special duties and obligations that, as a whole, constitute the special field of private law of banking transactions.[1]

This private law of banking transactions is modified and completed by special legislation on the protection of customers and investors. The most important laws to be named are the Law on General Conditions of Contract of 1976 (*Gesetz über Allgemeine Geschäftsbedingungen*; AGB-Gesetz), the Law on Consumer Credits of 1990 (*Verbraucherkreditgesetz*) and the Law on Trading Securities of 1994 (*Wertpapierhandelsgesetz*). The Law on General Conditions of Contract (AGB-Gesetz) does not focus on the banker–customer relationship but deals with all kinds of general conditions of contract or standard form contracts as used in the various areas of commerce and industry. But it is true that many court decisions under this law deal with making contracts. The Law on Trading Securities is equally not confined to banking transactions in the

---

1. On the German private law of banking transactions, see Canaris, *Bankvertragsrecht*, 3rd edn, vol. 1 (1988); Claussen, *Bank-und Börsenrecht* (1996); Horn, in: Heymann, *Handelsgesetzbuch*, vol. 4 (1990) Anh. § 372 Bankgeschäfte; Kümpel, *Bank-und Kapitalmarktrecht* (1995); Schimansky, Bunte and Lwowski, *Bankrechts-Handbuch* (1997); Schwintowski and Schäfer, *Bankrecht* (1997).

proper sense but includes the wider subject of financial services. Only some provisions of this Act can be qualified as private law; the major part deals with the supervision and control of financial services.

The prudential supervision of banks in Germany is carried out through the Federal Office for the Supervision of Credit Institutions (*Bundesaufsichtsamt für das Kreditwesen*) under the Law on the Supervision of Credit Institutions of 1961 (*Kreditwesengesetz*). The law does not establish a legal distinction between commercial and investment banking. German banks, as a rule, are allowed to carry on simultaneously all kinds of banking transactions (under what is known as a universal banking system). Supervision laws, although they protect the bank customer, do not give him the right to bring claims against the state or supervisory office on the grounds of a violation of supervisory duties. Thus, the German Law on the Supervision of Credit Institutions provides that the Supervisory Office exercises its supervision exclusively in the public interest (Art. 6 III Kreditwesengesetz).

THE BASIC BANKER–CUSTOMER RELATIONSHIP

Various contracts

The bank customer normally enters into a number of different contracts with his bank, e.g. relating to the opening of a bank account, a loan, the buying and selling of securities, or the use of a safe. The typical basic contract is on the use of a bank account for receiving and executing payments by remittance, cashing cheques, debit notes, or the use of cheque cards and credit cards. The contract on a bank account can be analysed in German law as contract of agency (*Geschäftsbesorgung*; Art. 675 BGB).[2] In order to make full use of such an account, this typical contract must be accompanied by other special contracts such as a contract on the use of debit notes or the use of a cheque card or credit card or other multifunctional cards used in modern electronic payment systems.

As a result, the typical banker–customer relationship can be described as a bundle of different contracts. The role of the bank is different in each of these contracts. Sometimes the bank renders its services on a continuing basis when carrying out payments and receiving money for the customer under a contract relating to a bank account. A continuing and often long-term contractual relationship over a certain period of time is established also by a credit contract; in a typical consumer credit contract, repayment is to be made by instalments together with interest payment. In other cases, the contact between bank and customer is rather short-lived, e.g. when a bank buys or sells securities for its customer. In such a case the bank may act as a broker or as an investment

2. See Heymann and Horn, *Handelsgesetzbuch*, vol. 4 (1990), Anh. § 372 Bankgeschäfte 1 no 5 *et seq.*; BGH ZIP 1996, 1079, 1081.

adviser, or the bank may itself become the seller or buyer of the securities involved.

The banker–customer relationship as a whole

Besides these differences, the various contracts between bank and customer normally have some similarities and common features. Invariably, the bank must use due diligence and care when handling the customer's affairs. It must provide proper information and disclosure, and it must observe strict standards of fairness. Another common feature of these different contracts is the fact that the banks invariably use uniform general conditions of contract as a basis for the contractual relationship with the customer.

The common features of the different contracts existing between a bank and its customer and the fact that normally general conditions of contract are used in these contracts have led some authors to develop a theory that the relationship between a customer and his bank is based on a so-called general banking contract. This general banking contract is said to be concluded when the first contact between the bank and its customer takes place. The contract is seen as the source of the duties of care and diligence described and as the contractual basis for the application of the general conditions of contract used by banks.[3] The theory of the general banking contract, however, does not give much help in solving particular legal problems. It is true that the banker–customer relationship can be seen as a whole. But this relationship is more an economic and factual one than a legal one. Lawyers must define the standards of diligence and care with respect to a particular contract, promise or precontractual situation, and on the basis of tortious liability.[4]

The applicable law in cross-border transactions

German private international law (conflict of law rules) as contained in the Introductory Law to the German Civil Code recognises the principle of party autonomy, i.e. the freedom of the parties to a contract to choose the law applicable to this contract (Art. 27 EGBGB). In their general conditions of contract, the banks propose German law as the applicable law (No 6(1) AGB-Banken 1993), and if the customer accepts these conditions, a choice of law to this effect is agreed. Even if these general conditions are not made part of the contract, an express or implicit choice of German law can often be found because, normally, the banks would conclude contracts only under the law of their main place of business.

In the absence of an express or implicit choice of law, Art. 28 EGBGB comes

3. Pikart, WM 1957, 1238; Herold and Lippisch, Bank-und Börsenrecht, 2nd edn (1962), pp. 33 *et seq.*; Rümker, ZHR 147 (1983), 27, 28 *et seq.*; Baumbach and Hopt, HGB, 29th edn (1995), (7) Bankgeschäfte A/6 m.w.N.; Claussen, Bank-und Börsenrecht (1996), pp. 60 *et seq.*
4. Horn, "Die Rechtsbeziehung Bank–Kunde", in: Wiegand (ed.), *Aktuelle Probleme im Bankrecht* (Berner Tage für die juristische Praxis 1993), Bern 1994, pp. 89 *et seq.*

into play. This rule prescribes that national law is applicable where the gravity of
the contract can be found. The decisive criterion here is which party owes the
performance characteristic for this type of contract. This normally leads again to
the law of the German bank.[5]

Where a foreign customer concludes a contract with a German bank, Article
29 brings the special EEC rules on consumer protection as contained in the
Convention on the Law Applicable to Contracts[6] into play. Thus, the contract
may be subject to the law of the customer's domicile if certain requirements are
met, i.e. the contract is preceded by an advertisement in the country of the
customer, and the customer accepts the contract in his own country, and there is
not express choice of law (Art. 29(1)3 and (2) EGBGB).

Where a customer concludes a contract with a foreign subsidiary of a German
bank, the law of the place of that subsidiary is normally applicable under the
aforementioned rule. There may be, however, a situation where a customer who
also has business relations with the German headquarters of this German bank,
wishes to keep all his contractual relationships with this bank under the same
law, i.e. German law. This is the question of an express or implicit choice of law.
If no indication of such an intention of the parties can be found, the rule prevails
that the applicable law for each contract must be found individually.

International customs and practices will be taken into account by German
courts in the interpretation of cross-border contracts. These customs and
practices can be found in semi-official publications as promulgated, e.g. by the
International Chamber of Commerce (Paris), or they can be seen in uniform
contractual patterns as used in many types of contracts relating to cross-border
financial transactions, e.g. bank guarantees, standard clauses in loan contracts,
bank syndicates for loans or the issue of securities and others. German doctrine
and practice recognises the freedom of parties to refer to internationally
recognised rules (*lex mercatoria*) in their arbitration clauses.

Variation and termination of contracts

Many contracts between the bank and its customer are long-term contracts, e.g.
the contract on a bank account or a loan contract. During the lifetime of such
contracts, there arises quite frequently the need to adapt them to changed
market conditions or other circumstances. In such cases, the bank and the
customer have to enter into negotiations about the variation of the contract. In
many areas of the banking business, where we find many thousands of contracts,
however, individual negotiations about a contract variation are not feasible.
Here, the General Conditions of Contract may open two ways. (1) The bank
may send information about the proposed change and ask his customer to
contradict within a fair period of time, if he does not agree. (2) The bank may
have reserved a contractual right to change unilaterally a certain condition of the

---

5. Reithmann and Martiny, *Internationales Vertragsrecht*, 5th edn (1996), No. 1066.
6. Of 19 June 1980.

contract, e.g. the interest rate. Such an agreed right of unilateral variation of a contract is generally recognised in the German Civil Code (Art. 315). The party that exercises this right must respect general standards of fairness; if these standards are violated, the court may be invoked (Art. 315(3) BGB).

The banks, in the General Conditions of Contract used by all private banks, also reserve the right to change these general conditions. No 1(2)2 General Conditions of Banks says that if a bank sends new general conditions to its customer, and the customer does not contradict within four weeks, he is deemed to have agreed to these new conditions. Whilst a right to such change can be recognised under Article 315 BGB as to fees, interest, and compensation, it is doubtful whether it can also be recognised as to the change of other contractual conditions. Here, an agreement of the customer other than by mere silence appears to be necessary.

A long-term contract may be terminated by a lapse of time agreed in the contract or by giving notice according to the conditions of the contract. In addition, it is generally recognised in German law that there exists for all long-term contracts an extraordinary right of giving notice when a serious change of circumstances or a misconduct by the other party makes the continuity of the contract unfairly burdensome for one party for the future. Such an extraordinary right to give notice is also contained in the General Conditions of Contract used by banks (No 18(2) AGB-Banken 1993).

BANK FEES, INTEREST, AND OTHER PRICES AND COMPENSATION

The bank customer owes his bank a number of fees, interest charges and other prices and compensation contractually agreed. Many contracts between a bank and its customer can be characterised as contracts of agency. This applies, for example, for a contract on a bank account and accompanying contracts, such as a contract on the use of cheques. Under a contract of agency (Geschäftsbesorgung: Arts. 675, 662–674 BGB), the customer must pay the amount necessary to carry out his order, e.g. an order to transfer money from his account by way of remittance (Arts. 669 and 670 BGB). The bank is entitled to deduct this amount automatically from the account credit of the customer. If the bank, in turn, receives money by remittance in favour of its customer, the bank is obliged to credit this amount to the account of the customer, according to its duty as agent (Art. 667 BGB). In addition, the customer has to pay the fees contractually agreed for such services.

According to the great variety of different bank services, there is a great number of different fees and compensation, and it would not be possible to agree individually on them case by case. Instead, the banks have drawn up large indices of fees for their various services that can be inspected by the customer. The fees and prices owed under one given contract may be composed of different elements, e.g. the contract on a bank account may prescribe a monthly flat fee plus a small fee for every entry into the account, plus an amount for mailing out account statements to the customer plus interest for an account debit.

There is an ongoing debate in German jurisprudence and literature about the question whether courts may control the fees and prices asked by banks. It is generally held that the freedom to charge is part of the principle of freedom of contract as recognised by the Constitution (Art. 2 GG). Fees, prices and compensation contained in indices drawn up by the banks are, however, general conditions in the sense of the law on general conditions of contract (AGB-Gesetz). The amount and adequacy of fees, prices, and compensation is, however, not subject to control by the courts (Art. 8 AGB-Gesetz). Only general conditions surrounding the prices and fees, such as rules on how to calculate such a fee, are subject to court control. The banking industry, however, was upset by a decision of the Federal Court that a bank is not allowed to charge a fee if a customer collects his own money in cash from his account in the bank's office, as this was seen as a natural corollary of a customer's right to have his money at his disposal in his bank account. In the same decision, the right of the bank to charge a fee for cash payments of a customer in favour of his account was denied.[7] This decision was criticised for two reasons: (1) because it disregarded the freedom of contract with respect to prices, and (2) it prevented the banks from allocating prices according to costs. Cash transactions in the offices of the banks do cause comparatively high costs that, as a consequence of this decision, must be covered by other income and, in the end, be borne by other customers using other services of the bank. In a later decision, the Federal Court recognised the right of a bank to allocate its prices according to costs and, generally, to split prices, e.g. to ask a flat fee for an account and other fees according to the number of the account entries.[8] The amount of interest to be paid under loan contracts is freely agreed upon between the customer and his bank. In consumer contracts, the bank must precisely describe in writing all prices, including disagio, interest, and other fees (see below, Consumer and Investor Protection). There is no price control as to the amount and adequacy of interest rates. The freedom of contract, however, is generally limited by the principle that contracts violating good faith are not valid (Art. 138 BGB). The courts have used this rule to define maximum limits of interest rates in consumer credit. They declare a consumer loan contract invalid where the interest rate is more than twice as high as the average interest rate ascertained each month by the Federal Bank in light of market conditions.[9]

7. BGHZ 124, 274 = WM 1993, 2237.
8. BGH WM 1996, 1080 = BGHZ 133, 10 = ZIP 1996, 1079. For the whole problem, see Horn, *WM Sonderbeilage* Nr. 1/1997.
9. BGHZ 98, 174, 176 *et seq.*

GENERAL CONDITIONS OF CONTRACTS AND THEIR CONTROL BY THE COURTS

Uniform general conditions of contract for banks

The banking industry uses uniform standard conditions of contract in their contracts with customers and other banks. These uniform conditions have been drafted by the leading associations of banks and are invariably used by all members of these associations. One uniform set of such conditions has been drafted by the association of German private banks, another one by the association of savings banks, and a third one by the association of cooperative banks. These general conditions form an important legal basis for the daily business of banks. In addition to these general conditions used in every contract with the customer, the banks use general conditions confined to particular banking transactions, and standard form contracts.

The banks have constantly reformed and redrafted these uniform conditions. The current set of rules was introduced in 1993 and is, for the first time, well structured according to the main activities and duties of the parties.[10] Furthermore, it is much more easily understood by the ordinary customer than before. The association of private banks, when drafting these new rules, hired linguists and public media agencies to make the new rules as transparent and understandable as possible. This is in line with legal doctrine promulgated by the Federal Court that general conditions of contract are subject to the general principle of transparency.[11]

The law on general conditions of contract

The uniform general conditions of contracts for banks and other similar sets of rules used in other areas of the economy are subject to the Law on General Conditions of Contract of 1976 (AGB-Gesetz).[12] This law applies also to the standard form contracts used by banks. The law aims to protect not only the consumer in the proper sense, but the customer in general, i.e. every person who is confronted with a set of general conditions used by the other party and proposed for inclusion in a contract. The protection of the law extends not only to the private customer but also to the merchant (Art. 24 AGB-Gesetz). The law is aimed more at maintaining general standards of fairness in contractual relationships than at dealing with special issues of consumer protection alone.

Under the law, general conditions of contract form part of the contract with the customer only if this contract contains an express reference to these general conditions and if the customer has had an opportunity to inspect the text of these

---

10. Horn (ed.), *Die AGB-Banken 1993* (1994), pp. 65–133.

11. BGHZ 106, 42, 46; BGHZ 106, 259, 264; 112, 115; Horn (ed.), *Die AGB-Banken 1993* (1994), pp. 65–133.

12. On the application of this law to the general conditions of contract of the banks see Horn, in: Wolf, Horn and Lindacher, *AGB-Gesetz*, 3. Aufl. 1994, Anh. § 23.

conditions before the conclusion of the contract (Art. 2). Unusual clauses which a customer need not expect will not become part of the contract (Art. 3). Clauses that, in an unfair way, are to the disadvantage of the customer are void (Art. 9–11). Under the law, the courts have declared void a great number of clauses used in many different general conditions of contract in many areas of economic life. This way, the law has exercised a considerable impact on contractual practice in Germany. Many sets of general conditions of contract in many industries have had to be totally rewritten.

In 1993, the European Union issued a Directive on unfair clauses in consumer contracts,[13] which is designed for consumer protection. In Germany, it was widely held that the highly developed jurisprudence on the German Law on General Conditions of Contract takes care of most issues addressed in this Directive and that little change in German legislation was needed. Nevertheless, a new Article 24a has been inserted into the German law on general conditions of contract. The new article protects a consumer against unfair conditions drafted by the other or a third party, even if such clauses do not form part of general conditions of contract used in other cases.

The test of fairness of general conditions used by banks

Article 9 of the German Law on General Conditions of Contract says that clauses in general conditions of contract are void if they place the other party in a disadvantageous legal position that violates the standards of fairness. An example of the test of fairness being applied by the courts to the general conditions of banks is found in the problem of over-collateralisation of loans. Bank loans to traders and manufacturers are often secured by the transfer of ownership of goods or the assignment of movables to the bank. Under a typical contract, ownership of goods in a warehouse is transferred to the bank (security ownership; *Sicherungsübereignung*), but the borrower is allowed to sell the goods and replace them with new goods, so that the flow of goods necessary for trade is not impeded. The economic effect of such security is not very different from that of a floating charge in English law. In a similar way, a borrower, by a global contractual clause, may assign to the bank a certain volume of movables to be obtained by him in the future (*Globalzession*).

The Federal Court has long held that such security contracts can be illegal and void under Article 138 BGB and Article 9 AGB-Gesetz, if the economic value of the security given (movables or goods) grossly exceeds the amount of the credit extended by the bank.[14] The argument is that such over-collateralisation reduces the borrower's capacity to obtain other loans because of a lack of security which might otherwise be offered to new lenders. As a legal consequence, some senates (departments) of the Fenderal Court have tightened the requirements for fair and proper clauses on securing of loans. They held that all standard clauses

13. Directive No. 93/13/EEC, 5 April 1993.
14. BGHZ 72, 308, 311.

relating to security for loans are void if they do not contain a precise ceiling (*Deckungsgrenze*). The ceiling must reflect the bank's justified need for security and is therefore to be calculated as an amount of the credit extended plus a small margin for interest and costs. Every clause which does not contain such a ceiling is void.[15] The ceiling must be expressed as a specific amount.[16] Moreover, the contract must contain a clause giving the borrower the right to ask the bank to give back any collateral in excess of the amount required by law (*Freigabeklausel*).[17] These requirements are not very practical because, in a typical case, the amount of credit may change every day.[18]

In order to trigger such a clause on the return of collateral to the borrower, the value of the goods transferred or the movables assigned must be ascertained. Accordingly, there must be methods of calculating the value of these goods or movables prescribed in the contract. The Federal Court held that the nominal value of movables assigned could exceed the amount of the credit by 50 per cent.[19] If the ownership of goods is transferred, their value may exceed the ceiling by 20 per cent.[20] The court went on to require a contract to provide precisely how the value of securities should be determined, e.g. how the value of goods in a warehouse with constantly changing stocks should be calculated.[21] In the opinion of the Federal Court, the purchase price of goods could provide an indication of the minimum economic value of the security.[22] This is, however, not in line with economic reality, if we think of seasonal goods or other goods with a fast depreciation (e.g. computers).

This jurisprudence stirred up a heated debate among banking lawyers because it threatened the validity of hundreds of thousands of security clauses in credit contracts. Another senate of the Federal Court held that the contract need not contain a clause on the return of securities (*Freigabeklausel*) because such a right already exists as an implied clause under the contract and follows from general principles of good faith. Therefore, this senate has invoked the Great Senate of the Federal Court to decide on the validity of such collateral agreements.[23]

The principle of transparency

Banks' fees and other prices are, as such, not subject to any control by the courts under the Law on General Conditions of Contract (AGB-Gesetz). In a free economy, prices should be left to be determined by the play of market forces. The German market for banking services is highly competitive, as Germany is

15. BGHZ 109, 240, 242 = WM 1990, 51, 53; BGH WM 1992, 813; BGH WM 1993, 139, 140.
16. BGH WM 1992, 813.
17. BGHZ 109, 240, 246 = WM 1990, 51, 52 f. (concerning global assignment); BGH WM 1992, 813 (concerning transfer of ownership of goods in a warehouse).
18. Horn, *Die AGB-Banken 1993* (1994) p. 121.
19. BGHZ 98, 303, 316, *et seq.* = WM 1986, 1545.
20. BGH WM 1993, 139.
21. BGH WM 1992, 813.
22. BGH WM 1992, 815.
23. BGH, ZIP 1997, 632 *et seq.*

the European country with the highest number of branches of banks in every town. On the other hand, fees are often determined by a complicated network of general contractual clauses. In this respect, the Federal Court has adopted the principle of transparency.

The leading case decided by the Federal Court concerned a widely used standard clause relating to the repayment of principle and the calculation of the interest rate in consumer and other private loans.[24] The decision concerned loans repayable in monthly, quarterly, or yearly instalments. These instalments normally contained two elements: the interest due, and a partial repayment of principal. In the critical clauses the interest was calculated on the basis of the amount outstanding at the end of the preceding year, irrespective of the fact that in the meantime, this amount might have been diminished substantially through further repayment instalments.

The Federal Court considered the general rule that interest on a credit should be calculated according to the amount of the loan outstanding at the time when the interest accrues. The clause in question obviously deviated from this rule to the detriment of the borrowers. The Federal Court admitted that this does not necessarily amount to a violation of the law,[25] but held that the clause violated the principle that general conditions of contract must be clear and transparent. This requirement of transparency was violated by a complicated clause that determined the amount outstanding at the end of the previous year to be relevant to the interest calculation in a way that a customer would not easily understand.[26]

Some German banks suffered a loss of millions of Deutschmarks as a result of this decision. The banking industry resolved the problem for the future not only by avoiding such clauses banned by the Federal Court, but also by disclosing the effective annual interest rate of a loan (calculated on the basis of all credit costs to be borne by the customer) as distinct from the nominal interest rate. This disclosure requirement, in the meantime, has been imposed by the Law on Consumer Credits.

THE BANK'S DUTIES OF CARE AND DILIGENCE

Due diligence when serving the customer

Under its various contractual and precontractual relations with its customer, described above, the bank owes due diligence when serving the customer. The duties of care and diligence need not be expressly agreed upon. Under German legal doctrine and jurisprudence, such duties follow from the precontractual relationship under the principle of fairness (Art. 242 BGB) and, when a contract

---

24. BGHZ 106, 42, 47.
25. Federal Court, as cited.
26. BGHZ 106, 42, 49 ff.; BGHZ 112, 115, 117 et seq.; Köndgen NJW 1989, 943, 948, 950; Horn, in: Wolf, Horn and Lindacher, AGB-Gesetz, 3. Aufl. 1994, § 23 no 715.

is concluded, are implied duties of this contract. The bank must use due diligence and care when handling the customer's affairs. It must provide proper information and disclosure, and must observe strict standards of fairness. In particular, it must disclose whether there is a conflict of interest between the bank and its customer; for example, when the customer instructs his bank to buy securities, the bank must make clear whether it acts as a commission agent (Art. 383 HGB) or as a seller of these securities. Furthermore, it must carry out the contract according to the stock exchange price ruling at the time when the contract is carried out and, finally, it must abstain from any unfair influence on the price (front running and the like).

In the affluent Western societies, there is a growing market for administering other people's wealth, and banks and others have increasingly become active in this field of trust administration. Here, the bank must find out which kind of administration the client wants, and which type of investment and what chances and risks he prefers. Once the bank has found out the customer's expectations, and which type of investment is suitable for him, the bank's duty is not so much a duty to give current information and advice as to make careful investment decisions on behalf of the customer. It must, for example, take care that a portfolio management has an adequate distribution of risks,[27] and it must not expose too large a part of the fortune to high risk investments.[28]

Confidentiality. Right to give information about the customer

As a rule, the bank must keep the customer's affair confidential; in particular it must not give information about his assets with the bank or about his plans for certain financial transactions, unless the customer has given his consent.[29] The duty does not have an express statutory basis but is derived from the contractual relationship between the bank and the customer, which implies a general fiduciary duty.[30] Bank secrecy covers all "facts the customer wants to be held confidential".[31] This duty of the bank to observe bank secrecy (*Bankgeheimnis*) includes the right of the bank to refuse testimony in a civil procedure (Art. 383 I, no 6, 384, no 3 ZPO). In a criminal procedure, however, the bank has no such right (Art. 53 Code of Penal Procedure (StPO)). The tax authorities have a limited right to ask for information from the bank (Art. 30a AO); in a procedure for tax fraud, however, the bank has an unlimited duty to inform the authorities (Art. 385 AO).

It is a widely used commercial practice in Germany to ask a bank to give

---

27. BGH WM 1994, 834, 386 = ZIP 1994, 693, 694.
28. OLG Hamm WM 1996, 669; Horn and Balzer, EWiR 1996, 499 *et seq.*; OLG Frankfurt/M., WM 1996, 665; Horn and Balzer, EWiR 1996, 589 *et seq.*
29. BGHZ 27, 241; 95, 362, 365; Heymann and Horn, *HGB*, vol. 4 (1990), Anh. § 372 Bankgeschäfte 1, no 44.
30. Rehbein, "Rechtsfragen zum Bankgeheimnis", ZHR 149 (1985) pp. 139, 140 *et seq.*; Sichtermann, Feuerborn, Kirchherr & Terdenge, *Bankgeheimnis und Bankauskunft* (1984) pp. 111 *et seq.*
31. BGHZ 27, 241, 246.

standard information about a customer's general creditworthiness. This information is normally given in general terms without disclosing precise figures. The information is only passed on to another bank representing the party that seeks this information. Furthermore, the information is only given if the customer has agreed to it.

Business customers normally agree to such information being given in order to enhance their credit standing, since a refusal of a bank to give any information about that customer might damage his credit standing more than relatively adverse information would. A general consent to such information being given is contained in the general conditions of contract agreed between the bank and its customer. The general conditions make a distinction between a business customer and a private customer, the latter being often less inclined to disclose information about his wealth. The bank will not give any information about its private customer unless he expressly agrees to it.

Besides the principle of confidentiality of banks as part of the private law as described, there exists a particular duty under the legislation on personal data protection.[32]This protection of personal data is guaranteed by the German Constitution.[33] The duty of confidentiality of a bank is subject to limitation not only in the aforementioned cases when the bank is asked in a criminal procedure or a procedure on tax fraud, but also in special situations of conflict of interest to be described below.

The duty of confidentiality is further limited by special rights to information granted under the German Civil Code, even to persons who are not customers of the bank. For example, Art. 402 BGB grants the assignee a right to information.[34]

Conflict of interest. Multifunctional bank

The bank must do its best to avoid any conflict between the interests of its customer and its own interest. If the bank sells or buys securities for its customer, acting either as a commission agent (Art. 383 Commercial Code) or as a trader in securities, it must see to it that the contract is executed under the conditions most favourable to the customer. The bank must not execute or sell at a higher price than the securities exhange rate at the time of the transaction. Under the new Financial Services Act of 1994 (*Wertpapierhandelsgesetz*; see *infra*), banks and other enterprises rendering financial services must organise their business in such a way as to avoid conflicts of interest with their customers. Under the law on the supervision of banks of 1961 (*Kreditwesengesetz*), German banks are allowed to carry out simultaneously all kinds of financial transactions. In particular, there is no legal division between commercial and investment banks. As a consequence, banks sometimes not only lend money to a business, but also

---

32. *Bundesdatenschutzgesetz* (Federal Law on Data Protection) of 1990, BGBl. I, pp. 2954 *et seq.*
33. Federal Constitutional Court, BVerfGE 65, 1, 45 = NJW 1984, 419.
34. For further examples, see Horn, ZBB 1997, 139.

hold shares in it. In addition to owning shares in the respective company, the bank may also exercise voting rights on behalf of other bank customers which are shareholders of this company. Not infrequently, representatives of banks are members of the supervisory board of the company. As a consequence, banks have considerable internal information which other investors or debtors do not have. The legislature has taken various steps to limit the danger of conflicts of interest in this respect; for example, under Article 128 Company Law (*Aktiengesetz*), the banks are obliged to pass on all relevant information about the shareholders' meeting to the customer, to ask him whether he will give proxy to the bank or wishes to exercise his voting rights himself, and ask him for his instructions on how to vote.

A bank, furthermore, may be involuntarily involved in a conflict of interest between two customers. If customer A wants to obtain payment from customer B who is no longer creditworthy, and both A and B are customers of the bank, and the bank knows about customer's B situation, it must warn customer A, weighing the interests of both customers in the situation given.[35]

Information and advice in financial services: liability of banks

Banks must give proper information and advice to their customers as investors when they render financial services for them. These duties can be exemplified by two types of cases: (1) commodity futures and (2) bonds.[36]

Commodity futures

Over the last two decades, many German investors have been encouraged by German brokers and investment advisers to buy futures on the London commodities market. In the early years of this kind of investment, customers were not properly informed about the limited chances of profit and the high risk of a loss when investing in an open position in commodity futures. Moreover, they were not informed about the fact that the additional fee charged by the German broker or adviser virtually destroyed any chance of making a profit. In a number of decisions, the Federal Court insisted on full written disclosure of these risks. The court confirmed decisions of the lower courts that a violation of these duties made the broker or adviser liable to the investor for damages. The violation of such a duty of disclosure and advice constitutes a breach of a precontractual duty (*culpa in contrahendo*) as described and a tortious liability for wrongful prejudice to the investor's property (Art. 826 BGB).[37] The disclosure required in the prospectus or other printed material for sales promotion used by the broker or adviser or banks must point clearly to the high risks of loss and small chances for a profit, and must clearly set out the additional

35. BGHZ 107, 104. OLG Hamm ZIP 1982, 1061; *cf.* OLG Köln WM 1990, 1616 = NJW-RR 1990, 755 with a note by Vortmann, EWiR 1990, 869.
36. For a general overview on the duties to inform, warn and advise, see Vortmann, *Aufklärungs- und Beratungspflichten der Banken*, 4. Aufl. 1996.
37. BGHZ 105, 108, 110.

costs resulting from the fees of the German broker or adviser. Even if these strict disclosure requirements are fulfilled, however, they may not afford protection against precontractual and tortious liability, if the text and layout of the prospectus are designed to play down the risks and lead the customer to believe that the particular skills of the adviser or broker or bank would help the investor to overcome the risks and hence make a safe profit.[38]

Bonds

In 1988 and 1989, a number of German banks placed German mark debentures issued by the Australian company Bond Financial Ltd. with their German customers. As early as June 1988, the Australian Rating Agency had given these debentures a "BB" rating, followed in December of the same year by a "B" rating. Nevertheless, the debentures were admitted to the Frankfurt Stock Exchange in March 1989. The admission was soon followed by a "CCC" rating, which indicated an imminent insolvency of the issuer. Some of the sales of these debentures to German customers had taken place after this date. The banks relied on the prospectus used for admission to the Stock Exchange; they did not know of the negative ratings. Bond Financial Ltd. went bankrupt and the debentures became worthless. Some large German banks voluntarily paid back the purchase price of the debentures to their clients; others did not, and were sued by the investors.

The Federal Court held the banks liable for breach of a contractual duty of care. This duty of care stems from a special contract with the client to give appropriate information and advice. This contract is concluded when the customer approaches the bank or broker and asks him to find a suitable capital investment, and this order is accepted. This particular contract on information and advice must be distinguished from the purchase contract or the contract on commission agency that is necessary to carry out the investment. Under this contract, the bank is required to use due diligence to learn first the essential facts relating to the customer and his needs and expectations about the investment he wants; and the bank must give its recommendations for an investment suitable for this particular customer. Moreover, the bank must gather the relevant facts or information concerning the investment in question and evaluate the risks involved. In the case decided, this meant that a bank, even if it was a small rural savings bank, must either abstain from recommendations for Australian securities, or must get appropriate information about the Australian market, including information from the leading Australian rating agency. When the German Federal Court defined the standards of due diligence to be used by banks and brokers when giving investment advice to their customers, the definition was inspired by the rule of suitability that is part of the US capital markets law.[39]

38. BGH ZIP 1991, 1207.
39. *NASD Rules of Fair Practice*, manual § 2152, 2051, 2052; SEC, Exchange Act Rule 15b, 10–3, 17 CFR § 214, 15b, 10-3 (1977).

Later decisions, however, showed that the Federal Court did not intend to provide disappointed investors relying on information from other sources the undeserved chance to recover their losses from the bank effecting the transactions. The court denied the existence of a contract to give advice if the customer gives the bank a specific order relying on information not received from the bank. By this specific order the customer implicitly declares that he neither needs nor wants the advice of the bank.[40] It seems that the courts, in considering the existence of a contract to give advice, rely heavily on the knowledge of the customer concerned. If the customer has a certain knowledge in trading securities, the requirements to be met for the assumption of a contract to give advice seem to be higher.[41]

This is in line with the ideas underlying the new Law on Trading Securities of 1994. It requires a bank to ask at the beginning of every relationship for information on the customer's knowledge and the objectives of his investment. The customer has to be informed about the risks of the class of transactions he wants and is able to effect.[42]

SECURED TRANSACTIONS

The German Civil Code provides for a system of securities for creditors. There are personal securities, where the creditor receives another debtor for his claim. The civil code provides for only one type of a personal security: the contract of suretyship (*Bürgschaftsvertrag*; Arts. 765–777 BGB). The surety agrees to be liable to the creditor for performance to him by a third party (Art. 765 BGB). This undertaking must be in writing (Art. 766 BGB), unless the surety is a merchant (Art. 350 HGB). The surety is basically liable only to the extent that the (main) debt for which he has stood surety actually exists; he can use against the creditor any defences available to the third party (i.e. the main debtor; Arts. 767, 768 BGB). This way, the liability of the surety is made accessory (*akzessorisch*) to the main debt. A suretyship, therefore, does not always enable the creditor to execute swiftly on the security. Banking practice has developed, however, a type of a surety where a creditor can ask for payment "on first written demand", and the courts have recognised this unusual type of contract of suretyship, if a merchant is the surety.[43]

For some time, the courts have equally recognised a contract of "guarantee" (i.e. indemnity) not specifically regulated in the Civil Code. Under such a contract of guarantee (*Garantievertrag*), the guarantor promises to pay a specified sum of money (or, in rare cases, to perform another duty if a defined risk materialises). Unlike the surety, the duty of the guarantor is independent of

---

40. BGH WM 1996, 906 with note Zeller, EWiR 1996, 641; Schäfer, WuB IG 1—9.96.
41. OLG München WM 1994, 236; *cf.* Horn ZBB 1997, 139.
42. On the liability of a bank violating these duties, see Horn, ZBB 1997, 139, 149 *et seq.*
43. BGHZ 94, 244, 246 = NJW 1979, 1500; *cf.* Horn, NJW 1980, 2153; BGH ZIP 1996, 172, 173.

the existence or amount of the underlying debt or, to put it in terms of German legal doctrine, his liability is non-accessory (*nicht akzessorisch*). This type of independent undertaking is also very common in today's practice of securing international trade transactions, and, as such, is widely recognised internationally.[44]

Besides the contract of suretyship and the contract of guarantee, German legal practice uses a cumulative assumption of debt (*Schuldbeitritt*). Under such a scheme, the principal debtor finds another person who is willing to be liable to the creditor along with him. Finally, a common form of personal security in commerce occurs when a person accepts, endorses, or even draws a bill of exchange in order to help someone else to obtain credit. Banks themselves offer their customers such an "*Aval-Kredit*".

In addition to personal securities, the German Civil Code provides for real security in assets. Since German property law respects the principle of specificity, such a security can be created only in precisely identified individual things or rights, not in a collection or stock of things. The floating charge is unknown to German law, although, in practice, forms of security have been developed that are not unlike it in their result. Real security, or *Pfandrecht*, entitles the person for whose benefit it is created to obtain satisfaction of a claim or money debt by executing on a specified thing (Arts. 1113, 1191, 1204, 1273 BGB).

A real security in a movable or chose in action (claim) is created by a pledge in such an asset (Pfandrecht; Arts. 1204, 1273 BGB). A real security in real estate is created by a mortgage (*Hypothek*; Art. 1113 f. BGB), or a land charge (*Grundschuld*; Art. 1191 BGB). Pledges and mortgages are "accessory" rights, as they give a right to obtain satisfaction only to the extent that the secured claim exists. A land charge (*Grundschuld*), however, is an independent right (not accessory), and the creditor does not need to prove the existence of the underlying secured claim.

The principle of publicity runs through the security law of the BGB. Publicity for mortgages and land charges is achieved by registration in the land register (*Grundbuch*). In the case of pledges of movables, possession must be transferred to the creditor, and the pledgor must give up possession entirely (Art. 1205 BGB). In the case of a pledge of a chose in action (Art. 1280 BGB), notification to the debtor is required.

These two requirements were found to be tiresome in practice: a merchant cannot give up possession of his goods in order to raise a credit since he needs them to trade with, and people were reluctant to disclose the amount of the securities they were giving. Today, therefore, the pledge is hardly ever used in order to raise credit, except in the form of the pledge of negotiable instruments, almost always with a bank (*Lombardkredit*). Nevertheless, the pledge is still important insofar as the bank agrees with its customers that all assets of the

---

44. Horn and Wymeersch, *Bank-Guarantees, Stand-by Letters of Credit and Performance Bonds in International Trade* (Deventer 1990).

customer that are found in the possession or disposition of the bank (e.g. assets in a bank account) are under a pledge to secure any claims of the bank against the customer.

In order to secure trade transactions today, a pledge is not often used; instead the supplier of goods retains ownership of the goods until he is paid (*Vorbehaltseigentum*). A bank that extends credit to a merchant and accepts goods in his possession as security agrees with him on a fiduciary ownership of the goods (*Sicherungsübereignung*). In both cases (Vorbehaltseigentum, Sicherungsübereignung), the creditor need not obtain possession in order to establish and maintain these securities. This way, the merchant is in a position to trade with the goods. The bank agrees with the merchant that goods in a specified room in a warehouse are in the ownership of the bank, but the merchant is allowed to trade with them and to bring new goods into this room. This way, a legal effect comparable to that of a floating charge is achieved.

If a customer offers choses in action as a security, again the pledge is not used; instead, the chose in action is fully assigned to the creditor. Very often, a great number of choses in action are transferred to the bank (*Globalzession*) in this way. Here again, the borrower is allowed to collect the money secured by these choses in action and to put other choses in action (specified in advance) into this security pool. Such a global assignment of choses in action typically accompanies every agreement on the fiduciary ownership of goods. Here, the debtor is entitled to sell the goods but he assigns in advance his payment claims out of the sales contracts. He is allowed to collect the money, however, unless he goes bankrupt.

CONSUMER AND INVESTOR PROTECTION

Legislation on consumer credits, on general conditions of contract, and on financial services

In the area of private law, the European Union has issued a number of directives and recommendations on consumer protection. The most important initiative in this field is the Directive on Consumer Credits that has been made part of national consumer credit legislation.[45] The German legislature has enacted a law on consumer credits.[46] Under this legislation, banks are obliged to conclude credit contracts with private customers in writing, and to include in the contract certain precisely prescribed information about the most important conditions of the credit, in order to give the borrower a full picture about his rights and duties, in particular, about the economic burden of the credit. The German Law on

45. Council Directive of 22 December 1986 for the approximation of the laws, regulations and administrative provisions of the Member States concerning consumer credit (87/102/EEC, O.J. L 42/48, 12 February 1987); Council Directive of 22 February 1990 amending Directive 87/102 EEC for the approximation of the laws, regulations and administrative provisions of the Member States concerning consumer credit (90/88 EEC O.J. L 61/14, 10 March 1990).
46. Verbraucherkreditgesetz of 17 December 1990 (BGBl. I p. 2840).

Consumer Credit has extended the scope of its application to all private credit, irrespective of the credit amount, and thus goes markedly beyond the scope of the EC Directive.

Another important piece of legislation on consumer protection is the aforementioned German Law on General Conditions of Contract (AGB-Gesetz). The German law is not just a consumer protection law, but aims at protecting every customer against the restriction of their contractual freedom that would result from unilateral formulation of the contractual conditions. We have seen that under this law German courts and legal doctrine have developed a highly sophisticated system of customer protection against unfair or surprising general conditions and form contracts. The new EC Directive of 1993 on Unfair Terms in Consumer Contracts[47] has been implemented in the German law by inserting a new Article 24a (AGB-Gesetz). As the German Law on General Conditions of Contract already protects the consumer to a large extent, only a few changes were necessary to make the law applicable also to cases where no general conditions are used, but a contract is preformulated by one party, and to cases where the consumer is unfairly influenced when entering into the contract.

The German Law on Financial Services of 1994 (*Wertpapierhandelsgesetz* (WpHG))[48] is equally inspired by EEC Law, namely the Council Directive of 10 May 1993, on investment services in the security field (93/22/EEC, O.J. L 141/27, 11 June 1993). This law lays the foundation for a German capital market law or securities law as a new body of law that is close to banking law but not entirely a part of it. The new law provides for a federal authority for the supervision of the trade in securities and it establishes a number of duties for all enterprises active in the field of financial services. These enterprises must exercise due diligence when serving the customer. They must organise their business in a way that enables them to render the necessary information and advice, and to avoid conflicts of interest with their customers (Art. 32 WpHG). They furthermore must gather the necessary information about the customer, his knowledge, experience, and investment expectations (Art. 31 WpHG). On the basis of this information, the enterprise rendering the financial service can give the customer the information and advice appropriate for him and recommend those investments that suit his needs and expectations. These duties are established in the public interest and are not private law in the proper sense. But they support and underline the private law duties of due diligence, disclosure and advice discussed above that a bank owes to its customer and that are a basis for its contractual and tort liability.

Besides the protection granted on the level of the individual contract between the bank and its customer, some additional protection is provided by the supervision laws. Though the Law on the Supervision of Financial Services explicitly states that the supervision is carried out only in the public interest, the deposit guarantee funds for the protection of savings in case of a collapse of a

---

47. Council Directive 93/13/EEC of 5 April 1993, O.J. L 95/29, 21 April 1993.
48. 26.7.1994, BGBl. I, pp. 1749 *et seq.*

bank grant the customer at least minimal compensation. This type of fund, which has existed in Germany for some time, is now made mandatory on the European level by a Council Directive of 1994.[49]

The aforementioned legislation as well as the jurisprudence on the liability of banks towards customers and investors follow two principal ideas: to protect the customer of a bank as well as the investor taking advice from a bank, and to contribute to the transparency of the markets for banking and other financial services. The principle of freedom of contract is maintained as a basis of a free market economy. But this principle of freedom of contract is put into a new framework. In this respect, German law is in line with the tendencies to harmonise the legal systems of the members of the European Union on the basis of EEC Directives and recommendations.

NORBERT HORN

49. Council Directive 94/19/EC of 30 May 1994.

CHAPTER 5

ITALY

The Italian legal environment for banking activity has been transformed by the Unified Banking and Credit Act (U.A.), a new and in many ways innovative law, which represents the end of a process of renewal of financial legislation which began during the middle of the 1980s and ended with the issue of the legislative Decree of 1 September 1993, No 385. The law was later slightly modified by the legislative Decree of 23 July 1996, No 415, on investment services, which gave banks the possibility of engaging directly in activities relating to investment services. The legislative Decree No 415/96 has now been replaced by the Financial Intermediation Unified Act through the legislative Decree of 24 February 1998, No 58. The new law is divided into three parts. The first two of them—similar to Decree No 415/96—concern the regulation of institutions authorized to engage in investment services and the discipline of financial markets. The third part, completely new, concerns corporate governance in listed companies.

THE UNIFIED BANKING AND CREDIT ACT: A REVIEW

The Presidential Decree (DPR) of June 1985, No 350, which, with significant delay, implemented the First Banking Directive, may be considered the first step towards the new legal banking system, which had remained almost unchanged since the 1936/38 Banking Act.[1] After the Decree No 350/85 many other regulations followed, giving rise to a need for coordination: the laws reforming public banks, the one regulating banking groups, the regulation of non-banking institutions, the laws on consumer credit and the transparency of banking transactions and, finally, the legislative Decree of 14 December 1992, No 481, which implemented the Second Banking Directive, are some of the measures taken by the Italian legislature over recent years.

With the issue of the Unified Banking and Credit Act,[2] most of the regulation

---

1. For complete reconstruction of the history of the banking legal system see R. Costi, *L'Ordinamento Bancario*, Il Mulino, Bologna, 1994 pp. 41–70.

2. In regard to the Act see generally: C. Lamanda, "Il Testo Unico delle leggi in materia bancaria e creditizia", in *Note economiche*, no 3, 1994, pp. 474 *et seq.*; *Commentario al Testo Unico in materia bancaria e creditizia*, edited by F. Capriglione, Cedam, Padova, 1994; *La nuova legge bancaria*, edited by M. Rispoli Farina, Jovene, Napoli, 1995.

concerning the financial sector has been unified and coordinated, removing discrepancies and doubts arising from the previous recent legislation. That is not to say that the Act represents a mere rearrangement of banking regulations, for it also introduces some important new features, even if the new Italian financial legal system is the result of a long process of innovation.[3]

The Act is divided into nine Titles, each dealing with different sectors of regulation, and covers almost all banking regulation—apart, for example, from the discipline of the annual and consolidated accounts of banks and other financial institutions—as well as the regulation of non-banking institutions. However, the Decree cannot be considered a general law on the financial sector as some financial activities, such as those dealing with securities and insurance, are still ruled by separate legislation.

Title I concerns credit authorities[4] and introduces two important general principles. Article 5.1 fixes the aims of banking supervision, stating that credit authorities must exercise their powers to ensure the sound and safe management of the supervised institutions, the stability of the market, the efficiency and competitiveness of the financial system and the observance of credit legislation. The rule reaffirms the principle according to which the credit authorities are not free in their activity but have defined limits. According to Article 5.2, the credit authorities exercise their powers not only over banks but over banking groups and financial intermediaries as well. Still, with regard to the powers of credit authorities, Article 6 regulates them in relation to Community law. The rule establishes the principle that the supervisory powers must be exercised according to Community provisions and that the credit authorities apply the regulations and decisions of the European Community and take steps with regard to recommendations concerning credit and financial matters. The principle enacts a sort of system of direct applicability of Community rules, making the credit authorities directly responsible for compliance with them.

Title II of the U.A. is entitled "Banks". The law drops the Community term "credit institution" and goes back to the traditional one of "bank". The Title opens with the definition of banking activity, which according to Article 10.1 consists of "taking savings from the public and granting credits".[5] Banking activity is the reserve of banks that, besides taking funds and granting credits, may pursue "any other financial activity", including all the activities subject to mutual recognition (listed in Art. 1.2), within the limits fixed by specific regulations.[6] In other words, Article 10 of the Act confirms the lawfulness of the "universal bank" within the Italian credit system.

Defining the expression "taking savings", Article 11 of the Act establishes a

3. It should be noted that most of the novel features examined were introduced by the most recent legislation, and in particular by Decree No 481/92.

4. See R. Costi, *op. cit.*, pp. 71–142.

5. See R. Costi, *op. cit.*, pp. 145–160 and F. Belli, "Teorie creditizie e legislazione bancaria: la 'Banca Universale' e il Testo unico", in Rispoli-Farina, *La nuova legge bancaria*, Jovene, Napoli, 1995, pp. 73 *et seq.*

6. For example, Decree Law No 58/98 on financial services.

general regulation of the business concerning the collection of repayable funds. The rule prohibits persons or undertakings that are not banks from engaging in the business of taking repayable funds from the public, either in the form of deposits or in other forms. The article makes some exceptions to the prohibition. It shall not apply to the cases expressly cited, in particular to: Member States; international bodies of which one or more Member States are members; Member States' local authorities; third countries and specially authorised foreign subjects; the taking of repayable funds performed by companies through the issue of bonds within the limits fixed by the Civil Code; companies whose securities are negotiable in a controlled market, within the limits fixed by the credit authorities; undertakings whose collection of funds is carried out by banks or institutions performing insurance or financial activities, within the limits fixed by credit authorities; institutions performing insurance or financial activities subjected to specific prudential regulation.

Besides the definition of banking activity, Decree Law 481/92 first, followed by the Unified Act, has provided for a legislative de-specialisation of the banking sector, removing the basic distinction between credit institutions taking repayable funds at sight or in the short term (*aziende di credito*) and institutions allowed only to collect in the medium or long term (*istituti di credito*). The banking legal system now knows only a single category of subjects empowered to carry out banking activity: banks. The task of de-specialisation performed by the Unified Act is not limited to this: the Act also repeals the laws on specific categories of banking institutions, such as Act 1929 on Casse di Risparmio and Banche del Monte, Act 1937 on Casse rurali e artigiane (now Banche di credito cooperativo) and the Decree 1948 on Banche popolari, bringing to an end a process starting with the reform of public banks.[7] According to the new banking legal system, all banks are regulated by the Unified Act 1993. The Act still contains a few special articles dealing with special categories of banks, although they cover only a few aspects and mainly aim to put all banks on an equal basis of competition.[8]

Italian undertakings wishing to carry out banking activity within the territory of the European Community must apply for the authorisation of the Bank of Italy; the authorisation is granted if the stipulated conditions are fulfilled, but the credit authority may deny authorisation if "it does not appear assured [of] the sound and safe management" (Art. 14.2). On the contrary, the establishment of branches is not subject to authorisation, either for Italian banks or for Community banks. In the latter case Article 15.3 only provides for a communication to be given by the home country authorities to the Bank of Italy stating the intention of the Community bank to establish a new branch within the Italian territory. However, both the Bank of Italy and the Consob have the power to indicate to the competent authority of the home Member State and to the bank the conditions under which, in the interest of the general good, the branch's activities must be performed.

7. Carried out by Legislative Decree 356/90 and the Law No 287, of October 1990.
8. Arts. 29 to 32 refer to Banche popolari and Arts. 33 to 37 to the Banche di credito cooperativo.

The case is different as regards the regulation provided for by the Act for third country banks wishing to establish a branch within the territory of Italy. To establish the first branch, the foreign bank must have the authorisation of the Treasury, given by decree, in agreement with the Foreign Affairs Ministry, after having consulted the Bank of Italy. Authorisation is given in conformance with the reciprocity condition (Art. 14.4). According to Article 15.4, for the establishment of other branches besides the first, third country banks require further authorisation granted by the Bank of Italy.

With regard to the freedom to provide financial services without the establishment of branches, Article 16 U.A. states that Italian banks are free to provide their services within the Community but must ask the Bank of Italy for authorisation if they want to do so within the territory of third countries; the Community banks are free to provide their services within the territory of Italy after the Bank of Italy has been informed of their intention by the competent authority of the home country; the third country banks, however, must request authorisation from the Italian Central Bank.

Finally, it is interesting to point out that, according to Article 17 U.A., the Bank of Italy, according to the directives of the Interdepartmental Committee for Credit and Savings (CICR), regulates activities not subjected to mutual recognition by Community banks within Italian territory.

Returning to the de-specialisation process, with regard to credits, the Unified Act has cancelled most of the special credits provided for by different items of legislation, maintaining only a few provisions concerning a limited number of special credits: land and public works credit (Arts. 38–42), agricultural and fishing credit (Arts. 43–45), and secured credit (Art. 48); however, the Act recognises a general capacity of any bank to exercise any kind of credit. With particular regard to facilitated credits, Article 47 of the Act states that any bank, including therefore foreign banks, may grant facilitated credits, provided that they are ruled by an agreement with the public administration and are part of the business normally carried out by the bank.

The discipline concerning special credits is completed by a regulation of securities. While Article 39 U.A., concerning mortgages, does not introduce new features, Article 46 represents an interesting evolution of Italian securities law regarding the lien on movable goods. According to the new regulation, medium and long-term credits granted by banks to businesses may be secured by special priority on non-registered movable property; the priority may concern plant, capital goods, raw materials, finished products, stocks and "credits (including those arising in the future) deriving from the sale of such goods".

Title III of the Unified Act concerns the supervision of banks and banking groups; it reproduces and coordinates the provisions of the Decree Law 481/92 on the powers of the Bank of Italy in its supervisory activity (Arts. 51 to 58), of the Decree Law 356/90, which introduced a general regulation of banking groups (Arts. 59 to 64), and of the Decree Law 528/92 on consolidated supervision (Arts. 65 to 68).

As far as foreign banks are concerned, it seems interesting to point out that Article 55[9] empowers the Interdepartmental Committee for Credit and Savings (CICR) to limit—within the cases allowed by Community law—the supervisory powers of the Bank of Italy on Community banks established within Italian territory. With regard to consolidated supervision, Article 69 of the Act enacts a mechanism of collaboration between the credit authorities of Member States, giving the Bank of Italy the power to promote ways of cooperation with the authorities of the other Member States and to agree with them on the sharing of competencies for the consolidated supervision of banking groups engaged in activities within more than one Member State.[10]

Subsequently, Title IV deals with banking crises and reproduces the discipline provided for by the Banking Law 1936–38, as already slightly amended by the legislative Decree 481/92.[11] It is interesting to examine the discipline concerning foreign banks. According to Article 78 the Bank of Italy may either prevent branches authorised within Italian territory from initiating any further transactions or may order their closure, should the authority ascertain that the institution is not complying with the legal provisions concerning its activity, or there is a situation of irregular management, or, in the case of extra-Community branches, their "own funds" are not sufficient.[12]

As far as Community banks are concerned, Article 79 empowers the Bank of Italy to require institutions not complying with regulations on branches or the performance of financial services to put an end to the irregular situation, giving notification of this to the home Member States authorities. Should the competent authority of the home Member State not take the necessary steps, when the irregularities may be prejudicial to the general interest or when, in emergencies, precautionary measures are needed to protect the interests of depositors, investors or others to whom services are provided, the Bank of Italy may take the necessary measures. Such measures include the possibility of preventing institutions from initiating further transactions and the power to close the branch office, and the Bank of Italy must in any case communicate such measures to the competent authority.[13] According to Article 95, in the case of withdrawal of authorisation by the competent authority, the branch established in Italy may be submitted to compulsory administrative liquidation.

Title V U.A. regulates "subjects operating in the financial sector".[14] These are institutions engaged in the assumption of shareholdings, granting of credits in any form, payment services and foreign exchange trading. The regulation is not new, as it was included in Law No 197 of 5 July 1991 concerning money laundering. However, the Unified Act has instituted a few important

9. As already provided for by Art. 24 legisl. Decree 481/92.
10. As already provided for by Art. 6, sub-section 1 legisl. Decree 528/92.
11. See R. Costi, *op. cit.*, pp. 641–727.
12. The article reproduces Art. 29 legisl. Decree 481/92.
13. The article reproduces Art. 30 legisl. Decree 481/92.
14. See S. Cotterli, "Gli intermediari finanziari nel Testo Unico sul credito", in *Banca, Impresa Società*, 1994, no 1, pp. 89 *et seq.*

modifications and has afforded the discipline a more appropriate footing. In fact, the regulation concerns bodies engaged in some of the activities typical of banking but whose debit side is not represented by repayable funds taken from the public[15] and which, therefore, need to be subject to less strict control by the public authority. The regulation establishes three different levels of discipline: the first concerns institutions carrying out the above-mentioned businesses not concerning the public: such bodies are only required to register on a special list and have the duty of ensuring the honourableness of the persons directing the business and of the natural or legal persons that have qualifying holdings. The second level of discipline is provided for bodies which deal with the public; Article 106 U.A. stipulates the conditions for entry on the list of bodies allowed to carry out the business of assumption of shareholdings, granting of credits in any form, payment services and foreign exchange trading with the public. The article dictates the form of company and requires the existence of minimum funds; it sets rules regarding the professionalism and honourableness of the persons directing the business and the honourableness of shareholders; and it imposes some duties of transparency. The regulation of the third level has been enacted on the basis of the consideration that there are undertakings which, in view of the business carried out, their size and debt-to-net-worth ratio, must be subjected to a stricter regulation. Article 107 U.A. gives the Bank of Italy a wide range of supervisory powers, in order to ensure the "proper running" (*regolare esercizio*) of such undertakings, whose precise identification is delegated to the Treasury Ministry.

Title VI of the Unified Act governs the transparency of financial transactions, making a coordination between Law No 154 of 17 February 1992 on the transparency of banking services and the rules on consumer credit included in Law No 142 of 19 February 1992.[16]

Title VII of the Unified Act contains only one article, though it represents one of the most interesting new features introduced into the financial legal system by the new banking law. The rule concerns the issuing of movable values and coordinates the discipline on the access to the securities market. According to Article 129 U.A. the issue of securities, as well as the offering of foreign securities within Italian territory, exceeding the limits fixed by the Bank of Italy,[17] must be communicated to the credit authority itself. The aim of the notification is to enable the Bank of Italy to exercise the power to defer the issue or the power of veto on the issue in cases, generally fixed by the CICR, which might endanger market stability. There are some exceptions to the regulation, which does not apply to state securities, shares, the issue of shares of national investment movable funds, or the marketing of shares of investment funds of Member States when complying with the Community regulation. Other exemptions may be

15. Excluded for possible issue of bonds allowed to societies in accordance with the Civil Code.
16. See further pp. 89–91 and 102–104.
17. The limit must in any case exceed a thousand million lire. The duty of communication also concerns any separate issue exceeding the limit occurring within the span of twelve months.

provided for by the Bank of Italy, in accordance with the CICR general directives.

Finally, Titles VIII and IX, respectively, provide for the sanctions and the final transitional provisions.

The Unified Banking and Credit Act makes the Italian banking legal system more in keeping with a modern European banking market and the requirements of Italian and foreign banks, evidencing the lawfulness of the universal bank model and definitively providing a technical and objective approach to banking regulation. If, on the one hand, the new law has given credit authorities a wide range of powers in order to fix many aspects of the regulation, on the other it has removed most of the discretion in their application, making evident the aims and limits of regulation and supervision.

THE BASIC BANKER–CUSTOMER RELATIONSHIP

In general, protection of consumers for financial services is provided through the regulation of financial transactions or of those engaging in a financial activity. As explained above, in both these areas in Italy banks are (mainly) governed by the Unified Banking and Credit Act. Concerning the regulation of financial transactions in particular, Title VI of the Unified Act focuses on the transparency of financial transactions, establishing coordination between the previous law on the transparency of banking services and regulations governing consumer credit.

Besides the Unified Act, there are some regulations introduced by the Italian Bankers' Association (ABI) which play an important role in the banker–customer relationship. Apart from the interbank agreement on business terms (NBU),[18] the ABI has recently issued a Code for the self-regulation of banking and financial transactions, setting out behavioural rules to be followed by signatory banks. Among other aspects of the banker–customer relationship, these rules concern proceedings before the Banking Ombudsman, a committee established in 1993 by the ABI itself, whose task is to consider complaints from banks' customers.

The Unified Banking and Credit Act: the transparency of business terms

According to Article 115.1 U.A. the banks, alongside the financial institutions coming under Title V of the Act, are bound to comply with the regulation,[19]

18. After the issue of Law No 287 of 10 October 1990 (Antitrust Act) and Law No 52 of 6 February 1996 (Art. 25 on unfair terms in consumer contracts) the NBU lost some of its importance. It has undergone in-depth revision, and the ABI, in accordance with the measure taken by the Bank of Italy, has pointed out that the NBU is not binding on the associated banks but is provided by way of example only. See *Provvedimento della Banca d'Italia 12 dicembre 1994*, No 12; ABI, *Bollettino dell'Autorità Garante della Concorrenza e del Mercato* No 49, 1994, p. 75. See also *Norme bancarie uniformi e condizioni generali di contratto, I Contratti*, 2, 1996, p. 152.

19. The Treasury Ministry is given the power to broaden the application of the regulation to other subjects (Art. 115, subs. 2).

which provides for a system of complete transparency with regard to the prices, rates and terms of financial transactions.

Under Article 116.1 U.A. the economic terms of agreements must be published in every place open to the public. Specifically, these terms include rates of interest, prices, charges for communications with the customer and any other economic conditions relating to the services offered. Reference to standard commercial practice is not allowed.

Moreover, the article provides specific regulations on state securities, which not only impose duties as to publicity, but also lay down principles to be respected. Under the new law the Treasury Minister, after consulting the Bank of Italy, fixes the criteria and the parameters for the calculation of the possible maximum fees banks may charge customers when placing securities, and for the determination of yields. The Treasury Minister also establishes the banks' additional duties of publicity, transparency and public promotion in relation to the placing of public securities (Art. 116.2).

Under Article 116.3 U.A., the CICR has the power (a) to issue instructions on the form and contents of publications, (b) to establish uniform criteria for the calculation of interest rates and of any other matters which affect the transaction economically, and (c) to fix the information included under subsection 1, which must be given in advertisements and in offers of any kind. The authority also has the power, after consulting the Bank of Italy and the CONSOB, to establish the transactions and services to be published.

Article 117 U.A. sets out requirements with regard to contracts. Agreements must be in written form (otherwise the contract is null) and a copy, which must specify every economic condition, must be given to the customer (Arts. 117.1–117.3 and 117.4).

Under Article 117.5 any possibility of varying either the interest rate or any other price or term to the disadvantage of the customer must be expressly stated in the contract and specifically signed by the customer. Moreoever, clauses which provide rates, prices and terms more unfavourable to the customer than those made public are null and void, as are clauses which refer to commercial usage (Art. 117.6).

In cases of nullity or a lack of specific indications, all that is applicable is the minimum (for lending transactions) or maximum (for borrowing transactions) nominal rate on Treasury Bills issued within 12 months from the date of the contract. As far as the other conditions are concerned, only those published will apply. Where there has been no publicity, nothing is payable to the bank (Art. 117.7).

Furthermore, according to Article 118 U.A., concerning duration of contracts, in the case of changes disadvantageous to the customer, written notice must be given and the customer will have the right, within 15 days, to withdraw from the contract, retaining the old terms for settlement of the account. As far as these contracts are concerned, a clear and complete report must be given to the customer at the expiration of the contract or at least once a year (Art. 119.1). In particular, in the case of current accounts, an account statement must be sent to the customer at least annually, unless the customer asks to receive it at half-yearly, quarterly or monthly intervals (Art. 119.2). With regard to the validity of the statement, Art. 119.3 stipulates that the content of the statement is considered to be approved by the customer if he does not lodge a written complaint with the bank within 60 days from the date of receipt. The article therefore lays down a duty on the customer's part to check the bank statement; after 60 days the statement becomes binding as to the state of the account. However, an error can always be rectified by the court.

Article 120 U.A. covers the delicate problem of the date of value. In practice, interest in favour of the account holder starts to accrue from the date of deposit in the case of deposit of money or of cheques issued by or drawn on the bank itself.

Article 127 fixes two important principles: the possiblity of waiving Title VI only in favour of the customer and the power on the customer's side only to request the invalidity of the contract.

Finally, it must be noted that the regulations on transparency empower the Treasury Ministry, the Bank of Italy and the CICR to complete the regulatory framework with regard, for example, to the subjects to which it shall apply, state securities, types of transactions regulated and, more generally, to the definition of practical aspects of the provisions.

The Code for the self-regulation of banking and financial transactions

The Code for the self-regulation of banking and financial transactions was issued by the ABI at the end 1996. It provides behavioural rules to be complied with by banks in their relationships with customers. Any bank signing the agreement binds itself to follow a number of general principles, such as:

(a) carrying out its activities with transparency, diligence and professionalism;
(b) always providing the customer with precise information about the economic terms of their agreement;
(c) helping the customer in the understanding of financial services;
(d) granting descretion;
(e) making the Code known among its employees in such a way that they will comply with it, etc.

The Code, like the NBU, is an agreement of a contractual nature, and therefore it is only binding on banks in their relationships with each other. However, it will constitute an important guideline for the competent judicial authority in determining the contents of the principles of fairness and of good faith as referred to in the Italian Civil Code.

The Banking Ombudsman

During autumn 1992 the ABI started the process of drafting the "Agreement for the formation of the Office for customer complaints and the Banking

Ombudsman", which came into effect on 15 April 1993; by the end of 1997 nearly all banks had subscribed to it.[20]

The agreement provides for the establishment of a Complaints Office at every banking institution, whose task is to consider complaints from customers.

Any customer (individual person or corporate body) may present a claim to the Office with regard to any question, of any vlaue, arising out of the relationship with the bank and related to the bank's behaviour, apart from managerial decisions, such as whether or not to grant credit.

The Office must reply to the customer within 60 days from the presentation of the complaint and its decision will be binding on the bank but not on the customer. If his claim is not upheld (or if he gets no answer from the Office) the customer may have recourse to the Ombudsman.

The Ombudsman is a Committee of five members: two of them are appointed by the ABI, two are appointed respectively by the Consiglio Nazionale Forense and by the Consiglio Nazionale dei dottori commercialisti (Italian Law Society and Accountants' Association), and its president is appointed by the Governor of the Bank of Italy. The members are appointed for a three-year term and they can be reappointed only once.

The Ombudsman, located in Rome, is required to reply to claims within 90 days after their receipt. Its sphere of competence is limited to disputes that:

(a) have not already been submitted to the judicial authorities or to an arbitration board;
(b) have already been submitted to the Complaints Office of the bank;
(c) do not exceed 5 million lire in value.

The Ombudsman's resolutions are binding on the bank, which must therefore comply with the decision if the claim is upheld. If it does not, the Committee fixes a term for compliance, and if the bank has still not fulfilled its obligations on expiration of this period, the Ombudsman will make the default public by publication in the press at the bank's expense. In any case, customers always retain the right to submit their dispute to the competent ordinary court.

CONFIDENTIALITY

Italian banking legislation does not provide any definition of banking secrecy. Many theories have been advanced to justify the existence of this institution: I shall dwell upon two of them.[21] Under the first theory—recognised also by the jurisprudence[22]—the legal basis of banking secrecy has to be found in commercial usage. As a matter of fact, it says, banks have traditionally treated as confidential their relationships with customers and, on the other hand, customers have always expected banks to treat their business with

20. See ABI, *La banca e l'arbitrato*, a cura di F. Riolo, Bancaria Editrice, Roma, 1994.
21. See R. Costi, *L'ordinamento bancario*, Bologna, Il Mulino, 1994; N. Salanitro, *Le banche e i contratti bancari*, Torino, UTET, 1983; G. Molle, *La banca*, Milano, Giuffré, 1987.
22. See the Supreme Court decision No 2147 of 18 July 1974.

confidentiality. Therefore banking secrecy has become a legal custom, and a liability in contract arises every time the bank gives information about its customer without his prior consent.

A second theory, which seems to be preferable, links the existence of banking secrecy to the principle of fairness provided for by Article 1175 of the Civil Code, which requires that: "A debtor and creditor shall behave in accordance with the principle of fairness." The article sets out the duty of a contractor, in this case the banker, not to disclose any information on the personal or financial situation of its customers. The obligation of secrecy is limited by the principle of fairness. This means that secrecy does not have any legal relevance if disclosure is required for the protection of other interests which are considered more worthy. It is not possible, for example, for banks to raise banking secrecy as a bar to disclosure when required by a judge to answer questions in civil or penal proceedings.

With regard to an accused person raising banking secrecy in criminal proceedings, the Code of Criminal Procedure of 1988 includes two articles of relevance. The first is Article 248, according to which:

To find out the things to be attached or to verify other circumstances useful to the inquiry, the judicial authorities or the judicial police officers delegated by the judicial authorities can examine acts, documents and correspondence with banks. In case of refusal the judicial authorities may conduct a search.

Article 255 provides:

The judicial authorities can levy a distress on banks of documents, securities, values, money lodged in a current account and of any other thing, even if put in a security box, when they have established grounds that are relevant to the crime, even if they do not belong to the accused person or are not registered under his name.

There is also a special regulation on banking secrecy regarding tax administration. It can be said that, in practice, as regards banking secrecy the tax authorities do not face any limitation on their investigations, especially after the approval of the Law of 30 December 1991, No 413.

In 1972 and 1973 there was a tax reform which gave banking secrecy very limited importance, further reduced by the DPR 15 July 1982, No 463.

Under those laws, the tax authorities can, in the cases expressly provided for by Article 35 DPR September 1973, No 600, and Article 51 *bis* DPR 26 October 1972, No 633, ask the banks for data and information regarding identified subjects by name or class. In case of non-compliance with the request, the tax authorities (and tax investigators) can have direct access to data and information concerning the accounts (Art. 33 DPR 600/73 and Art. 51 *bis* DPR 633/72).

The Financial Law of 1992 (Law of 30 December 1991, No 413) is intended to exclude banking secrecy with respect to the tax authorities. Under Article 18, the tax authorities and inspectors can always (not just in the cases provided for by Articles 35 DPR 600/73 and 51 *bis* DPR 633/72) ask the bank for a "copy of the accounts kept on the taxable person, with the details of every transaction

connected to or relating to such accounts, including third-party securities".
Further information, data and specified documents relating to the accounts can
be asked for through a specific questionnaire (Art. 32.1, DPR 600/73, as
amended by Art. 18.1, Law No 413/91).

Law No 413/91 however, repealing Articles 35 DPR 600/73 and 51 *bis* DPR
633/72, gives the power to the tax authorities to investigate in every
circumstance and with no limitation. On the other hand it removed an
important power which those articles bestowed. Under the previous articles, a
tax investigation could also cover the accounts of a spouse or minor children
living with the person being investigated, and, in some circumstances, unlimited
liability companies (Art. 35.11 DPR 600/73 and 51 *bis* DPR 633/72).

Moreover, Law No 197 of 5 July 1991, concerning money-laundering,
establishes the obligation on certain institutions, including banks, to identify
those who make one or more transactions of any kind through them which
amount to more than 20 million lire. They must also provide the date and reason
for the transaction, complete personal data and the written authorisation of the
person making the transaction or on whose behalf the transaction has been
made. This must be filed within 30 days of the date of the transaction. The data
must be kept for a period of at least 10 years. Where an institution fails to
comply, the employees responsible for the transaction face a penalty of 5 million
to 25 million lire. Moreoever, a person responsible for the office must inform
their legal representative about any "questionable transaction" such as, for
example, transactions not justified by the activity or the economic capacity of
the person making them.

Finally, mention must be made of Law No 675 of 31 December 1996
concerning the protection of persons and other subjects in relation to the
handling of personal data (the so-called Privacy Bill). The law deals with the
confidential nature of personal data, imposing duties for all collection,
recording, arrangement and use of personal data. These must be handled in a
lawful way and according to fairness, and recorded only for specific, clear and
proper purposes. Moreoever, the data collected must be relevant, complete and
not excessive with regard to the purposes for which they are collected and then
processed. The new regulation also applies to banks when they collect and deal
with information concerning customers; in particular, they must ask for clients'
consent to the transmission of data within the financial system. Moreover,
customers have the right to always be informed about the data handled; this
duty to inform the customer only ceases to apply if the collection, processing and
transmission of the data are required by law.

THE MULTIFUNCTIONAL BANK

The situation in Italy has undergone profound change since issue of the Unified
Act and the legislative Decree No 415 of 23 July 1996[23]—replacing Law No 1 of

23. *Gazzetta Ufficiale* No 186 of 9 August 1996, Serie generale, Suppl. ord.

2 January 1991—which empowered Italian banks to engage directly in any financial activity (the U.A.), including the securities business (Decree 415/96).[24]

The involvement of a single institution in a variety of activities generates the need to set up an adequate system aimed at avoiding conflict of interest in the relationship between customers and financial institutions. The latter may give priority or preference to their own interests and behave without sufficient transparency.

As far as the banking system is concerned, the Bank of Italy recommends banks which intend to develop and diversify their activities to adopt a conglomerate structure. In the view of the supervisory authorities, a conglomerate structure ensures adequate legal separation between group members engaging in different activities (loans business, investment and financial transactions, business assistance, etc.). Moreover, the conglomerate model should prevent the risk of a crisis in one part of the group affecting other companies in the group.

Law No 218 of 30 July 1990 gives the Bank of Italy wide powers of control over banking groups. These powers are in addition to those of an informative nature already operating in consolidated supervision.

The Bank of Italy has issued instructions aimed at achieving the separation between bookkeeping and organisation required by the law. In particular, the basic records of the transactions carried out by every organisation specialising in the different activities must be drawn up in such a way as to allow an individual survey. Moreover, the records relating to different kinds of transactions must be properly protected in order to avoid access to them by operators from other sectors. Every single activity must be run by separate structures, each having a separate hierarchy of officials, with equal rank and with managerial autonomy.

The new regulations on investment services provide for rules of access to the investment business, conduct of business, supplier's organisation, contracts, supervision of suppliers, etc. In particular, as regards the problem of conflicts of interest, under Article 21.1 subs.(c) Decree 58/98, the provider of investment services must be organised in such a way that conflicts of interest are minimised, and must act in a manner that ensures that the customer is always guaranteed transparency and fair treatment.[25]

Apart from this rule, in Italian financial law there is no specific provision concerning conflict of interest. The only provision which could possibly be

24. Law No 1 of 2 January 1991 reserved the activity of dealer and broker exclusively to new companies called SIM (Società di Intermediazione Mobiliare), which must establish themselves in accordance with legal requirements. An Italian bank which intended to act in the field of dealing and brokerage was therefore forced to set up an SIM. Banks were allowed to engage in other investment business (giving of specific advice about dealing, portfolio management, placing a security issue, etc.) directly. Decree 415/96 has now been replaced by Decree 58/98.

25. Under Art. 6 of the previous Law No 1/91, it is not possible to make transactions with or on behalf of the customer if there is a direct or indirect conflict of interest in the transaction, unless the customer is informed in writing about the nature and extent of the company's interest, and a preliminary and definite authorisation has been given. A complex form of controls, directed by CONSOB (National Commission for listed companies and the stock exchange) and the Bank of Italy (which must reciprocally coordinate their activities), is also provided.

relevant is contained in the general legal provisions (in particular in the Civil Code) which stipulate that where directors of companies find themselves in a situation which gives rise to a conflict with the company's interests they should abstain from voting. This regulation is of course not sufficient to guarantee the stability and fair trading practices of banks and financial institutions.

However, as regards the administrative regulation of the matter, legislative Decree No 58/98 empowers the National Commission for listed companies and the stock exchange (CONSOB), after consulting the Bank of Italy, to provide rules about the conduct to be adopted in its relationship with customers, having regard to the necessity to minimise the risk of conflicts of interest (Art. 6.2), to ensure that private portfolio management is in conformity with the specific needs of the investor, and the duty to provide information.

Finally, it should be noted that legislative Decree No 58/98 provides for a system of "separation of property". Under Article 22 of the Act, in the case of investment business each customer's investments and money, held by a bank for any reason, form property separate from that of the bank or of other customers for all intents and purposes.

Therefore, creditors of the bank or of other customers cannot take legal action to secure this property. On the other hand, customers' creditors may only act within the limits of the property of the individual customer.

Unless written acceptance is given by the customer, the bank cannot use any client's financial securities or money, held by the bank for any reason, for its own interests or those of other customers.

THE LIABILITY OF BANKS FOR ADVICE

Banks have a huge amount of information of every kind on customers and their activities, on companies, on the financial market and its trends, etc.—all of which is information they need to carry on their activities and which can be considered functional to them. In the modern banker–customer relationship banks are often requested to make different use of that information, both because they receive a direct request from a client or even from persons with whom they do not have a contractual relationship, and because customers expect their banks to advise them in financial matters.

Until now the Italian legal system, when facing the problem of the responsibility of a bank for advice, charged the banks with extracontractual liability when possible, on the basis of Article 2043 of the Civil Code:

Any negligent or fraudulent action, which causes unfair damage to someone else, obliges the one who had done the action to indemnify the loss.

In the few decisions, all regarding the dissemination of wrong or false information by a credit institution, the courts actually imposed extracontractual liability on the bank on the basis of the remark that the damage in those cases concerned "the right to decide freely in activity concerning personal property (Art. 41 Constitution) with reasonable reliance on the veracity of the statements given by anyone, . . . without being damaged by false or wrong statements given with negligence or fraud".[26] The possibility of applying Article 2043 of the Civil Code was linked to the circumstance that the information given by the bank was incorrect and that, in any event, the bank had not behaved with perfect diligence. The diligence required of a bank cannot be compared with that required of "information agencies". As a matter of fact this kind of activity is considered a "courtesy activity", as evidenced by the fact that it is normally given free of charge, and not regarded as a professional activity. That means that the negligence of the bank may only arise in a communication which has been given without attention to the information already held by the bank (thus it cannot be a request to the bank for additional research); consists of a mistake in referring to that information; or is advice which does not make allowance for the information held by the bank.

Law No 1 of 2 January 1991, Decree Law No 415/96, and now Decree Law No 58/98 have affected these matters. As we said, the latter permits banks to engage directly in investment services (an activity which Law No 1/1991 made the exclusive preserve of Securities Firms—Società Intermediazione Mobiliare or "SIMs") and provides some general principles and behavioural rules which the bank is obliged to follow when supplying investment services. According to Article 21, SIMs and banks must:

1. behave with diligence, correctness and transparency[27] in caring for the client's interest;
2. acquire all necessary information from the client and act in a manner ensuring that the customer is always adequately informed;
3. Organise themselves in such a way that conflicts of interest are minimised and act in a manner that guarantees the customer transparency and fair treatment in all circumstances;
4. be organised—also with regard to internal control—in a way that ensures the efficient supply of services; and
5. provide independent, safe, sound management and adopt every measure to safeguard the customer's rights with regard to securities and money.

Finally, it must be pointed out that according to Article 23 of Decree Law No 58/98, in the trial of claims for damages caused to the customer during the provision of investment services, the onus is on banks (and SIMs as well) to prove that they have acted with the necessary specific diligence.

26. From the leading case of the Court of Cassation, 4 May 1982, No 2765, *Giurisprudenza italiana*, 1983, 1, 1, 876.

27. The word "correctness" must be understood in the context of Art. 1175 of the Civil Code (good faith), meaning that consideration must be given to the ways and means on the basis of which the supply of services has been made. "Professionalism" should simply indicate that the diligence used has to be commensurate with the professionalism exercised by the debtor (Art. 1176, 2, C.C.).

CONSUMER PROTECTION

In the field of consumer protection the regulations of the Civil Code on the general conditions of contracts generally have wide importance. In the context of problems concerning the banker–customer relationship it is useful, even though there is now a specific regulation on the transparency of banking transactions.

With the "European Law 1996", Parliament introduced new regulations on unfair terms on contract, supplementary to the previous regulations on the general conditions of contracts contained in the Civil Code. Article 25 of Law No 52 of 6 February 1996 introduces a new section to the Civil Code dedicated to "Consumer contracts" (Arts. 1469 *bis*–1469 *sexies*).[28]

Most banking contracts are drawn up using standard contracts. The relationship between the banker and the customer represents a typical example of a relationship between a powerful contracting party who can impose certain rules, and a weak one, whose choice consists only in agreeing or refusing to agree, without the possibility of modifying the content of the contract.

A matter connected with the problems concerning private law rules is the law of procedure and, generally speaking, access to justice. Many problems are linked with this: the first concerns the long duration of civil trials and high court costs.

Italian law provides for a form of simplified scheme for the handling of small consumer complaints, where a body (*giudice di pace*) is authorised to pass judgment in less important cases (5 million lire of value at most), as well as a more informal and rapid procedure, where the parties have the power to represent themselves personally (only for cases of a value less than 2 million lire). This law was approved on 2 August 1991, and for a certain period was blocked by the President of the Republic because of lack of finance. Finally, it came into effect on 1 May 1995.

An important obstacle lies in the difficulty experienced by consumer groups in bringing individual claims, also due to the problematic relations between the legal profession and collective organisations. In Italy there is no form of legal aid for consumers.

The general conditions of contract and the law on unfair contract terms

The Italian Civil Code of 1942 was the first in Europe to have a specific provision[29] designed to ensure control over the general conditions of contract.

28. See G. Romagnoli, *Clausole vessatorie e contratti d'impresa*, Cedam, 1997; G. Lener, "La nuova disciplina delle clausole vessatorie nei contratti dei consumatori", *Foro italiano*, 1996, I, c.145; G. De Nova, "La novella sulle clausole vessatorie e la revisione dei contratti standard", *Rivista di diritto privato*, 2/1996, p. 221.

29. On the subject see *Le condizioni generali di contratto nella giurisprudenza*, a cura di E. Cesdro, Padova, Cedam, 1989. On the applicability of this to the banking contracts see " 'Trasparenza' bancaria e diritto 'comune' dei contratti", in *Banca, borsa e titoli di credito*, 1990, p. 297.

Articles 1341 and 1342 of the Civil Code contain a specific principle on consent, where the real intent of a contracting party is ignored and its knowledge or even its negligent lack of knowledge is considered sufficient. On the other hand, for any "vexatious contract clauses" specific written acceptance is required. In particular, sub-section 1 of Article 1341 places upon the party which dictates terms the onus of putting the other party in the position of being able to find out about the contract clauses. The counterpart, in his turn, must check the existence and the contents of the clauses. The provision states:

The general conditions of contract prepared by one of the two contracting parties are effective as far as the other party is concerned if, at the moment of the conclusion of the agreement, the latter knew them or should have known them by using ordinary diligence.

It cannot be said for certain that this rule has entirely fulfilled the *ratio* of protection of the weaker contracting party. Fifty years after the Civil Code came into effect it could certainly be said that the main effect of sub-section 1 has been to worsen a customer's position, considering the fact that it imposes on him or her an obligation to know something about contract clauses. As far as banking transactions are concerned, this is certainly contradictory: the user of banking services, especially of those most commonly used, for example the current account, is the "person in a hurry". To require that he or she examine closely barely legible terms, which are obscurely worded and difficult to comprehend, just because they are written on the form, is not practical. For this reason the rule gives the customer only an apparent protection; it seemingly confirms the power of the banker to put into the contract any kind of term, which cannot be negotiated or modified by the customer. As a matter of fact, in Italian jurisprudence it is sufficient that general conditions are printed in a form which can be read and easily interpreted.

There are some clauses, peremptorily listed in Article 1341 of the Civil Code, sub-section 2, which have to be approved precisely in writing under penalty of nullification. These are "vexatious clauses", among which, in the banking sector, are those limiting the liability of the bank. In this category of clauses, Italian jurisprudence has placed, for example:

1. a clause in a contract with a bank to collect documents of credit, which exempts it from liability in case of payment on non-presentation of the documents;
2. a clause according to which the bank is not responsible for delays or errors in or non-delivery of communications and orders of customers;
3. a clause of the Uniform Banking Regulations (NBU) concerning safe-deposit boxes, where it is provided that the maximum value of the boxes' contents is automatically fixed at a certain amount.

With regard to safe-deposit boxes, the Italian Supreme Court has confirmed that a clause which fixes the maximum compensation payable at a certain amount is unlawful.[30] However, this ruling, even though it does not directly

30. Sent. No 4604 of 3 November 1989.

address the problem, has raised the question which may arise from the use of another clause, which obliges a customer not to keep in a safe-deposit box anything having a value higher than that fixed in the contract. This kind of clause is always used by banks, and the judgment of the Supreme Court seems to implicitly approve it. However, the court has deemed this condition unlawful insofar as the limitation on liability constitutes a case of fraud or serious fault on the part of the bank.[31]

In addition to the articles already examined, the Civil Code now contains new regulations on unfair terms in consumer contracts.[32] According to Article 1469 *bis*, these apply to contracts concluded between a seller or supplier and a consumer, that is—as under Article 121.1 U.A.—"any natural person acting for purposes outside his own business or profession".

If, on the one hand, the new regulation has wider scope than that concerning general contract conditions—because it applies to any contract when concluded between a consumer and a seller or supplier and not only to standard contracts—on the other it does not cover any contract concluded by customers but only those of consumers.

The new law establishes some general principles, the most important of which are:

(a) In the case of written contracts the terms offered must always be drafted in plain and intelligible language. Where there is doubt about the meaning of a term, the interpretation most favourable to the customer shall prevail (Art. 1469 *quater*, sub-section 1).

(b) Contractual terms which reflect rules of Law or provisions of principles of international conventions to which all Member States or the Community are party shall not be regarded as unfair (Art. 1469 *ter*, sub-section 3).

(c) Individually negotiated contractual terms shall not be regarded as unfair; however, in the case of pre-formulated contracts, the burden of proof that terms have actually been individually negotiated shall be incumbent on the seller or supplier.

(d) Contractual terms shall be regarded as unfair if, in spite of good faith, they cause a significant imbalance in consumers' rights and obligations arising under the contract (Art. 1469 *bis*, sub-section 1).

(e) There are some terms (Art. 1469 *bis*, sub-section 3 lists 20 terms) which shall always be regarded as unfair, unless proved otherwise.[33]

(f) Unfair terms are not binding on the customer and the contract shall continue to bind the parties (Art. 1469 *quinquies*, sub-section 1).

31. Sent. No 5421 of 7 May 1992, *Giurisprudenza italiana*, I, 1993, 1, p. 369.

32. On the subject, see G. De Nova, "La novella sulle clausole vessatorie e la revisione dei contratti standard", *Rivista di diritto privato*, 2/96, p. 221; G. Romagnoli, *Clausole vessatorie e contratti d'impresa*, Cedam, 1997; G. Lener, "La nuova disciplina delle clausole vessatorie nei contratti dei consumatori", *Foro Italiano*, 1996, V, cc. 175–176.

33. The list of unfair terms largely reproduces the terms listed in the Annex of Directive 93/13/EEC on unfair terms in consumer contracts.

Of course the regulations examined here also apply to banks, and in fact the ABI has responded by modifying its standard contracts.[34] For example, it has deleted the condition establishing the competence of judicial authorities in places other than that in which the consumer is resident or domiciled.[35]

In particular, with regard to financial contracts it should be noted that the regulations examined provide for some waivers: in the case of a contract of indefinite duration concerning financial services, if there is true and just cause the provider can terminate the contract without notice, giving immediate communication to the consumer, and he may also modify terms of the contract, giving the consumer reasonable notice and the right to terminate the contract (Art. 1469 *bis*, sub-section 4). Moreover, if there is a valid reason, the provider is empowered to modify the economic terms without notice but must inform the consumer immediately; in this case the consumer again has the right to terminate the contract (Art. 1469 *bis*, sub-section 5).

The new legislation on unfair terms has met the need, pointed out by some Italian writers, to make it possible to rule a group of clauses null and void even in the case of specific written acceptance (lawful terms under Article 1341), because of their capacity to distort the balance of the contract in favour of the party dictating the terms, contrary to the principle of fairness.

Group actions in Italian civil proceedings concerning compensation for damages to consumers

There is no doubt that the greatest problem arises from the absence in Italian law of any reference to forms of collective suits.[36] In order to take legal action, the plantiff must be the holder of a violated right; no form of group action is provided for by ordinary or specific legislation. Article 2909 of the Civil Code states the *res judicata* has effect only insofar as the parties in the proceedings or their heirs are concerned. Therefore, at present, the only instrument which can be used by a collective association to ask for compensation for damage is to obtain a general or special power of attorney from each of the injured consumers. The reform of these matters is of primary importance to ensure the effectiveness of collective redress in the event of a multiplicity of small injuries to various subjects. It is sometimes said (wrongly) in Italy that the introduction of instruments such as class actions or public interest actions are incompatible with the role of the judge and with the structure of civil proceedings. It should be stressed that these systems presuppose a strong consumers' organisation, an element which is lacking in Italy. A 1981 government bill (the "Spadolini Bill")

34. See ABI, Circolare 23 febbraio 1996: Attuazione della direttiva n.93/13/CEE concernente "le clausole abusive nei contratti stipulati con i consumatori", *Banca, borsa e titoli di credito*, I, 1996, p. 585.

35. This particular unfair term is not included in the Annex to the EEC Directive.

36. On the subject, see M. Bessone, "La tutela civilistica dei consumatori e gli strumenti del controllo giurisdizionale", in *Rassegna del Diritto Civile*, 1981 p. 983 and Denti, "Interessi diffusi", in *Novissimo Digesto Italiano*, Appendice, IV, Torino, 1982 and U. Ruffolo, *Interessi collettivi o diffusi e tutela del consumatore*, Milano, Giuffré, 1985.

would have conferred on private authorities with a public interest the capacity to take legal action in defence of interests of a community group represented by them. Recently some members of Parliament supported a bill giving to consumers' associations the right to take legal action before civil judges on behalf of consumers singly or as a group. It is not likely that this law will be soon approved by Parliament as a whole.

On this matter the Law 52/96 on unfair terms in consumer contracts has introduced a principle according to which consumers' associations, as well as associations of sellers or suppliers and the Chamber of Commerce, are empowered to sue sellers or suppliers (as well as their associations) and ask the judge for a decree which prohibits the use of the unfair contractual terms (Art. 1469 *sexies* Civil Code).

Moreover, the Law of 30 July 1998, No 281, concerning the regulation of consumers' rights, empowers the most representative national consumers' organisations to take some legal actions. According to Article 1.2 of the law, consumers have a right to correctness, transparency and fairness in their agreements concerning goods and services. Consumer organisations may ask the judge for an injunction against behaviour contrary to consumers' rights. They may ask as well for measures to stop consequent possible damage to consumers and may also ask for the publication of the decree in local newspapers.

Consumer credit

With the "European Law 1992", Parliament has introduced a number of new laws concerning several older Community Directives, including nos 87/102 and 90/88 on consumer credit. In 1993, the regulation concerning consumer credit by way of the Law No 142 of 19 February 1992 was included in the U.A. The possibility to grant consumer credit has been limited to banks, "bodies operating in the financial sector" (ruled by the U.A. under Articles 106 and next) and sellers (only through delay of payment).

Under Article 121.1 U.A. consumer credit must be understood as:

the providing, in the performance of a commercial or professional activity, of credit in the form of an extension of payment, or in the form of a loan, or any other financial help in favour of a natural person (consumer) who acts, in this context, for goals extraneous to its possible contracting or commercial activity.

The regulation does not cover credit transactions concerning:

1. contracts with which "a party binds itself, against a price, to make, in favour of the other party, a periodic or continuing supply of services of goods" (Art. 1559 C.C.), but only those contracts that are in a written form and where a copy has been given to the consumer;
2. credit contracts for an amount less than 300,000 Italian lire and higher than 60 million Italian lire; and

3. independently of their value:
   (a) credit contracts on "soft conditions", like the ones repayable in one instalment within 18 months and with no interest charge (predetermined expenses, or out-of-pocket expenses are permitted);
   (b) credit given for the purchase, preservation, repair or improvement of land or immovable property;
   (c) "pure" hire contracts, thus excluding contracts for lease.

The law also covers the case of intervention by a third party in a financial transaction. In particular, the global cost of intervention must be included in the annual percentage rate (APR) (Art. 122.3). The annual percentage rate (TAEG = Tasso annuo effettivo globale) will be calculated in accordance with the formula indicated by the EC Directive and the method prescribed by the CICR (Art. 122.2). The APR should always appear in any advertisement of consumer credit which contains the rate of interest or any other cost of the transaction, possibly with a typical example (Art. 123.2).

Moreover, according to Article 123.1, it applies to the consumer credit transactions described in Article 116 U.A., concerning the publication of the economic terms of banking transactions.[37]

Article 124 U.A. provides, generally, for the content of the credit document. According to Article 117.1, recalled by Article 124.1, credit transactions must be in writing and a copy of the document must be given to the customer (otherwise the contract is null (Art. 117.3)). Moreover, according to Article 124.2, the documents must contain:

1. the amount and method of the financial transaction;
2. the number, amount and final date of the individual instalments;
3. the APR;
4. the conditions, in detail, under which the APR may be changed;
5. the amount and the reason for the expenses excluded from the APR, or "a realistic estimate of them" (otherwise nothing is due to the creditor);
6. the security if any; and
7. insurance expenses, excluding the ones that must be included in the APR (insurance in favour of the creditor in the case of death, invalidity or illness of the consumer).

Furthermore, in consumer credit agreements for the purchase of determined goods or services, the document must, on pain of nullity, contain:

1. a description of the goods or services which are the object of the contract;
2. the cash price, the price fixed in the agreement and the amount, if any, of a deposit; and
3. the terms of transfer of property to the consumer, in the case that it is not direct.

37. See p. 90.

In the hypothetical event of absence or nullity of contractual clauses, they are replaced in conformity with the following rules:

1. the APR will be the minimum nominal interest rate on state securities (or other securities indicated by the Treasury Minister) issued within 12 months from the agreement;
2. the due date of the credit is within 30 months; and
3. no guarantee or insurance is provided for the creditor;

According to Article 125.2 the possibility of prepayment or of cancellation of the contract is the prerogative of the consumer only, who may take advantage of it at any time, without expense or penalty. In all cases the consumer has the possibility of prepaying his debt, and in this event he has the right to an equal reduction of the total cost of credit.

Article 126 U.A. deals with the particular case of credit opened in a current account, which must, on pain of nullity, contain:

(a) the limit, and the due date if fixed;
(b) the annual interest rate and the detail of the expenses, including the conditions under which they can be changed (outside of which nothing is payable to the bank); and
(c) the terms and conditions for cancelling the contract.

SECURITY

As a matter of principle, the general regulation of security[38] does not change when the secured creditor is a bank. There are mainly two special rules on banking securities: Article 2787, final sub-section, of the Civil Code, and Article 67, final sub-section, of the bankruptcy law.[39]

Article 2878 C.C. concerning requirements for the pledge of movable assets, establishes that:

If . . . the pledge is evidenced by a ticket or any other document of an institution which, properly authorised, carries on professionally credit transactions on pledge, the date of the document may be determined by any element of proof.

The article provides an exception to the principle of the "true date" operating as a general rule in the law of pledge. The Court of Cassation has interpreted the exception in the sense that it is always applicable to those credit institutions which are authorised in general to engage in banking activity.[40]

The provision provided for by Article 67.3 of the Bankruptcy Law is similar, but the interpretation given to it by the jurisprudence is different. The rule states

---

38. On the law concerning security in general, see F. Gazzoni, *Manuale di diritto privato*, Napoli, ESI, 1991; and A. Torrente e P. Schlesinger, *Manuale di diritto privato*, Milano, Giuffré, 1991.
39. For further details see M. Bussoletti, "Garanzie bancarie", in *Digesto*, Torino, UTET, 1990. See also, G.B. Portale, *Le garanzie bancarie internazionali*, Milano, Giuffré, 1989.
40. See lately Cass. S. U., 15.4.1976, in *Giurisprudenza Commerciale*, 1976, II, p. 597.

the exemption from bankruptcy for revocation for "the bank of issue, the institutions authorised to the credit transactions on pledge, as far as those are concerned, and the mortgage banks". In the jurisprudence the rule is not applicable to every credit institution that is generally authorised to exercise banking activity, but only to credit transactions on pledge done by state pawnshops and similar bodies.[41]

The action in bankruptcy for revocation is based on the consideration that all the acts done by an insolvent entrepreneur (even if not yet declared bankrupt) are prejudicial to creditors. Therefore, when an entrepreneur is insolvent and the third party knew of his insolvency, any disposal made by the entrepreneur is ineffective as against creditors. In particular, the following are invalid, except if the third party proves that it did not know that the debtor was insolvent:

1. discharging debts due and payable which have not been effected by cash or other normal means of payment, if made within two years from the adjudication of bankruptcy;
2. pledges and mortgages given within two years of the adjudication of bankruptcy for pre-existing debts not yet due;
3. pledges and mortgages given within one year from the adjudication of bankruptcy for due debts.

In this connection, it is useful to bear in mind a particular problem concerning remittances made on an overdrawn current account within the year prior to bankruptcy.[42] Will the bank have to pay them back to the bankrupt? The Court of Cassation thought so at first, but has changed its opinion more recently. In accordance with recent authority of the Supreme Court,[43] if the overdrawn current account was assisted by a regular, not revoked credit opening, Article 67.2 is not applicable. On the contrary, if the opening of credit was revoked or, as often happens, there was never an opening of credit and the bank simply allowed the account to be overdrawn, the bankruptcy action for revocation applies and the bank will have to repay those amounts to the bankrupt, thus becoming simply one of the creditors in the bankruptcy itself.

A particular problem as regards security concerns banking guarantees. Until recently banks have made very large use of a particular form of guarantee: the *fidejussion omnibus*,[44] a personal security which, accompanied by the clause *omnibus*, is characterised by having general validity, giving a guarantee to the bank in respect of any debts, even future debts, incurred by the customer. The

---

41. See Cass. 30.1.1985, no 579, in *Giurisprudenza Commerciale*, 1985, II, p. 588 and Cass. 16.1.1987, no 7649, in *Foro Italiano*, 1988, I, p. 823.

42. On the problem, see F. Maimeri, A. Nigro, V. Santoro, *Contratti bancari, Le operazioni in conto correnta*, Milano, Giuffré, 1991; and M. Arato, *Operazioni bancarie in conto corrente e revocatoria fallimentare delle reimesse*, Milano, Giuffré, 1991.

43. Cass., 18.10.1982, no 5413, in *Banca, borsa e titoli di credito*, 1983, II, p. 8.

44. For further details, see M. Viale, "Fideiussione omnibus", in *Contratto e impresa*, 1990, pp. 276 *et seq.*; and A. Di Majo, "La clausola omnibus nella fideiussione e parametri valutativi", in *Contratto e impresa*, 1991, pp. 19 *et seq.*

guarantor's position this way becomes particularly grave, considering that he guarantees a sequence of debts not determined when the security is granted. The validity of this guarantee is therefore in doubt because of the indeterminate nature of the object secured.

Moreover, this kind of security presents a few other problems, being largely exempt from the general regulation of the Civil Code on the *fidejussion* by a number of clauses provided for by the Interbank Agreement. First, under Article 8 of the Interbank Agreement, and in derogation of Article 1939 C.C., the *fidejussion omnibus* is also valid when the principal obligation has been declared void: the guarantor still secures the return of the amount granted by the bank. Secondly, by way of exception to Article 1945, the guarantor is obliged to repay the bank as soon as a request is issued in written form, even in the case of opposition by the debtor. Finally, the bank, under the Interbank Agreement, has no duty to inform the guarantor about the situation of the secured debtor: it may continue to grant credit to the latter even when it is aware of his bad financial position, without being authorised by the guarantor, and not even informing him. However, the ABI has recently recommended that banks cancel every term which (a) excluded the duty of the bank to inform the guarantor about the accounts situation and generally about its relationship with the beneficiary of the secured credit, and (b) modified Article 1945 C.C. to the extent that the guarantor raised objections.[45] Until now the courts have mainly confirmed the validity of the *fidejussion omnibus*, both in relation to the indeterminate nature of the object secured[46] and with regard to the clauses provided for by the Interbank Agreement.[47] But the law on the transparency of banking transactions and the regulation on unfair terms in consumers contracts will have an important impact on the *fidejussion omnibus*.

Article 10 of Law No 154/92, modifying Article 1938 of the Civil Code, has established that the guarantee of future or conditional debts must provide the maximum amount secured from the beginning. The article states that:

The fidejussion may be given also for a conditional or future obligation with the anticipation, in this last case, of the maximum amount secured. . . .
The previous quitclaim by the guarantor to make use of the release is not valid.

There is also a problem concerning the "pledge omnibus".[48] In this case, goods held in pledge for a determined obligation may secure all the customer's bank credits, present and future. The clause is valid as far as the relationship

---

45. See ABI, Circolare 23 febbraio 1996: Attuazione della direttiva n.93/13/CEE concernente "le clausole abusive nei contratti stipulati con i consumatori", *Banca, borsa e titoli di credito*, I, 1996, p. 588.

46. See Cass. 1.8.1987, no 6656, in *Banca, borsa e titoli di credito*, 1988, 11, p. 145 and Cass. 18.7.1989, no 3362, in *Foro Italiano*, 1989, I, c. 2750.

47. Among others see Cass. 12.11.1988, no 6142, in *Banca, borsa e titoli di credito*, 1989, II, p. 412; Cass. 8.2.1989, no 786, in *Giurisprudenza italiana*, 1989, I, p. 1517; Cass. 20.7.1989, no 3387, in *Giustizia civile*, 1990, I, p. 395.

48. On the argument see G. Sicchiero, *L'engineering, la joint venture, i contratti di informatica, i contratti atipici di garanzia*, Torino, UTET, 1991.

between the bank and its customer is concerned, but it cannot be raised against other creditors.[49]

Finally it should be noted that, as above mentioned, Article 46 U.A. states that medium and long-term credits granted by banks to businesses may be secured by special priority on non-registered movable property; the priority may concern plant, capital goods, raw materials, finished products, stocks and "credits, future as well, deriving from the sale of such goods".

ENVIRONMENTAL LIABILITY

The Italian legal system does not contain any regulation specifically concerned with the liability of a bank, in relation to its lending activity, for environmental damage caused by its customer. On the other hand, there is a regulation on compensation for environmental damage.[50] Under Article 18 of Law No 349/86, the perpetrator of an act damaging to the environment is obliged to compensate the state for the damage. The action for environmental damage has to be commenced before a civil judge. Environmental protection associations may intervene in the judgment. When it is not possible to assess the amount of damage, this is determined by the judge according to what is equitable, taking into account the gravity of the individual negligence, the sum required for restoration and the profit derived by the offender from his behaviour. In the judgments where this law has been applied, the problem of the liability of a bank which provided the finance for a work that turned out to be injurious to the environment has never been considered.

It would seem that the liability of a bank can probably not be excluded when the documentation to obtain the loan can easily verify that the work financed was prejudicial to the environment. As a matter of fact, Article 18 of Law No 349/86 provides for the liability to compensate for damage not only by the direct perpetrator of the pollution, but also "anyone who negligently or fraudulently causes environment damage". There is no doubt that a bank which grants a loan for the execution of work dangerous to the environment is acting contrary to the duty of care and it may be considered as a joint cause of the detriment. In this case, therefore, the bank will probably be held liable for compensation "within the limits of its individual liability" (Art. 18, sub-section 7, Law No 349/86), that is, in relation to the causal contribution which its behaviour has had in the creation of the pollution.

SIMONETTA COTTERLI

---

49. Cass. 19.6.1971, no 1927, in *Rivista di diritto civile*, 1974, II, p. 212.
50. On the subject see A. Costanzo and C. Verardi, "La responsabilitá per danno ambientale", in *Rivista trimestrale di diritto e procedura civile*, 1988, 3, p. 691.

CHAPTER 6

THE NETHERLANDS

THE BASIC BANKER–CUSTOMER RELATIONSHIP

General

Unlike the law of certain other European countries, Dutch law does not specifically provide for a "banking contract" which would cover the entire relationship between bank and customer. Some authors in the Netherlands[1] believe that a so called "relation agreement" comes into existence when a customer engages the services of a bank for the first time. However, this view is not generally held.[2] Most people look at the relationship in a pragmatic way: a combination of qualified and unqualified contracts, governed by the general rules of contract law, and the General Banking Conditions.

Qualified and unqualified agreements

Under Dutch law a distinction is made between qualified (*benoemde*) agreements and unqualified (*onbenoemde*) agreements. Special statutory provisions apply to a specific type of qualified agreement, in addition to the general rules of the law of contract which apply to all agreements whether qualified or not.

Certain aspects of the relationship between bank and customer in the Netherlands can be seen as separate qualified agreements. For instance, a loan or credit granted by the bank to a customer and a savings deposit made by a customer with his bank can both be qualified as a loan agreement (*verbruikleen*). When a customer gives instructions to his bank to make certain payments this can be qualified as a mandate (*opdracht*) under Dutch law. Giving securities to be looked after by the bank constitutes a custody agreement (*bewaargeving*).

An essential relationship is the bank account agreement (*bankrekening overeenkomst*). This agreement has elements of a mandate (i.e. orders for crediting or debiting an account) and of lending (i.e. a positive balance) and borrowing (i.e. maintaining an overdraft). In addition the bank account is a *"rekening-courant"* ("current account") in which mutual claims of the bank

---

1. See C. van Ravenhorst, *De Bankovereenkomst*, 1991, pp. 17 *et seq.*
2. See, for instance, W.A.K. Rank, *Geld, Geldschuld en Betaling*, 1996, p. 221.

and the customer are set off against each other. The Dutch Civil Code contains a specific provision for continuous set off in a current account arrangement.[3] Usually, the entire relationship between the bank and a customer will consist of one or more qualified agreements combined with various unqualified elements.

General law of contract—implied terms

In addition to the provisions applying to certain qualified agreements, the general rules of the law of contract apply to the relationship between bank and customer. An essential rule of Dutch contract law is that the contents of an agreement are not exclusively determined by what the parties have expressly agreed, but also by customs and by the principle of "reasonableness and fairness".[4] This concept is comparable to the English concept of "implied terms". The contents of an agreement can be interpreted, supplemented and even, under certain circumstances, set aside by the principle of reasonableness and fairness. Another important aspect of Dutch contract law is the law on general conditions. These regulations have had and will continue to have an impact on the General Banking Conditions (*Algemene Bankvoorwaarden*).

The General Banking Conditions

The General Banking Conditions (GBC) apply to virtually all retail banking transactions in the Netherlands. The present text of the GBC, which has been in force since 1 February 1996, is the result of consultations between the Association of Dutch Banks (*Nederlandse Vereniging van Banken*) and representative consumer and business organisations. The GBC apply to general banks, savings banks and cooperative banks in their dealings with both private and business customers. In addition to the GBC, banks use specific conditions for certain banking products, such as eurocheques, foreign currency accounts, custody of securities, etc. A few provisions of the GBC should be mentioned at this stage.

Due care

In the GBC,[5] banks have undertaken to exercise "due care" in rendering their services (*dienstverlening*).[6] However, this obligation has been made subject to the proviso that a bank is not obliged to make use of information of which it has knowledge, but which is not in the public domain. According to the GBC this type of information includes price-sensitive information.

3. Art. 6:140 Civil Code.
4. Art. 6:248 Civil Code.
5. Art. 2, General Banking Conditions.
6. The applicability of the duty of due care to the broad field of "rendering of services" is new in the 1996 GBC. The previous GBC which came into force on 1 January 1988 referred to due care in executing orders from customers and in performing obligations under any agreements and transactions with customers.

The duty of care should be seen as complementing the general rule of contract law that agreements should be performed in accordance with "reasonableness and fairness". It is, among other things, the basis on which a customer may expect the bank to keep information about him confidential. The GBC state that in exercising this due care, the banks will, to the extent possible, take into account the interests of the customer.

Bank statements

Bank statements reflect the transactions carried out by the bank at the customer's request and the changes in the customer's financial position. As such, they are part of the basic banker–customer relationship.

The GBC[7] impose a duty on the customer to check the correctness of all statements of account, written confirmations or any other statements from the bank and to check immediately whether his instructions to the bank have been duly followed. If the bank has made mistakes, it must rectify them. However, if the customer has not contested the contents of a bank statement within 12 months after its receipt, he is deemed to have approved its contents. After this period the customer's right to complain has lapsed, unless the bank made an error in calculation. Such errors are not included in the "implied approval".

As pointed out above, the principle of "reasonableness and fairness" in Dutch contract law may, under certain special circumstances, set aside the contents of an agreement. In principle, the customer loses his rights to have mistakes (with the exception of calculation errors) corrected after 12 months. It would, however, still be possible that a court, considering the special circumstances of a particular case, would rule that the bank acted against "reasonableness and fairness" by invoking the 12-month period of limitation in the GBC. In that case the contractual right of the bank would be set aside. Note that the GBC do not impose the 12-month period of limitation on the banks! They may correct mistakes and make claims against a customer after the 12 months until the normal civil law period of limitation expires.

CONFIDENTIALITY

General[8]

There is no explicit statutory provision which imposes an obligation of secrecy on banks in the Netherlands. In Dutch civil law, such obligation is nevertheless assumed to exist. The Dutch Criminal Code does contain secrecy provisions but these do not apply to banks. Exceptions to the civil law confidentiality obligation of banks apply when banks have to testify in proceedings or give

7. Art. 12, General Banking Conditions.
8. See, for a general discussion, Marc S. Groenhuijsen and Frank Molenaar, "Bank confidentiality and governmental control of exchange operation and of their unlawful effects", in Netherlands Reports to the Fourteenth International Congress of Comparative Law, 1995.

information to the tax inspector. Also, on the basis of the legislation on the prevention of money-laundering, banks are under a statutory duty to report "unusual transactions".

Confidentiality under civil law

Neither any Act nor the General Banking Conditions explicitly provide for confidentiality by banks, but an obligation of secrecy is generally assumed to exist. As far as Dutch contract law is concerned, the obligation on the bank to keep its customers' information confidential follows from the general principle that the contents of an agreement are also determined by customs and "reasonableness and fairness".

The duty of "due care" contained in the General Banking Conditions is believed to be an additional basis for banks to assume an obligation of secrecy. The Complaints Committee for the Banking Business has ruled several times on the basis of the General Banking Conditions that a bank has a basic obligation of secrecy.[9]

A civil law obligation of secrecy is also recognised in the Dutch law of tort. Under the law of tort, a person can be held liable for damages resulting from a breach of a generally required duty of care ("*zorgvuldigheid die in het maatschappelijk verkeer betaamt*"). Breach of a bank's obligation of secrecy could, under certain circumstances, be considered a breach of this duty of care and therefore tortious.

Finally, the Privacy Act[10] provides for an obligation of confidentiality in respect of "registered personal information", i.e. a collection of personal information concerning various persons managed by automated means or, for ease of consultation, systematically compiled. Article 11 of the Privacy Act states that registered personal information can only be disclosed to third parties if such disclosure is in accordance with the purpose of the registration or required pursuant to a statutory provision, or when the registree has given his consent. The Dutch Association of Banks has adopted a Privacy Code on the basis of the Privacy Act.[11]

Confidentiality under criminal law

Under Article 272 of the Dutch Criminal Code, disclosure of a secret by a person who knows or should know that he has a duty of secrecy pursuant to his office or pursuant to a statutory provision is a criminal offence. This obligation of secrecy under criminal law has not been accepted by the courts in respect of banks. A decision of the Court of Appeal in Amsterdam confirms this.[12] A bank had

---

9. Case nos 8626, 8716, 8745, 8765 and A9160 of the Complaints Committee for the Banking Business.
10. Privacy Act (*Wet Persoonsregistraties*) of 1 July 1989, Official Gazette (*Staatsblad*) 1988, 480.
11. Privacy Code (*Privacy Gedragscode Banken*) of 16 May 1995.
12. Amsterdam Court of Appeal, 18 December 1974, NJ 1975, 441.

provided a Dutch civil law notary with information on the amount of credit outstanding to one of its customers. The Court of Appeal decided that this did not constitute a criminal offence within the meaning of Article 272.

Exceptions to the civil law obligations of secrecy

A person who is called to testify in civil or criminal proceedings in the Netherlands is in principle obliged to appear in court.[13] Violation of this duty to appear and testify is a criminal offence, unless the witness has a valid excuse. Such valid excuse exists if the witness has a statutory right to be excused (*verschoningsrecht*). The question arises whether directors or employees of a bank have such a statutory right. The answer is no. Under civil and criminal law, a statutory "right to be excused" exists for, among others, those who are bound to secrecy pursuant to their profession or office (for instance: solicitors, doctors and clergy). Case law on this point shows that courts in the Netherlands have so far denied bankers this right. Legal authors seem to hold the same view. Therefore, a banker will have to breach his obligation of secrecy if he is called to testify in civil or criminal court proceedings.

Various other exceptions to the bank's obligation of secrecy exist under both civil and criminal law. An important exception is the right of inspection by the tax authorities. Pursuant to the General Act on state taxes,[14] the tax inspector may require a bank to give access to find facts for the determination of taxes to be imposed on a certain customer of the bank. The tax inspector may also ask the bank to give any further information which may be relevant for the imposition of taxes on the given customer. Since 1984, a code of practice (*fiscale gedragsregels*) issued by the Ministry of Finance, provides for guidelines to be followed by banks when the tax inspector uses his right of inspection. It should be noted that the tax inspector may seek access in two ways, by giving the name of the customer and by giving the bank account number.

Another exception is the bank's duty on the basis of the Consumer Credit Act (as discussed below) to register the granting of consumer credits with the Central Office for Credit Registration. Finally, the courts have held that under certain circumstances the bank may have a duty to provide information about the financial position of a customer to a third party granting security for the obligations of the customer to the bank.[15]

Prevention of money-laundering

The Netherlands has implemented the Money Laundering Directive[16] and the recommendations of the Financial Action Task Force on money-laundering,

13. Art. 191 Code of Civil Procedure; Art. 218 Code of Criminal Proceedings.
14. Algemene Wet inzake Rijksbelastingen of 28 August 1959, as amended.
15. Hoge Raad, 1 June 1990, NJ 1991, 759; also Hoge Raad 3 June 1994, RvdW (Jurisprudence Weekly) 1994, 126C.
16. EC Directive of 10 June 1991 on prevention of use of the financial system for the purpose of money-laundering (L 166/77).

through two pieces of legislation: the Disclosure of Unusual Transactions Act[17] and the Identification Financial Services Act.[18]

The Disclosure of Unusual Transactions Act requires banks[19] to notify the Disclosures Office (*Meldpunt Ongebruikelijke Transacties*) of any unusual financial transaction which is carried out or is intended to be carried out. The notification obligation is not imposed on individual employees of the banks, but on the banks themselves. A transaction is considered to be unusual on the basis of criteria—referred to in the Act as "indicators"—which are determined from time to time for a maximum period of six months. The indicators are set by the Ministers of Finance and Justice following consultation with the Disclosures Office and a committee established to provide guidance to the Disclosures Office. They can be divided into objective and subjective criteria. Transactions meeting the objective criteria include:

— cash transactions exceeding Dfl. 1 million;
— cash transactions exceeding Dfl. 25,000, involving currency exchanges;
— giro transactions exceeding Dfl. 25,000 by non-account holders involving foreign countries.

If one of the objective indicators is met, the transaction must be reported to the Disclosures Office. In the case of subjective indicators, the bank is required to make a disclosure, if in its view one or more of the criteria have been fulfilled. These include:

— transactions suspected to be linked to money-laundering activities;
— a customer's expressed preference for transactions below the threshold of Dfl. 25,000 (*smurfing*).

The Disclosure of Unusual Transactions Act contains rules indemnifying persons, who reasonably made a notification in compliance with the Act, against civil and criminal liability.

The Identification Financial Services Act requires banks and other financial institutions to establish the identity of a customer prior to performing a financial service. Financial services include:

— taking custody of securities, banknotes, coins, precious metals and other valuables;
— opening an account on which a balance may be held in the form of moneys, securities, precious metals or other valuables;
— hiring out of a safety deposit box;
— providing a service in respect of a transaction or a number of related transactions with a value or a joint value of at least Dfl. 25,000.

17. Wet melding ongebruikelijke transacties of 16 December 1993, Official Gazette 1993, 705, as amended.
18. Wet identificatie bij financiële dienstverlening of 12 December 1993, Official Gazette 1993, 704, as amended.
19. The disclosure obligation is imposed on "each person who in the course of his profession or trade performs a financial service (as defined in the Act)".

The Act provides for certain exceptions to the identification requirement, notably where a financial service is rendered for a client whose identification had already been established.

In addition to specific legislation, changes have been made to the Criminal Code and the Code of Criminal Proceedings to further combat money-laundering. These changes include the use by the public prosecutor of more and better methods to trace and seize moneys obtained by criminal means and the extending of provisions regarding the receipt of stolen property (*heling*).

THE MULTIFUNCTIONAL BANK

General

Traditionally, banks in the Netherlands have been involved in a wide range of financial services. The services of these "general" banks include brokerage, investment advice and the arranging of new issues. All general banks are Admitted Institutions of Amsterdam Exchanges N.V. and, as such, are allowed to conduct business on the Amsterdam (AEX) Stock Exchange. It is quite common, for instance, for a Dutch bank to have its credit department and its brokerage or new issues department within one legal entity. As a result, a bank may sometimes be confronted with a conflict of interest. For instance, a customer of the brokerage department seeking advice on the purchase of securities may have an interest in receiving certain information on a company which is a client of the credit department. In such a case the banks must choose between a customer's interest in receiving certain information and the bank's interest in withholding information in order to prevent insider dealing. To a certain extent, the setting up of "Chinese walls" within the banks might solve this dilemma.

Chinese walls[20] and insider dealing

Dutch banks have for some time now built "Chinese walls". Their use is closely connected with the prevention of insider dealing. The most important pieces of legislation aiming to prevent the use of insider information are the recently amended and extended provisions of Articles 46 *et seq.* of the Securities Act.[21] The principal provision states that a person having insider information may not conclude or procure transactions in securities listed, or shortly to be listed, on a recognised stock exchange in or outside the Netherlands. There are a limited number of statutory exceptions from this prohibition, including a so-called

20. See, for a general discussion, M.C.M. van Dijk, "Chinese Muren, papieren tijgers", in TVVS 1997, nr. 8 (pp. 235–240).
21. 1995 Act on the supervision of the securities trade (*Wet toezicht effectenverkeer 1995*) of 31 December 1995, as amended.

"Chinese walls exception". In addition, the Act allows for further exemptions to be granted by ministerial decree.[22] The Securities Act, furthermore, contains provisions regarding the disclosure of insider information as well as certain transactions in securities and requires issuing institutions to set internal regulations in accordance with ministerial guidelines. Several other regulations also contain rules regarding insider dealing, including the General Regulations and the Further Regulations for Admitted Institutions with which Admitted Institutions of Amsterdam Exchanges N.V. must comply.[23]

Under these rules, banks, as Admitted Institutions, are under an obligation to provide for adequate arrangements to avoid the passing of price-sensitive information from one department to another.

In view of the stock exchange rules, in 1991 the Association of Dutch Banks introduced a code of conduct in respect of the separated handling of price-sensitive information. The code of conduct, which took effect on 1 April 1991, recommends certain action in setting up Chinese walls. The code of conduct requires the banks to make a physical or, alternatively, a clear procedural division between its credit, issues and brokerage departments. Furthermore, the banks must inform their customers that Chinese walls are in place and that certain price-sensitive information will, as a result of the Chinese walls, not be conveyed to the customers and not be used by the banks in rendering services. Under the code of conduct banks must appoint an officer to enforce compliance (*toezichthouder*). The banks' employees must be made subject to various obligations to comply with the Chinese walls and to ensure their effect.

The use of Chinese walls will help banks to avoid insider trading. However, at least until the introduction of the "Chinese walls exception" mentioned above, it was considered doubtful whether their use could always prevent banks from incurring criminal liability.[24] The new rules have not yet been tested.

For Chinese walls to be effective in terms of a bank's position *vis-à-vis* its customers, a contractual arrangement would be necessary. The proviso discussed above to the duty of due care as included in Article 2 of the General Banking Conditions aims to achieve this.

22. The revised provisions were proposed following the collapse of a high profile prosecution on the basis of the current provision. For a discussion of the new provisions, see S.E. Eisma, "Nieuwe wettelijke bepalingen inzake voorwetenschap", Ondernemingsrecht 1999, No 3.

23. Art. 7(e) General Regulations (*Algemeen Reglement*) and Art. 5 Further Regulations for Admitted Institutions (*Nadere Regeling Toegelaten Instellingen*). The Listing Rules of the AEX Stock Exchange (*Fondsenreglement*) also required listed companies to adopt internal regulations (Appendix IX: Model Code for the prevention of insider dealing). Following the coming into force of the new provisions of the Securities Act this requirement has been repealed.

24. See Prof. M.S. Groenhuijsen, *Strafbaar misbruik van voorwetenschap en "Chinese walls"*, 1991.

LIABILITY OF BANKS FOR INVESTMENT ADVICE

Basis of liability

Liability for incorrect advice must be considered under two heads: liability for breach of contract (*wanprestatie*) and liability for tort (*onrechtmatige daad*).

Contractual liability may arise when a bank, in rendering advice, breaches a specific contract with a client for the rendering of advisory services. It is more likely, however, that there will not be a specific contract. The bank may then be liable for a breach of its duty under the General Banking Conditions and the general rules of the law of contract to exercise "due care" in its relation to its customer.

The bank's incorrect advice may also constitute a tort. Under the Dutch law on tort, it is among other things tortious to act in violation of a "generally required duty of care" ("*zorgvuldigheid die in het maatschappelijk verkeer betaamt*") or, in other words, to be negligent. This negligence may, in addition to breach of contract, be a basis on which a bank may be sued for giving incorrect advice.

It is difficult to indicate when exactly, under Dutch law, a bank will be liable for incorrect investment advice.[25] It will depend on the circumstances of the case. A relevant circumstance might be the customer's expertise or experience in respect of a contemplated action or transaction.[26] An inexperienced customer will require more care by the bank than an experienced customer. The duty of care may force the bank not only to warn a customer against the risks of a transaction, but even to refuse to carry out a transaction for its customer. This applies in particular to high-risk transactions such as dealings in options.[27]

However, the bank is not under a general obligation to prevent a customer from carrying out his own risky investment policy or to warn him about the risks of his investment policy.[28]

Exclusion of liability

Under Dutch law a party to a contract is in principle permitted to exclude liability for breach of contract and/or for tort in all circumstances except wilfulness (*opzet*) or gross negligence (*grove schuld*) of this party. Exclusion by a party of liability for breach of contract or tort by its employees is permitted in all circumstances, even if an employee's act was wilfully or grossly negligent.

The General Banking Conditions contain several limitations on the liability of

---

25. See on liability of banks in general: I.P. Michiels van Kessenich-Hoogendam, *Aansprakelijkheid van Banken*, 1987, Serie Praktijkboekhandleidingen.
26. For instance Hoge Raad, 1 June 1990, NJ 1991, 759 and Hoge Raad 3 June 1994, RvdW 1994, 126.
27. Hoge Raad, 23 May 1997, RvdW 1997, 128.
28. Hoge Raad, 24 January 1997, NJ 1997, 260.

banks.[29] These limitations are less far reaching than an exclusion of liability, except wilfulness or gross negligence, as referred to above.

Invoking a contractual limitation or exclusion of liability may, under certain circumstances, be considered to violate the principle of reasonableness and fairness. Under certain circumstances, it might be unreasonable for a bank to invoke the exclusion in the General Banking Conditions, even though the contractual exclusion itself is valid under Dutch law. In such case the bank will be liable notwithstanding the contractual exclusion.

The landmark case on the exclusion of liability by a bank is the *Saladin/HBU* decision of the Supreme Court of the Netherlands (*Hoge Raad der Nederlanden*) of 19 May 1967.[30] In this case the Supreme Court had to consider a bank's liability for incorrect investment advice and the effect of the bank's contractual exclusion of liability. The bank (HBU) had, on its own initiative, rendered advice to a Mr Saladin, who had no expertise in financial matters, to purchase certain securities. The transaction was recommended by the bank as very advantageous and very safe. Mr Saladin purchased the securities but discovered soon afterwards that the transaction was very unsafe and that his investment was virtually worthless. He sued the bank on the basis of breach of contract and tort and claimed damages as a result of the transaction. In the proceedings, the question whether the bank was liable in tort never needed to be resolved. The bank had excluded all liability for the transaction in a letter of confirmation to Mr Saladin. The central question of the proceedings was therefore whether the bank could reasonably invoke the contractual exclusion of liability even if the bank had committed a tort.

The Supreme Court decided that the answer to the question of liability depended on "various circumstances". One of these circumstances might be the position of the parties in society and their relation to each other. The Supreme Court does not decide on factual matters. It could therefore only decide whether the Court of Appeal had given a reasonable decision in denying Mr Saladin's claim on the basis of the bank's contractual exclusion of liability. The Supreme Court did find that the decision of the Court of Appeal in this case was reasonable. Mr Saladin therefore lost his case in the final instance. If the bank had not excluded its liability, the matter would probably have been decided in Mr Saladin's favour.

The bank as lead manager

The position of a bank in its capacity as lead manager of an issue of securities has come under scrutiny in recent years. In the important *Co-op* case,[31] the Hoge Raad ruled on the responsibility of a lead manager for—and liability in respect of—a prospectus, based on tort. The principal facts of the *Co-op* case are as follows. In June 1987 and July 1988 the wholly-owned Dutch subsidiary of the

29. Arts. 3, 27 and 31 General Banking Conditions.
30. NJ 1967, 261.
31. HR 2 December 1994, NJ 1996, 246.

German corporation Co-op AG ("Co-op") issued two series of bonds which were guaranteed by Co-op and listed on the Amsterdam Stock Exchange. Both prospectuses contained the annual accounts of Co-op, including the consolidated balance sheet, the consolidated profit and loss account and a statement of auditor's approval. The last page of each prospectus contained a statement on behalf of ABN-AMRO Bank as lead manager ("ABN-AMRO") and the other members of the syndicate to the effect that the information in the prospectus as provided by the syndicate was true and accurate and that in the opinion of the syndicate no information had been omitted the inclusion of which could alter the substance of the prospectus. By the end of 1988, ABN-AMRO became aware of unfavourable financial information about Co-op. This information was published and in consequence the prices of the bonds fell. A number of bondholders formed an association and brought a class action against ABN-AMRO. The accounts of Co-op appeared not to consolidate a large number of affiliated companies of Co-op. Had these been consolidated, the accounts would have shown a deficit of around two billion Deutschmarks. The legal framework for prospectus liability under Dutch law is formed by a special category of tort dealing with the providing of misleading information.[32] In essence, a person commits a tort by publishing or making available misleading information in relation to goods or services offered by that individual, on his behalf or another person's behalf, in the course of a business or profession.

The claim of the bondholders association was based on the view that ABN-AMRO had committed a tort towards the bondholders who had purchased the bonds in reliance on the information contained in the prospectuses. According to the association, ABN-AMRO had made misleading statements insofar as it had determined the contents of the prospectuses which contained incorrect and incomplete information. Also, the association claimed that ABN-AMRO had acted unlawfully by advising investors to purchase bonds after it had become public that Co-op was in a bad financial position or in any case by not warning the investors about the risk of such purchase. The Supreme Court ruled against ABN-AMRO. The most important part of the decision relates to the position of ABN-AMRO as lead manager. It follows from the Supreme Court's judgment that the bank which acts as a lead underwriter in an offering of securities is in principle responsible for the contents of the prospectus. The mere fact that certain statements in the prospectus do not originate from that bank, but from others such as auditors, does not discharge the lead manager from its responsibilities. ABN-AMRO's claim that it was not under an obligation to verify the financial information supplied to it by Co-op's auditors was rejected, notwithstanding the fact that the prospectuses contained an auditor statement. The extent of a lead manager's verification obligations was not precisely set by the Supreme Court.[33] Also, somewhat cryptically the

32. Arts. 6:194 and 6:195 Civil Code.
33. Admitted Institutions introducing a new listing on the AEX Stock Exchange are subject to due diligence requirements; see Art. 11 Listing Procedure Rules (*Reglement Procedure Beursnotering*).

court stated that a lead manager should not be considered as having (co-)determined the contents of a prospectus if the prospectus states in clear and unambiguous terms that certain statements in the text are not prepared by it and that it does not accept responsibility for the accuracy of statements prepared by other persons. The responsibility statement included in the Co-op prospectuses did not meet such requirements. It is yet unclear to what extent a disclaimer can limit or indeed prevent liability of a lead manager for misleading statements in a prospectus.

SECURITY

General

In this section the main forms of security available under Dutch law will be discussed. Furthermore, attention will be given to the granting of security in group financing transactions. In Dutch legal practice, the potential problems related to this form of financing are of particular interest. Finally, the law applicable to the granting of security in a multi-jurisdictional context will be addressed.

Forms of security

A distinction is made between security in the form of rights *in rem* (*beperkte rechten*) and contractual security. The main difference between the two types of security lies in the creditor's position in case of the debtor's bankruptcy. This position is much stronger if the creditor holds security in the form of a right *in rem*: in principle, the encumbered goods do not form part of the bankrupt's estate and the creditor is entitled independently to enforce his security right in order to settle his claims.

The rights *in rem* which are most frequently used by bankers are the rights of pledge (*pand*) and mortgage (*hypotheek*). A right of mortgage can be created on registered goods (e.g. real property, ships and aircraft). A valid mortgage requires a notarial deed which must be filed with the competent public register.

A right of pledge can be created over all goods which do not require a mortgage and can, in principle, take two forms: the traditional pledge (*vuistpand*) and the non-traditional pledge (*bezitloos pand*). A traditional pledge requires that the pledgor transfer his power over the object of the pledge to the pledgee or a third party, which is created simply by a notarial or a private deed. However, a non-traditional pledge created by private deed is only valid upon filing of the deed with the competent register. The range of objects over which a pledge can be created is wide: it can be used to encumber movables, but may also be created over registered claims and shares in book entry form. It can therefore be particularly helpful to banks. In this context two remarks should be added. First, unlike a lot of other jurisdictions, Dutch law does not recognise the concept of a "floating charge". In addition, more than 95 per cent of the securities listed on the AEX Stock Exchange are transferred by way of giro transfer pursuant to the Act on Securities Transactions by Giro.[34] This Act provides for specific rules for the creation of a pledge over securities within the giro system.[35]

Apart from the rights *in rem*, security can be obtained through contractual arrangements. These include the subordination of claims, surety (*borgtocht*) and guarantee (*garantie*). Contracts of surety and guarantee are usually entered into with third parties securing obligations of the debtor. Unlike the guarantee, for which there are no specifically statutory provisions, the contract of surety is regulated by the Civil Code.[36] One essential feature of the surety is its accessory nature: the relation between the original debtor and the creditor. This feature is generally unacceptable to banks and they will therefore demand a guarantee which imposes direct and independent obligations on the guarantor towards them. To avoid any chance of the surety provisions in the Civil Code being applicable, the guarantee should specifically state that the arrangement is not to be considered a right of surety.

Group financing

The structure of group financing transactions varies depending, *inter alia*, on the structure and financial requirements of the group and the wishes of the (syndicate of) lending banks. Sometimes a facility is granted to the holding company of the group. In that case, the holding company will on-lend the money to its group companies if so required and, in doing so, will act as an "internal" bank.[37] Alternatively, a number of group companies can collectively act as borrower,[38] thus having direct access to the bank's facility.

Variations on both types of financing exist. However, a common feature of most group financing transactions is that a number of group companies grant security, irrespective of receiving (directly or indirectly) any proceeds of the banking facility.

The granting of security by one company for the benefit of another company, where the relevant companies do not form part of the same group, gives rise to a number of issues potentially affecting the strength of such security. These issues include the following.

Ultra vires

The granting of security by a company for the benefit of another company may, depending on the relevant circumstances,[39] be considered to be *ultra vires*.

34. Wet giraal effectenverkeer of 8 June 1977, as amended.
35. Arts. 20 *et seq.*, Act on Securities Transactions by Giro.
36. Art. 7:850 Civil Code.
37. See, in relation hereto, J.M.M. Maeijer, *Financiële kruisverbanden en andere aspecten van concernfinanciering*, 1987, pp. 71 *et seq.*
38. Dutch law provides for the possibility of co-debtorship, Art. 6:6 (New) Civil Code.
39. Hoge Raad, 7 February 1992, NJ 1992, 438 and Hoge Raad, 16 October 1992, NJ 1993, 98.

Under Dutch company law[40] the concept of *ultra vires* means that a (legal) act performed by the company may be annulled if through such act the company's objects were transgressed. The possibility to annul a (legal) act is subject to the condition that the other party was or should have been, without the need for any investigation, aware of the transgression of the company's objects. The annulment on the grounds of *ultra vires* can only be invoked by the company itself or, in the case of its bankruptcy, the receiver (*curator*).

Fraudulent conveyance (actio pauliana)

A creditor and, in the event of bankruptcy, the receiver is able to invoke the annulment of a legal act which has been performed by the debtor if such act was voluntarily performed and the debtor knew or should have known that such act would prejudice the position of its other creditors.

Tort (onrechtmatige daad)

As a general rule of Dutch law, each person has to act in accordance with a generally required duty of care ("*zorgvuldigheid die in het maatschappelijk verkeer betaamt*"). In failing to meet such standards a person may, under certain circumstances, commit a tort. This rule may be relevant to banks if the security obtained from a company prejudices the position of the other creditors.[41]

Liability for improper management

A receiver may take action against the directors of a bankrupt company if they have grossly neglected their tasks ("*kennelijkeonbehoorlijke taakvervulling*") and such negligence is an important cause of the bankruptcy.[42] A similar claim can be made against others who, not being directors, in fact significantly influenced the management of the company. If a claim is successful, the defendants can be held liable for the deficit in the accounts of the bankruptcy estate.

In recent years the question has been raised regarding to what extent the issues listed above apply to group financing transactions.[43] This debate intensified as a result of the failure of a number of industrial conglomerates in the Netherlands in the 1980s: it appears that the structure of financing of these groups might have accelerated the collapse of these groups.[44] It seems that, in practical terms, the risk of group financing transactions being affected as a result of *ultra vires* and fraudulent conveyance is fairly limited. Claims of liability on the basis of tort in general or improper management appear to be more effective. In this context the

---

40. Art. 2:7 Civil Code.
41. Hoge Raad, 20 March 1959, NJ 1959, 581; see also Hoge Raad, 9 May 1986, NJ 1986, 792.
42. Arts. 2:138 and 2:248 Civil Code.
43. See J.W. Winter, *Concernfinanciering*, 1992.
44. See, *inter alia*, J.M.M. Maeijer and P. van Schilfgaarde, *Financiële kruisverbanden*, t.a.p.

extent of the knowledge which banks have of the group of companies they finance and their influence on the management of such companies, may be relevant. Detailed knowledge and significant influence on management may lead to increased standards of care and, consequently, result in incurring liability.[45]

Security in a multi-jurisdictional context

The granting of security in a multi-jurisdictional context has long given rise to uncertainty for banks. This holds in particular for the creation of security rights over registered claims, i.e. rights of one person against one or more other persons. In 1997, the Supreme Court rendered an important judgment in the *Hansa/Bechem* case regarding the law to be applied to an assignment of a registered claim which is also considered to be relevant to the creation of security rights.[46] According to the Supreme Court, the 1980 Rome Convention on the law applicable to contractual obligations does not only apply to the contractual arrangement between an assignor and an assignee to assign a registered claim, but also to the assignment itself, i.e. the *in rem* aspects of the assignment.

Similar to other civil law jurisdictions, Dutch law distinguishes between the contractual relationship between an assignor and an assignee and the *in rem* aspects of the assignment by which the transfer of the legal title to the right from the assignor to the assignee is effected. Although the *Hansa/Bechem* decision was rendered in connection with an assignment of a registered claim, it is generally accepted that the legal analysis underpinning the Supreme Court's judgment would also apply to the creation of security rights over registered claims. This means that if the agreement to grant security is governed by the law of a particular jurisdiction, the law of that jurisdiction also applies to *in rem* aspects of the creation of the security right.

It should be noted that, according to the 1980 Rome Convention,[47] the relationship between the assignee (or the holder of a security right) and the debtor of the registered claim as well as the conditions under which the assignment can be invoked against the debtor are determined by the law governing the registered claim. That law also governs the assignability of the registered claim and any question whether the debtor's obligations have been discharged.

The Supreme Court did not address the question of the exercise of rights and remedies within the Netherlands, by the holder of a foreign security right. It is likely that, if a security right granted under foreign law is enforced in the Netherlands, the Dutch courts will compare the foreign security right with available security rights under Dutch law and will choose the security right available which most closely resembles the foreign security right. The secured person's rights and remedies would then be exercised subject to Dutch law

45. See Hoge Raad, 19 February 1988, NJ 1988, 487 (note that the defendant in this case was not the bank but the parent company).
46. Hoge Raad, 16 May 1997.
47. Art. 12 para. 2 1980 Rome Convention.

applicable to execution and to other provisions of Dutch civil procedure. Also, the ranking of the foreign security interest would probably be determined in a similar way.

CONSUMER PROTECTION

General

In recent decades, consumers' rights have been the object of increasing attention. This has resulted in a variety of new legislation. This section will focus on two sets of legislation which are of particular importance to bankers and their customers: the provisions on general conditions in the Civil Code and the Consumer Credit Act.

General conditions

The Civil Code contains specific provisions with respect to general conditions. In Article 6:231 of the Code, general conditions are defined as one or more written statements which are intended to be used in a number of agreements. The provisions which reflect the essence of the agreement do not qualify as general conditions. It is understood that such essential provisions are those without which it is not possible to reach an agreement; for example, in a sale and purchase agreement the price and quantity of the goods are considered to be essential.

A provision in general conditions may be annulled if:

1. such provision places an unreasonable burden on the other party (i.e. the consumer); or
2. the user of the general conditions has not offered the other party a reasonable opportunity to take cognisance of the conditions.

The provisions on general conditions are primarily intended to protect individuals. The Civil Code therefore provides that, if used in respect of individuals who do not act in the course of a profession or trade, certain conditions are *per se* unreasonably burdensome (usually referred to as the "black list"). Other provisions are considered to be *prima facie* unreasonably onerous (the "grey list").[48] As the aim of the legislation is to protect individuals against abuse of general conditions it is evident that certain parties cannot invoke the protection of the statutory provisions (for example, large companies) as fully described in the Civil Code.

The General Banking Conditions qualify as general conditions under the Civil Code. Therefore, the banks will have to reckon with the statutory provisions when drafting the Conditions. In relation to this it can be argued that the GBC contain provisions which appear on the "grey list".[49]

48. Arts. 6:236 and 6:237 Civil Code.
49. See H.R. Sollie, *De Nieuwe Algemene Voorwaarden*, 1990, p. 44.

Consumer Credit Act

The Consumer Credit Act[50] which, *inter alia*, implements the EC Consumer Credit Directive,[51] sets out the rules for professionals granting credit to consumers. A few of the detailed provisions of the Act will be highlighted.

The parameters of the Act show that its applicability is both restricted and broad. On the one hand, the Act protects individuals who do not act in the course of a profession or trade and only applies to credit transactions up to an amount of Dfl. 50,000. On the other hand, the Act covers a wide range of credit transactions including traditional loans, purchase by instalments, mail order credits and credit card transactions, as well as certain overdraft arrangements. However, the applicability of the Act is subject to the condition that the consumer obtains (part of) the credit for a period of at least three months.

The Act provides for a number of rules designed to protect the consumer: the giver of credit is obliged to make available to the consumer, without charge and in writing, the conditions on the basis of which he is prepared to grant the credit. Furthermore, the giver must obtain written information as to the creditworthiness of the consumer prior to entering into a transaction for credit exceeding Dfl. 2,000. In relation hereto he may obtain information from the Central Office for Credit Registration. Also, a credit transaction can only be entered into in writing. The Act contains rules as to the contents of the agreement.

The Act prohibits anyone acting as a giver of credit from presenting himself as such, without a licence. In practical terms this requirement does not affect banks, because all credit institutions which are licensed under the Act on the supervision of the credit system and supervised by the Dutch Central Bank, are eligible for a licence. To protect the consumer further, the Act provides that certain onerous provisions in a credit agreement are null and void; others can be annulled on the request of the consumer. Finally, the Act imposes restrictions on the security which may be obtained by the giver of credit.

It follows from the above description that the Act provides elaborate protection for consumers obtaining credit. This is of particular importance as the Act covers almost all consumer credit transactions: more than 90 per cent of such transactions relate to credits of less than Dfl. 50,000.

JULIE A. ROELVINK* AND LODEWIJK J. HIJMANS VAN DEN BERGH**

---

50. Wet van 4 juli 1990, Staatsblad 395, houdende regels met betrekking tot het consumentenkrediet.

51. EC Directive of 22 December 1986 for the approximation of the laws, regulations and administrative provisions of the Member States concerning credit (87/102/EEC) as amended on 22 February 1990 (90/88/EEC).

* Formerly Advocaat, De Brauw Blackstone Westbroek, London (1993 edition only).

** Partner, De Brauw Blackstone Westbroek, Amsterdam.

CHAPTER 7

SPAIN

THE ORGANISATION OF THE SPANISH BANKING SYSTEM: LEGAL ASPECTS

The influence of EEC law

As a result of Spain's entry in the EEC with effect from 1 January 1986, it was necessary to incorporate *en bloc* the then-existing Community regulations, in particular in respect of banking. In order to make the most urgent modifications to Spanish laws resulting from such incorporation, Act (*Ley*) 47/1985 was enacted on 27 December 1985, conferring upon the Government the power to issue provisions under law to adapt to Community law the matters regulated in the laws listed in the annex thereto; such matters included banking.[1]

In particular, the process of adaptation of Spanish banking law to Community law has followed the different stages of bank harmonisation.[2] First of all, in what has come to be called the "first stage of harmonisation", which covers the conditions of access to the banking profession and exercise thereof, Act 47/1985 gave rise to Legislative Royal Decree (*Real Decreto Legislativo*) 1298/1986 on adaptation of the regulations of credit institutions.[3] With regard to the "second stage of harmonisation", relating to the control of credit institutions, in addition to the basic regulation contained in Act 13/1985 of 25 May, it is also worth noting the modification introduced in Act 13/1992 of 1 June on equity and consolidated supervision of financial institutions, which responds to the need to include the Community regulations (in particular, Directives 89/299, 89/646 and 89/647) in Spanish law. The third and definite

---

1. See in this respect, F. Sánchez Calero, *Instituciones de Derecho Mercantil* (Madrid, 20th edn, 1997); E. Angulo Rodríguez, "La adhesión española a la CEE y la ordenación bancaria", in VV.AA. *Estudios de Derecho público bancario*, Madrid, 1987, pp. 71 ff.; and J. Sánchez-Calero Guilarte, "La armonización bancaria: autorización, control y estructura de bancos y sucursales", in VV.AA. *Libre circulación de capitales en la CEE*, Valladolid 1990, pp. 33 ff.

2. With regard to such stages, see P. Maestre Casas, "El mercado único: un nuevo marco jurídico para la actividad bancaria" in *La Ley*, 29 June 1990, p. 4 ff. See also D. Augustin, "Hacia la Europa de los bancos", in *Revista de Derecho Bancario y Bursátil (RDBB)*, 31 (1988), pp. 507 ff. and P. Clarotti, "El libro blanco de la Comisión de las Comunidades Europeas sobre el perfeccionamiento del mercado interno y la banca", in *RDBB*, 22 (1986), pp. 241 ff.

3. See F. Sánchez Calero, "Adaptación de la normativa de los establecimientos de crédito al ordenamiento de la CEE" in *RDBB* 23 (1986), pp. 463 ff.

stage has been achieved by Act 3/1994, of 14 April, which adapts the Spanish Law on credit institutions to the Second EC Directive on Banking Coordination, introducing as well other modifications of the financial markets. The Act has been further regulated by Royal Decree (*Real Decreto*) 1245/1995, of 14 July, on the creation of Banks, trans-border activities and other matters concerning the legal status of credit institutions.[4]

Public control of credit institutions

Public intervention in the Spanish banking system has several objectives: the protection of customers who entrust their savings to credit institutions, control of the granting of credits and loans insofar as this increases the money supply and, finally, the wish to control the political power that credit institutions acquire as a result of the economic power gained from the funds at their disposal.[5] This public control is exercised by the Ministry of Economy and Finance (which authorises the incorporation of credit institutions and has the power to penalise) and the Bank of Spain (*Banco de España*).[6]

The Bank of Spain holds a special position in Spanish banking law, not only because it is a state entity performing a public function and having a considerable degree of autonomy in respect of public administration, but also because it performs the normal functions of a central bank. In particular, it is responsible for carrying out monetary policy, acting as bank for the State and the Treasury, and serving as a bankers' bank. Secondly, it is responsible for the senior management, coordination and inspection of all credit institutions, and has significant powers regarding the imposition of penalties and temporary intervention. Thirdly, it manages several different services, i.e. the Claims Service (*Servicio de Reclamaciones*), the National Electronic Clearing Service (*Servicio Nacional de Compensación Electrónica*), the headquarters for recording the National Debt and the Risk Information Headquarters (*Central de Información de Riesgos*).

Act 13/1994, of 1 June on Autonomy of the Bank of Spain has adapted the legal status of the Bank in order to enable its incorporation into the European Central Banks System, according to the provisions of the Maastricht Treaty. Thus, the Act defines the Bank of Spain as a public law body, with full legal personality and full power to act both publicly and privately. It is independent from the Administration. Its functions are divided between those related to

4. See J. Cadenas Coronado, "Derecho comunitario de la competencia en el sector bancario", in *RDBB*, 45 (1992), p. 167 ff., and J.O. Llebot Majo, "El mercado interior del crédito en al ámbito de la CEE", in *RDBB*, 38 (1990) pp. 373 ff.

5. See A. Jiménez Blanco, "Supervisión bancaria y responsabilidad administrativa" in *RDBB* 20 (1985), pp. 823 ff., and S. Martin Retortillo, "Estudio preliminar", in VV.AA., *supra* n. 1, pp. 15 ff.

6. See S. Martin Retortillo, *Crédito, banca y cajas de ahorro. Aspectos jurídico-administrativos*, Madrid 1975, and G. Perez de Armiñan, "Poder politico, sistema financiero y marco jurídico", in *RDBB*, 33 (1989), pp. 109 ff. In particular on the Act on Discipline and Intervention of 1988, see E. García de Enterria, "Significado general del Anteproyecto", in *RDBB*, 28 (1987), pp. 702 ff., and S. Martin Retortillo, "Reflexiones sobre la Ley de Disciplina e Intervención Bancaria" in *Revista de Administración Pública* 118 (1989), pp. 7 ff.

monetary policies, interest rates, and treasury and public debt services. Its management bodies are the Governor, the Assistant Governor, the Managing Council and the Executive Committee. Their organisation has been developed by Standing Orders approved by Resolution of the Managing Council of 14 November 1996.

Moreover, the Act on Discipline and Intervention of Credit Institutions of 29 July 1988 (*Ley de Disciplina e Intervención de las Entidades de Crédito*) grants the Bank of Spain a power of regulation, which it exercises through Circulars (*Circulares*).[7]

Credit institutions

Legal concept

Under Spanish law and in pursuance of Article 1 of Legislative Royal Decree 1298/1986 of 28 June (in the text given in Art. 39 of Act 26/1988 of 29 July), credit institutions are defined as companies which have as their typical and normal activity the obtaining of funds from the public in the form of deposits, loans, temporary assignment of financial assets and similar forms involving the obligation of return or repayment, using such funds for the granting of credits on its own account. They are, therefore, entrepreneurs whose activity consists of intermediation in credit and who, moreover, provide their clientele with a number of different services constituting accessory operations, pursuant to Article 38 of the Banking Act of 31 December 1946. The concept is therefore functional and extensive and does not take into account the form or structure of the subject performing such activity; moreover, it has been directly influenced by Directives 77/780/EEC and 89/646/EEC.[8]

Kinds of credit institution

After defining the concept of the credit institution, Article 1.2 of Legislative Royal Decree 1298/1986 lists the different kinds of credit institution, giving an initial impression of heterogeneity of such institutions. Indeed, the list groups together corporate enterprises (private banks) and foundational enterprises (savings banks); enterprises having the structure of a corporation (private banks) and others having a cooperative nature (credit unions); entities having the legal nature of public institutions (Official Credit Institute) and others subject to private law.[9]

7. See H. Hernández Marqués, "Las potestades de dirección y supervisión. Especial referencia a las del Banco de España", in VV.AA., *supra* n. 1, pp. 115 ff. On the regulatory power of the Bank of Spain, see in particular J.R. Parada, "Valor jurídico de la Circular" in *RDBB*, 2 (1981), pp. 311 ff., and T.R. Fernández, "Los poderes normativos del Banco de España" in *RDBB*, 13 (1984), pp. 7 ff.

8. See F. Sánchez Calero, "La delimitación de la figura de entidad de crédito y la de otros sujetos" in *RDBB*, 28 (1987), pp. 709 ff. and T.R. Fernández, "Comentario al artículo 1" in VV.AA., *Comentarios a la Ley de Disciplina e Intervención de las Entidades de Crédito*, Madrid 1989, pp. 29 ff.

9. See F. Barco Gorostegui, "Real Decreto sobre creación de entidades de crédito de ámbito operativo limitado", in *RDBB*, 35 (1989), pp. 675 ff.

OFFICIAL BANKS

The legal regulations of official banks in Spain contain both public and private provisions, which reveal, on the one hand, the intense administrative intervention in this sector and, on the other, the desire for the activity of such banks to be performed through competition on equal conditions with other credit institutions. In particular, Law 25/1991 of 21 November establishes a new organisation of public credit institutions with the following structure:[10]

First, the Spanish Banking Corporation (*Corporación Bancaria de España*) has been established as a state-owned company with the status of a credit institution and the stature of a bank, to which the ownership of the shares representing the capital of official credit institutions has been transferred.

Secondly, the Official Credit Institute (*Instituto de Crédito Oficial*, ICO) has been given the legal status of a State Financial Agency, according to the Sixth Additional Provision of Royal Decree Law 12/1995, of 28 December 1995.

Thirdly, Corporación Bancaria de España, S.A. holds the capital of official credit institutions, which are subject to the specific legislation on official credit contained in Acts 33/1987 and 13/1971. Although these official credit institutions are subject to the general legislation on corporations, they have a number of special characteristics. They must: obtain administrative approval of their Articles, have a Board of Directors and two Managers appointed by the Chairman of the entity and hold a General Meeting composed of a sole shareholder, etc. At present, this category of credit institutions comprises Banco de Crédito Industrial, Banco de Crédito Agrícola, Banco de Crédito Local de España, Banco Hipotecario and Caja Postal. Special reference should be made to the peculiar situation of Banco Exterior de España: although this institution is entrusted with the management of the public service of official export credit, part of its capital is held by private persons. The commercial name of the group (which is under a process of privatisation) is Argentaria.

PRIVATE BANKS

A private bank under Spanish law is a private corporation that normally and for profit performs the activity of intermediation in indirect credit, with no restriction on its operations and with authority to receive sight deposits.

Private banks are credit institutions, founded as corporations (*sociedad anónima*), regulated by Royal Decree 1245/1995. Their main characteristics are: minimum stock capital of 3,000 million pesetas, fully paid in cash, with nominative shares; the corporate purpose must be limited to the normal activities of a credit institution; the Board of Directors must have at least five members; they must have a proper administrative and accounting organisation, including adequate procedures of internal control; and the stockholders with a significant share must be *suitable*.[11]

10. I. Guayo Castiella, "Estudio de la nueva Corporación Bancaria de España, S.A., particularmente a la luz del Derecho comunitario europeo", in *RDBB*, 44 (1991), pp. 939 ff.
11. See M. Broseta Pont, "Referencia al régimen de los bancos", in *RDBB*, 28 (1987), pp. 739 ff.

SAVINGS BANKS

Savings banks are entrepreneurial ventures with a foundational structure and a private-law nature that exercise banking activities without any functional restrictions. The administrative authorisation of these enterprises is subject to requirements similar to those of private banks in respect of documents, and they are required to have endowment funds that are not fixed, but depend on the population of the municipalities in which they operate, fluctuating between 150 million and 750 million pesetas, pursuant to the provisions of Decree 1838/1975. Act 31/1985 of 2 August reformed the internal organisation of savings banks, establishing new regulations for their management bodies, which are the General Meeting (or Assembly), the Board of Directors and the Control Committee.[12]

CREDIT UNIONS

These are regulated in Spanish law by Act 13/1989 of 26 May, which must be coordinated with the General Law of Cooperatives (*Ley General de Cooperativas*) 3/1987 of 2 April and the different provisions issued by the Autonomous Communities. When the principal object of the credit union is to provide financial services in the rural environment, it is called a *Caja Rural*.[13] Further developments have taken place due to the Regulation on Credit Unions, approved by Royal Decree 84/1993, of 22 January.

FINANCIAL ESTABLISHMENTS OF CREDIT

Act 3/1994 restricted the concept of credit institutions, putting aside the so-called "Credit institutions with a limited scope of operation", which became "financial establishments of credit" (*establecimientos financieros de crédito*).[14] They are regulated by the First Additional Provision of Act 3/1994 and Royal Decree 692/1996 of 26 April. Their main corporate purpose must consist of one or several of the following activities: loans and credits, factoring, leasing, issuance and management of credit cards, issuance of bills of guaranty, etc. They are not allowed to get funds from the public and they are subject to the surveillance of the Bank of Spain.

12. See J.M. González Moreno, *Naturaleza y régimen jurídico de las Cajas de Ahorros*, Madrid 1983, and J.E. Soriano García, in VV.AA., *supra* n. 1, pp. 391 ff. Recently, see the articles by F. Sánchez Calero, J.M. González Moreno, M. Aragon Reyes, J.A. Santamaría Pastor, A.J. Tapia Hermida, X. Añoveros Trías de Bes and R. García Villaverde, in the monographic edition of *RDBB*, 43 (1991), pp. 557 ff.
13. See J.M. Carcelen Conesa, "La nueva regulación de Cajas de Ahorros y Cooperativas de Crédito en el marco constitucional" in *RDBB*, 12 (1983), pp. 849 ff., and C. Balaguer Escrig, *El crédito cooperativo. Régimen jurídico estatal*, Madrid 1990.
14. On factoring companies, in particular, see recently J.A. Corrales Romero, "Aspectos institucionales de las compañías de fáctoring", pp. 69 ff. and R. Prado Iglesias, "Entidades de fáctoring", pp. 155 ff., both in VV.AA., *Jornadas sobre fáctoring*, Madrid, 1992. On leasing companies, see J.L. Piñar Mañas, "Comentario a la Disposición Adicional Séptima" in VV.AA. *supra* n. 8, pp. 179 ff. On money market brokerage companies, see R. Ortega Fernández, "Las sociedades en el mercado de dinero" in *RDBB*, 3 (1981), pp. 553 ff.

GENERAL CHARACTERISTICS OF BANKING

Rules of solvency and equity

One fundamental characteristic in the regulation of credit institutions in Spanish law is the imposition, necessarily through formal law, of the obligation to respect a number of specified ratios between assets and liabilities, or between resources and investments. In this respect, a number of bank ratios are imposed by Act 26/1983 of 26 December on cash ratios, and Act 13/1985 on investment ratios, equity and information obligations of money brokers; those laws have subsequently been extended by regulation. In this respect, Act 13/1992 of 1 June on equity and supervision on a consolidated basis of financial institutions is especially important, since that Act, which aims to adapt Spanish provisions to several EC Directives (namely 89/299, 89/646 and 89/647), contains provisions not only regarding credit institutions and their groups, but also on brokering companies and agencies (*sociedades de valores* and *agencias de valores*), management companies of the stock exchanges and the securities clearing and settlement service and its groups, insurance companies and their groups, other consolidated groups of financial institutions and mixed, non-consolidated groups of financial institutions.[15]

Bookkeeping of credit institutions

The regulation of bookkeeping of credit institutions is much more detailed and complex than for other entities. In this respect, the Ministerial Order (*Orden Ministerial*) of 31 March 1989 granted the Bank of Spain the power to establish and modify the accounting regulations and models of financial statements of credit institutions in accordance with Article 48 of Law 26/1988. Such financial statements may either be public, intended to inform third persons, or confidential, to give information to the Bank of Spain so that it can adequately perform its duties of supervision and control. The Bank of Spain can also establish the form, frequency and term of publication or rendering of both kinds of statements and, moreover, it may require individual credit institutions to provide information supplementary to that given in the confidential financial statements. The Bank of Spain must apply homogeneous publishing principles to all credit institutions within the same category, in accordance with the principles established in the EC Directives on the subject, and must respect accounting principles, such as that of cautious valuation, and the fact that these entities receive funds from third persons. The models of accounting statements are compulsory for credit institutions, which may not modify them or make any omissions, although they may break down the items included thereon in

---

15. See J. Piñares Leal, "Coeficientes" in VV.AA., *supra* n. 1, pp. 253 ff. Solvency of credit institutions is regulated by Royal Decree 1343/1992 (amended by Royal Decrees 538/1994 and 2024/1995), Order of 30 December 1992 (amended by Order of 23 July 1993) and Circular 5/1993 of the Bank of Spain (amended by Circulars 2/1994 and 3/1997).

pursuance to the Bank of Spain Circular 4/1991 of 14 June. Furthermore, Act 13/1985 reinforces the requirements in respect of accounting; it authorises the Bank of Spain to establish an obligation to make public certain reports on the financial structure which may be considered important for shareholders and depositors.

Directors and managers of credit institutions

The special rules regarding the directors of credit institutions under Spanish law have basically been enacted in response to two concerns: first, the concern that the supervision, control and sanction of these entities should be effective, for which reason the members of the Board of Directors, general managers and the like are subject to the regulations on discipline and intervention contemplated in Act 26/1988; secondly, both the Act of 27 July 1968 and some of the provisions of Act 3/1985 of 2 August respond to the concern about the excessive economic power of credit institutions, by establishing a system of incompatibilities whereby the chairmen, directors and senior personnel of private banks are prohibited from holding similar positions in other banks, and from sitting on more than four Boards of Directors of Spanish companies. Moreover, except in certain cases, the directors of banks are prohibited from holding the representation of rights conferred on shares deposited at said banks.[16]

BANK CONTRACTS UNDER SPANISH LAW

Sources of law

The Spanish legislation on bank contracts mainly affects the external aspects thereof; so far as its substance is concerned, it is largely developed and performed in accordance with the Commercial Code (*Código de Comercio*) and under the principle of freedom of contracting contemplated in Article 1255 of the Civil Code (*Código Civil*). The efforts of lawyers and courts to fit modern bank contracts within the old moulds of the Commercial Code increasingly produce cases where the new contractual models do not fit into the established types.[17] The bank contracting regulations in Spanish law are based on the principle of imperfect self-regulation, since the contents do not depend on the will of the parties equally; instead the banks, through general contracting conditions, impose the contract outline on their clients.

16. See J. Cadenas Coronado, "Incompatibilidades y limitaciones de altos cargos de la banca privada" in *RDBB*, 5 (1962), pp. 117 ff., and J. Quijano González, "Responsabilidad administrativa en la reciente legislación de crédito, seguro y mercado de valores: algunas cuestiones sustantivas" in *RDBB*, 34 (1989), pp. 293 ff.

17. This phenomenon was dealt with by the great scholar, Professor Joaquín Garrigues, *Contratos bancarios*, Madrid 1975, pp. 13 ff. More recently, see R. García Villaverde, "Tipicidad contractual y contratos de financiación", in VV.AA., *Nuevas entidades, figuras contractuales y garantías en el mercado financiero*, Madrid 1990, pp. 3 ff.

Bear in mind the importance both of bank customs and of the Articles and Regulations of the Bank of Spain and the private banks, contemplated in Article 310 of the Commercial Code.[18] However, the former are difficult to apply within modern banking enterprises and generally crystallise in general conditions, and the contractual nature of the latter (in the case of private banks) makes them a contractual outline that is imposed upon the client and, by reference, also causes them to incorporate the general conditions.

Therefore, the principal source of law in this respect is the general conditions stipulated by the banks. In this respect, and in the absence of a law on general contracting conditions in Spain, reference must be made to the applicability of Article 10 of the general Act on the defence of consumers and users of bank contracting, 26/1984 of 19 July.[19] The requisites established in Article 10 for the general bank contracting conditions are determined by the fact that such conditions come within the scope of subjective and objective application of such provision. First, the client must be a consumer or user, as defined in Article 1.2 and 1.3 of Act 26/1986. Secondly, the credit institution establishing the general conditions must be classified as a company or group of companies, according to the definition of credit institutions contained in Article 1 of Legislative Royal Decree 1298/1986. From an objective point of view, the general conditions of bank contracting must be incorporated into clauses, conditions or stipulations which, in general, apply to the supply, promotion or sale of products or services, which presents no difficulty in the scope of banking. The immediate consequence of the inclusion of the general bank contracting conditions in pursuance of Article 10 consists in the enforceability of the requisites of specification, clarity and simplicity of the text, delivery of documents and good faith and fair balance of the considerations. The last requisite excludes, among other things, the unfair clauses that disproportionately or unfairly prejudice the consumer or produce a situation of imbalance, unfair credit conditions, price increases for accessory services, financing, deferral, surcharges, etc., absolute limitations on liability, etc. In this respect, although some of the requisites contained in Article 10 of Act 26/1984 are developed in the specific bank

18. See J. Garrigues, *supra* n. 17, pp. 16 ff. and M. García Amigo, "En torno al atículo 310 del Código de Comercio" in *Revista de Derecho Privado* (1964), pp. 836 ff. More recently, see M. Aragon Reyes, "Las fuentes. En particular el problema de los Estatutos de los Bancos y de las Circulares del Banco de España", in R. García Villaverde, (ed.), *Contratos bancarios*, Madrid, 1992, p. 19 ff., and J.L. García-Pita y Lastres, "Seguridad jurídica, fuentes del Derecho y tutela del usuario en las normas sobre contratos bancarios de los Estatutos y Reglamento del Banco de España", in *Foro Gallego*, no 184, 1997, pp. 3 ff. V. Cuñat Edo, "Las fuentes reguladoras de la actividad contractual bancaria", in *Estudios de Derecho Bancario y Bursátil, en homenaje a Evelio Verdera y Tuells*, Madrid 1994, Tome I, pp. 605 ff.

19. See J. Azorin Roncero, "La Ley General de Protección de los derechos de usuarios y consumidores. Operaciones bancarias" in *Revista General de Derecho*, no 490–491 (1985), pp. 211S ff.; J.A. García-Cruces González, "Contratación bancaria y consumo" in *RDBB*, 30 (1988), pp. 259 ff.; C. Vázquez Iruzubieta, "Consideraciones sobre la incidencia de la Ley del Consumidor en los contratos bancarios" in *RDBB*, 17 (1985), pp. 129 ff.; and F. Rodríguez Artigas, "La contratación bancaria y la protección de los consumidores. El defensor del cliente y el Servicio de Reclamaciones del Banco de España", in García Villaverde (ed.), *supra* n. 18, pp. 923 ff.

regulations referred to in the following section, others are not contemplated in such regulations, so they are the principal means of protection of the consumer or user of bank services. In particular, Act 7/1995 of 23 March on Credit Consumption, which incorporated EC Directive 87/102/EEC (amended by Directive 90/88/EEC) stands as an example.

System of bank transparency and customer protection

Under Spanish law there is a set of legal and public regulations which directly affect bank contracting, insofar as its external forms and the requisites for informative transparency are concerned. Such regulations are contained basically in Article 48.2 of Act 26/1988 of 29 July on Discipline and Intervention of Credit Institutions[20]; they are developed in the Ministerial Order of 12 December 1989 on interest rates and fees, rules of procedure, information to the customer and publicity of credit institutions, and in the Circular 8/1990 of the Bank of Spain of 7 September on transparency of operations and customer protection which has been amended by Circular 3/1996, of 26 February.[21] This mass of legislation deals mainly with three aspects affecting bank contracting:

1. There is a set of provisions dealing with the written formalisation and delivery to the customer of the duly signed contractual documents by credit institutions.[22] In this respect, credit institutions must provide their customers with copies of the contract documents, the rates of fees and charges and the applicable valuation rules.
2. There is a set of provisions designed to guarantee the transparency of the conditions applied by credit institutions to their loan and deposit operations. In turn, these provisions impose on such institutions a double obligation in respect of information: on the one hand, they are obliged to inform the Bank of Spain of their interest rates and the information that they publish; on the other, they must display on a permanent notice board in each of the offices open to the public all information to be provided to their customers.
3. The necessary rules have been set down to ensure that publications regarding loan and deposit operations include all the necessary details to inform the client about the terms and conditions of such operations and guarantee the administrative control thereof. Indeed, bank publications, which cover "all forms of communication whereby operations, services or financial products are offered, or information is provided on them,

20. See the comment on this article by T.R. Fernández, "Comentario al artículo 48", in VV.AA., *supra* n. 8, pp. 152 ff.

21. See F. Rodríguez Artigas, *supra* n. 19, pp. 945 ff. and C. Sánchez Miguel, "Entidades de crédito. Transparencia de las operaciones y protección de los clientes", in *RDBB*, 41 (1991), pp. 129 ff. S. Rivero Aleman, *Disciplina del crédito bancario y protección del consumidor*, Pamplona 1995.

22. See R. Illescas Ortiz, "Los contratos bancarios: reglas de información, documentación y ejecución, in *RDBB*, 34 (1989) pp. 261 ff.

irrespective of the means of communication used", must comply with two conditions. First, there are substantial requisites for clarity, precision and respect for the competition, to give information on the characteristics of the financial offer and an adequate description of the product or service offered. On the basis of these substantial requisites, a second, formal requisite is imposed, according to which all publications issued by credit institutions on financial operations, services or products in which explicit or implicit reference is made to their cost or yield for the public is subject to prior authorisation by the Bank of Spain, which will examine the publications and may require the credit institutions to rectify or terminate publication thereof.[23]

Banking ombudsmen and the Claims Service of the Bank of Spain

Although they are included within the set of rules considered under the preceding heading, it is advisable to make separate reference to the rules of Spanish law which deal with both the Banking Ombudsman and the Bank of Spain's Claims Service.[24]

First, the institution of the Ombudsman is not specifically regulated under Spanish law, although it is referred to implicitly in both the Order of 12 December 1989 and the Bank of Spain Circular 8/1990, which establishes that the Bank of Spain's Claims Service may reject any claims that have not been previously submitted to the Ombudsman or equivalent body of the entity in question, provided that such body exists and fulfils the necessary requirements. Unlike other countries, such as England since 1985, where there is a sole Ombudsman for all banks, in Spain there are several ombudsmen, appointed by different private banks and savings banks. The private-legal nature of this institution, which has had considerable success in recent Spanish practice, makes the duties of ombudsmen fundamentally reconciliatory in nature and excludes from their sphere of operation such matters as the bank's relationship with its employees or shareholders, the decisions of the bank to grant a credit or otherwise, the issues contained *sub iudice*, etc. With regards to their *modus operandi*, when an ombudsman is presented with a claim, he will try to achieve a friendly solution between the parties, which will be binding and the case will consequently be deemed closed. Should such friendly solution not be attained, the ombudsman shall, within a period of no more than two months, issue a detailed resolution, which is binding on the bank but is merely a proposal for the client. The latter may, therefore, accept it or have recourse to either extrajudicial

23. See C. Lema Devesa, *et al.*, *Regulación jurídica de la publicidad financiera y bancaria*, Madrid, 1985; J.A. Gómez Segade and C. Lema Devesa, "Problemas jurídicos de las invocaciones publicitarias al ahorro" in RDB, no 18 (1985), pp. 247 ff.; and J.M. Cuesta Rute, "Las responsabilidades de las administraciones públicas por alegaciones publicitarias de contenido financiero" in RDBB, 18 (1985), pp. 263 ff.

24. See F. Rodríguez Artigas, *supra* n. 19, pp. 958 ff. and J. Sánchez-Calero Guilarte, "En torno a los banking 'ombudsmen' ", in *RDBB*, 26 (1987), p. 436.

avenues, such as the Bank of Spain's Claims Service, or judicial avenues to resolve the issue. It is important to note here that the ombudsman will take into account both the legal provisions applicable to the case and commercial customs and good banking practice, seeking at all times a fair solution for the issue in question.

Secondly, the Bank of Spain's Claims Service (contemplated in the Ministerial Order of 3 March 1987, created by the Executive Committee at its session on 26 May of the same year and regulated in the Bank of Spain Circular 24/1987 of 21 July) is currently regulated in the provisions of Chapter II of the Ministerial Order of 12 December 1989 and Chapter 11 of Circular 8/1990.[25] The principal function of the aforesaid Service is to receive and process claims regarding specific operations that affect them and which customers of credit institutions may make in respect of any actions of the latter institutions that might breach the rules of discipline or good banking customs and practice. The first limitation on the Service is in the competence attributed by law to the ordinary courts of justice to determine the correct interpretation and extent of the private legal relations established between the credit institutions and their clients. This, however, does not prevent the Service from giving its opinion on whether, in their private legal relations, the credit institutions have breached the legislation on discipline and good banking customs and practice. The actions of the Service conclude with the issue of a report, which has limited effect, since it is not binding on either the customer or the credit institution.

Bank secrecy and bank information

Although there is no doubt that the initial basis of bank secrecy is in the relationship of trust that always exists between customer and bank,[26] the interest of the State and, more particularly, the tax authorities in obtaining information from banks on their customers has made it necessary to analyse the legal basis for such secrecy.[27] In this respect, an effort has been made to find grounds in the right to personal and family privacy established in Article 18.1 of the 1978 Spanish Constitution. However, such grounds are arguable in view of certain judicial resolutions, such as those contained in the judgment of the Supreme Court of 29 July 1983, the judgment of the Constitutional Court of 26

25. See F. Rodríguez Artigas, *supra* n. 19, pp. 953 ff., and S. Sánchez Miguel, "La protección del usuario a través del Servicio de Reclamaciones del Banco de España", in *Estudios sobre consumo* no 10, pp. 57 ff.

26. See J. Garrigues, *supra* n. 17, pp. 47 ff.; L. Cazorla Prieto, *El secreto bancario*, Madrid 1978; and R. Jiménez de Parga, "El secreto bancario en el Derecho español", in *Revista de Derecho Mercantil*, 113 (1969), pp. 379 ff.

27. See J.M. Otero Novas, "El secreto bancario. Vigencia y alcance", in *RDBB*, 20 (1985), pp. 725 ff. and J.M. Embid Irujo, "Contrato bancario y cuenta corriente bancaria. Las prestaciones: El llamado 'sevicio de caja'. El secreto bancario. El deber de información. La responsabilidad", in García Villaverde (ed.), *supra* n. 18, pp. 105 ff.

November 1984 or the ruling of the latter court of 23 July 1986.[28] From the point of view of ordinary legislation, Article 23 of the Articles of the Bank of Spain should be remembered.

In order to determine what information is covered by bank secrecy, the Spanish system may be classified as a mixed system, between the systems of enumeration and those having a general clause. Furthermore, the recent reform of the Corporations Act allows the information incorporated in annual accounts to be excluded from that covered by secrecy, in view of the obligation to deposit such accounts at the Trade Registry (*Registro Mercantil*) so that they can be examined by members of the public. Moreover, an external limit on secrecy is imposed by the duty to collaborate with the tax authorities, imposed on credit institutions by the Law on Urgent Measures of Tax Reform of 14 November 1977.

With regard to the duty of secrecy, it should be remembered that bank information is contemplated as a duty of the bank, which should be available both to its clients and, on certain occasions, to third persons requesting information on the customers of the bank. Such limits on the contents of such information as are imposed arise, on the one hand, from the need for the bank to specify the technical details of the operation in respect of which the information is requested and, on the other hand, from the requirement for the information to be in accordance with the experience and technical competence of the customer requesting it. The duty to provide information is especially important in relation to the duty to supply a statement in respect of the current bank account.[29] There is also special legal significance in the fact that if a customer receives information on a transaction and expresses no reservation or doubt in respect thereof, this may be considered by the bank to be a tacit expression of acceptance of such transaction.

CREDIT INSTITUTIONS AND STOCK MARKETS

The system established by the 1988 Stock Market Act

The Stock Market Act 24/1988, of 28 July, established a new legal system on that market which affected all its sectors and all the subjects operating on it. The passing of the Act has made it necessary to review the role of credit institutions on the stock market. Moreover, the new regulations of the Spanish Stock

28. See E. Piñel Lopez, "El Tribunal Constitucional y el secreto bancario", in *RDBB*, 17 (1985), pp. 123 ff.; J. Aguilar Fernández-Hontoria, "La defensa de la intimidad como nuevo límite a las obligaciones de información tributaria (Sentencias de 18 de junio y de 29 de julio de 1983. Alcance y Posibilidades ulteriores)", in *RDBB*, 12 (1983), pp. 829 ff.; *Idem*, "De nuevo en torno a la defensa de la intimidad como límite a las obligaciones de información tributaria", in *RDBB*, 17 (1985), pp. 71 ff.; *Idem*, "El segundo pronunciamiento constitucional sobre el secreto bancario: el auto del Tribunal Constitucional de 23 de julio de 1986. Un comentario de urgencia", in *RDBB*, 21 (1986), pp. 851 ff.; *Idem*, "Secreto bancario" in VV.AA., *supra* n. 1, pp. 299 ff.; and I.G. Fajardo García, "Fundamentación y protección constitucional del secreto bancario", in *RDBB*, 39 (1990), pp. 571 ff.
29. See J. Sánchez-Calero Guilarte, "Consideraciones en torno a algunos aspectos de la cuenta corriente bancaria" in *RDBB*, 23 (1986), pp. 644 ff.

Market coincided in time with the establishment of homogeneous public legal regulations applicable to all credit institutions as a result of the enactment of Law 26/1988 of 29 July, on Discipline and Intervention.[30]

As regards the activities of brokers on the stock market, the Stock Market Act established a double mechanism for classifying their principal activities and reserving them for certain brokers, with a system of variable authorisations. Firstly, Articles 70 and 71 of the Stock Market Act classify the typical activities of such market, and which of them will be converted into considerations of some bank contracts. It must be underlined that the list of standard activities substantially coincides with one included in Section A of the Annex enclosed to Directive 93/22/EEC, of the European Council, of 10 May 1993, on investment services on securities.

Secondly, Article 76 of the Stock Market Act reserves the normal performance of those activities to brokering companies and agencies and other brokers, including credit institutions.[31]

The consequence of this process of classification and reservation of activities is that credit institutions may perform practically all the typical activities of the stock market. However, such institutions are permanently excluded from being able to trade on stock exchanges, which relegates them to a secondary role, since in order to perform stock exchange transactions they must always operate in collaboration with a stock exchange brokering company or agency which, moreover, is a member of a Stock Exchange, pursuant to Article 65 of the Stock Market Act (see also Chapter One of Royal Decree 726/1989 of 23 June, on Management Companies and members of Stock Exchanges, Stock Exchange and Collective Guarantee Companies (*Sociedad de Bolsas y Fianza Colectiva*).

The structure of brokers within the Spanish Stock Market, which excludes credit institutions from being members of the securities markets (the so-called *mercados secundarios de valores*) will be modified in the near future by the Act amending the Stock Market Act, whose draft was published in the *Boletín Oficial de las Cortes Generales* (the Parliament gazette), on 12 February 1997. On one hand, this Act would enable the credit institutions to become members of the securities markets (*mercados secundarios* or placement markets, as opposed to the *mercados primarios* or issuance markets); on the other hand, it will adapt the Stock Market Act to the legal requirements of Directive 93/22/EEC concerning the single passport for investment companies.[32]

Multifunctional banking groups on the Spanish Stock Market

The legal treatment of these groups falls basically under two heads. First, and from a functional or operative point of view, the fact that the Stock Market Act

30. See A.J. Tapia Hermida, "Los contratos bancarios de depósito, administración y gestión de valores negociables", in García Villaverde (ed.), *supra* n. 18, pp. 609 ff. A.J. Tapia Hermida, *El contrato de gestión de carteras de inversión*, Madrid 1995.
31. See A.J. Tapia Hermida, *supra* n. 30, pp. 616 ff.
32. See A.J. Tapia Hermida and J. Sánchez-Calero Guilarte, "La adaptación del Derecho español del mercado de valores al Derecho comunitario", in *RDBB*, 44 (1991), pp. 982–983.

has excluded credit institutions from stock exchange trading indicates the desire to create an "affiliation" process of the "parabanking" activities of credit institutions on the stock market (which process is clearly contemplated in point 13 of the Preamble to the Act). In short, the legislator, aware of the traditional importance of credit institutions on the stock market and that these institutions are the only entities with sufficient financial capacity to support or promote the creation of a network of brokering companies and agencies, tried to encourage such specialisation. Secondly, the existence of multifunctional banking groups acting on the stock market is important for the purpose of supervision of the solvency and equity of groups of financial institutions. In this respect, the Act 13/1992 of 1 June, on Equity and Consolidated Supervision of Financial Institutions, stresses the primacy of the solvency aspects of groups of financial institutions fundamentally from the point of view of banking. Indeed, after such Law establishes that consolidatable groups of credit institutions must maintain a sufficient volume of equity and a capital adequacy ratio equal to or higher than the percentage determined in the regulations, it indicates that in order to fulfil the capital adequacy ratio and the operative and investment limitations, credit institutions must consolidate their accounting statements with those of the other financial institutions with which they make up one decision-making unit (Arts. 6 et seq. of Act 13/1985 of 25 May, in the text given in Art. 1 of Law 13/1992).[33]

The activities of credit institutions on the Spanish Stock Market

The primary stock market

Traditionally, credit institutions and, more specifically, private banks have been providing securities issuers with brokering services in the placement of securities issues.[34] These banking services, which channel accessory or neutral transactions, have been classified, from a legal-commercial point of view, as commission agreements, since they are concerned with the management of the business of third parties. A distinction is made between the mediation in the placement of securities, which is called a simple commission agreement, and the underwriting of such placement, called a guarantee commission (typified in Art. 272 of the Commercial Code).

The Stock Market Act reflects this distinction in the list of activities contained in Article 71; Article 71.c refers to the activity of "intervening, directly or indirectly on behalf of the issuer, in the placement of securities issues", while Article 71.d refers to the activity of "underwriting the subscription of securities issues". Both activities may be performed by credit institutions with an unlimited scope of operation (pursuant to Art. 76.2.a of the Stock Market Act), while other credit institutions may perform only the first activity (pursuant to Art. 76.2.b and c of the Act).[35]

---

33. See Tapia Hermida and Sánchez-Calero Guilarte, *supra* n. 32, pp. 979 ff.
34. See J. Garrigues, *supra* n. 17, pp. 661 ff.
35. See F. Vega Perez, "Intervención bancaria en la emisión y colocación de valores negociables", in García Villaverde (ed.), *supra* n. 18, pp. 541 ff.

These activities of credit institutions on the primary stock market are performed within the legal framework established by Title III of the Stock Market Act. Therefore, Chapter V of Royal Decree 292/1992 of 27 March, on issues and public offerings of securities, regulates the "professional activities relating to issues or public offerings". It distinguishes between two types of function that may be performed by credit institutions having unlimited scope of operation, namely acting as "placement and marketing entities" (Art. 30) or as the "management entity" of an issue (Art. 31).[36]

Finally, it is worth remembering the references made in the 1989 Corporations Act (*Ley de Sociedades Anónimas*) (Art. 21.1) to credit institutions in the successive foundation processes of corporations.

Secondary stock markets

Traditionally, banks have issued the vast majority of stock exchange orders without being able to finally execute them. This occurred in the stock exchange system existing prior to the coming into force of the Stock Market Act, when securities could only be traded on the stock market by stockbrokers. In the system established in Act 24/1988, the banks are still authorised to receive orders from national or Spanish investors regarding the trading of any securities and forward such orders to other entities authorised to execute them (Art. 71.a); such entities, with regard to stock exchange trading, are *Sociedades* and *Agencias de Valores y Bolsa* (stock exchange brokering companies and agencies) (pursuant to Art. 70 and Title IV of the Stock Market Act, and the provisions of Royal Decree 726/1989). The points that were made on the necessary modifications that arose from the adaptation of the Directive on investment services should be remembered here.

It should be added that credit institutions are authorised to "negotiate with the public, on their own account or on behalf of third persons, national or foreign securities not listed on an official secondary market" (Art. 71.f of the Stock Market Act).

In addition to forwarding orders to be executed on the stock exchange, credit institutions with unlimited scope of operation may also "act as members of the Securities Clearing and Settlement Service" (Art. 71.h of the Stock Market Act). In particular, the provisions whereby the financial institutions directly involved in the clearing and settlement processes of securities may hold shares in the capital of such Service (Art. 54 of the Stock Market Act) have been developed in Title III, Chapter II of Royal Decree 116/1992 of 14 February, on representation of securities by means of account entries and clearing and settlement of stock exchange transactions.

As it has been said, the reform of the Stock Market Act in order to incorporate the European Directive on Investment Services into Spanish law enables

36. See A.J. Tapia Hermida, "El desarrollo reglamentario del régimen de las emisiones y ofertas públicas de venta de valores", in *RDBB*, 45 (1992), pp. 301 ff.

institutions to become members of the securities market (*mercados secundarios de valores*).

Other activities of credit institutions on stock markets

In pursuance of the Stock Market Act, credit institutions may "grant credits directly related with the purchase or sale of securities" (Art. 71.i); "manage securities portfolios for third persons, in which case they may not negotiate on their own account with the holder of the securities being managed" (Art. 71.j); and "act on behalf of stock holders as depositaries of securities represented in the form of certificates, or as administrators of securities represented in account entries" (Art. 71.k).[37]

In addition to the above activities, there are others that affect the stock market, dealing with aspects related with Collective Investment Institutions. In particular, credit institutions may "handle, on behalf of the issuer, the subscription and redemption of participations in unit trusts and negotiate the transfer of such units, on their own account or on behalf of third persons" (Art. 71.p), and "act as depositaries for Collective Investment Institutions" (Art. 71.l). It should be mentioned that credit institutions dominate the area of collective investment institutions, since they act, on the one hand, as parent companies of the management companies of such institutions and, on the other hand, as depositaries thereof (see Arts. 27, 28 and 29 of Law 46/1984 of 26 December, regulating Collective Investment Institutions).

LEGAL SYSTEM OF INSOLVENCY OF CREDIT INSTITUTIONS

The crisis in the Spanish banking system in the 1970s and 1980s has left its mark in the aim of Spanish banking law to establish both rules to prevent economic crises and measures to remedy the consequences on depositors of any insolvency of credit institutions.[38]

Intervention and substitution measures

With regard to preventive measures, when a credit institution is in an exceptionally grave situation that puts at risk the effectiveness of its equity or its stability, liquidity or solvency, it may not be necessary to intervene in such institution or provisionally to replace its administrative or management bodies.

37. See Tapia Hermida, *supra* n. 30, pp. 624 ff.
38. See F. Sánchez Calero, "Las crisis bancarias y la crisis del Derecho concursal", in *RDBB*, 11 (1983), pp. 533 ff.; E. Piñel López, "La crisis bancaria desde la óptica del Derecho", in *RDBB*, 11 (1983), pp. 553 ff.; *Idem.*, "El anteproyecto de Ley concursal desde la perspectiva bancaria", in *RDBB*, 15 (1984), pp. 575 ff.; and A. Rojo Fernández-Río, "Aspectos civiles y mercantiles de las crisis bancarias", in *RDBB*, 29 (1988), pp. 113 ff.

Such measures will be adopted by the Bank of Spain, informing the Ministry of Economy and Finance of its decision, after hearing the credit institution in question, save when the credit institution itself has requested such measures. Title III of the Law on Discipline and Intervention of Credit Institutions (Arts. 31–38) establishes, consequently, two types of preventive measures, each with different consequences.[39] First, in the case of intervention, the acts and resolutions of any of the bodies of the credit institution will not be valid and may not be carried out without the express approval of the appointed controllers. Secondly, in the case of replacement of the board of directors, the provisional directors will act as controllers in respect of the agreements and resolutions of the General Meeting or Assembly of the credit institution.

The system of deposit guarantee funds

If, in spite of the aforesaid preventive measures, a credit institution becomes insolvent, funds are guaranteed by the *Fondo de Garantía de Depósitos en Entidades de Créditos* (Fund of Deposit Guarantee in Credit Institutions), which is regulated by Royal Decree 2060/1996, of 20 December, as a result of the reform process initiated by Royal Decree Law 12/1995, of 28 December. Royal Decree 2606/1996 was aimed at the incorporation of Directive 94/19/EEC, of 30 May 1994, on Guarantee Funds, as well as at the coordination of the different funds in credit institutions, savings banks and credit unions. Such Funds provide a guarantee for the clients' deposits of the various credit institutions, and they act as means for prevention and restructuring on crisis situations. The management bodies of the Funds are the Managing Commissions (*Comisiones Gestoras*), composed of eight members each, four on behalf of the Bank of Spain and the other four representing the respective credit institutions. Their assets are obtained by contributions from its members, consisting of 2 per cent deposits which are guaranteed by the Fund. The Bank of Spain only makes contributions on an exceptional basis, in order to protect the stability of the whole system affected by the Funds. Membership is compulsory both for the Spanish credit institutions and for branches of foreign banks, distinguishing therein between the European Community and the non-EC ones.[40]

FERNANDO SANCHEZ CALERO

39. See J.L. Villar Palasi, "Medidas de intervención y sustitución", in *RDBB*, 28 (1987), pp. 730 ff. J.L. García-Pita, "Las medidas de intervención y sustitución de órganos de las Entidades de crédito en la Ley 26/1988, de 29 de julio", in *Cuadernos de Derecho y Comercio*, 7 (1990), pp. 47 and ff.
40. See F. Sánchez Calero, "El Fondo de Garantía de Depósitos Bancarios", in *RDBB*, 1 (1981), pp. 11 ff., and A Jiménez Blanco, "El Fondo de Garantía de Depósitos en establecimientos bancarios" in VV.AA., *supra* n. 1, pp. 175 ff. J. García de Enterría, "La reforma del régimen del Fondo de Garantía de Depósitos en establecimientos bancarios", in *RDBB*, 55 (1994), pp. 569 and ff. and C. Salinas Adelantado, "La nueva regulación de los Fondos de Garantía de Depósitos, in *RDBB*, 66 (1997), pp. 431 and ff.

CHAPTER 8

SWEDEN

INTRODUCTION

Among financial companies, banks hold a special position in that in principle they alone have the right to receive deposits into accounts and to borrow from the Central Bank. Deposits function as a means of payment; consequently, banks play a vital part in the payments system. In addition, banking business is characterised by a considerable scope both where deposit services and lending operations are concerned. These functions give banks a public utility dimension. These days, banks offer a wide range of financial services in other areas, too. Hence, the importance of banks and banking to the individual citizen has kept increasing in recent years. The banker–customer relationship is steadily developing and becoming more complex.

This chapter deals with some of the issues that affect the relationship between customer and bank. In Sweden, it is natural to present this from a consumer-protection perspective. I have attempted to present, without going into too much detail, the relevant issues in a way that facilitates general discussion.

BANKING ACTIVITIES: A REVIEW

Several different institutions are active in the Swedish credit market. The banks have traditionally been regarded as the most important. They play a central part in the world of business, and they possess most of the business branches that operate in the capital and credit markets today.

Banking in Sweden comprises three categories of banks: banking companies, savings banks and cooperative banks. These three banking institutions differ, partly because they form different kinds of associations. The association pattern of the commercial banks corresponds with that of business companies. The savings banks have no owners and can be compared to trusts. These days, a savings bank may alter its form of association and become a banking company.[1] Finally, the cooperative banks are organised as cooperative associations. Each banking category is covered by a special Act of Parliament which contains rules

1. The relevant legal text is found in SFS 1991:371.

pertaining to association law. The actual banking activities are regulated by an Act which applies to all three types of banking; the Banking Business Act (BBA).

The history of banking in Sweden extends further back in time than in most other countries. Even so, banks must be regarded as rather a late component in economic development.[2] The first Swedish commercial bank proper was established in 1830. That was the Scanian Private Bank (*Skånska Privatbanken*) in Ystad. The first savings banks came into being during the first part of the nineteenth century. The Savings Bank of Gothenburg (*Göteborgs Sparbank*) was the pioneer in 1820.[3] The cooperative banks are a more recent phenomenon. They were created during the twentieth century, after 1915, when a Parliamentary decision made it possible to establish this type of bank.[4]

Basically, the characteristic picture of development up to 1968 is one of three different banking categories, each operating within its own sector.[5] The commercial banks were used by businesses; small savers turned to the savings banks; and the cooperative banks were used by farmers. This pattern was to a great extent the outcome of the banking legislation then in force. In principle, this subdivision prevailed up to, and including, 1968; but certain changes took place in the orientation of banks even before that year. The 1950s and 1960s saw the increasing use of commercial banks by the general public.

The year 1968 is certainly an important year in the context of Swedish banking: it witnessed the introduction of coordinated banking legislation for banking activities, and this meant that the business branches of the three different categories were made to coincide in all essential respects.[6] Subsequent developments show that the savings banks and cooperative banks have been moving closer and closer to the field of activities traditionally associated with commercial banks.

Deregulation

In the 1980s, the rules of the game were altered for banks and, indeed, for the credit market as a whole.[7] The old regulations were felt to be dated, ineffective or capable of distortions. These were regulations that prevented market forces from controlling developments in, for instance, the capital market.

This change of rules suggests that the National Bank wished to push credit policies in a more market-orientated direction as far as the banks and some other institutions are concerned. The shift had, in my view, a great effect on banking developments in the 1980s. The significance of the changes has been discussed in various quarters; some maintain that it was in fact negligible. Regardless of what one might think about this issue, these alterations certainly influenced the

2. *Green Paper*, SOU 1984:27, p. 7.
3. *Green Paper*, SOU 1984:28, p. 7.
4. *Green Paper*, SOU 1984:29, p. 7.
5. Government Bill 1986/87:12, p. 165.
6. Government Bill 1986/87:12, p. 165.
7. *Green Paper*, Ds 1990:84, p. 24.

development of Swedish banks during the period concerned, both favourably and unfavourably.

Tougher competition

In the last few years, Swedish banks have experienced greater competition than before. Deregulation, which affected competition between banks, played a vital part in this process.

The number of participants in the credit market has increased in the last few years. In addition to banks, finance companies and the "intermediary institutions" (credit companies and mortgage institutions) are currently operating there, increasing the pressure of competition on banks. Another type of institution whose importance in the credit market is steadily increasing is the insurance company. Insurance companies are expected to possess excess capacity for investment in the capital markets.

A number of foreign subsidiary banks have now set up operations in Sweden. This development may have had some influence on competition in the banking area, but so far that influence has probably been slight.

Shifting business

Banking activities and competition insofar as it relates to banks are obviously being affected by the gradual shift in respect of trading operations that is taking place in the capital and credit markets. One such shift that has been the subject of much discussion in recent years is the one currently affecting banks and insurance companies.[8] In consequence of the alteration in the law in 1991 mentioned above, it is now possible for banks and other financial enterprises on the one hand and insurance companies on the other to own each other's shares and to form part of the same group. Shifting business, or the effacement of boundaries between various finance institutions, must be held to form a very important issue in the capital-cum-credit market changes now in progress.

Risks

Banks run many risks in their activities. This exposure to hazards of various kinds has increased sharply over the last few years. The growing internationalisation of banking is one reason for this development; augmented competition is another. Banks which make mistakes in assessing risks may have to face serious consequences. In the 1980s and early 1990s, the credit losses accounted for by Swedish banks increased dramatically. Today, they are at a more acceptable level.

8. Government Bill 1990/91:154, p. 65.

Banking legislation

Along with the other credit institutions, banks have an important part to play in society; and they carry a heavy burden of responsibility for the financial situation of society as a whole as well as for that of individual citizens. Hence it is natural for public bodies to possess some insight into, and exert some control over, their operations. The actions of banks are governed by comprehensive legislation. In addition, the banks are supervised in different ways—and for different purposes—by several authorities.

In 1987, part of the reform process regarding banks was completed.[9] The laws that have regulated the activities of the various banking institutions from that year onward may be described in the following manner.

The Riksbank Act (*Lagen om Sveriges Riksbank* 1988) prescribes that the National Bank of Sweden, the Riksbank, is in charge of credit and currency policies. It also has a duty to promote a secure and efficient system of payments transactions. In addition, the law contains directives on such matters as the nature of the business it is required to engage in.

Banking legislation of 1987 comprised, as I have mentioned above, the Banking Business Act, which applies to all banks, and the three Acts which cover the different types of banking institutions, namely the Banking Companies Act, the Savings Banks Act, and the Cooperative Banks Act. A new Act concerning cooperative banks was implemented in 1995 (*Lagen om medlemsbanker*) and from 1 January 1999 banking companies are regulated by the Companies Act and the Banking Business Act.

The Banking Business Act contains regulations concerning the kinds of business activities that a bank is allowed to engage in, as well as certain other regulations which apply to banking operations: granting credit, capital cover, auditing, bookkeeping, damages, and inspection by public organs.

The Companies Act, the Savings Banks Act, and the Cooperative Banks Act contain rules on how the three different types of banks in Sweden should be set up and organised, etc.

As a result of Sweden's joining the European Community, several changes in banking legislation were implemented. New Acts were added, too, such as the Act (1994:2004) on Capital Adequacy and Large Exposures, etc. (CALE).

CONSUMER PROTECTION

Background

In the last few decades, consumer protection has come to assume a central position in Sweden. There are several reasons for this development. Generally speaking, people have more money to spend these days and the market has multiplied. All this has raised popular consumption to a very high level. This is a

9. Government Bill 1986/87:12, p. 168.

favourable development, of course, but it has given rise to problems, too. One major problem has been, and still is, the frequency with which consumers find themselves in an inferior position when acting in various markets. As a result, national authorities have come to the conclusion that it is important to try to satisfy consumer interests by way of introducing active consumer policies. Sweden is something of a pioneering nation where consumer protection is concerned.

Up to about 1970, consumer protection was mainly geared to consumer guidance,[10] although there were also measures aimed against limited competition and intended to promote competitive pricing. In the late 1960s, it was widely felt that consumer guidance had yielded too little benefit to the poorest consumer groups. The new key idea was that producers should be subjected to direct persuasion and thus not merely indirectly affected by way of consumer guidance.[11]

In Sweden, legislation is the main method of implementing the intentions of the powers that be where consumer policies are concerned.[12] From a legal point of view, six chief objects of consumer protection may be distinguished, listed here in no particular order:

1. to protect consumers against harmful limitations in competition and unreasonable pricing,
2. to protect consumers against improper marketing strategies and devices,
3. to ensure that consumers receive reliable and sufficient information,
4. to protect consumers against substandard and useless goods,
5. to protect consumers against one-sided agreement clauses and financial hazards,
6. to provide consumers with easily accessible and efficient means by which they can protect their rights in cases of dispute.[13]

Regarded from the perspective of legal practice, three main types of consumer-protective legislation can be distinguished: market law; property law; and procedural law.[14]

The objective of market legislation is to protect consumers as a collective group, whereas property legislation—that is, the consumer-protective legislation which belongs wholly within the province of civil law—aims primarily to protect the individual consumer.

Consumer protection and banking

A number of fundamental protective interests gave rise to special legislation on finance institutions and financial markets.[15] Those interests have constituted the

10. Ulf Bernitz, *Svensk Marknadsrätt*, 1981, p. 219.
11. *Ibid.*, p. 220.
12. *Ibid.*, p. 225.
13. *Ibid.*, p. 226.
14. *Ibid.*, p. 226.
15. *Green Paper*, SOU 1991:2, p. 16.

point of departure with regard to the supervision of institutions and markets, too. Protective interests in the financial field have been the subject of recent discussion in several Government Commissions, especially in the Credit Market Committee, the Insurance Activities Committee, and the Securities Market Committee.[16]

In the financial field the relevant protective interests may be grouped under three main headings:[17] stability, consumer protection, and efficiency. The boundaries between these areas are not very clearly defined.[18] Consumer protection is the only aspect that will be dealt with here.

There are two main reasons for the special importance of consumer protection in the credit area. First, miscalculations may entail serious financial consequences for the individual customer.[19] Secondly, there is an "information asymmetry" between the parties.[20] Consumers may be said to be at a disadvantage in relation to credit institutions. Consequently, the consumer-protection interest plays an essential part in the field of financial operations. Still, there can be no question of doing away with, or even minimising, all sorts of risk-taking on the part of consumers.[21] One of the main functions of the financial market is to redistribute and spread risks.

The public may turn to one or several of the following organisations in cases where a bank, for example, is believed to have acted erroneously as far as the consumer is concerned.

The Finance Inspection Board

The Finance Inspection Board is a fairly small public authority working on a national basis.[22] The Board supervises banks as well as other institutions. A complex set of legal rules prevails in the area overseen by the Board. Some of the relevant Acts invest the Board with what one might call a "door-keeper function".[23] Consequently, the Finance Inspection Board influences—and in some cases determines—the question which actors are to be allowed access to the credit market and to the securities market.

Many of the extant rules that define the operations of the Finance Inspection Board were intended to safeguard the interests of banks or of other supervised objects.[24]

The Finance Inspection Board operates a scheme of "soundness supervision". The protection of consumers is one obvious motive[25] behind such a scheme; the

16. *Green Paper*, SOU 1991:2, p. 16.
17. *Ibid.*, p. 16.
18. *Ibid.*, p. 16.
19. *Green Paper*, SOU 1991:2, p. 19.
20. *Ibid.*, p. 19.
21. *Ibid.*, p. 20.
22. G. Svensson, A. Björklind, S. Holmberg and S. O. Wärnslund, *Får banken göra så här?*, 1989, p. 13.
23. *Ibid.*, p. 14.
24. *Ibid.*, p. 14.
25. *Ibid.*, p. 16.

demand for "soundness" was primarily probed in connection with the settling of complaints from the general public. In principle, the Finance Inspection Board no longer deals with individual complaints from the general public; such matters are primarily handled by the Public Merchandise Complaints Board and by the Consumers' Bank Bureau. Naturally, the consumer aspect is taken into account in the supervising activities of the Finance Inspection Board. It is, however, brought to bear on other occasions as well, for instance when a bank intends to introduce new forms of agreement.[26]

The Public Merchandise Complaints Board (PMCB)

If a customer has a claim of a financial nature and the bank will not agree to settle it, he may turn to the Public Merchandise Complaints Board, the PMCB. The only qualification is that he must be involved in a dispute with his bank as a private individual, not as a tradesman.

Reports to the PMCB must be made in writing, and a definite claim must be made in order for the PMCB to be able to assess the matter. Unlike a court of law, the PMCB cannot hear witnesses or other oral testimony. Hence, the PMCB is bound to dismiss matters where such evidence is necessary for a proper assessment to be made.

A decision announced by the PMCB constitutes a recommendation as to how the dispute should be solved. In other words, the decision is not compelling in the way that a court judgment is. As a rule, though, PMCB recommendations are adhered to. There is no appeal against a decision made by the PMCB, but a dissatisfied party may bring the matter before a court of law.

Every year, the Public Merchandise Complaints Board addresses a number of cases involving a consumer and his/her bank; in 1994/95, 488 such cases were registered.

The Consumers' Bank Bureau

The Consumers' Bank Bureau (the CBB) is an independent advisory agency which provides guidance on questions in the fields of banking and trading in securities; it does so free of charge. The Bureau is also constantly in touch with people in charge of complaints in banks and other relevant institutions, and it keeps them, as well as the relevant authorities, informed about consumer issues that come to the Bureau's attention.

Courts

Anyone who has a claim of a financial character which a business will not agree to settle may turn to a court of law (the local district court) in order to have the matter tried. This is done by bringing a suit, instituting legal proceedings.

26. *Ibid.*, p. 16.

Granting of credit and consumer protection

Over the last 10 years developments in the consumer credit area have been rapid. This applies, among other things, to technological progress, which has taken us a considerable distance along the road to what is usually referred to as "the cashless society". Developments in this area have been associated with new forms of payment negotiation and new types of loans.[27] Another significant factor in this respect is the vigorous expansion of consumer credit that took place in the late 1980s, chiefly as a result of the deregulation of the credit market.[28] In a variety of ways, these developments have been favourable for consumers; but for some people they led to severe difficulties. Quite a few people found themselves unable to cope with the growing burden of debt, ending up in the "debt trap" with its concomitant personal and social problems. A number of inquiry committees have been working on consumer-credit issues.[29] For example, in October 1990, the Insolvency Commission (Ju 1988:02) proposed a Debt Clearance Act in a partial report (SOU 1990:74). As the Act has been implemented, over-indebted individuals who do not run business operations are in certain circumstances to be given the opportunity to rid themselves of their debts, wholly or partly.

The problem of the growing indebtedness of households contributed to the drafting of a proposal for a new Consumer Credit Act. Now enacted, the main objective of this Act is to reinforce consumer protection in several respects. It should be regarded as part of the current reform work aimed at strengthening the position of consumers in various fields. The following paragraph sketches a few components of the Consumer Credit Act which might be of interest.[30]

The Act contains a number of rules aimed at strengthening consumer protection in various ways. One concerns the general obligations of tradespeople and prescribes, among other things, that a tradesman should observe "generally accepted standards of credit granting" in his dealings with consumers (s. 5). According to the main rule, credit agreements must be in writing and signed by the consumer. An agreement which has not been settled in writing will still be valid except in respect of terms that are to the consumer's disadvantage (s. 9). The right of the lender to raise the rate of interest during an ongoing credit period is restricted. The circumstances pertaining to changes in interest must be set out in the agreement, and the interest rate cannot be raised unless certain events specified in the Act have taken place (s. 11).

The lender must not demand a charge for the loan unless such a charge has been expressly mentioned in the agreement and refers to a cost incurred by the lender for the credit concerned. The agreement must state the conditions in which charges may be altered during an ongoing agreement period (s. 12). The

---

27. *Green Paper*, Ds 1990:84, p. 24.
28. *Ibid.*, p. 24.
29. *Ibid.*, pp. 25–26.
30. Government Bill 1991/92:83, Ny konsumentkreditlag. The Act has now been adopted by the Parliament.

consumer is entitled to redeem a credit in advance without having to pay any charges. When the rate of interest is fixed for the whole agreement period, or for part of it, the lender is also entitled to reasonable compensation for any interest loss if he has provided for it in the agreement (ss. 20 and 24).

THE BASIC BANKER–CUSTOMER RELATIONSHIP

Banking legislation supplies the fundamental rules governing the operations of a bank. In most cases, the relations between banks and their customers are regulated by agreements. Such agreements may apply to deposits or to loans.

In previous years, the Finance Inspection Board received a large number of complaints from the general public.[31] When a citizen asks the standard question "Can a bank really act this way?" what he wants to find out is whether the bank has acted in accordance with the legislation and agreements in force. Although the Finance Inspection Board is not a court of law, its decisions may be said to supply a valuable source of material for anyone who wishes to establish what "sound banking practice" really means.[32] Today, the Public Merchandise Complaints Board and the Consumers' Bank Bureau have largely taken over the functions of the Finance Inspection Board where this question is concerned. Even so, previous decisions made by the Finance Inspection Board are still regarded as highly significant when it comes to determining the implications of "sound banking practice". Generally speaking, it is unusual for a bank customer to go to court in order to have a case tried. However, only a court of law is authorised to decide whether a bank should pay compensation for any damage suffered by the customer. A court case of relevance to this issue is reviewed below.

The following pages attempt to explain some fundamental rules in banking while conveying an idea of what constitutes "sound" or "generally accepted" banking practice in some areas of central importance to the banker–customer relationship.

Deposits

Chapter 2, s. 1 of the Banking Business Act makes it clear that receiving deposits from the public constitutes the principal activity of banks. A licence to run banking operations entails an obligation to receive such deposits. However, the obligation to receive deposits is not unconditional.[33] For example, a bank must not accept deposits under circumstances which would mean that the bank's representative became guilty of a criminal offence, say that of receiving stolen property. A bank may also occasionally have reasons for turning down an individual customer's application for a deposit account; the customer may, for

31. Svensson *et al.*, *op. cit.*, p. 17.
32. *Ibid.*, p. 26.
33. Government Bill 1990/91:154, p. 91.

instance, have abused a previous account or acted dishonestly towards the bank in some other way.[34] In Sweden, an Act on money laundering became valid in 1994. Whenever a banking transaction concerns an amount larger than SEK 110,000, and the customer is unknown, proof of identity must be requested. If the bank suspects that the transaction is in any way related to money laundering, it must not go ahead.

A special Act on the protection of bank deposits has been in force in Sweden since 1 January 1996. The Swedish deposit guarantee applies both to previous and future payments into certain accounts. If a deposit payment comes under the guarantee, the client is entitled to compensation corresponding to the amount deposited as well as to accrued interest up to the bankruptcy decision. The right to compensation from the guarantee is limited to SEK 250,000 per client and institution.

Normally, then, a bank is required to provide an "ordinary" account for members of the public—an account geared to the depositing of money without any restrictions as to amounts, depositing procedure, demands for regular savings or deposits, etc.[35] This does not prevent the bank from imposing special terms on savings in special types of accounts, as long as these terms are reasonable, have a distinct purpose, and do not involve discrimination.[36]

According to accounts regulations, every account holder is obliged to keep detailed notes on deposits and withdrawals. Still, the bank must not neglect to provide the customer with information on the current position of the account.[37] To the question whether statements regarding the balance of an account are binding, the Finance Inspection Board replied[38]:

Only the account holder himself is in a position to know about all deposits and withdrawals that have been made or ordered during any one day, and only he is able to possess information on the correct account balance at any given moment. Hence, the responsibility for ensuring that no overdraft arises normally rests with the account holder. The primary function of those balance statements that are supplied by banks in cash dispensers, on bank statements of account, or in other ways is to provide a service the purpose of which is to guide the checking-up procedures undertaken by customers themselves when scrutinising their own notes regarding their accounts. Consequently, these bank statements are not binding in a legal sense.

Withdrawals from accounts

It is fairly common for banks to be authorised to make withdrawals for certain ends. However, such a right to withdraw does not permit the bank to create an overdraft.[39] Should that situation arise, the bank ought to wait until sufficient funds are available in the account.

34. *Ibid.*, p. 91.
35. The Finance Inspection Board, Supervision Case 5/86.
36. *Ibid.*
37. The question of information on accounts has been touched on by the Finance Inspection Board in connection with the following Supervision Cases: 19/87, 20/84, 21/88.
38. The Finance Inspection Board, Supervision Case 44/87.
39. The Finance Inspection Board, Supervision Case 29/87.

In this context, the case of *WH Finans* v. *Östgöta Enskilda Bank* is relevant. The point at issue was the bank's liability when payment to a bank customer had been delayed. The Supreme Court declared[40]:

The penalty in cases of delayed payment is not necessarily limited to the obligation to pay interest on overdue payment (cf. Govt. Bill 1975:102, pp. 97f., and NJA 1967, p. 195). The reasons for an additional obligation to pay damages are especially strong when—as in the present case—the payment in question was due from a bank, with regard to which stringent demands in respect of punctuality may be made. When delayed payment entails indemnity liability, this liability usually applies independently of any error on the debtor's part, subject to the restrictions that might obtain under any *force majeure* provisions. In the present case, no circumstances prevail which might lead to a deviation from the principle of strict liability.

One condition that must be fulfilled if indemnity liability is to apply, however, is that the damage that has arisen may be held to have been foreseeable.

Granting of credit

Chapter 2, ss. 13–19 of the Banking Business Act contain provisions regarding the proper ways of *granting credit*. The initial passages prescribe that credit may only be granted if the borrower can be expected to fulfil the terms of the loan, and that satisfactory security should, in principle, be provided. More specialised rules on certain conditions involved in the granting of credit follow. Loans entailing a right to postponed repayment may only be granted in certain cases (ss. 14 and 15a). A bank may only in certain cases reserve the right to a share in the profits from operations which the bank itself is not allowed to conduct (ss. 15 and 15a). A bank must not grant loans to employees etc. on terms other than those which the bank normally applies (s. 17). The provisions on credit shall also be applied to any guarantee commitments that the bank might undertake (s. 18). The date of expiry of a loan must be settled in such a way that it agrees with the terms governing the bank's own obligations (s. 19).

Credit assessment by a bank is normally a two-stage business.[41] The first stage is primarily devoted to determining the prospective borrower's financial position, profitability, and potential. The second consists of security probing. When allocating the credit available, a lender must not apply improper considerations.[42] On a few occasions, the Finance Inspection Board has criticised banks which granted credits for markedly speculative purposes. Still, the existence of a fairly minor element of speculation need not mean that banks are not allowed to participate.[43] In addition, the Finance Inspection Board has stated that banks should take a restrictive line in respect of large credits to private individuals when the purpose of the credit is to reduce taxes.[44] The customer, and the purpose of the loan, must be known to the bank.[45] In this

40. NJA 1991 217, p. 227.
41. Svensson *et al.*, *op. cit.*, p. 76.
42. The Finance Inspection Board, Ethical Announcements No. 6 and 10.
43. The Finance Inspection Board, Supervision Case 133/87.
44. The Finance Inspection Board, Ethical Announcements No. 46.
45. The Finance Inspection Board, Supervision Case 50/86.

context, it should perhaps be pointed out that banks must not contribute to transactions which may subsequently be found to be invalid.[46] There is no appeal against decisions as regards credit made by banks.[47]

Guarantees

In most cases of credit granting where the security consists of a personal guarantee, the guarantee in question is drawn up in such a way that the guarantor is liable as for a debt of his own. Consequently, the lender may approach the guarantor directly, without first having demanded payment from the chief debtor. According to customary procedure, however, the demand should primarily be directed to the latter.[48] In some situations the bank is obliged to inform the guarantor of what the guarantee commitment actually implies.[49] This responsibility applies to the borrower as well.

Normally, a guarantor can only dispose of his liability by repaying the loan. If, however, the guarantor is able to show that the bank failed to make a thorough credit assessment, the guarantee undertaking may be significantly reduced. The same applies if the bank withheld information on the borrower's previous debts and difficulties over payments, or on the implications of the guarantee.[50]

Charges

Many complaints to the Finance Inspection Board concern the question of various kinds of charges.[51] Charges and fees make up a considerable source of income for banks. The banks maintain that the imposition of charges mainly serves to minimise costly transactions. The Finance Inspection Board has compiled an index listing bank charges for the most common banking sevices.[52]

The principal attitude of the Finance Inspection Board is that banks should not charge for services that belong within the sphere of traditional, fundamental banking operations, such as deposits and withdrawals.[53] The Finance Inspection Board may agree that exceptions from this rule are permissible, if the basic services are utilised to an abnormal extent.[54]

BANK SECRECY

The rules on a banker's duty of secrecy are found in Chapter 1, s. 10 of the Banking Business Act. The relevant statute reads as follows:

46. The Finance Inspection Board, Statement of 15 April 1983.
47. The Finance Inspection Board, Supervision Cases 55/86 and 56/86.
48. Svensson et al., op. cit., p. 99.
49. The Finance Inspection Board, Supervision Case 79/85.
50. The Public Merchandise Complaints Board, Case Nor. 91/R134.
51. Svensson et al., op. cit., p. 125.
52. Ibid., p. 125.
53. The Finance Inspection Board, Supervision Case 109/87.
54. The Finance Inspection Board, Supervision Case 112/87.

The relations of individuals to a bank may not be disclosed without legal cause. In the public sector, however, the provisions of the Secrecy Act (1980:100) apply.

One vital reason for the existence of bank secrecy is that the individual customer does not want unauthorised persons to learn of his financial circumstances known to the bank. However, bank secrecy certainly would not have possessed such staying-power throughout the ages if purely individual bank–customer interests had been its sole support. The explanation of its power must be sought in its importance to the function of the banking system and in the fact that the objective of bank secrecy is not only that of safeguarding bank customers, it is also intended to protect the bank itself, business, and society at large.[55]

Banking operations may be abused in various ways, for example in the context of tax evasion. A wish to prevent abuse of this sort has led to a limited reduction of bank secrecy in Sweden. The purpose of the rules on bank secrecy has been, and still is, that of avoiding such abuses while maintaining desirable confidentiality.[56]

The secrecy provision itself only states that the relations of a private individual with his bank must not be divulged without legal cause. The somewhat vague expression "without legal cause" was not defined in the preparatory legislative materials.[57]

Under the secrecy regulation, the bank is sometimes obliged to divulge requested information. In other cases, it has a right, but is not compelled, to part with information. A brief recapitulation of a few cases may illustrate the significance, and the extent, of bank secrecy.[58]

Customer's consent

Since the interest of bank customers in not having their dealings with the bank unnecessarily disclosed forms an important reason for bank secrecy, the duty to remain silent may of course be affected by the customer's consent. Such consent can be revoked at any time.

Internal information within the bank

"Disclosure without legal cause" cannot be held to apply to such internal information within the bank as is called for by the loyal interests of the bank itself. Hence, information may be transmitted from one department to another, thus enabling the bank to safeguard the interests of the customer.

55. Nial Håkan in collaboration with Per Ola Jansson, *Banksekretess*, 1987, 5th edn, p. 17.
56. *Ibid.*, p. 18.
57. *Ibid.*, p. 18.
58. This paragraph relies on Nial Håkan's work *Banksekretess*, written in collaboration with Per Ola Jansson, 1987, pp. 33 ff.

Information to tax authorities

The Taxation Act (1990:224) and the Act on Income Tax Returns and Salary Statements (1990:325) have invested tax authorities with considerable powers which enable them to obtain information on the relations of an individual to banks. These Acts have also restricted the banks' duty to observe secrecy by prescribing that they are obliged to submit various kinds of information.

Testimony in a court of law

The general obligation of citizens to give evidence before a court of law also applies to directors of the board, members of a bank's management, its auditors and employees. That does not mean that when in the witness box he should happily disclose everything he knows about a person's relations with the bank. He should restrict his evidence to matters of importance in the case.

Information to the Public Prosecutor and to the police

According to currently valid law, a police authority is not entitled to compel a bank employee to part with information in the context of a police investigation. However, Chapter 23, s. 13 of the Judicial Procedures Act allows for the possibility of interrogating witnesses under certain circumstances in connection with a preliminary investigation in a criminal case. However, this can only take place if there is a patent reason for suspecting a person of having committed a crime. In view of this, it is not considered inadmissible to submit information in the context of a criminal enquiry even if no such witness interrogation has been called for.[59]

Credit information

In all kinds of credit operations, it is obviously very much in the lender's interest that he should be able to obtain information on the borrower's solvency in order to ensure that the latter will be able to repay the loan. Credit-rating particulars are as essential to the credit system as to business in general. In order to prevent wrongful credit granting, banks are held to be entitled to provide certain information about customers without infringing bank secrecy rules.

A bank is hence considered to have a right to submit information about a customer to other banks and to a credit-information company jointly owned by the banks themselves—the Upplysningscentralen UC—that the customer in question has gravely neglected his liabilities towards the bank or been guilty of any other improper conduct. Naturally, no information may be passed on if there is reason to suspect that it will be used in an improper manner.

59. Government Bill 1986/87:12, p. 212.

THE MULTIFUNCTIONAL BANK

A vital task, involved in several legislation projects, has been that of solving problems concerned with setting up boundaries between various institutions in the market, considering the legal conditions that should apply to new institutions, and creating rational business regulations for different kinds of financial institutions. The following observations relate to the banking sector.

Since 1 July 1987, banks have had greater opportunities for joining groups than they had before.[60] "Financial groups" is a term often used in this context. Nowadays it is possible for a bank to form part of a group as a parent company and also as a subsidiary. For a bank to be able to join a group as a subsidiary, the Finance Inspection Board's permission is necessary. In such a case, the provisions in the Banking Business Act concerning banking operations and supervision apply.[61]

Recently, the rules on banking operations have been altered so as to keep banking activities abreast of current developments.[62]

In addition to traditional banking business and to the acquisition of securities for its own portfolio, or for trading purposes, banks may conduct the following types of business: credit negotiation; payments service; the provision of guarantee commitments; factoring; financial leasing of chattels; and counselling.[63] In certain circumstances, too, banks are now entitled to acquire shares in non-banking companies.

Clearly, then, modern banks run extensive and manifold operations, and this can cause a variety of problems. The application of different protective rules to bank groups was touched on in a previous section. An issue often discussed abroad is how to solve conflicts of interest due to the different types of business conducted within a bank, bearing in mind that the bank is obliged to treat its customers with all due care and circumspection. One fundamental reason for the emergence of such conflicts is that the various departments of a bank have access to different kinds of information. The question is whether the knowledge of certain particulars on the part of one bank department implies that all the bank's departments should be regarded as being informed of them. That would mean that a bank department is, due to the demand for care and circumspection, obliged to take account of this information when dealing with customers.

To Swedish banks, the problem is a familiar one, but there has been virtually no discussion of it. Nor have the Bankers Association or the banks themselves issued any guidelines on these matters. Apparently the current attitude in Sweden is that a bank should not be regarded as forming one information unit; each department is thus an independent entity where information is concerned. Consequently, a bank department is not obliged to pay attention to the supply of information accessible to other departments when dealing with customers. Bank

60. Government Bill 1986/87:148 and Government Bill 1992/93:89
61. Government Bill 1992/93:89, p. 199.
62. Government Bill 1992/93:89, p. 186.
63. *Ibid.*, p. 186.

secrecy—which also prevails in inter-departmental contexts—favours this stance, too. If this were not the case, the obligation to observe due care in relation to one customer might, for instance, entail a failure to honour that obligation in relation to another.

In some cases, information must not spread within a bank in consequence of the laws on insider trading.

THE LIABILITY OF BANKS FOR ADVICE

A bank may give counselling in a variety of situations. Banks may give advice on legal matters, on the acquisition and sale of shares, and on how to minimise taxes. Counselling has increased rapidly over the last few years. In several respects, banks may be regarded as highly qualified counsellors. Questions regarding the liability of banks for erroneous advice have recently been debated a good deal, especially in the context of financial advice related to the purchase and sale of shares. The unfavourable decline in the stock exchange is the chief reason for this. The following paragraphs survey the extant rules on liability, focusing on the basis for liability.

A few cases from lower courts refer to the liability of banks for faulty counselling. Disputes of this kind are usually settled out of court and in conjunction with the bank's insurance company. Hence, guiding principles will mainly have to be derived from general lines of reasoning regarding the responsibilities of counsellors on the basis of contract law.

A bank is obliged to conduct its business with care, and it must compensate its client for any damage caused deliberately or through negligence.[64] When the issue of culpability is determined, it is important to decide whether the actions of the bank in relation to the client appear to be negligent. Attention should, in this context, be paid to conditions which are specific due to the fact that the advice in question was given by a bank. The liability of a bank may be regarded as an instance of professional liability. Consequently the bank, in its capacity as expert, carries a responsibility towards its clients which is linked with the special knowledge that the bank is assumed to possess. A legally and financially ignorant person should be able to entrust problems he cannot solve himself to his bank. The customer must hence be able to rely on the advice his bank gives him.

A number of cases heard by the PMCB have primarily been concerned with the content and extent of the counselling commission. Due to the modes of operation employed by the Complaints Board, it was unable to deal with several of these cases.

A distinction should be made between legal advice and "suitability advice".[65] Obvious errors of judgement with regard to legal advice should entail indemnity

64. B. Bengtsson, *Särskilda avtalstyper*, 1971, p. 172.
65. Bengtsson, *op. cit.*, p. 173.

liability. If the legal situation is unclear, the bank is held to be obliged to advise the client accordingly. The degree to which a bank is obliged to give a client such information varies, depending on who the client is.[66] In certain situations, a bank is considered to have an obligation to inform the client of effects in legal areas other than the ones involved in the main issue.[67] For instance, it may be obliged to tell the client that a transaction entails certain effects in terms of taxation, even though the consultation proper was mainly concerned with the transaction itself. If the relevant advice concerned questions as to how the client should act in financial matters, it is reasonable for the bank to command a wider margin of error. Assessing financial affairs is a risky business. Banks should have considerable scope for discretionary judgement. Anybody who relies on financial assessments made by a bank must be aware of the fact that those who place their faith in information of this kind run a considerable risk.

A bank should also be obliged to provide information in connection with giving certain kinds of advice. In particular, it should supply information on matters related to the question that elicited the advice.

SECURITY

This section raises some currently debated problems concerning liens over bank safe-custody accounts containing securities, or "depots" (the latter term will be used in the discussion). The increased use of depots in the administration of property and investments has lent some urgency to these issues. The "speciality principle" is a fundamental principle in the Swedish law of property.[68] In broad terms, it means that a lien can only refer to individually designated objects. Another fundamental principle prescribes that no valid lien can exist if the pledger has a legal or factual opportunity to make use of what has been pledged without being compelled to obtain the pledgee's consent in each case.

These days, securities are rather frequently pledged on terms whose ability to satisfy fundamental requirements under lien law may well be called into question.[69] This is the case when a depot is pledged. In such a case, the object of the pledging operation is not certain designated securities; it is a collective unit. Usually, a bank account is attached to the depot, and that account is pledged, too. The reason for this choice of pledge is that it offers a convenient way of conducting transactions with the depot. If the pledgee is to have the benefit of lien with regard to a depot, the shares or securities in it must have been placed there by order of the pledger.[70] Shares that belong to the pledger but have not been put in the depot are not affected by the relevant lien. In respect of the

---

66. NJA 1994, s. 598.
67. NJA 1992, s. 502.
68. T. Håstad, *Några problem rörande panträtt i en värdepappersdepå i Festkrift till Henrik Hersler*, p. 309.
69. *Ibid.*, p. 310.
70. *Ibid.*, p. 319.

borrower's legal right to conduct transactions with the depot, a degree of uncertainty prevails. A further complication arises in those cases where the borrower only pledges part of the depot. Still, the question is whether this mode of pledging is not compatible with currently valid law after all.

The first issue for detailed consideration is the partial pledging of a depot. One question in this context is whether the pledged portion must be specified, so that certain objects are listed or part of the total stock is kept separate. The doctrine may be taken to mean that separation must take place if lien effects are to arise.[71] Professor Torgny Håstad, however, is of the opinion that there is no factual reason for insisting that the pledged amount be separated when the quality of the stock is homogeneous.[72] This is, for example, the case if a person who owns Volvo shares only pledges a certain number of those shares. The same thing should, according to Håstad, apply if the stock is of uneven quality but certain kinds of goods belonging to it are distinguishable due to their particular character.[73]

What happens, then, when a partial lien is defined as a certain amount in a depot of uneven quality? If the pledger is cut off from the right to control the entire depot, probably the pledging does not necessarily conflict with the speciality requirement.[74] At first sight, such a pledger does not appear to have much of an opportunity to conduct transactions with the depot. Several considerations, according to Håstad, favour the situation where the pledger has access to the pledged assets—provided the pledgee possesses satisfactory legal and factual control of the pledge—being able to withdraw shares from the depot and put in new ones after having obtained the pledgee's consent in every individual case.[75] This procedure probably would not mean that the lien is not valid. The legal situation is uncertain. Such a view facilitates depot-pledging operations in banks.

Sometimes the question of transactions has not been expressly laid down in the credit agreement. The reason might be that the lender simply assumes that the borrower is not entitled to make use of the pledge without the pledgee's consent. Usually, however, the right of disposal is regulated in an agreement. The following form of words is frequently employed:[76]

In consequence of the pledging, the pledger may not utilise the pledged property without the pledgee's consent in each individual case. Such consent is hence required for every action that affects the pledged property, such as the exchange or sale of the same—even if the purchase-sum is paid into the pledged account—or the purchase of new securities for the pledged account.

In this context, a few words should be said about liens with regard to companies which apply an account-based securities system according to the Act on Shares

71. Ulf Göransson, *Traditionsprincipen*, 1985, p. 510.
72. Håstad, *op. cit.*, p. 331.
73. *Ibid.*, p. 331.
74. *Ibid.*, pp. 336 ff.
75. *Ibid.*, p. 339.
76. Form No. 75 of the Swedish Bankers Association.

Accounts. The system refers to "VPC companies"; it was introduced in 1989–90, and it meant that share certificates were abolished for these companies. The legal implications that used to be associated with share certificates are attached to account entries instead.

Under s. 1, ch. 6 of the Act on Shares Accounts, anyone who has been registered as shareholder in a shareholder's account is authorised to transfer liens as regards his shares to another person. Once the lien has been registered in the pledgee's name in the shares account, the latter is authorised to utilise this right.[77] As a result, the pledging must not, for instance, be removed from the VPC records without the pledgee's consent.[78] Furthermore, the pledgee is protected from the pledger's creditors once the pledging has been entered in the daily records, provided an entry in the shares account is subsequently made as well.[79]

ENVIRONMENTAL LIABILITY

One question which has not given rise to much discussion in Sweden is whether a bank may be held liable for damage to the environment caused by a borrower, if the bank is the lender. It is likely that a bank will be liable for environmental damage in such a situation, if the relevant damage arose in connection with criminal activity and the bank could be held to have contributed to that activity.

KRISTER MOBERG

Note: The case law contained in this chapter is based on information available up to Summer 1997.

77. Government Bill, 1988/89:152, p. 113.
78. *Ibid.*, p. 113.
79. *Ibid.*, p. 113.

CHAPTER 9

A UNITED STATES COMPARISON

INTRODUCTION

The banker–customer relationship in the United States is largely a matter of contract law (as embodied in the judicial case law of the various states[1]) and of commercial law (as embodied in state Uniform Commercial Code (UCC) statutes and as such statutes are interpreted in state judicial decisions[2]). While this general statement is essentially correct, it is not terribly meaningful after an initial glance: it only becomes meaningful when the multi-dimensions (including the regulatory, institutional, and operational environments) respecting the banker–customer relationship are better understood. For example, it is important to understand what in fact a "banking institution"[3] is and is not, as this may well make a difference as to how the legal relationship is viewed. In addition, the legal relationship may be affected by what type of customer is involved: is it an individual or a wholesale depositor, a sophisticated commercial or a consumer borrower, or a user of other services (e.g. trust services)? Further, the contractual and commercial underpinnings of the banker–customer relationship may be overlaid with, influenced by, and reshaped by special common law doctrines such as that of "special relationship", "good faith and fair dealing", wrongful set-off, and even possibly fiduciary duty (or quasi-fiduciary duty).

Moreover, particularly in the United States, the banker–customer relationship can be affected by the regulatory environment applicable either to a particular banking institution (e.g. deposit and lending regulations for federal commercial banks are not necessarily coextensive with the regulations for thrift institutions and credit unions) or to a particular type of customer (e.g. a consumer requiring consumer protection). Further, the nature of the US judicial process, with its widespread use of jury trials and availability of punitive (i.e.

1. See, *inter alia*, Symons Jr., "The Bank–Customer Relation: Part I—The Relevance of Contract Doctrine", 100 Banking LJ 220 (1983); and "Part II—The Judicial Decisions", 100 Banking LJ 325 (1983).
2. See, *inter alia*, J. White and R. Summers, *Uniform Commercial Code* (4th edn 1995); and F.H. Miller and A.C. Harrell, *The Law of Modern Payment Systems and Notes* (2nd edn 1992).
3. This term is used in this chapter in a generic sense to cover institutions exercising a "depository" function, and generally would cover commercial banks, thrift institutions and credit unions.

exemplary) damages under various "contort" and bank liability theories can exacerbate the practical liability aspects of the banker–customer relationship in the United States.

The purpose of this chapter is to provide perspectives on some of the main considerations respecting this relationship so that a non-US observer can better appreciate the complexities of this relationship as it exists and operates in the United States.[4]

THE CONTEXT: DEFINING A "BANKING INSTITUTION" AND ITS REGULATORY ENVIRONMENT

Whilst banking institutions operate in significant numbers in the United States (e.g. over 10,000 commercial banks and 6,000 bank holding companies, over 1,200 thrift institutions, and several thousand credit unions) and play a substantial role in the US economy and financial markets, there does not appear to be any clear or precise definition of a "bank".

Legal perspective

Though the US Supreme Court has proffered its views on the nature of a commercial bank on several occasions,[5] the legal reality is that defining a bank is essentially the function of the legislature. However, in the United States, there are 50 state legislatures and the US Congress, all of which (from time to time) have employed differing definitions of "bank" in various of their state and federal statutes for differing purposes.[6] Today, however, the operative term is not solely "bank" but also "the business of banking". Recent judicial decisions have given broad deference to the bank regulators in determining the definitional embrace of this phase.[7]

Organisational perspective: main forms of banking institutions

In the United States, the main forms of banking institution comprise *commercial banks*, *thrift institutions*, and *credit unions*.

Commercial banks

Commercial banks developed as depository institutions with defined investment powers and with broad lending powers. Their source of funds was primarily

4. For more comprehensive and detailed analyses, see Matthew Bender's multi-volume treatise on *Banking Law* (updated as of 1998) ("Matthew Bender Treatise").

5. E.g. *Oulton* v. *German Savings & Loan Society*, 84 US (17 Wall.) 109, at 118 (1873); and *United States* v. *Philadelphia Nat. Bank*, 374 US 321, at 326.

6. E.g. separate definitions of "bank" exist under the National Banking Act, state banking codes, the UCC, the federal securities laws, the federal tax code, the 1956 Bank Holding Company Act (as amended), and the Federal Deposit Insurance Act.

7. See *NationsBank of N.C., N.A.* v. *Variable Annuity Life Ins. Co.*, 513 US 251 (1995).

short or intermediate term deposits. The receipt of demand deposits, at least until recently, was unique to commercial banks. While commercial banks relied primarily on deposits as a source of funds, recent events have made these banks explore other avenues for obtaining funds such as bulk individual and corporate deposits, the commercial paper markets and retail purchase agreements. Commercial banks also engage in a number of depository related and non-depository services related to their primary banking functions. Under most federal and state banking laws, commercial banks can only engage in statutorily or regulatorily expressed powers or implied powers incidental to primary banking functions.

The most significant economic impact of commercial banks arises from their ability to create money and credit, to facilitate payments to the management of the "checking account" (i.e. current account) system, and to extend short-term loans to meet business needs.[8] Commercial banks may be chartered under national or state "enabling" statutes.

Thrift institutions (savings associations)

Thrift institutions (which can be state or federally chartered) were originally special investment financial intermediaries for the encouragement of thrift, and (in the case of savings and loan associations) of facility home mortgages.[9] In the late 1970s and early 1980s, federal legislation expanded the powers of thrift institutions to include many which were similar to those of commercial banks. However, more recently (in light of the financial crises in the thrift industry), Congress and regulators are taking a more restrictive approach to thrift powers.[10] Under recent legislation, such institutions are now dubbed "savings associations".

Credit unions

Credit unions originated in nineteenth-century Germany and grew in popularity in the United States during the twentieth century. Credit unions are cooperative groups that pool the savings of their members, who share some common bond, and primarily make personal loans to these members, often at favourable rates of interest. Federal credit unions have been given expanded powers by recent federal legislation.[11] Under regulatory policy, federal credit unions are now

8. See generally M.K. Lewis and K.T. Davis, *Domestic and International Banking* (1987). Also on regulatory dimensions, see E.G. Corrigan, "Are Banks Special?" Fed. Res. Bank of Minn. Annual Report (1982). Also for a modern perspective, see R. Cranston, *Principles of Banking Law* (1997).
9. See Friend *et al.*, *Study of the Saving and Loan Industry* (4 vols. 1969).
10. At present most savings banks are state chartered; however, recent federal restrictions on state savings banks may make federal savings banks a predominate form of savings banks in the future. Recent federal legislation sets forth various emergency provisions facilitating the conversions of state savings associations into a merger with federal associations or even with commercial banks.
11. See Moddy & Fite, *The Credit Union Movement, Origins and Development 1850–1970* (1971).

permitted to determine their own eligibility requirements for membership; however, recently there has been a significant judicial and political struggle under way as to whether credit unions may have such broader based membership.[12]

Other "bank-type" institutions

Not all bank-type institutions are formally banks. More and more, in the current deregulated financial market environment in the United States, other forms of non-bank financial institutions are increasingly coming into direct competition with banking institutions for sources of funds and customers. One example would be money market funds. These funds are mutual fund vehicles (often organised by investment banking firms) that invest in a portfolio with money market instruments. Although under the supervision of the federal Securities Exchange Commission (SEC), money market funds are not subject to bank regulations such as legal reserve requirements, investment requirements, routine supervisory examinations equivalent to banks, and are not subject to a host of other regulatory requirements that control many aspects of bank operations. As such, these forms of financial institutions have been viewed as direct competitors of banks for deposits and for customers. Other non-bank financial institution competitors may include life insurance companies (regulated by state authorities), investment banking firms (regulated by federal and state securities authorities), pension funds (regulated under federal retirement laws), finance companies and mortgage banking firms (generally unregulated).[13]

Unless otherwise indicated, this chapter will limit its focus to commercial banks, in particular national banks (i.e. banks chartered under the National Banking Act).

Operational perspective

Banking institutions in the United States operate either as "unit" banks, branches, or as part of bank holding company systems. Many banks also have significant "correspondent" relationships with other banks. The manner in which the organisational and operational structure of the bank is configured may often affect the regulatory structure and legal environment within which a particular banking institution and its customers co-exist.

Unit banking

Unit banking involves the conduct of a bank's business operations through a centralised facility (with auxiliary facilities to the extent permitted by law). Unit

12. While the US Supreme Court has recently ruled against the credit union's concept of a broad-based membership, at August 1998, the US Congress has passed legislation largely undoing the court's decision and favouring the credit union industry and regulators. President Clinton has stated publicly that he intends to sign such legislation when presented to him.

13. See J. Norton and S.C. Whitley, *Banking Law Manual* § 1.04 (1997) (hereinafter cited as *BLM*).

banking results not so much from economic preference, but from federal and state restrictions on branch banking and geographic activities. There still are several states that have geographic restrictions on banking. However, the Riegle-Neal Interstate Banking and Branching Efficiency Act of 1994 has significantly expanded geographic banking opportunities (though preserving various state "opt-out" rights).[14]

Branch banking

Branch banking entails multiple office banking. Under federal law, the ability to branch is left essentially for federal purpose as a matter of state law and preference under the 1927 McFadden Act.[15] The liability of the branch is essentially imputed to that of the main banking facility, as there is no corporate distinction between the head office and the branch. Even though branch banks or offices may, in an economic sense, constitute distinct business entities or even lines of business, they are not separate legal entities. The parent (i.e. head office) bank owns the property of the branch, is liable for the debts of the branch, and is responsible for its operations.[16]

Holding company operations

The primary example of group banking in the United States today is the use of bank holding companies, by which a parent entity may have one or more wholly-owned banking subsidiaries and one or more wholly-owned non-banking subsidiaries. Bank holding companies are primarily regulated by the Federal Reserve Board (FRB) under the Bank Holding Company Act 1956, as amended.[17] Except in emergency takeover situations, this Act prohibits multi-bank holding companies from acquiring a bank in another state, unless the law of the state in which the bank is to be acquired and is domiciled expressly so provides.[18] The non-banking subsidiaries of bank holding companies, however, operate across state lines to perform many functions "closely related to banking".[19] The 1994 Riegle-Neal Act, referred to above, significantly expands interstate banking opportunities.

14. See Pub. L. No. 103-328, 108 Stat. 2338 (1994). Generally on bank geographic restriction/expansion issues, see *BLM*, Ch. 17.

15. 44 Stat. 1228 (1927); codified at 12 USC § 36.

16. See generally *BLM*, Ch. 17, particularly on liberalising aspects of the 1994 legislation.

17. See 12 USC § 1841 *et seq*. On legal aspects concerning banking holding companies, see Beckeford, *Bank Holding Company Compliance Manual* (1997).

18. So called "Douglas Amendment" of 1970, 12 USC § 1842(d).

19. The Bank Holding Company Act (12 USC § 1843(c)(8)) limits the activities and powers of the non-bank subsidiaries to those activities "closely related to banking". The FRB was given a broad regulatory power to define such term and it does so through its "Regulation Y" (12 CFR § 225). Over the past decade, the Federal Reserve Board (largely through its "Section 20" order powers) has expanded and continues to expand and to reshape the definitional and substantive content of what "closely related to banking means" (e.g. permitting increased securities powers within the bank holding company structure).

In 1956 there were only 53 registered bank holding companies in the United States; in 1970, there were 121 bank holding companies; but in recent years, there were over 6,000 bank holding companies controlling over 9,000 banks and having assets approximating 3 trillion dollars.

Correspondent relationships

Regardless of whether a bank operates through a unit, branch, or holding company, banks frequently have formal or informal cooperative relationships with other banks, particularly in geographical areas in which they do not have banking facilities. This relationship, which is important domestically and internationally, is called a "correspondent" relationship.

The cornerstone of many correspondent relationships is the network commercial banks use to facilitate the intricate, nationwide cheque-collection system which would be subject to both federal regulation (e.g. FRB Regulation J) and state law (e.g. UCC). Banks also correspond on a number of other matters including letters of credit, compensating balances, loan payments and disbursements, loan participations, and international matters. These activities may involve different types of legal relationships (contractual or commercial) between the various banks and any customers involved and may be heavily influenced by bank industry practices. Also many larger banks seek deposits from smaller banking institutions on a continuing basis.[20]

Impact of regulatory environment

As the term "bank" is subject to legislative vagaries, the regulations of these institutions are also subject to a highly fragmented regulatory system in the United States. What must be remembered is that the overall regulatory environment within which a US bank operates (which is often largely determined by the nature, practices and attitudes of a particular regulator) is extremely important in the shaping of the character and practices of the bank itself. For example, regulatory rules and attitudes concerning depository or lending relationships can determine the way in which a bank approaches its depositor or borrower, or vice versa.[21]

The present bank regulatory system is fragmented among various independent regulatory bodies, which lends itself to regulatory redundancy, complexity and inefficiencies and which presents significant costs to banking institutions. This fragmentation is directly attributable to an historical fear of undue concentration of financial power in the hands of banking institutions and the ensuing belief that the statutory framework should separate the various classes of financial institutions.[22]

20. See generally Fischer, *American Banking Structure*, Ch. 3 (1968).
21. See, *inter alia*, Norton, "Being Competitive in a 'Reregulated' Banking Environment: The Case of Commercial Lending Activities of Banking Institutions", 11 Okla. City U.L. Rev. 547 (1986).
22. See generally Hackley, "Our Discriminatory Banking Structure", 55 Va. L. Rev. 1421 (1969).

In addition, the regulatory scheme for banking institutions in the United States is a "dual banking system" of state and federal regulation and regulators, and even the federal regulation is fragmented among various regulatory authorities.[23] In order to determine the laws applicable to a specific banking institution, it is important to ascertain under which law the institution is chartered and who is the responsible regulator.

With respect to commercial banks (which may be federally or state chartered), their regulation is as follows:[24]

1. National banks are chartered and supervised by the Comptroller of the Currency (Comptroller or "OCC"), are members of the FRS and are insured by the Federal Deposit Insurance Corporation (hereinafter "FDIC").
2. State chartered banks are regulated by the relevant state bank authorities, and may choose to become members of the FRS. If a state bank becomes a member of the FRS, it must be insured by the FDIC.
3. State banks may choose to be insured by the FDIC without becoming members of the FRS.
4. Unless otherwise required by state or federal law, state banks may choose to operate independently from the FRS and the FDIC (a possibility becoming obsolescent, legally and practically).

Prior to the passage of the 1989 Banking Act (FIRREA) commercial banks were not eligible for membership in the Federal Home Loan Bank System (FHLBS) respecting federal savings banks. Presently, commercial banks may be eligible for such membership if they satisfy certain statutory and regulatory requirements.

With the 1987 Competitive Equality Banking Act (CEBA) legislation, Congress essentially put a moratorium on the legislative deregulation efforts of the late 1970s and early 1980s.[25] Understandably (but in part regrettably) with the collapse of the savings and loan industry and significant troubles in the commercial banking industry, the subsequent enactment of the 1989 FIRREA legislation unfolded as a piece of reactive legislation.[26]

Congress, through FIRREA, totally reorganised the supervisory structures and standards of thrift institutions, subsumed the thrift insurance fund under the administration and supervision of the FDIC, substantially restricted the activities and investments of thrift institutions, and granted the FDIC its full "wish list" for enhancement of regulatory enforcement powers. The original

---

23. See, *inter alia*, Scott, The Dual Banking System "A Model of Competition in Regulation", 30 Stan. L. Rev. (1977).

24. On regulation of commercial banks generally, see, Matthew Bender's multivolume *Banking Law* treatise (1998).

25. On CEBA, see *BLM*, § 2.05 [7]. For discussion of earlier deregulation period see Norton, "The 1982 Banking Act and the Deregulation's Scheme", 38 Bus. Law 1627 (1983).

26. On FIRREA, see Norton and Gail, "A Decade's Journey from 'Deregulation' to 'Supervisory Reregulation': The Financial Institutions Reform, Recovery and Enforcement Act of 1989 (FIRREA)", 45 Bus. Law 1103 (1990).

congressional plan of deregulation had been derailed by congressional tax reform, serious adverse economic conditions in significant parts of the United States, and an increasingly restrictive approach to bank and thrift regulation. For many in government, the philosophy of deregulation came to be seen as discredited and was abandoned in favour of enhanced supervisory reregulation in prudential supervision and regulatory enforcement areas. The earlier vision of the compatibility and dynamics of deregulated, but "safe and sound", banking and thrift industries was being shelved. In 1991, significant additional banking federal banking legislation (covering domestic and foreign banking institutions) was passed, again directed primarily at prudential supervisory concerns.[27]

What all this means for the banker–customer relationship is that this relationship today sits within a highly complicated and uncertain regulatory environment, and one in which the regulators' concerns for prudential supervision and tough civil and criminal enforcement (i.e. "supervisory reregulation" and "regulatory micromanagement"[28]) may be creating a chilling effect within the banking industry and may be adding significant burdens, costs and restrictions to the banking industry that will only lead to further noncompetitiveness of the US banking industry. In fact, the 1991 Act now brings foreign bank operations in the United States substantially under the same supervisory reregulation web.[29]

THE BANK–DEPOSITOR–CUSTOMER RELATIONSHIP

Nature of bank accounts[30]

Background

At common law in the United States, state courts made no distinction between a deposit and an account, and did not adopt a universal definition of the term "deposit". Generally, courts concluded that a deposit occurred when a customer placed money with a bank for safekeeping subject to withdrawal upon the depositor's demand or pursuant to rules and regulations to which the depositor and the bank had agreed. A "depositor" was simply one who placed money with the bank. At common law, the depository relationship was essentially a contractual relationship which normally (unless it was a "special account") gave rise to a debtor (bank)–creditor (depositor) relationship.[31]

27. FDIC Improvement Act of 1991 and RTC Refinancing, Restructuring and Improvement Act of 1991, Pub. L. No. 102-242, 105 Stat. 2236 (19 Dec. 1991). For further discussion see *BLM*, § 2.05 [11].

28. See presentation made by Gail and Norton, "The US Banking Reform Legislation of 1991: More Regulatory Micro-Management and Supervision" (Paper presented to 10th Annual Conference of Association of European Banking Teachers, Bangor, September 1992).

29. Title VIII of the FDIC Improvement Act of 1991 is the Foreign Bank Supervision Enhancement Act of 1991, which is discussed by Gail, Norton and O'Neil in 26 *The International Lawyer No. 4* (Spring 1992).

30. For further discussion and specific citations regarding the subject matter of this section, see *BLM*, Ch. 11, from which portions of this section are derived.

31. See generally Matthew Bender treatise *op. cit.*, n. 24, Vol. 1, Ch. 9.

However, in modern times, the definition of "deposit" in the United States has been altered by statute, and the meaning of this term may vary according to the statute under which it is defined (e.g. for commercial purposes under state UCC statutes or for deposit insurance purpose under federal law). Yet, a banker–customer transaction that is not defined as a deposit by one or more statutes may nevertheless still be properly classified as an account pursuant to another statute, to the common law, or to the law of contracts.

Modern statutory definitions

REVISED ARTICLE 4 OF UCC

Revised Article 4 of the UCC deals with "Bank Deposits and Collections". Article 4, like other modern statutes, uses the term "account" in lieu of the term "deposits". An "account" is defined as "any deposit or credit account with a bank, including a demand, time, savings, passbook, share draft or like account, other than an account evidenced by a certificate of deposit".[32]

FEDERAL PURPOSES

Federal banking statutes have also defined the term "deposit", and the statutory definition of the term may vary according to the purpose of the statute under which it is defined. For example, the Federal Deposit Insurance Act provides that a deposit is

the unpaid balance of money or its equivalent received or held by a bank in the usual course of business and for which it has given or is obligated to give credit, either conditionally or unconditionally to a commercial, checking, savings, time, or thrift account, or which is evidenced by its certificate of deposit, or a cheque or draft drawn against a deposit account and certified by the bank, or a letter of credit or a traveller's cheque on which the bank is primarily liable.[33]

FRB Regulation D governs reserve requirements of depository institutions, and adopts a similar definition of "deposit".[34]

Types of bank deposits and accounts

Deposits

Bank deposits are customarily classified by type, customer, or duration.

CLASSIFICATION BY TYPE

Deposits are, by type, either general deposits or special deposits. A special deposit is made when the bank and customer agree, either expressly or impliedly, that the money or item deposited is for a specific purpose other than a

---

32. Revised UCC § 4-104(1)(a). See also UCC § 9–105(1)(e).
33. 12 USC § 1813(1).
34. 12 CFR § 204.2(a)(1). For purposes of the federal Truth in Savings Act, yet another definition is given for an "account". See FRB Regulation DD, 12 CFR § 230.2(a). An account is generally not a "security" under federal securities law.

general credit or account, is deposited for safekeeping, and will be returned upon the customer's demand.[35] All other accounts are general accounts, absent a mutual agreement that the account is to be held for a special purpose.[36]

The distinction between general and special accounts is important for three reasons. First, title to the deposited funds is determined by the type of account. If funds are deposited into a special account, the customer retains title; if funds are deposited in a general account, title passes to the banking institution. Secondly, the legal relationship is determined between bank and depositor by the type of account. A special deposit creates a bailee–bailor relationship; a general account creates a debtor–creditor relationship.[37] Finally, the uses to which a bank may put deposits are determined by the type of deposit. A special deposit must be segregated, and the bank may not use a special deposit in its general banking operations; a general deposit becomes part of the bank's general fund that may be commingled with other funds and used in general banking operations. Whether an account is classified as general or special depends upon the intention and understanding of the parties as expressed in their agreement, and upon the surrounding circumstances.[38]

CLASSIFICATION BY CUSTOMER

A deposit may be established by various customers, including an individual, multiple parties, a partnership, a corporation, or a public entity.

Funds in an individual account may be deposited and withdrawn by only one natural person.

Multiple party accounts are established in the names of two or more persons, and include joint accounts, payable-on-death (POD) accounts, and trust accounts. A joint account is in the name of several persons who may deposit or withdraw funds from the account. In the event of death, the survivor becomes the account holder. Many states have adopted the Uniform Probate Code to regulate ownership of multiple party accounts. These state statutes typically define a joint account as: "an account payable on request to one or more of two parties whether or not any mention is made of survivorship."[39] A POD account is defined as:

an account payable on request to one person during [one's] lifetime and on [one's] death to one or more POD payees, or to one or more persons during their lifetimes and on the death of all to one or more POD payees.[40]

35. 12 USC § 24 (Seventh) expressly authorises national banks to receive deposits.
36. See *Mid City Nat'l Bank* v. *Mar Bldg. Corp.*, 339 N.E. 2d 497 (Ill. 1975).
37. E.g. *Martin* v. *First State Bank*, 490 S.W.2d 208 (Tex. Civ. App. 1973).
38. Cf. *McGhee* v. *Bank of America National Trust & Sav. Ass's*, 131 Cal. Rptr 482 (1976) (special deposit) with *Mid-City Nat. Bank* v. *Mar Bldg. Corp.*, 339 N.E.2d 497 (Ill. 1975). The common mortgage loan escrow account for taxes, insurance and the like is a special account but ordinarily does not create a fiduciary obligation. However, a bank becoming an escrow agent to facilitate a transaction with or between third parties most probably will take on fiduciary duties.
39. See Uniform Probate Law § 6–101(4), 8 ULA 520 (1983).
40. *Ibid.* § 6–101(10), 8 ULA 521 (1983).

A trust account is an account in the name of a trustee, for the benefit of others. The relationship is established by the type of trust account, and by the deposit agreement with the institution. The subject of the trust is the funds on deposit in the account.[41]

Partnership accounts generally are established to maintain partnership funds. A bank should require evidence that the person opening the account or withdrawing funds from the account is authorised to do so. A general partner is authorised to open a partnership account because of his status as agent for the partnership; a limited partner may or may not have this authority, depending upon the terms of the limited partnership agreement. Under certain circumstances, a bank may be liable for misappropriation or wrongful withdrawal of partnership funds by a partner.[42]

Corporate accounts present similar authorisation concerns. A bank should secure a corporate resolution of authorisation, providing that the person with whom it is dealing is in fact authorised to establish the account. If the bank releases corporate funds to a person not authorised to use the account, it may be liable to the corporation.[43]

Public fund accounts may also be established in a banking institution. In the absence of an agreement between the parties, public deposits are general deposits. Unlike deposits from private customers, deposits by the federal government must be secured by specifically identified assets.[44] In addition, national banks may accept deposits from states or political subdivisions of states, and may pledge assets to secure these deposits to the same extent as other banking institutions located in the state in which the national bank is located.[45]

CLASSIFICATION BY DURATION

Deposits are classified by duration as either demand deposits or time deposits. Demand deposits are judicially defined as deposits that are payable at any time the depositor chooses (subject to reasonable limitations).[46] Many checking accounts are within this definition, and demand is made by writing a cheque. Time deposits are defined judicially as deposits made for a specified period of time. These include Christmas club deposits, vacation club deposits, and certificates of deposit payable on a certain date. Statute and regulation (e.g. FRB regulations) may affect whether a deposit is a time deposit, savings deposit or demand deposit.

Congress has authorised two new types of savings deposits, the Negotiable Order of Withdrawal (NOW) account and the automatic transfer account. A NOW account permits a bank customer to transfer money from an interest

41. *Ibid.* at § 6–101(14), 8 ULA 521 (1983).
42. See generally *Michie on Banks and Banking* § 41 (1973 as suppl.).
43. E.g. *Movie Films, Inc.* v. *First Security Bank*, 447 P.2d 38 (1968).
44. 31 CFR §§ 202–203.
45. E.g. *Inland Waterway Corp.* v. *Young*, 309 US 517 (1940), *reh. den.*, 309 US 698 (1940).
46. E.g. *Mallett* v. *Tunnicliffe*, 136 So. 346, *reh. den.*, 137 So. 238 (Fla. 1931).

bearing account to a third person by using a negotiable instrument of withdrawal, an instrument similar to a cheque: a NOW account is, in effect, a checking account that draws interest.[47] An automatic transfer account permits a bank automatically to transfer funds from a depositor's savings account to this checking account: this account is available only to individual depositors.[48]

MONEY MARKET INSTRUMENTS

The 1982 Banking Act directed the establishment of an account that is "directly equivalent to and competitive with money market mutual funds". This account, which normally is subject to minimum monthly balances and numbers of transfer restrictions, would not be considered a "transaction account" for Federal Reserve requirements. This account was established and, generally, is available to all types of bank customers (including commercial customers), and has no interest ceiling. Provided certain limitations are met, these accounts are not subject to FRB reserve requirements. The account is insured by the federal insurance agency, and has no minimum maturity requirements.[49]

These new depository instruments should, if properly structured, substantially supplant most of the innovative depository instruments offered in an attempt to provide a near market return to depositors. These instruments also provide a competitive means to lure back traditional sources of bank funds that shifted into money market mutual funds. However, the actual packaging and pricing of this new account has proved troublesome for many banking institutions.[50]

Other accounts

TRUST ACCOUNTS

The Comptroller and the Office of Thrift Supervision have the power to grant to national banks and federal savings associations, respectively, the authority to act as trusts or to act in other fiduciary capacities. If authorised, banking institutions may accept trust accounts.[51]

A trust is a fiduciary relationship in which one person or entity (i.e. a banking institution) is the holder of title to the property, with an equitable obligation to keep or use the property for the benefit of another. To create a valid and enforceable trust, certain requirements must be met. Each element must be described with clarity and certainty. First, there must be an intent (written or

---

47. See 12 USC § 1832.
48. See Internal Revenue Code § 128.
49. See 1982 Garn-St Germain Banking Act, § 327 and 47 Fed. Reg. 53710 (No. 29, 1982).
50. E.g. maintenance of minimum balance and the number and manner of transfers may create pricing and marketing problems.
51. For national bank authority, see 12 USC § 92a and 12 CFR § 9; for federal thrifts, see 12 USC §§ 46(n)(1) and 12 CFR §§ 545.17; 550; and while federal credit unions do not have general trust powers, they may act as trustees and custodians of pension plans. 12 CFR § 724.1.

oral as determined as a question of fact) to create a trust by the settlor. Also the subject matter or "trust principal" must be identifiable. Further, a trustee must be named (by the settlor or court) to maintain or use the subject matter of the trust. Finally, a trust must have an identifiable beneficiary: failure to name a beneficiary defeats the trust.[52]

If a trust is accepted by the board of directors of a banking institution, it must be administered according to federal and state law, and according to the terms of the trust instrument.[53]

REPURCHASE AGREEMENTS (REPOS)

In an effort to compete against nondepository financial institutions, banking institutions now offer repurchase agreements. These agreements are not deposits, but rather are typically in the form of debt obligations of banking institutions that are secured by a US Government obligation or a pool of these securities. A repurchase agreement (which may be subject to various bank and securities regulatory requirements) is an instrument that enables a banking institution to "purchase" funds from a customer subject to an obligation to repay the funds, plus interest, on a specified date. A repurchase agreement is a hybrid instrument that describes a transaction which has both "sale-repurchase" and "borrowing" aspects.[54]

FEDERAL RESERVE FUNDS

Another type of bank account, available only to banking institutions, are federal reserve funds. Federal reserve funds, or "fed funds", are deposits placed in Federal Reserve District Banks by depository institutions.

SAFE DEPOSIT BOXES

A further account offered by banking institutions is the safe deposit box. The legal relationship between the banking institution and the safe deposit box customer is generally considered to be that of bailee and bailor. The bailment requires the banking institution to exercise ordinary care or the degree of care that an ordinarily prudent person would use with his own property of similar description.[55] Some courts, however, consider the legal relationship between the institution and its customer to be that of landlord and tenant. These courts reason that the institution does not have custody of the contents of the safe

52. See generally, ALI, *Restatement of Trusts (Second)*, and Bogert, *Law of Trusts*.
53. See generally 12 CFR § 9, 11(a).
54. See *inter alia*, Porter, "Eighty-nine-day Agreements for the Sale and Repurchase of Fractional interests in Government Securities", 98 Banking L.J. 343 (1981); and Waters, "Sale of Retail Repurchase Agreements and Loan Associations—Issues for Legal Counsel and Bank Management", 43 Ala. Law 283 (1982).
55. E.G. *Nat. Safe Deposit Co.* v. *Stead* 95 New 973 (Ill. 1911), aff'd 232 US 58 (1914); and Stein, "Safety Deposit Vault or Leased Metal Box: The Responsibility of a Bank to its Customer", 18 McGill L.J. 45 (1972).

deposit box since the customer retains a key or combination to the box, and therefore the institution cannot be held to the standard of care required of a bailee. State law generally governs the rights of third parties to access or remove the contents of the box.[56]

Services related to accounts

BRANCHES, REMOTE TERMINALS AND AUTOMATIC TELLERS

Banking institutions also compete for funds by offering convenient access to bank services. Services may be available at branch banks, remote terminals and automatic teller machines.[57]

Some states may prohibit remote terminals if the terminals are included within the definition of a branch bank.[58] It has been the policy of the Office of Thrift Supervision (OTS) and its predecessor agency, the FHLBB, to permit the intrastate establishment of federal S & L branches when the branch will not harm other local thrift and home financing institutions.[59] Remote terminals may be established anywhere with OTS approval, including across state lines. Banking institutions are relying on remote terminals to a greater degree, because the cost of establishing a remote terminal is less than the cost of establishing and maintaining a branch bank.[60]

DEBIT AND CREDIT CARDS

Another service offered by banking institutions to their customers is the bank card. The use of bank credit cards has increased steadily since they were first issued in 1959.[61] All banking institutions are authorised to issue credit cards.[62]

A typical credit card program includes three distinct legal agreements:

1. the agreement between the card holder and the issuing bank;
2. the agreement between the merchant and the issuer; and
3. the sales agreement between the merchant and the cardholder.

Numerous state and federal statutes govern the relationship between the bank, the cardholder, and the merchant. At the state level, the UCC is sometimes applied by analogy to govern credit card disputes.[63] However, the revised UCC

---

56. *Carples* v. *Cumberland Coal & Iron Co.*, 240 N.Y. 187, 148 N.E. 185 (1925).

57. Federal credit unions may, if the common bond requirement is satisfied, branch world wide.

58. 12 USC § 36.

59. 12 CFR § 545.14.

60. *Id.*; "Supermarket ATMs Join Arsenal of Weapons in Texas Teller Battle", Sav. & Loan News, 15 August (1981).

61. Clontz, "Bank Credit Cards Under the Uniform Commercial Code", 87 Banking L.J. 888 (1970).

62. 12 CFR §§ 7.7378, 701.21.3.

63. Davenport, "Bank Credit Cards and the Uniform Commercial Code", 1 Val. U.L. Rev. 218 (1966).

specifically excludes credit and debit card slips from the definition of "item" and therefore from the scope of Article 4. At the federal level, the Consumer Credit Protection Act limits the cardholder's liability for purchases made with a lost or stolen credit card.[64]

During the 1970s, banking institutions established electronic fund transfer (EFT) services that enable customers to transfer funds among their bank accounts, to make deposits and withdrawals from their accounts, and to pay for goods or services by transferring funds from their account to the merchant's account at the point of sale.[65] These services are available through debit or EFT cards. Some states have enacted EFT laws, [66] and the federal Consumer Credit Protection Act provides the basic framework establishing the rights, liabilities and responsibilities of participants in the EFT system.[67]

Premiums and fees

Banking institutions often use premiums and finders' fees to attract and to retain deposits. Premiums are paid in cash, merchandise or credit. A premium is generally considered to be interest paid on a deposit, unless it is considered a legitimate advertising or promotional expense.[68] A finders' fee is a payment made by an institution for the introduction of a depositor to a bank. Finders' fees are considered to be interest to the depositor for purposes of determining the interest rate ceiling.[69]

Regulatory impact on the deposit transaction

The classic regulatory restraint on deposit transactions was FRB Regulation Q which set maximum interest rates to be paid on deposits.[70] Though, as part of the 1980s federal deregulation efforts, these requirements have been phased out, a new federal "truth-in-savings" statute has been enacted (1991 Truth in Savings Act).[71] This Act is designed to require the clear and uniform disclosure of:

1. the rates of interest payable on deposit accounts by depository institutions, and
2. the fees that are assessable against deposit accounts so that customers can make a meaningful comparison between the competing claims of depository institutions respecting deposit accounts.

The FRB is to prescribe implementing regulations and to publish model forms

64. 15 USC §§ 1642–1645.
65. Geva, *The Law of Electronic Funds Transfer* (Matthew Bender) (1997).
66. *Id.* At § 6.03[3].
67. 15 USC § 1693, 12 CFR § 205. See generally Penney and Baker, *The Law of Electronic Transfer Systems* (1980, as suppl.).
68. See, generally, 12 CFR § 1204.109.
69. See Karr and Rhoads, "The DIDC and Premiums", 98 Banking L.J. 700 (1981).
70. See FRB's prior Regulation Q (repealed), 12 CFR § 217 (1979).
71. On 10 September 1992, the FRB issued a 45-page truth-in-lending regulation (Regulation DD), with 155 pages of related commentary, model disclosure forms and sample forms.

and clauses. The FRB has also been given broad enforcement authority. Consumers of bank lending services were highly protected under federal and state consumer laws; now the FRB under the Act is extending consumer-type protection to depositors.

The traditional depositor protection has been federal deposit insurance, which currently provides $100,000 protection per account (with complicated FDIC rules often being manipulated to provide coverages in excess thereof and with FDIC practices in some situations providing greater coverages). Insurance premiums paid by depository institutions have been based on flat-rate formulae; but governmental concern for the "moral hazards" of such insurance is shifting the insurance basis to that of a "risk-based" formula; previous "loopholes" permitting excess coverage recently have been eliminated by Congress; and the "too big to fail" doctrine curtailed. At present, the entire federal deposit insurance scheme remains under Congressional scrutiny.[72]

Another deposit area of recent federal regulation has concerned brokered (i.e. wholesale) deposits. In particular, poorly capitalised institutions may be precluded from acquiring such deposits.[73] A further type of federal deposit account regulation is that of FRB reserve requirements.[74]

Legal relationship of a banking depositor customer[75]

A general account creates a debtor–creditor relationship, and a special account and a night deposit creates a bailor–bailee relationship. The duties and liabilities of the bank and the customer are determined by the legal nature of the relationship.

Background

The law does not require a particular procedure to establish an account. However, the institution and the customer must mutually assent to the deposit, either expressly or impliedly. If the parties do not expressly agree to the terms of an account, the law will imply terms based on the usual banking relationship.[76]

The terms that govern checking and savings accounts are generally embodied in a signature card or passbook that a customer signs when the account is opened.[77] A signature card incorporates by reference the rules of the institution. Passbooks include printed rules which:[78]

72. See, e.g., Comment: "Deposit Insurance—What Now?", in E.L. Symons, Jr. and J.J. White, *Banking Law*, at 729 (3rd edn 1991).
73. See Gail and Norton, *op. cit.*, n. 28.
74. See discussion below.
75. For more specific discussion see *BLM*, at § 11.03; and Symons, Jr., *op. cit.*
76. E.g. *Taylor v. Equitable Trust Co.*, 304 A.2d 833 (Md. 1973).
77. The bank–customer relationship will generally be governed by UCC Article 4 and various federal disclosure requirements.
78. See UCC §§ 3–404, 3–405, 3–406, 4–401 and 4–406.

1. release the institution from liability if the institution pays funds to an imposter;
2. require presentation of the passbook for withdrawal; and
3. delineate requirements for cheques and other deposits, and for examination of statements and cancelled cheques.

Contractual terms are also included in deposit slips. The customer is bound by the terms appearing on a deposit slip to which he has access, but he is not charged with knowledge of, or assent to, terms that appear only on an institution's copy of the deposit slip. If the deposit slip is the contract, extrinsic evidence cannot be introduced to change the terms contained in the deposit slip. The deposit slip should set out clearly what the institution is required to do.

If the institution and the customer have embodied the terms of their deposit agreement in a written contract (i.e. a signature card or passbook), the contract generally is conclusive as between the customer and the institution. In the absence of fraud, duress or mistake, a court will be bound by the terms of the agreement, and may not consider extrinsic evidence.[79] The contract is formed when the institution accepts and acknowledges the deposit. Accordingly, the legal relationship is determined at the time the account is established. The money deposited is consideration for the obligation of the institution to repay the deposit. The contract will be interpreted so as to effectuate the intent of the parties.[80] The courts will generally enforce terms that impose limitations upon the institution and the customer. Some courts, however, will not enforce clauses exculpating the institution from liability for failure to exercise reasonable care.[81]

Creation and nature of the relationship

The legal relationship between a banking institution and its customer is created by an express or implied contract.[82] If the deposit is a general deposit, title to the money passes to the institution, and a debtor–creditor relationship is created. Thus, the institution assumes an obligation to the depositor to repay the funds, and the funds become the property of the institution.[83] If a deposit is a special deposit, the relationship between the institution and customer is that of bailor and bailee. The bank has a duty as bailor to return the deposit to the depositor, and the deposit may not be commingled with the institution's other funds.[84] Some courts consider depositors to be beneficiaries of a fiduciary relationship with the bank or (at least) of a quasi-fiduciary duty resulting from a special relationship of trust and confidence.[85] Whether this is a generally held judicial precept is questionable.

79. E.g. *Bennett v. First Nat. Bank*, 443 F.2d 518 (8th Cir. 1971).
80. See *Western Nat. Bank v. Hawkeye-Security Ins. Co.*, 380 F. Supp. 508 (D. Wyo. 1974).
81. E.g. *Hy-Grade Oil Co. v. New Jersey Bank*, 350 A.2d 279 (NJ 1975).
82. See *Johnson v. Stamets* 148 NW 2d 468 (Iowa 1967).
83. See *Meyer v. Idaho First Nat. Bank*, 525 P.2d 990 (Idaho 1974).
84. E.g. *Mid-City Nat. Bank v. Mar Bldg. Corp.*, 339 N.E. 2d 497 (Ill. 1975).
85. See discussion by Miller and Harrell, *op. cit.*, n.2, at § 9.03.

Duties and liabilities of the bank

GENERAL DEPOSITS

When title to a general deposit passes to the banking institution, it assumes the risk of loss if the deposit is lost, destroyed or stolen. Thus, if an institution pays out funds upon presentment of a lost or stolen passbook, it may be liable to the account owner for the fraudulently withdrawn funds. In the absence of an agreement limiting the bank's liability, the courts are divided as to the extent of an institution's liability in these cases. Some courts hold that an institution is absolutely liable for payments made upon presentment of a lost or stolen passbook. Other courts impose liability only if the fraudulent withdrawal of funds resulted from the institution's failure to exercise reasonable care. Generally, a banking institution breaches its duty of reasonable care if it fails to compare the signature on the signature card with the signature on the withdrawal order. In some cases, where an institution's employee doubts the identity of the person making a withdrawal, it may be under duty to require identification.[86]

The duties and liabilities of a banking institution with regard to checking account transactions are governed by Article 4 of the Uniform Commercial Code. Article 4 provides that an institution is liable for:

1. wrongful dishonour;[87]
2. failure to act promptly on a cheque or other item;[88]
3. ignoring a stop payment order; or[89]
4. paying a forged cheque.[90]

Article 4 is not limited to checking accounts.[91]

New Article 4A of the UCC deals with issues (including liability) relating to "funds transfer".[92]

SPECIAL DEPOSITS

A banking institution must exercise reasonable care as bailee of a special deposit. If the institution exercises reasonable care, it will not be held liable for loss, destruction or theft of the deposit. The loss or theft of a special deposit, however, raises a presumption that the institution has acted negligently. Thus, the bank has the burden of proving that it exercised reasonable care. If the institution is acting as a gratuitous bailee, receiving no compensation for

86. See revised UCC § 3-501(b)(2); see also *Annotation*, 68 ALR 3d 1080 (1976).
87. UCC § 4–402.
88. UCC § 4–301 and 4–302.
89. UCC § 4–403.
90. UCC § 4–406.
91. E.g. a savings withdrawal order would be covered. *Cf.* broad definitions of "item" at revised UCC § 4–104(a)(9).
92. The subject of the banker–customer relationship under UCC Arts. 4 and 4A is highly complex and would require separate, extensive discussion outside the scope of this chapter. For an introduction into these matters, see Miller and Harrell, *op. cit.*, n.2, particularly Chs 4–10.

holding the special deposit, some courts limit liability to actions that are grossly negligent.[93]

NIGHT DEPOSITS

If a customer leaves a deposit in a banking institution's night depository, the legal relationship created is that of bailor–bailee. Therefore, the institution must exercise ordinary care to protect the deposit.[94] If the deposit is a general deposit, risk of loss is not assumed by the institution until it takes some unequivocal act with respect to the deposit such that a debtor–creditor relationship is created. An "unequivocal act" is an act or series of acts by a bank that objectively evidences that a deposit has been made, and that the depositor is not required to take further action (e.g. entering the deposit in a passbook, or crediting the account of the depositor).[95]

Prior to the institution's taking an unequivocal act, it generally is liable with respect to the night deposit only if it is negligent.[96] The depositor must show that a deposit was made or a bailment created, and must prove that the bank was negligent. If the trier-of-fact determines that the bank receives a deposit and that the depositor sustained a loss, the burden is upon the bank to show that it acted with reasonable care. Banking institutions may include in their night depository agreements a clause excluding the bank from liability if the night deposit is lost, stolen or destroyed. The courts are split concerning the enforceability of these clauses. Section 4-103 of the UCC provides that: "no agreement can disclaim a bank's responsibility for its own lack of good faith or failure to exercise ordinary care or can limit the measure of damages for such lack or failure."

FIDUCIARY DUTY OF DISCLOSURE

The law may impose a fiduciary or quasi-fiduciary duty of disclosure upon a banking institution.[97] As a general rule, a banker–customer relationship does not create a fiduciary duty of disclosure. However, a number of courts have held that if an institution assumes a "special relationship" of trust or confidence (as discussed above) with a customer, it assumes a fiduciary duty to disclose material facts. ("Materiality" is a question of fact to be determined in light of all the circumstances.) The duty may arise, for example, if the bank has acted as a financial adviser to a depositor for many years, and where the depositor has relied upon this advice.[98]

---

93. On the issue of "reasonable care", see, *inter alia, Owosso Masonic Temple Ass'n v. State Savings Bank*, 263 NW 771 (Mich. 1936); on the "gross negligence" standard, see *Miller v. Viola State Bank*, 246 P 517 (Kan. 1926).
94. See, *inter alia, Phillips Home Furnishing, Inc. v. Continental Bank*, 331 A.2d 840 (Pa. 1974).
95. E.g. *Bernstein v. Northwestern Nat. Bank*, 41 A.2d 440 (Pa. 1945).
96. E.g. *Bowling Corp. v. Long Island Nat. Bank*, 292 NYS 2d 562 (1968).
97. See *Annotation*, 70 ALR 3d 1344 (1976).
98. *Cf. Baylor v. Jordan*, 445 So.2d 254 (Ala. 1984).

Duties of the customer

A depositor owes a banking institution a duty of due care in its transactions with the bank. This duty includes a duty:

1. to report stolen cheques or a stolen passbook;
2. to draft withdrawal instruments carefully and unambiguously; and
3. to otherwise engage in reasonable conduct with respect to the account.[99]

In addition, the UCC provides that when a bank sends the customer an account statement, the customer has a duty to examine the statement reasonably and promptly, and to notify the bank of any alteration or unauthorised signature. A customer's failure to conduct an examination and to notify the bank when required will relieve the bank from liability.[100]

Termination of the relationship

The relationship between a bank and a customer, in the absence of a contractual provision to the contrary, is terminable at the will of either party. The bank may terminate the relationship by tendering the full amount of the deposit, and some courts require the bank to give reasonable notice prior to closing the account. A customer generally may terminate the relationship by withdrawing the funds from the account.[101]

Bank Secrecy Act

The Anti-Drug Abuse Act of 1986 amended the Bank Secrecy Act.[102] The rules require banks to aggregate multiple cash transactions of which they have knowledge, for the purpose of triggering the $10,000 Currency Transaction (CTR) reporting requirement. They also provide procedures for verifying a customer's identity, requiring retention of transaction account records for five years, reducing the reporting period from 30 to 15 days, and clarifying certain exemptions and definitions. Banks must also have procedures for monitoring compliance.[103]

Set-off [104]

A banking institution may secure a debt owed by a customer by imposing the banker's lien or by exercising the right of set-off. The bank account may also be

---

99. See *George Whalley Co.* v. *Nat. City Bank of Cleveland*, 380 N.E.2d 742 (Ohio 1977).
100. UCC §§ 4–406 and 407.
101. See generally *Elliot* v. *Capital City State Bank*, 103 NW 777 (Iowa 1905).
102. 12 USC § 1829b, 12 USC §§ 1951 *et seq.*, 31 USC §§ 5311 *et seq.*
103. See 31 USC §§ 5311 *et seq.*; 31 CFR parts 103 *et seq.*; Pringle & Allen, "Currency Transaction Reports, Criminal Referrals, and the Right to Privacy", 46 Consumer Fin. L.Q. Rep. 33 (1992).
104. For further discussion regarding the subject matter, see *BLM*, § 11.04(2), and Ch. 18 to *Lender Liability: Law and Litigation* (LL) (eds J. Norton and W.M. Baggett, 1997 latest update).

subject to garnishment by another creditor of the customer.[105] This section discusses the more commonly used right of set-off only.

When a depositor is indebted to a banking institution on a matured obligation, the institution has the right, subject to certain limitations, to set off, or reduce, the indebtedness by charging the debt to the customer's account. Although many states have authorised the right of set-off by statute, this right may exist even without express statutory authority. The right of set-off is derived from the law merchant, and from the equitable principle that "a man should not be compelled to pay one moment what he will be entitled to recover back the next". Set-off is also based on the theory that the depositor has impliedly consented to the set-off.[106] Loan agreement provisions often elaborate upon and expand a bank's common law right of set-off.

To exercise the right of set-off lawfully, the following requirements must be met:[107]

1. the debtor–creditor relationship must exist;
2. the funds must be owned by the debtor;
3. the indebtedness must be an existing one;
4. the debt must have matured;
5. a mutuality of obligation must exist; and
6. there must be an absence of deposit restrictions.

However, various legal theories exist for a borrower–depositor to bring a suit for wrongful set-off. The theories include[108]:

1. breach of the deposit contract, which also may entitle a successful plaintiff to reasonable attorney's fees;
2. wrongful set-off;
3. wrongful dishonour, if the set-off results in the wrongful dishonour of the depositor's cheques, which is often the case;
4. intentional interference with contractual relations;
5. intentional infliction of mental anguish and emotional stress;
6. conversion, which may be best plead if a special account is involved;
7. breach of a duty of good faith, if a special relationship or a prior contrary or mitigating course of conduct existed between the banking institution and the debtor;
8. negligence, but this may give rise to the application of the comparative negligence doctrine, which would not be available otherwise; and

105. On garnishment see, *inter alia*, Robison, "Creditor's Remedy: Garnishment of the Bank Account", 40 Ala. Law 438 (1979).
106. See Loyd, "The Development of Setoff", 64 U.Pa.L.Rev. 541 (1916).
107. See *FDIC* v. *Pioneer State Bank*, 382 A.2d 958 (N.J. 1977).
108. See discussion in Ch. 18 of LL, *op. cit.* This also discusses in detail various statutory and common law and constitutional limitations on the right of set-off and the sundry legal issues involved with competing claims of holders in due course, secured and garnishing creditors, the federal tax authorities, and trustees in bankruptcy. For a recent case considering a bank's set-off liability, see *Reliance Insurance Co.* v. *U.S. Bank of Washington, N.A.*, 9th Cir., 29 April 1998.

9. a claim under a state Deceptive Trade Practices Act (assuming the plaintiff can prove he or she was a consumer), which might allow special damages and reasonable attorney's fees.

Although a banking institution may have a right to set off an account, set-off is generally characterised as a privilege that may be waived by the institution. Thus, the institution is not liable to the depositor if it fails to set off the account.[109] The institution is also not liable, in most states, to sureties, indorsers, or others secondarily liable on the debt if it fails to set off an account, even though sufficient funds are available in the debtor's account to pay the debt at maturity.[110] In a few states, persons secondarily liable are released from liability on a debt if a banking institution fails to set off the debtor's account and the account would have been sufficient to satisfy the debt on the date the debt became due. In no event, however, is the institution under a duty to set off an account belonging to a person secondarily liable on the debt.[111]

THE BANKER (LENDER)–CUSTOMER (BORROWER) RELATIONSHIP

Legal bases of lending powers

The lending powers of banking institutions are derived from statute, and may be expanded upon or defined by statutory and judicial notions of "incidental" or implied powers, or (for non-bank lending subsidiaries of bank holding companies) by the statutory concept of "closely related to banking" powers.

Specifically with respect to national banks, these institutions derive their lending powers primarily from the National Banking Act. They are empowered to discount and to negotiate promissory notes, drafts, bills and exchanges, and other evidences of indebtedness, and to lend money on personal security.[112] Under the 1991 Banking Act,[113] the federal bank regulators are required to promulgate comprehensive real estate regulations concerning such matters as loan-to-value value appraisal standards, and aggregate lending limitations as to real estate related loans.[114]

The investment powers of banking institutions are also statutorily based. For example, national banks may invest only in:

1. obligations of the US Government and its agencies;

---

109. E.g. see discussion in *Doctor* v. *Riedel*, 71 N.W. 119 (Wisc. 1897).

110. See *Merdith* v. *First Nat. Bank*, 271 S.W.2d 274 (Ky. 1954).

111. *Cf. First Nat. Bank* v. *Petlz*, 35 A.218 (Pa. 1996) with *Bank of America Nat. Trust & Sav. Ass'n* v. *Liberty Nat. Bank & Trust Co.* 116 F. Supp 233 (W.D. Okla.), aff'd 218 F.2d 831 (10th Cir. 1955).

112. 12 USC 24 (Seventh).

113. Federal Deposit Insurance Corporation Improvement Act of 1991, § 304.

114. See joint agencies real estate lending standards, 57 Fed. Reg. 62, 890 (1992); text corrected 58 Fed. Reg. 4460 (1993); codified at 12 CFR pts 34, 208, 365, 545 and 563.

2. assessment and revenue bonds issued by states and their political subdivisions;
3. foreign corporate or government bonds;
4. domestic debt instruments; and
5. stock in corporations that engage in bank-related activities.[115]

Limitations on available funds

Banking institutions primarily derive their funds for loans and investments by accepting deposits and by borrowing from non-depository creditors such as central banks, other banking institutions and the general public. Borrowing limitations on banking institutions may be statutory, regulatory or supervisory. Limitations on funds available for loans and investments include reserve requirements, liquidity requirements and practices, and permitted investment requirements.

FRB reserve requirements

All "depository institutions" (which would include all federally insured banking institutions and all banking institutions eligible for federal insurance) are required to maintain legal reserves pursuant to statute and to FRB Regulation D. Regulation D provides three categories of deposits for purposes of reserve requirements: transaction accounts, non-personal time deposits and Eurodollar liabilities. Regulation D provides, from time to time, specified percentage reserve requirements for each of the above categories of deposits.[116]

Liquidity requirements

National banks (unlike federal savings associations and federal credit unions) are not subject to any formal liquidity requirements. However, such banks are subject to liquidity requirements via the bank examination and supervisory processes and the formal bank "CAMEL" rating system (the "L" being for liquidity).

Single borrower lending limits

The National Banking Act contains a specific limitation, under 12 USC s. 84, on the amount of money that may be loaned to a single borrower (other federal banking institutions are subject to equivalent limitations). This limitation is commonly called the "single borrower" limitation. The primary objective of this limitation is to safeguard the bank's depositors by spreading the loans among a relatively large number of persons engaged in different lines of business. 12 USC

---

115. See 12 CFR § 1.
116. See 12 CFR § 204.

s. 84 sets a single borrower lending ceiling 15 per cent of a national bank's unimpaired capital and surplus, and the creation of an additional fully secured 10 per cent ceiling.

The 1982 Banking Act conferred upon the Comptroller authority to prescribe implementing regulations and to issue rules for aggregation or combination of loans. These aggregation regulations are highly complex and fact sensitive and comprise general aggregation rules and specific rules for partnerships, corporate groups, and foreign governments. Special attribution rules apply to guaranty situations, and the single-borrower rules contain sundry exemptions and exceptions, special situations (e.g. advances and commitments and loan participations) and special definitions.[117]

The single-borrower rules impose liability upon directors of a national bank for knowingly violating, or knowingly permitting a bank office or agent to violate, any provision of the National Banking Act, including the lending limit provisions. Accordingly, a director who consents to, or participates in, an excessive loan is liable for damages suffered by the bank, its shareholders or other persons. In assessing liability, the full amount of the lent credit that exceeded the lending limit (not simply the excess) and any subsequent money lent is the maximum potential liability, and a responsible director will be liable for such amounts until all of the outstanding amounts of such credits have been paid in full.[118] A disagreeing director should formally dissent from approving such loan(s).

Violations of the statutory lending limit provisions will be cited by the Comptroller in its examination report, may form the basis of an administrative enforcement action, and may give rise to a derivative cause of action by a bank shareholder.

In addition to the statutory liability under the National Banking Act, directors of national banks have common law duties to exercise due care, prudence and undivided loyalties in their role as directors of the bank.[119] It should be noted that a banking institution may not raise the statutory lending limitation as a defence to avoid or limit its underlying contractual obligations with a non-conspiring borrower. Conversely, a borrower or guarantor cannot raise a bank lender's limit violations as a defence to payment on a violative loan.

Credit allocation

Banking institutions are subject to statutory requirements that directly affect credit allocation. Examples of such requirements are found in the Community Reinvestment Act and the Equal Credit Opportunity Act. In addition, the regulatory agencies have recently been enforcing common "fair lending" guidelines.

---

117. See 12 CFR § 32. For further discussion of single borrower lending limits, Norton, "Lending Limits on National Banks Under the 1982 Banking Act", 101 Banking L.J. 122 (1984).
118. See *Larimore* v. *Conover*, 1775 F.2d 890 (1985), rev'd 789 F.2d 1244 (7th Cir. 1986); and *Tirso del Junco* v. *Conover*, 682 F.2d 1338 (9th Cir. 1982), *cert. den.* 103 S. Ct. 74.
119. See § 410 of the 1982 Garn-St Germain Banking Act.

Community Reinvestment Act (CRA)

The primary purpose of the CRA is to encourage financial institutions to meet the credit needs of the local communities they serve, consistent with the safe and sound operation of the institution. This purpose is achieved through examination of these institutions by the appropriate federal financial supervisory agency. The CRA applies to all "regulated financial institutions" (i.e. an institution whose deposits are federally insured). The CRA does not establish specific requirements for bank performance, but seeks to use the bank's examination and application processes as a device for fostering acceptable "standards of performance". The standard for assessing the performance of each financial institution is subjective; it asks whether each institution serves the convenience and needs of the community in which it is chartered to do business.[120] The CRA particularly affects examination and application (e.g. acquisitions) standards and the Statute (and related regulations) are being aggressively enforced.

Equal Credit Opportunity Act (ECOA)

The ECOA became effective on 28 October 1974 and has been called the first civil rights statute to deal with consumer credit.[121] The premise of the statute is that all consumers and business should have an equal opportunity to obtain credit. While not expressly directed to the allocation of credit, the ECOA does prohibit a lender from allocating or extending credit on a discriminatory basis. This prohibition covers both bank and non-bank lenders and covers all forms of credit transactions (including even the application stage).

As amended, the statute prohibits discrimination on the basis of sex and marital status, race, colour, religion, national origin, age (provided the applicant has the capacity to contract), and receipt of public assistance benefits. The ECOA prohibits discrimination against a person who in good faith exercises a right under the Consumer Credit Protection Act (CCPA). The FRB has the statutory responsibility to implement the ECOA and has done so through its Regulation B. Regulation B provides the following general rule:[122]

A *creditor* shall not *discriminate* against an *applicant* on a *prohibited basis* regarding *any* aspect of a *credit transaction*. [emphasis added]

Fair Lending Initiative

In March 1994, the federal banking regulators issued an "Interagency Policy Statement" to clarify, regroup and even redefine what constitutes lending discrimination.[123] Through regulatory enforcement practices, the bank

120. See 12 USC §§ 2901 *et seq.*
121. See 15 USC §§ 16901 *et seq.*
122. See 12 CFR § 202.4.
123. See 59 Fed. Reg. 18266 (15 April 1994).

regulators and US Justice Department, effectively, are trying "to mix and match" disparate provisions under differing pieces of federal legislation (*e.g.* Equal Credit Opportunity Act, Fair Housing Act, Community Reinvestment Act, Home Mortgage Disclosure Act and the 1994 Riegle-Neal Act) in order to maximise and expand enforcement in the so-called "fair-lending" area.[124]

Loans to special borrowers (affiliates and insiders)

Federal banking laws restrict extensions of credit to, and investments in, special parties including:

1. bank examiners (as to whom there is generally an absolute prohibition)[125]; and
2. loans to affiliates and insiders (as to which there are severe limitations).[126]

Also, there are federal bribery laws and regulations respecting officials and employees of federal banking institutions that are very comprehensive, with broad definitional embraces and with stiff civil and criminal penalties.[127]

Usury violations

Banking institutions are subject to limitations respecting maximum rates of interest on loan transactions. These limitations have traditionally been a matter of state law, and these laws often vary as to whether the transaction is consumer or personal, or is business or commercial in nature. The comprehensiveness and severity of state usury laws vary considerably from state to state, with some states even having no usury laws.[128] However, federal pre-emption statutes, over the past decade or so, have been enacted in certain lending areas,[129] with national banks having their own special federal usury statute.[130] Violation of usury laws may result in severe statutory penalties.[131] It is possible to purge usury violations under certain conditions, although this may not always be practical.[132] In commercial loan transactions the structuring of transactions may be made so that through valid choice of law provisions the most advantageous usury treatment for the lender can be obtained.

---

124. For detailed analyses of recent fair lending initiatives see Vartanian, Ledig *et al.*, *The Fair Lending Guide* (2 vols. 1998).
125. See 12 USC § 210.
126. See 12 USC § 371c on affiliate loans, as discussed in detail in *BLM*, at § 8.06; and FRB, "Regulation O", 12 CFR § 215 on insider loans.
127. E.g. Comprehensive Crime Control Act of 1984 (as amended).
128. See generally Norton *et al.* (eds), *Commercial Loan Documentation Guide*, Ch. 20 (1997).
129. E.g. Monetary Control Act of 1980, §§ 501 *et seq.*
130. See 12 USC § 95.
131. E.g. 12 USC § 96.
132. See *Helms* v. *First Ala. Bank of Gadsen, N.A.*, 386 So.2d 450 (Civ. App. Ala. 1980). For detailed discussion of US usury laws, see, *inter alia*, J. Norton and M. Baggett, *Lender Liability*, Ch. 13 (1997).

Legal considerations: commercial loans

A commercial loan may involve a number of special legal considerations involving securities credit ("margin" requirements),[133] antitrust (e.g., antitying arrangements),[134] and interlocking directorate restrictions.[135] Bankruptcy law,[136] securities laws (e.g., with participation arrangements)[137] and truth-in-lending laws[138] must also be considered. Pervasive lender liability concerns have become looming during the past decade. This section will consider briefly the questions of fiduciary and other lender liability theories.

Fiduciary duties

The general state of the law is that a lender, solely by virtue of the lending relationship, is not in a fiduciary position with the borrower, but is in a contractual, creditor–debtor relationship. Notwithstanding movements of the case law in the bank–depositor area to create a fiduciary relationship between a bank and its customers, such cases should (in the author's view) be limited to depositor situations (if then and only in special circumstances) and not extended to commercial, arm's length lending situations. This being said, however, additional facts and circumstances (including the nature of a pre-existing lending relationship, prior course of conduct, reasonable expectations of the borrowers, inordinate lender control, and ongoing rendering of advice to a borrower who relies on such advice) may give rise to a "quasi-fiducial" or "special relationship" between lender and borrower, which at minimum would create an implied lender duty of good faith and fair dealing.[139] In addition, under either the agency or inadvertent partnership theories, a fiduciary relationship may arise from the very nature of the theories themselves.

Obviously, if a fiduciary relationship exists, the lender will be deemed to have far greater duties than those arising under a loan contract (e.g. due care, undivided loyalty, confidentiality, fair dealing, material disclosure) and may be charged with the burden to show the fairness of the lender's conduct, and may have its claim subordinated in a bankruptcy proceeding.[140] A legal issue of concern to a bank is whether a fiduciary duty exists with respect to the use of information submitted to it by a borrower in connection with a loan. Prudent counselling may require the bank to assume that a fiduciary duty does exist concerning the dissemination of non-public information to a third party or to another department of the bank. In addition, dissemination of "inside"

133. E.g. FRB regulation on margin credit, 12 CFR § 221.
134. E.g. 12 USC § 1972.
135. E.g. FRB "Regulation L", 12 CFR § 212.
136. See LL, Ch. 8 (1992).
137. *Ibid.*, Ch. 6.
138. E.g. see FRB "Regulation 2", 12 CFR § 226.
139. *Cf. Commercial Colton Co. v. United Cal. Bank*, 209 Cal Rptr. 551 (1985) with *Copesky* v. *Superior Court of San Diego County*, 229 Cal. App.3d 678 (1991). The most recent trend is for the courts to deny the existence of any "special relationship".
140. See LL, at § 5.05.

information could have federal security law implications. The fiduciary standards on "insider" loans set forth in the Financial Institutions Regulatory and Interest Rate Contract Act of 1978 (FIRA), as enhanced by the 1991 Banking Acts and implementing federal regulation, are applicable to commercial loan transactions.

Emerging theories of lender liabilities

Litigation against lenders by disgruntled borrowers or affected third parties is increasing. These suits may be based on one or more of numerous innovative legal theories, commonly used theories being as follows.

CONTROL THEORIES

If a lender becomes so entwined in control over the conduct of a borrower and in a manner that goes beyond the bounds of prudent lending practices, a lender may find itself judicially characterised as the principal, partner or joint venturer, alter ego, or fiduciary of the borrower. This, in turn, could expose the lender to liability for third party claims against the borrower.[141] In addition, such degrees of inordinate control could, given the proper circumstances, create lender liability under federal securities,[142] tax,[143] and bankruptcy laws.[144]

COMMON LAW TORT AND FRAUD

The *Restatement (Second) of Torts* asserts that one who aids another may be liable to the other for physical harm resulting from his failure to exercise care to perform his undertaking if:

1. his failure to exercise such care increases the risk of harm; or
2. the harm is suffered because of the other's reliance upon the undertaking.

Building upon this theory of legal duties, borrowers have argued that where a lender provides specific assistance to a debtor or assumes control (directly or indirectly) over a borrower's business, and the debtor relies on the creditor, the lender is liable to the borrower for any failure to perform such assumed duties with reasonable care. In addition, in instances where a lender can be shown to have misrepresented a material fact to the borrower in order to coerce the borrower into some action, or shown to be otherwise in bad faith in the lending relationship, common law actions for misrepresentational fraud, duress and tortious interference may lie.[145]

141. E.g. *A.G. Jensen Farms Co.* v. *Cargill, Inc.*, 309 N.W.2d 285 (Minn. 1981).
142. See § 15 of federal 1933 Securities Act and § 20(a) of federal 1934 Securities Exchange Act.
143. See federal Internal Revenue Code §§ 3402, 3505 and 6672.
144. E.g. § 510 of Federal Bankruptcy Code (equitable subordination).
145. For a classic lender liability claim, see *State Nat. Bank of El Paso* v. *Farah Manufacturing Co.*, 678 S.W.2d 661 (Tex. Civ. App. 1984) (writ granted but dismissed by agreement).

UCC AND NON-UCC "GOOD FAITH"

UCC s. 1–203 states: "Every contract or duty within this Act imposes an obligation of good faith in its performance or engagement." "Good faith" [under UCC s. 1–201 (19)] is, in turn, defined as "honesty in fact in the conduct or transaction". This contract-based duty has been held in certain cases to apply to the conduct of lenders in enforcing security arrangements coming within the scope of the UCC.[146] If a "special relationship" is deemed to exist, a tort-based duty of "good faith" outside the UCC may be implied.[147] It is important (for damages and other purposes) to know that UCC bad faith claims are contractual (and not tort) claims.

ENVIRONMENTAL LAW CONCERNS

A lender may incur significant risk of liability under federal and state environmental laws with respect to its control over a borrower's property which has an adverse environmental impact.[148] Lenders who secure their loans through security interests in real property are becoming increasingly concerned with the impact on their interests of hazardous waste clean up statutes under federal and state laws, especially under the federal Comprehensive Environmental Response, Compensation and Liability Act (CERCLA). CERCLA imposes liability for the cost of hazardous waste clean up on a broad range of people, including former and current owners or operators of a site. Responsible parties are strictly liable, and liability is joint and several. Lenders can take advantage of certain narrowly drawn defences to liability.[149]

Asset classification, allowances for losses, and capital and CRA ratings

The various bank regulators employ loan classification procedures in their examination procedures. For example the Comptroller, FDIC, FRB and Conference of State Bank Examiners have adopted Uniform Guidelines for the classification of loans. This asset classification is: "substandard", "doubtful" and "loss".[150]

Related to the classification of assets is the responsibility of management of banking institutions to maintain an adequate allowance for loan losses and lease losses (ALLL), and to establish and follow a system of written procedures to ensure complete analysis of all factors pertinent to the evaluation of the ALLL. Failure to do so could result in an institution filing a false or misleading regulatory report (e.g. a "call report") or financial statement, which could lead

---

146. E.g. *K.M.C. Co.* v. *Irving Trust Co.*, 757 F.2d 752 (6th Cir. 1985).
147. Cf. *Kraus/Jewell* v. *Bank of America*, 248 Cal. Rptr 217 (1988) with *Copesky* v. *Superior Court of San Diego County*, 229 (Cal. App.3d 678 (1991)).
148. E.g. *US* v. *Maryland Bank and Trust Co.*, 632 F.Supp. 573 (D.Md. 1986).
149. In April 1992, the federal Environmental Protection Agency issued a "safeharbor rule" for secured lenders (40 CFR §§ 300.1100 *et seq.*); and the US Congress enacted the 1996 US Conservation Act to clarify and to minimise a secured lender's environmental liability.
150. E.g. FRB Reg. Serv. Locator No. 3-1501 (7 May 1979).

to regulatory action (including a cease and desist order, civil money penalties, or a suspension or removal order), or could result in a securities law violation.[151] Also, under the 1991 Banking Acts, the federal regulators have instituted a separate classification procedure (with significant functional consequences) for the capital adequacy of a federal banking institution.[152] All the above institution-related ratings can have a significant impact upon the decision-making and operational processes of the institutions in the lending area.

Capital adequacy regulation and capital-based supervision

Recent years have witnessed the rise of capital adequacy as a paramount concern of bank regulators. US banking institutions are subject to a rigorous risk-based capital adequacy scheme based on the Basle Accord. These regulations (backed up by significant enforcement authority) are having a substantial impact on bank growth, lending and off-balance sheet policies.[153]

The 1991 Banking Act also introduces a "capital-based" supervisory scheme which empowers the federal banking agencies to impose corrective measures on undercapitalised depository institutions, with the scope of mandatory and permissible measures becoming progressively restrictive as an institution's capital declines. Also, an institution's ability to engage in new powers, to take brokered deposits, and to pay dividends are becoming dependent on an institution's capital strength.[154]

Secured transactions

The taking of collateral to support a financing arrangement in the United States will normally be a matter of state commercial law, though other state and federal laws may apply depending on the type of collateral (e.g. real estate, aircraft, vessels, motor vehicles, etc.) or borrower (e.g. a consumer or agricultural borrower). Under state commercial law, Art. 9 of the UCC will apply to the attachment and perfection of security interests in personal property (including intangibles such as certain types of accounts) and fixtures. Article 8 of the UCC is also relevant as to security interests in investment securities (documented and undocumented), and Art. 7 as to warehouse receipts, bills of lading and other documents of title. Security interests in real property are generally governed by state real property, mortgage and foreclosure laws.[155]

The two key concepts under UCC Art. 9 are attachment, and perfection of the security interest. Assuming value is given and the debtor has rights in the collateral, attachment normally arises through a written security agreement

151. E.g. Comptroller of the Currency, *Banking Circular* No. 201 (31 May 1985).
152. See new § 38(b)(1) of the Federal Deposit Insurance Act.
153. E.g. see 12 CFR § 3. For further discussion, see *inter alia*, Norton, *Revising International Bank Supervisory Standards*.
154. See, *inter alia*, Gail and Norton, *supra*, n. 28.
155. See, generally, J. Norton *et al.*, *Commercial Finance Guide* (1997).

legally binding upon the debtor and third parties with notice or knowledge of the agreement. Perfection is a legal term of art which often determines the priority of the security interest and is accomplished (as provided under the Code) by the public filing of a "financing statement", or in some instances (e.g. securities or CDs) by possession, or in a few instances automatically by operation of law (e.g. small purchase money interests in consumer goods).[156]

Whether a security interest is legally attached and perfected will have significant legal consequences in the event the lender needs to realise upon the collateral and in the event the borrower becomes a debtor in a bankruptcy proceeding. The realisation of a security interest may be subject to (in addition to contract and UCC law, and, if relevant, bankruptcy law) common law restraints (some of which may be embodied under the UCC) as to unconscionability, "good faith", single-action rule, and adhesion contracts.

In summary, because of the existence of 50 state jurisdictions (which give rise to numerous conflict of laws problems), the complexities of the UCC (particularly Art. 9), the differing legal rules and practices as to differing types of collateral and the uncertainties created by bankruptcy law, secured lending in the United States is a highly specialised area of banking and legal practice.

The advent of asset securitisation

A popular, new balance sheet strategy for banking institutions is selling a portion of their loan portfolios to investors. In a technical sense, "asset securitisation" refers to the process of raising funds through the issuance of marketable securities backed by future cash flow from income producing assets. This process of "asset securitisation" has created a new generation of asset-backed securities, which were first introduced to the market place in 1985. These securities, similar to mortgage-backed securities, are backed by financial assets such as automobile or credit card receivables having a predetermined payment stream and an average life of over one year. The economic effect of asset securitisation may be thought of as the "conversion" of income-producing assets into marketable securities. The structuring of securitisation transactions can be highly complex involving a "pass-through", "participation", or secured debt structure.

In addition, nearly all publicly issued sale and debt structured asset-backed securities transactions have had sufficient credit enhancement to obtain one of the two highest investment grade ratings available. Securitisation in the United States is fraught with legal problems and concerns, including:

1. federal and state securities laws;
2. legal investment laws;
3. legal disclosure requirements;
4. Investment Company Act of 1940;

156. See, *inter alia*, A. Harrell (ed.), *The Law of Personal Property Secured Transactions Under the Uniform Commercial Code and Related Laws* (1992).

5. federal taxation;
6. accounting treatment;
7. bankruptcy and insolvency; and
8. special regulatory concerns (e.g. powers issues, finance subsidiary regulations, reserve requirements, collateralisation of deposits, and Glass-Steagall (see below)).[157]

TRUST FUNCTIONS

Banking institutions may establish certain trust relationships (which will be governed by a complex of state common and statutory laws and federal banking laws). This section focuses briefly on the agency powers as to national banks and on the trust powers of national banks with emphasis on the issue of self-dealing.[158]

Duties as agent

A bank may be given the power to act as agent for its customers and others in areas incidental to the ordinary business of banking. A bank's agency may be based upon and limited by a letter of instructions from its principal. However, a bank acting as agent usually is empowered to do all acts necessary and appropriate to accomplish the purpose of the agency. A bank may act as agent for both parties to a single transaction, provided it has the knowledge and consent of each. The rights and liabilities of the bank are determined by the general principles of agency in effect within its jurisdiction. As such, a bank serving as agent must exercise ordinary care to act according to the instructions of its principal. The bank must also act with loyalty and in good faith. A claim for damages in negligence for a breach of the duty of care owed a customer requires proof of a causal relationship between the bank's negligence and a specific loss. A breach of duty by the bank may be ratified or waived by the principal. Recovery may also be barred by laches.[159]

Banks are commonly made agents for the collection and remittance of claims, notes, and lease payments. A bank may, as agent for its customer, negotiate a loan. Banks not prohibited by their charter have the power to lend and invest money for their depositors. A bank is not liable for ordinary losses occurring as a result of such lending or investment as long as it exercises due diligence and good faith. State statutes and case law dictate the rights, duties, and liabilities of banks acting as trustees.

National banks may act as an agent for their customers in a variety of circumstances. Thus, for example, a national bank located in a town with a

---

157. See generally J. Norton *et al.* (eds), *Asset Securitization*, 2nd edn (1996).

158. For more detailed and broader discussion, see Comptroller of the Currency, *Handbook for National Trust Examiners*, and *BLM*, at § 4.03[1][d].

159. See generally ALI, *Restatement (Second) on Agency*.

population of 5,000 or less, may act as an agent for any insurance company, or for the procurement of real estate loans. National banks may act as agents for customers by providing messenger services by means of an armoured car or otherwise, so long as it is agreed that the messenger is an agent of the customer and not the bank. A national bank may act as a "finder" to bring together a buyer and a seller. National banks may act as an agent for a customer in disbursing pay to the customer's employees, either in cash or by crediting employee accounts. Also, a national bank may act in an agency capacity in providing securities brokerage services: such services may include buying and selling shares in mutual funds and units in unit investment trust publicly offered real estate limited partnership interests.[160]

Trust powers generally

Since 1962, the Comptroller of the Currency has been empowered to grant a national bank the right to act in a fiduciary capacity that state banks, trust companies, or other corporations that come into competition with national banks are permitted to act in under the laws of the state where the national bank is located. The grant and exercise of these powers will not be deemed to be in contravention of state laws whenever the laws of the state permit the state banks, trust companies, or other corporations that compete with national banks to exercise similar powers. The exercise of fiduciary powers is not one of the activities authorised for national banks by virtue of the bank's certificate to commence business. The exercise of these powers requires separate approval from the Comptroller. A limitation on the Comptroller's authority to grant fiduciary powers to national banks is that he cannot authorise activities that would contravene state law.[161]

The responsibility for the exercise of fiduciary powers by a national bank is vested in the bank's board of directors. The directors may delegate the administration of fiduciary powers to officers, employees, or committees. All officers and employees to whom the administration is delegated must be adequately bonded. The bank must have legal counsel to advise the bank and its trust officers on fiduciary matters. No employee can serve as a trust officer for two competing banks.[162]

The board of directors must formally accept fiduciary accounts; however, this responsibility may be delegated to an employee of the bank. Upon the acceptance of an account, a prompt review of the assets of the account is conducted. All assets held in a fiduciary account must be reviewed at least annually and within 15 months of the last review to determine the advisability of retaining or disposing of assets.

National banks exercising fiduciary powers are required to develop written

160. See generally *BLM*, Ch. 4.
161. See generally, 12 CFR § 9.
162. 12 CFR § 9.7(a)(1).

policies to ensure that federal securities laws are complied with and to ensure that national bank trust departments will not use material inside information in connection with any decision or recommendation to purchase or sell a security. Written policies must also cover decisions or recommendations to purchase or sell securities.

National banks exercising fiduciary powers must segregate assets held in a fiduciary capacity from the general assets of the bank, and must keep records of all transactions under the bank's fiduciary powers. Furthermore, the investments of each fiduciary account must be placed in the joint custody of two or more employees. A national bank may, however, permit assets of fiduciary accounts to be deposited elsewhere. The assets of each account must either be held separate from the assets of all other accounts, or adequately identified as property of the relevant account.

When a national bank with fiduciary powers seeks to render trust services requiring expertise that it does not possess, the services may be provided in several ways. The bank may act as co-fiduciary with another party. As an alternative arrangement, a national bank appointed as a fiduciary can contract with a bank or service corporation for information, advice, or facilities necessary to render adequate trust services. As a final alternative, another bank that is able to render adequate trust services can be appointed as fiduciary over the account with the bank seeking the services acting as a contact with the beneficiaries and performing duties of a local nature.

A national bank and an affiliated state bank can consolidate their trust operations provided the bank's trust assets and accounting are segregated. A national bank acting as custodian for other banks is not permitted to commingle the securities it holds in the fiduciary capacity with its own securities. Such commingling would violate 12 USC s. 92a(c) as implemented by 12 CFR s. 9.13(a). Bank owned securities may be placed under the control of the trust department if they are clearly identified and are segregated in a formal custodial account. Under 12 USC s. 92, 12 CFR s. 9 and Comptroller examination practices, special rules and requirements and standards exist for funds awaiting investment or distribution, investment of funds held as fiduciary, and collective investment funds.

Banks generally, when operating as a trustee, are subject to the common law "prudent person" rule in the administration of the trust, which standard has been interpreted as:

a trustee must only exercise *sound* discretion, conduct himself faithfully, and manage funds entrusted to him as men of prudence, discretion, and intelligence would manage their own affairs, having due regard for the safety of the corpus and probable income.[163]

Trust relationship and self-dealing concerns

As to the issue of self-dealing, unless authorised by the instrument creating the fiduciary relationship, by state law or by court order, funds held in a fiduciary

163. E.g. *First Alabama Bank of Montgomery, N.A.* v. *Martin*, 425 So.2d 415 (Ala. 1982).

capacity by a national bank cannot be invested in stock or obligations of, or property acquired from the bank or its directors, officers, employees, or from individuals or organisations with which there exists a connection or interest that might affect the exercise of the best judgement of the bank in making the investment or acquiring the property.[164]

The Comptroller of the Currency presumes that an advisory director and the immediate family of a director are individuals with whom there exists this connection. Director-related companies are presumed to be organisations with which there exists an interest that might affect the judgement of the bank unless these companies are national concerns whose securities are widely traded and acceptable as securities for fiduciary investment.[165]

A national bank cannot invest its fiduciary funds in its own stock unless authorised by the trust instrument, by court order, or by state law. This prohibition applies to purchases of bank stock and to acquisition of bank stock through exchanges or debt retirements. Similarly, a national bank in its fiduciary capacity cannot invest in bank property such as real estate loans or other loans sold by the bank through repurchase agreements. An exception to the rule occurs where the governing instrument authorises the retention of assets, in which case the settlor has waived the rule of undivided loyalty with respect to assets originally held in the account. In addition, repurchase agreements should not be purchased from or sold to the commercial department of the bank for a trust account unless authorised by the trust instrument, court order or state law. Any other transactions by a national bank trust department in its own bank repurchase agreements are considered to be in violation of the Comptroller's regulation.[166]

When authorised by the trust instrument a national bank in its fiduciary capacity can invest in the securities of its affiliates. Investment decisions must be made with sole reference to the needs of the account. Anything which indicates to the Comptroller that the bank was motivated by other considerations will prompt criticism, especially where the investment appears to constitute an undue percentage of account assets or the investment is inferior to others that might have been obtained.[167]

Property held by a national bank in a fiduciary capacity cannot be sold or transferred, by loan or otherwise, to the bank, its directors, officers or employees, or to individuals or organisations with which there exists a connection or interest that might affect the exercise of the best judgement of the bank in selling or transferring the property. The property also cannot be sold or transferred to affiliates of the bank or their directors, officers, or employees. However, property can be sold or transferred to these persons:[168]

164. 12 CFR § 9.12(a).
165. See generally *Comptroller's Trust Handbook*, Opinions 9.3410 and 9.34000.
166. *Ibid.*, Opinions 9.3000, 9.3220, 9.3225, and 9.3020; Comptroller's *Trust Banking Circular* No. 22; and 12 CFR § 9.12.
167. See *Comptroller's Trust Handbook*, Opinion 9.3300.
168. 12 CFR § 9.12(b).

1. if authorised by the instrument creating the fiduciary relationship, or by court order or state law; or
2. if the bank has been advised by its counsel in writing that it has incurred a contingent liability and it desires to relieve itself from the liability, in which case the sale or transfer can take place with the approval of the board of directors provided the fiduciary account is reimbursed in cash at no loss; or
3. if the bank is administering a collective investment fund, it may purchase for its own account from such fund any defaulted fixed-income investment held by such fund, if, in the judgement of the board of directors, the cost of segregation of such investment would be greater than the difference between its market value and its principal amount plus interest and penalty charges due; or
4. if required by the Comptroller of the Currency.

A sale of trust assets by a broker within a short period of time after their acquisition to a party with whom there exists a connection, or to an organisation in which there exists an interest that might affect the judgement of the bank, presumptively violates the self-dealing regulation, 12 CFR s. 9.12. However, if these assets have been held in inventory by a broker for a reasonable period of time, such as a year, and bona fide sales efforts have failed, the presumption is satisfactorily rebutted. Section 9.12 not only controls the sale of trust property to persons with whom there exists a connection that might affect the judgement of the bank, but also controls sales through these persons.

It is unlawful for a national bank to lend to any director, officer, or employee of the bank any funds held in trust by the bank in its fiduciary capacity. Any person making or receiving a prohibited loan is subject to a fine of not more than $5,000, or imprisonment for not more than 5 years, or both. The statute makes no exceptions with respect to the lending of trust funds to officers, directors, or employees of the bank.[169] Therefore, the statute would prevail over any authority contained in the trust instrument, beneficiary consent, or a court order purporting to authorise the transaction. Obligations of directors, officers, or employees received in kind do not come within the statutory prohibition unless the obligations are renewed or carried past their due in the discretion of the bank. Demand loans of officers, directors, or employees received in kind in a trust department should be paid within a reasonable time. In an estate, a reasonable time would normally be the period of administration. These obligations should not be transferred by a bank as executor to itself as trustee under the will.[170]

In recent releases concerning self-dealing, the Comptroller of the Currency has warned that trust departments which accept financial incentives must pass those incentives on to the accounts which have had their assets invested in the

169. See 12 USC § 92(a)(h).
170. *Comptroller's Trust Handbook*, Opinion 9.3650.

fund. Such financial incentives include discounts, rebates and other financial incentives. Consistent with the Banking Circular on this topic, an interpretive letter concluded that utilisation of hardware and software obtained by a mutual fund for purposes other than order entry in that fund was a conflict of interest under 12 CFR s. 9.12.[171]

TWO CONCLUDING OBSERVATIONS: EXPANDING POWERS (SECURITIES AND INSURANCE ACTIVITIES) AND THE RISKS OF THE JUDICIAL PROCESS

This part will briefly discuss banks' attempts to engage in the securities business and will conclude with some general observations on the business and legal risks inherent for banking institutions in the US judicial processes.

Expanding powers

The increasingly convergent and competitive environment between banking institutions and non-banking financial institutions, the legislative and regulatory deregulation process, the economic recession and the impact of capital adequacy regulations are some of the factors which in recent years have turned banking institutions' attention to fee-generating activities instead of (or in addition to) traditional lending activities. A prime area for bank movement has been the securities area; however, a major difficulty for banks to enter this and other areas of business opportunities (e.g. the insurance area, which is another prime business target) has been legal: federal statutes place very significant restraints on such new activities, and state statutes may have an impact also. In addition, such new activities raise numerous common law considerations (including those of legal duties and conflicts of interest).

To engage in any banking activity, the activity (under federal statute) must be either authorised expressly or impliedly as "incidental" to banking (for bank holding companies the similar, but not identical concept is "closely related to banking"). In addition, respecting securities activities, banking institutions run headlong into the federal Glass-Steagall Act of 1933. Also, statutory barriers exist respecting limitations on a bank's involvement in insurance activities.

Erosion

In the middle of the Great Depression of the 1930s, the United States Congress passed the Banking Act of 1933. Four provisions of this Act (ss. 16, 20, 21 and 32) have become popularly known as the Glass-Steagall Act. These provisions attempt to separate commercial banking from investment banking because

---

171. See Comptroller of the Currency, *Staff Interpretive Letter* 214.

affiliations between these institutions were perceived as one of the main factors which contributed to the stock market crash of 1929 and the Great Depression. By this separation, Congress sought to restore public confidence in the commercial banking system. As such, the roots of the Glass-Steagall "wall" are steeped in strong and broad public policy considerations.[172] The Glass-Steagall Act does not, however, create an absolute barrier between commercial and investment banking.[173]

The four Glass-Steagall provisions do not cover the same institutions; and, accordingly, the provisions have loopholes. For example, s. 16 applies *only* to national banks and state FRS member banks.[174] Section 20 covers national banks and FRS member state banks and their corporate affiliates (i.e. a bank subsidiary, a holding company parent of the bank, and a non-bank subsidiary of the holding company) that are "principally engaged" in the securities business.[175] Section 21 (the rough converse of s. 16) covers *any* institution that is simultaneously and directly engaged in the securities business and that of deposit-taking, but it does not embrace these institutions' affiliates.[176] Section 32 precludes interlocking management between an institution "primarily engaged" in the securities business and any FRS member bank.[177] The affiliation prohibited by this section relates only to national banks and FRS member state banks (and not to non-FRS state banks or to thrift institutions), but it would affect a covered bank's subsidiary or parent company (or subsidiary thereof) "primarily engaged" in the securities business, as well as any other "securities" firm having interlocking management with a covered bank. Thus, while comprehensive, the Glass-Steagall "wall" is not all encompassing. There are a limited number of opportunities for banking institutions and their lawyers to explore (or, perhaps more accurately, to exploit).

Today, the main inroads to the Glass-Steagall prohibitions are being made through FRB s. 20 orders under the federal Bank Holding Company Act and through judicial interpretations. In terms of the market-place realities, a number of banking institutions are exploring the outer boundaries of the "not principally engaged" exception in the securities business of s. 20 of the Glass-Steagall Act with respect to securities activities of bank affiliates.

Also, though the Glass-Steagall Act represents a significant barrier to expanding business opportunities in an increasingly competitive and homogeneous financial services market-place, the Act also clearly reflects the long-standing and overarching public policy concern in bank regulation: the "safety and soundness" of the American banking system.

---

172. See, *inter alia*, Norton, "Up Against 'The Wall': Glass-Steagall and the Dilemma of a Deregulated ('Reregulated') Banking Environment", 42 Bus. Law 327 (1987).

173. E.g. 12 USC § 24 (Seventh) buying and selling securities on the order of and for the account of their customers.

174. 12 USC § 24 (Seventh).

175. 12 USC § 377.

176. 12 USC § 378.

177. 12 USC § 78.

While the main battleground for product expansion of securities-related services by banking institutions remains the Glass-Steagall Act, another unresolved issue is the proper vehicle for conducting any permissible services. An example of this structural dilemma has been the debate between the regulators and Congress about how best to expand the securities and other powers of banks. For instance, the Treasury Department and the FRB would like to see any expansion of powers through separate non-bank subsidiaries of holding companies. This vehicle is thought to be more identifiable for regulatory purposes and would, to some degree, insulate the bank from liability or loss exposure (i.e. create "firewalls" between the securities subsidiary and the bank). The Comptroller, at times, has indicated that such an approach may stress form over substance, and he appears not to be concerned by direct bank or bank subsidiary involvement in selected securities activities, provided adequate regulatory safeguards are effected. Further, the consequence of recent lender movements into the investment banking area and specific involvement in highly leveraged acquisition financings will likely lead to an expansion of lender liability notions under agency, fiduciary duty, conflict of interest, control, special relationship and securities laws liability theories of liability.

Most recently what has occurred is a two-fold erosion of Glass-Steagall. First, the FRB has eliminated most of its prior § 20 "firewalls"[178] and the Comptroller of the Currency (as to national bank and their subsidiaries) has adopted an expansive deregulatory definition of the "business of banking" under its new "Operating Subsidiary Regulation".[179] The Op-Sub regulations not only regulatorily erode Glass-Steagall further but also diminish traditional limitations in a national bank's banking involvement in the insurance area.[180]

The risks related to US judicial processes

In recent years, much has been made of the risks for banking institutions under the US judicial system. Clearly, the environment for the banker–customer relationship (in its many forms as discussed above) unfolds within a highly legal environment. Add to this the propensity toward litigiousness of American society, and one can readily understand that risks of litigation are a real and significant element for banking institutions to do business in the United States.

To exacerbate the problem, jury trials are common in civil litigation in the United States and most commercial litigation arises in local state (as opposed to federal) courts. Further, in non-contract matters punitive or exemplary damages exist and are determined by the jury (subject to judicial review by the court). Also in contract-commercial matters consequential damages are similarly determined and can also turn into significant awards. However, the concept that

---

178. See Amendments to Restrictions in Board's Section 20 Orders Final Conditions to Board Orders, 22 August 1997.

179. See 12 CFR § 5.34 (1997). The Comptroller is relying on the recent US Supreme Court decision in *Nationsbank of N.C., N.A.* v. *Variable Annuity Life Ins. Co.*, 513 US 251 (1995).

180. See generally *BLM*, Ch. 17.

a losing plaintiff pays a defendant's attorney fees has not crept into the American system. Although these aspects of the American judicial system tend to become exaggerated by outside observers, such aspects do present real differences from European modelled systems.

Further disturbing to banking institutions has been the tendency of some American courts to confuse contract causes of actions with tort causes of actions (e.g. in various lender liability suits). The effect of this "contort" confusion has been to provide plaintiffs with a means to circumvent normal summary judgment procedures in contract causes of action, to "get" to the jury and to seek tort damages. Though, recently, the judicial trend appears to be to limit this "contort" approach, the concept of "duties" and responsibilities of banking institutions have expanded over the past decade of lender liability and consumer litigation. Equally important have been the numerous governmental suits against failed banking institutions and their management for negligence and breach of duty (along with numerous other alleged legal violations).[181]

Thus, the general nature of the US legal system, the litigious nature of American society, and the spate of private and government litigation over the past decade have come to embrace the banker–customer legal relations in a judicial straitjacket, which when added to the regulatory straitjacket on US banking institutions makes the legal dimensions of the banker–customer relationship in the United States all-encompassing.

JOSEPH J. NORTON

181. See generally Norton and Baggett, "The Alice in Wonderland of American Lender Liability Laws: Of Common Law, Statutes and Contorts", in *Banks and Risks*, 2nd edn (ed. R. Cranston 1996).

CHAPTER 10

EUROPEAN AND GLOBAL HARMONISATION OF THE LAW OF BANKING TRANSACTIONS

A EUROPEAN AND GLOBAL HARMONISATION OF THE LAW OF BANKING TRANSACTIONS

During the past few years, the European Community has most successfully promoted and advanced the harmonisation of the laws of the Member States. This has also included the law of banking regulation. One could even say that the European Community is developing into a community devoted to regulating banking law. These developments have previously been reported and analysed.[1]

May we then assume that a harmonisation of the law of banking *transactions* has been given second priority? Is there no need for such harmonisation?[2] Does the Community lack the necessary authority even to achieve harmonisation in the sphere of private law? Or are a "European Uniform Commercial Code"[3] and a "European Consumer Code" in part already evolving, but without the necessary public attention? Put more generally, what effects are the worldwide efforts towards harmonisation of commercial law, for example through the United Nations Commission on International Trade Law (UNCITRAL), having on legal harmonisation within the European Community? Will the globalisation of markets also be followed by a globalisation of commercial law? Is a "Global

1. R. Cranston, *The Single Market and the Law of Banking* (1991); M. Gruson and W. Nikowitz, "The Second Banking Directive of the European Economic Community and its Importance for Non-EEC Banks", 12 *Fordham Int'l LJ* 205 (1989); U.H. Schneider, "The Harmonization of EC Banking Laws: The Europa-Passport to Profitability and International Competitiveness of Financial Institutions", 22 *Law & Pol'y Int'l Bus.* 261 (1991); G.S. Zavvos, "Towards a European Banking Act", 25 *Common Mkt. L. Rev.* 263, 276 (1988); G.S. Zavvos, "Towards a Banking Integration in the European Community", 9 *Nw. J. Int'l L. & Bus.* 572, 573 (1985).

2. Schmidt-Leithoff, *Festschrift für Rittner* 597, 611 (1991) ("Einer supranationalen Privatrechtsordnung sollte auch im Hinblick auf die Idee des Wettbewerbs der Rechtsordnungen nicht vorschnell das Wort geredet werden.") ["There is even competition of legal systems. One should not hasten to plead for a supranational system of private law."]; Troberg, in *Der europäische Binnenmarkt 1992—Auswirkungen für die deutsche Finanzwirtschaft* 68 (Büschgen and U.H. Schneider eds., 1990) ("Brauchen wir ein europäisches Bank- und Versicherungsvertragsrecht? Meine Antwort bleibt verneinend.") ["Do we need a European law of banking and insurance transactions? My answer remains 'no'".].

3. Lecourt and Chevallier, "Chances et malchances de l'harmonisation des législations européennes", 1963 *Recueil Dalloz [Rec.D.] (Chronique)* 273, 276; see Lecourt and Chevallier, 1965 *Rec.D. (Chronique)* 147. In the 1960s Lecourt and Chevallier already called for a comprehensive harmonisation of commercial law: see also Ulmer, 1 *Juristen Zeitung* 47 (1992).

Uniform Commercial Code for International Business Transactions" evolving out of the worldwide efforts on the harmonisation of law, or will commercial law remain a part of each nation's system of private law?

Careful analysis and broad discussion are thus far lacking with respect to the European Community's authority and the concepts regarding harmonisation of private law,[4] the relationships between the various institutions that are working worldwide on harmonisation of private law, the differing levels of harmonisation, and the relationships among the various individual projects aimed at legal harmonisation. This chapter will attempt to describe these problems as they relate to the specific area of banking transactions law. First, we will address the preliminary issue of whether rules of transnational banking transactions law exist, that is, whether there are positive rules within a supranational, autonomous legal system applicable to the area of banking transactions. Then we will examine the question of which international institutions on a global level are engaged in harmonisation of banking transactions law and what specific attempts at harmonisation have been made. Finally, we will attempt to clarify the paths which the European Community is taking. This will involve discussion of the issues of whether an autonomous European law of banking transactions will arise, whether there will be a "European Uniform Code for Banking Contracts", and what relationship harmonisation within the European Community in the area of banking transactions law will have to worldwide harmonisation efforts.

TRANSNATIONAL LAW OF BANKING TRANSACTIONS

Cross-border financial services and the free flow of capital have achieved great practical significance within the past few years. In each individual instance, the key issue is which system of law is applicable, a codified or non-codified transnational law of banking transactions or a particular national legal system. If there is a transnational system of banking transactions law, then no great effort should be required to harmonise the various national laws of banking transactions.

When we pursue this preliminary issue, we are confronted by an almost boundless discussion. On the one hand, there is the view that a self-created law of international commerce,[5] a *lex mercatoria*, exists parallel to national legal

---

4. Müller-Graf, *Privatrecht und europäisches Gemeinschaftsrecht* 27 (1989); Hallstein, *Zeitschrift für ausländisches und internationales Privatrecht, begründet von Rabel* 28 *RabelsZ* 211 (1964); Rittner, 115 *Archiv für das Öffentliche Recht* 332 (1990); Rittner, 1990 *Juristenzeitung [J.Z.]* 842; see also Drobnig, in *Festschrift für Steindorff* 1141 (1990); Hauschka, 1990 *J.Z.* 521; Hauschka, 1989 *Neue Juristische Wochenschrift [NJW]* 3048; Kötz, in *Festschrift für Zweigert* 481 (1981); Mansel, 1991 *J.Z.* 529; Remien, 87 *Zeitschrift für vergleichende Rechtswissenschaft [ZfVR]* 105 (1988); U.H. Schneider, 1991 *NJW* 1985; Tilmann, in *Festschrift für Oppenhoff* 495 (1985); Armbrüster, 60 *RabelsZ* 72 (1996); Schurig, in *Festschrift für Grossfeld* 1089 (1989).

5. Kropholler, *Internationales Einheitsrecht* (1975); Stein, *Lex Mercatoria* (1995); Jacques Béguin, "Le développement de la lex mercatoria menace-t-il l'ordre juridique international?", 30 *McGill L.J.* 479 (1985); C.M. Schmitthoff, 28 *RabelsZ* 47 (1964) and "The Law of International

systems. This view holds that general principles, guidelines established by professional organisations, standard form contracts, typical commercial contract clauses, and decisions by international arbitration tribunals constitute objective and generally valid rules of a supranational private and autonomous legal system: "Il existe un droite, dont le source est ailleurs que dans l'Etat."[6] On the other hand, there is the view that these ideas are mistaken.[7] They are described as being based on incorrect theories of the sources of law, conceptually hazy, and based on improper legal policy.[8] This view asserts that only national law has a chance of being accepted.

In reply to these strict views, one could assert that, particularly in world commerce, other types of sanctions could secure the realisation of rules of conduct. A good example is the occasional inclusion of clauses in international loan agreements in which the contracting parties express some doubt that the agreements are even valid. At the same time, however, the clauses provide that each party must comply with the agreement despite the suspected invalidity. Therefore, if one bases doubts about the existence of a transnational law of banking upon theories about the sources of law merely on the grounds stated above, then it is perhaps not legal practice but legal theory which must be changed.

A greater problem is that, despite intensive research, it is scarcely possible to determine the rules of a transnational law of banking transactions. The view that favours the existence of a transnational legal order believes that, as a very minimum, the contracting parties have the option of entering into "agreements outside legal systems"; that is, that they may opt out of positive national legal systems and create their own framework for business relations or base these relations on internationally common form contracts, standard contract terms, and typical clauses. Examples which deserve mention in this regard are loan agreements used by international organisations without choice of law clauses and also banking agreements with negative or, more commonly, alternative choice of law clauses.

In the case of alternative choice of law clauses, the national law of the country in which the suit is first filed is to be applied. In Germany, a 1936 decision by the Supreme Court is still used as precedent for holding such "agreements outside legal systems" to be invalid.[9] The decision stated that:

[o]nly an ... unrestricted subjection to one certain power with jurisdiction to make laws

---

Trade, its Growth, Formation and Operation", in *The Sources of the Law of International Trade* (C.M. Schmitthoff ed., 1964); *cf.* W. Lorenz, in *Festschrift für Neumayer* 407 (1985) (Lorenz agrees with this point of view, but with reservations). *Contra* Lord Mustill, in *Liber Amicorum for the Right Honourable Lord Wilberforce* (M. Bos and I. Brownlie eds, 1987).

    6. "There is a system of law that has its source elsewhere than in the state." Philippe Kahn, *La Vente Commerciale Internationale* 36 (1961).

    7. Staub and Canaris, *Handelsgesetzbuch, Bankvertragsrecht* [Commentary on the Commercial Code, Banking Transactions Law] 6, margin no. 925 (4th edn).

    8. von Bar, *Internationales Privatrecht* 79 (1987).

    9. Judgment of the Reichsgericht (RG) [Supreme Court until 1945], in 1936 *Juristische Wochenschrift* 2058–59.

…, which also provides the guarantee necessary for the legal relationships between countries that the contractual relationship can if necessary be enforced even against the selfish will of both parties while complying with general needs in accordance with the common legal views of the states bound together by common customs and views.[10]

This theoretical dispute shall be left open here. One reason is that it is scarcely possible to determine the rules that could be attributed to a transnational law of banking transactions. Another is that in practice contracting parties have only a very limited interest in freeing themselves from all national legal systems; if they attempt to do so, no basis remains for finding the rules that, in a disputed case, would be used to fill any gaps in the contractual provisions.

GLOBAL HARMONISATION OF THE LAW OF BANKING TRANSACTIONS

Numerous institutions, differing levels of harmonisation

We must ask whether it is correct to speak of an international law of banking transactions at all. The purposes, namely facilitating transactions on the one hand and the consistent regulation of cross-border financial services on the other, can also be achieved by means of uniform or equivalent national systems of rules. Whether in that case the rules embodied in the particular national legal systems should be referred to as "international law of banking transactions" is merely a semantic question. The real developments can only be understood by examining the various forms of legal standardisation, the adaptation (harmonisation) of national laws, and the present practice in the handling of contracts.

First, numerous public institutions are involved in the area of legal harmonisation: institutions with autonomous law making authority, such as the European Community, and institutions without autonomous law making authority, that pursue the task of preparing measures for legal harmonisation either globally or regionally. Among these are UNCITRAL and the United Nations Conference on Trade and Development (UNCTAD), the Asian-African Legal Consultative Committee,[11] the Hague Conference on International Private Law, the International Institute for the Unification of Private Law (Unidroit), the Intergovernmental Organisation for International Carriage by Rail, the Organisation of American States, the Nordic Council, and many others.

Secondly, many private organisations are involved in legal harmonisation. The list of such organisations extends from the International Chamber of Commerce (ICC) to professional associations and academic institutions. The Secretariat of UNCITRAL[12] listed no less than 28 such institutions engaged in

---

10. *Ibid.*
11. See also Hu Wen-Zhi, "Cooperation Between Unidroit and the Asian-American Legal Consultative Committee", in *International Uniform Law in Practice* 91 (Unidroit ed., 1988).
12. *Current Activities of International Organizations Related to the Harmonization and Unification of International Trade Law*, UN Comm'n Int'l Trade L., UN Doc. A/CN.9/380, 1 July

harmonisation of international commercial law and almost 100 harmonisation projects. Anyone who is already involved in this work is unlikely to be surprised by these numbers.

The goals, concepts, and methods of harmonisation also differ greatly. Three basic directions can be distinguished. First, directly applicable supranational law is evolving within the European Community, including the area of banking transactions law. Secondly, uniform or equivalent national laws are being created by adapting existing laws. The adaptation can be limited to international conflicts law and can also encompass substantive law. The methods include international treaties, the drafting of model laws which are then recommended for adoption by the individual countries, and Directives and recommendations as in the European Community.[13]

Finally, the drafting and recommendation of standard contracts, typical contract clauses, guidelines for the drafting of contracts, and similar documents by international professional organisations and associations does not constitute legal harmonisation in the strict sense. Such form contracts drafted by involved business groups do not raise these rules to the level of a generally binding source of law.[14] Internationally consistent contract practice does lead, however, to a factual harmonisation of laws. Likewise, the decisions of international arbitration tribunals[15] do not constitute a harmonisation of laws in a strict sense, but are in fact a form of "creeping" or "spontaneous" harmonisation. This privatisation of the harmonisation of laws also has significant practical importance in the areas of banking transactions law.

Individual harmonisation projects by intergovernmental organisations

Before turning to legal harmonisation within the European Community, we should first be aware that these efforts must be viewed within the context of the international and global harmonisation process. Many of these harmonisation measures have landed in the "dead letter file",[16] but a number of them have achieved great practical significance.

A global harmonisation of laws is being attempted by UNCITRAL. One of the

---

1993. For a list of international organisations involved in legal harmonisation, see *Digest of Legal Activities* III (Unidroit ed., 8th edn 1988). For more information on "unified private law" and for an incomplete list of harmonisation measures, see Kegel, in *Internationales Privatrecht* 41 (6th edn 1987).

13. See G. Herrmann, "United Nations Commission on International Trade Law", in 5 *Encyclopedia of Public International Law* 297 (Rudolf Bernhardt ed., 1983); Kropholler, *supra* n. 5, at 106; Trompenaars, *Pluriforme Unificatie en Uniform Interpretatie* 55 (Deventer, Neth. 1989).

14. Lorenz, *supra* n. 5, at 407–8; W. Lorenz, **126** *Zeitschrift für das Gesamte Handels- und Wirtschaftsrecht* 146 (1963).

15. *Rechtsfortbildung durch Internationale Schiedsgerichte* (Böckstiegel ed., 1989); von Hoffmann, in *Festschrift für Kegel* 215 (1987).

16. A good example is the 1978 Uniform Rules for Contractual Guarantees compiled by the International Chamber of Commerce, which were replaced by new rules in 1989. For a discussion of the reasons for the replacement, see Kleiner, *Bankgarantie* 273 (4th edn, Zurich 1990).

original goals set for UNCITRAL was that it should draft "a common body of law governing international trade",[17] which would lead to a "Global Uniform Commercial Code for International Business Transactions". This has already been achieved in part. Following the impressive success of the UN Convention on Contracts for the International Sale of Goods[18] and a number of other successful projects, in particular the UNCITRAL Arbitration Rules,[19] and the Model Law on International Commercial Arbitration,[20] UNCITRAL adopted a Model Law on International Credit Transfers on 15 May 1992.[21] Work has already been completed on a UN Convention on International Bills of Exchange and International Promissory Notes[22] and on a UN Convention on Independent Guarantees and Stand-By Letters of Credit.[23] By contrast, work on an Agreement on International Cheques was discontinued in 1984.[24] There are further plans for internationally consistent rules for the assignment of receivables financing.[25]

The group of countries participating in Unidroit is smaller. Its efforts to draft an international agreement on general principles of the law of contract obligations reach far beyond banking transactions.[26] The Unidroit Agreement on International Factoring of 28 May 1988[27] is an attempt to create a legal framework by means of uniform provisions of law in the various countries to "facilitate international factoring and to maintain a balance among the interests of the various parties participating in a factoring transaction". This agreement has also found acceptance in the Federal Republic of Germany within interested

17. "Draft Basic Convention Establishing a Common Body of International Trade Law: Proposal by the French Delegation", 1 *YB UN Comm'n Int'l Trade L.* 288–91, UN Doc. UNCITRAL/III/ CRP/3 (1968–70).

18. UN Convention on Contracts for the International Sale of Goods, (1980), UN Doc. A/CONF.97/18, Annex 1, reprinted in 19 *Int'l Legal Materials* 668 (1980) (hereinafter UN Convention on Contracts).

19. *Report of the United Nations Commission on International Trade Law*, 31 UN GAOR, Supp. 17, at 34, UN Doc. A/31/17, para. 57 (1976), reprinted in 15 *Int'l Legal Materials* 701 (1976).

20. *Report of the United Nations Commission on International Trade Law*, 40 UN GAOR, Supp. 17 at 81–93, UN Doc. A/40/17 (1985), reprinted in 24 *Int'l Legal Materials* 1302 (1985).

21. U.H. Schneider, in *Legal Issues in International Credit Transfers* 451 (Hadding and U.H. Schneider eds., 1993).

22. See G.A.Res 43/165, UN GAOR, reprinted in *Studies in Transnational Economic Law: The Law of International Trade Finance* 629 (Norbert Horn ed., 1989) (hereinafter *The Law of International Trade Finance*); see also Schinnerer, *Zu den Konventionsentwürfen von UNCITRAL für ein internationales Wechsel und Scheckrecht* (Vienna 1983); Ganten and Jahn, 1987 *Die Bank* 394.

23. Reprinted in *UNCITRAL Yearbook 1995*, Part 1D.

24. Report of the United Nations Commission on International Trade Law, XV *YB UN Comm'n Int'l Trade L.* 6, no. 20, UN Doc. A/39/17 (1984). The Draft Convention on International Cheques is reprinted in *Basic Documents on International Trade Law* 451 (Chia-Jui Cheng ed., Dordrecht, Neth. 1986).

25. Bazinas, "An International Legal Regime for Receivables Financing: UNCITRAL's Contribution", 8 *Duke Journal of Comparative & International Law* 315 (1998).

26. Unidroit, *Principles for International Commercial Contracts* (Rome 1994).

27. M.R. Alexander, "Towards Unification and Predictability: The International Factoring Convention", 27 *Colum. J. Transnat'l L.* 353 (1989); Brink, 1990 *Finanzierung, Leasing, Factoring*

business circles and has now been adopted as a domestic statute.[28] However, interest in signing the Unidroit Agreement on International Finance Leasing of 28 May 1988 is so far lacking in Germany.[29]

Unidroit has also nearly completed work on a harmonisation of the law of security interests in movable goods.[30] The difficulties involved in this project caused the Commission of the European Community to discontinue work in 1979–80 on similar projects involving harmonisation of laws on security interests in real and personal property. For many years, harmonisation in some areas of the law of security interests has existed, namely through the Geneva Convention on the International Recognition of Rights in Aircraft of 1948, the Brussels Convention for the Unification of Certain Rules of Law Relating to Maritime Liens and Mortgages of 1926 and 1967, and the Geneva Convention on the Registration for Inland Navigation Vessels of 1965. The need for a consistent international system of law governing security interests in personal property has led Great Britain to consider following Canada's[31] lead in adopting the US law of security interests in personal property, Art. 9 of the UCC.[32]

The agreements initiated by the Council of Europe are limited to the European countries. These include two agreements regarding money debts, the European Agreement on Foreign Currency Obligations of 11 December 1967,[33] and the European Agreement on the Place of Payment of Money Obligations of 15 May 1972.[34] Also worthy of mention in this regard is the Convention Relating to Stops on Bearer Securities in International Circulation of 18 May 1970.[35]

26; R.M. Goode, in *Festschrift für Sauveplanne* 91 (1984); R.M. Goode, "Conclusion of the Leasing and Factoring Conventions", 1988 *J. Bus. L.* 347, 510; Rebmann, 53 *RabelsZ* 559 (1989) A.F. Reismann, "The Uniform Commercial Code and the Convention on International Factoring", 22 *UCC L.J.* 320 (1990); Sassoon, in *Current Problems of International Trade Financing* 247 (Ho Peng Kee and H.M. Chan eds, 1990); Sommer, 1988 *Finanzierung, Leasing, Factoring* 230; Basedow, 5 *Zeitschrift für Europaisches Privatrecht* 615 (1997).

28. German O.J. [=*Bundesgesetzblatt*] II of 9.3.1998, p. 172 and of 21.9.1998, p. 2375.

29. Basedow, 1988 *RIW* 1; Feinen, 5 *RIW* supp. 1 (1988); Feinen, 4 *RIW* supp. 1 (1986); R.M. Goode, "The Proposed New Factoring and Leasing Conventions", 1987 *J. Bus. L.* 219, 318, 399; R.M. Goode, "Conclusion of the Leasing and Factoring Conventions", 1988 *J. Bus. L.* 347, 510; Kronke, 190 *Archiv für die civilistische Praxis* 383 (1990); Nagano, in 1990 *World Leasing Year Book* 15; Nagano, in 1989 *World Leasing Year Book* 35; Poczobut, 51 *RabelsZ* 681 (1987); Stanford, 1989 *Finanzierung, Leasing, Factoring* 128; Stanford, in 1990 *World Leasing Year Book* 36.

30. See Revised Draft Unidroit Convention on International Interests in Mobile Equipment, February 1997 and Draft 1998, Study LXXII, Doc. 42, July 1998; Cuming, in *International Regulation of Aspects of Security Interests in Mobile Equipment*, Study LXXII, Doc. 1 (Unidroit ed., 1989).

31. von Kenne, *Das kanadische einheitliche Sicherungsrecht* (1981).

32. See Diamond, *A Review of Security Interests in Property* 14 (London: 1989).

33. See Küng, *Zahlung und Zahlungsort im IPR* 126 (Freiburg, Switz. 1970); Schönle, in *Festschrift für Werner* 817 (1984).

34. See Klingsporn, 1972 *Wertpapiermitteilungen [WM]* 1262; Ernst von Caemmerer, in *Festschrift für Mann* 16 (1977); von Hoffmann, in *Festschrift für Firsching* 126 (1985).

35. *Common Papers*, Eur. Parl. Ass., Doc. No. 4580 (1971); Gördel, 1971 *J.Z.* 217; Herber, 1971 *WM* no. 16, spec. supp. no. 3.

Privatisation of the harmonisation of laws

The factual harmonisation of laws is taking place on another level through uniform contract practice. This is also true for the law of banking transactions. On the one hand, in the market-place, for example in international loan agreements and international underwriting agreements, certain standards regarding contract design and typical clauses have evolved. These contract clauses are constantly adapted when new problems arise in practice. On the other hand, numerous non-governmental international organisations have drafted standard banking contracts and recommendations for the execution of banking contracts. This "privatisation of the harmonisation of law" is particularly apparent when relevant business groups draft standard form contracts or publish guidelines for contract design.[36] For example, the International Securities Market Association (ISMA) has worked on a Global Master Repurchase Agreement, the International Primary Market Association (IPMA) has published recommendations applicable to issues of debt instruments including equity-related debt instruments, and IPMA and the International Swaps and Derivatives Association (ISDA) have published a definition of the ECU. In addition, intergovernmental organisations such as the World Bank, United Nations Industrial Development Organisation (UNIDO), the Economic Commission for Europe, and other international institutions such as the European Bank for Reconstruction and Development have participated in the drafting of typical banking agreements and recommendations for the design of certain types of banking contracts.

Particularly well known are documents prepared by the ICC: the Uniform Customs and Practice for Documentary Credits,[37] the Uniform Rules for Collections,[38] the 1978 Uniform Rules for Contract Guarantees,[39] and the revised draft for a 1989 amendment on contract guarantees. Most recent are the ICC's "Guidelines on International Interbank Funds Transfer and Compensation"[40] and a draft of "Rules on Demand Guarantees". Also worthy of mention are the Model Rules on the Time of Payment prepared by the International Law Association.

This makes clear that there is a broad range of activities which are intended to bring about consistent international contract practice in the field of financial services.

---

36. See G. Delaume, *Transnational Contracts—Applicable Law and Settlement of Disputes: A Study in Conflict Avoidance* (1980).

37. The Uniform Customs and Practice for Documentary Credits is reprinted in *Law of International Trade Finance, supra* n. 22, at 607.

38. *Ibid.*, at 597.

39. The 1978 Uniform Rules for Contract Guarantees is reprinted in 2 *Studies in Transnational Econ. L.: The Transnational Law of International Commercial Transactions* 415 (N. Horn and C.M. Schmitthoff eds., Deventer, Neth. 1982).

40. International Chamber of Commerce (ICC) Publication No. 457.

THE EUROPEAN COMMUNITY AS A COMMUNITY OF COMMERCIALLY RELEVANT PRIVATE LAW

The design of private law through the European Community

When we attempt to analyse the place of the European Community in this international legal harmonisation process, we must first realise that the European Community is affecting private law in many differing ways.

First, Community law restricts freedom to execute and design contracts for legal transactions by means of legal requirements and prohibitions.[41] One example is Art. 7, para. 5 of the regulation on merger control.[42] This Article provides that the validity of a merger is dependent upon a decision made in accordance with Art. 6, para. 1 or Art. 8, para. 2 or 3.[43] Likewise, agreements between companies are null and void if they violate the Community's legal prohibition on restriction of competition. Thus, the issue of legal consequences, already discussed in relation to national law,[44] is also relevant in the Community for banking contracts when the conclusion or content of contracts violates European banking regulatory law, European capital markets law, and other laws. On the other hand, to some extent Community law supersedes national restrictions on the conclusion or contents of contracts.

Secondly, Community law also creates private law, sometimes with direct effects and sometimes through harmonisation of laws when Community Directives are adopted into national law.

Finally, the European Court of Justice also decides cases involving issues of private law, thus creating a body of European case law in the area of private law.

The special status of the Community in the harmonisation of laws process

As a rule, international institutions such as UNCITRAL or Unidroit can only draft international agreements, model laws, or recommendations for designing contracts. These institutions have no law-making authority of their own. Therefore, it is left to the individual Member States to decide whether to adopt a model law or to ratify an international convention. This is one reason why many harmonisation projects have had little success.

41. See also Judgment of Bundesgerichtshof (BGH) [German Supreme Court], 30 BGHZ 74; Bleckmann, *Europarecht* margin no. 504 (5th ed. 1990); Müller-Graff, *supra* n. 4, at 20; Hönn, in *Gedächtnisschrift für Geck* 321, 325 (1991). For the impact on private law of the interdiction of nontariff trade barriers in the EC, see Schaefer, *Die unmittelbare Wirkung des Verbots der nichttarifären Handelshemmnisse in den Rechtsbeziehungen zwischen Privaten* (1987); Hauschka, 1990 *Der Betrieb [DB]* 873.

42. Council Regulation 4064/89, 1989 O.J. (L395) 1 as amended by Council Regulation 1310/97, 1997 O.J. (L180) 1; see O. Sandrock and E. Van Arnheim, "New Merger Control Rules in the EEC", 25 *Int'l Law.* 859 (1991); P. Thieffry *et al.*, "The Notification of Mergers under the New EEC Merger Control Regulation", 25 *Int'l Law.* 615 (1991).

43. *Ibid.*

44. Huber, *Die Normen des Kreditwesengesetzes zur Verhinderung einer Bankinsolvenz und ihre Auswirkungen auf das Giroverhältnis* (1987); Lünterbusch, *Die privatrechtlichen Auswirkungen des Gesetzes über das Kreditwesen auf Einlagen- und Kreditgeschäfte* (1968).

By contrast, the European Community has independent law-making powers. These powers are not limited to individual areas of private or commercial law, but instead extend to all economically relevant areas of private law. Some doubts have, incorrectly, been expressed concerning this principle.[45] It is true that in the Treaty establishing the European Economic Community only some specific areas of private law are expressly listed and provision is made for harmonisation of laws in these areas. These include company law,[46] labour law,[47] and consumer protection law.[48] One should not conclude from this list, however, that it is intended to be exhaustive. Instead, Article 100 of the Treaty provides for more general authority[49] that extends to private law and can even constitute the basis for some harmonisation measures in the area of criminal law.[50] In accordance with this Article:

the Council shall, acting unanimously on a proposal from the Commission, issue directives for the approximation of such provisions laid down by law, regulation or administrative action in Member States as directly affect the establishment or functioning of the common market.[51]

Thus, the only dispute concerns whether a specific measure directly affects the functioning of the common market. In deciding whether this prerequisite is met, the competent organs of the Community have broad discretion.[52] With regard to the high degree of enthusiasm for travel throughout Europe, liability law concerning traffic accidents could be a topic of harmonisation, as could areas of banking transactions law such as surety law,[53] land mortgages, or the law of security interests in movable goods.[54] For example, in 1966 the Segre Report[55]

45. Rittner, 1990 J.Z. 842; see Grabitz-Langeheine, *Kommentar zum EWG-Vertrag* Art. 100, margin no. 29 (1989) ("only limited authority to harmonise"). For a broader view, see Groeben *et al.*, *Kommentar zum EWG-Vertrag* Art. 100 margin no. III 1 (2nd edn); Müller-Graff, *supra* n. 4, at 23; Tilmann, *supra* n. 4; Zweigert, in *Festschrift für Dölle* 401, 408 (1963).

46. Treaty Establishing the European Economic Community (EEC Treaty) Art. 54(3)(g).

47. *Ibid.*, Arts. 100a(3), 118.

48. *Ibid.*, Art. 100a(3).

49. See e.g., Eiden, *Die Rechtsangleichung gemäß Art. 100 EWGV* (1984); Kapteyn and Verloren van Themaat, *Introduction to the Law of the European Communities* 467 (2nd edn 1989); Oppermann, 1991 *Europarecht* 416, 431. For a more restrictive interpretation with regard to "necessity", see Bruha, 1986 *Zeitschrift für ausländisches öffentliches Recht und Völkerrecht* 1.

50. The topic of harmonising penal law is much disputed. See e.g., Council Directive on Prevention of the Use of the Financing System for the Purpose of Money Laundering, 1991 O.J. (L 166) 77. See generally Howarth [1989] *Journal of Criminal Law* 358; Johannes, 1968 *Europarecht* 63; Paridaens, 1989 *Nederlands Juristenblad [NJB]* 791.

51. EEC Treaty, Art. 100.

52. Grabitz-Langeheine, *supra* n. 45, margin no. 36; Birk, 1990 *Europarecht* supp. 1, at 23; see also Schwartz, in *Festschrift für Hallstein* 474 (1966).

53. Drobnig, in *Festschrift für Bärmann* 249 (1975).

54. For preparatory comparative legal studies, see Gravenhorst, "Mobiliarsicherheiten für Darlehens- und Warenkredite in den Ländern der Europäischen Gemeinschaften", Study for the Commission of the European Communities, XIV/405/71-D; see also U. Drobnig, "Report of the Secretary-General: Study on Security Interests", VIII *YB UN Comm'n Int'l Trade L.* 171, 213, UN Doc. A/CN.9/131 (1977).

55. "Der Aufbau eines europäischen Kapitalmarktes" ["The Construction of a European Capital Market"], Report of a Group of Experts of the Commission of the European Community (Brüssels 1966) (Prof. Segre, President).

reached the conclusion that one of the primary tasks of the Community was harmonising laws regarding land mortgages and introducing a uniform system of real property security interests in the Member States. Recently the Union Internationale du Notariat Latin[56] has again recommended the introduction of a uniform "Euromortgage".

Another example is the Fifth General Report of the European Communities, which in 1971 had already pointed out the substantial differences in the forms of security interests in personal property contained in the individual legal systems of the Member States.[57] The report found that these differences hinder the granting of loans across borders and make such loans substantially more expensive.[58] The differing laws also cause confusion regarding the existence, the extent, and the enforceability of claims, and this situation was found to affect the movement of capital and, in a broader sense, the conditions of competition between enterprises.[59] As already mentioned, however, work on legal harmonisation in the area of security interests in real and personal property was discontinued in 1979–80.

In analysing the issue of whether a harmonisation of laws is necessary, one must certainly consider at what level the harmonisation of private law should take place, for instance, through UNCITRAL and thus worldwide, or only through the European Community. This issue will be further discussed below.

The possibility of harmonising laws in the area of private law in general and specifically in the area of commercial law has already been exercised many times[60] and not only in the areas expressly listed in the Community Treaty. The harmonisation measures include travel contract law,[61] product liability law,[62] laws concerning commercial agents,[63] protection of computer programs,[64]

56. Union Internationale du Notariat Latin, Commission des Affaires Européennes, *Der Schweizer Schuldbrief und die deutsche Briefgrundschuld* (1988); Stöcker, 1991 *Der langfristige Kredit* 537; van Velten, 1991 *Weekblad voor Privaatrecht, Notariaat en Registratie [W.P.N.R.]* 241; Wehrens, 1988 *NotarZeitung* 181; Wehrens, "Die zukünftige Eurohypothek", in *Festschrift zum 85-jährigen Bestehen der niederländischen Vereinigung der Hypothekenbanken* (Deventer, Neth. 1991); Wachter, 1998 *WM* 49.
57. Commission of European Coal and Steel Community, European Economic Community, and European Atomic Energy Commission, *Fifth General Report on the Activities of the Communities* 140 (1971–72).
58. *Ibid.*
59. *Ibid.*
60. See, e.g. Grundmann, *Europäisches Schuldvertragsrecht* (1999); Hommelhoff, "Zivilrecht unter dem Einfluß europäischer Rechtsangleichung", 192 *AcP* 71 (1992); Remien, "Illusion und Realität eines europäischen Privatrechts", *JZ* 277 (1992); Filip de Ly, *Europese Gemeenschap en Privaatrecht* (1993); Müller-Graff, "Europäisches Gemeinschaftsrecht und Privatrecht", *NJW* 13 (1993); Taupitz, *Europäische Rechtsvereinheitlichung heute und morgen* (1993); Blaurock, "Europäisches Privatrecht", *JZ* 270 (1994); Schwartz, "Perspecktiven der Angleichung des Privatrechts in der Eropäischen Gemeinschaft", *SEuP* 559 (1994); Basedow, "Über Privatrechtsvereinheitlichung und Marktintegration", in: *Festschrift für Mestmäcker*, 347 (1996).
61. 1990 O.J. (L 158) 59; Abeltshauser, 1991 *Europäisches Wirtschafts- und Steuerrecht* 97; Tonner, 1990 *Europäische Zeitschrift für Wirtschaftsrecht* 409.
62. 1985 O.J. (L 210) 31.
63. 1986 O.J. (L 382) 17; Kindler, 1990 *RIW* 358.
64. See e.g., Directive on the Legal Protection of Computer Programs, 1991 O.J. (L 122) 42; Funke, 1991 *Europäisches Wirtschafts- und Steuerrecht* 161.

distance selling[65] and parts of banking transactions law and law of insurance contracts.[66]

The result is that the status of the European Community as a legal community is developing not only into a community of regulatory law but also increasingly, with some limitations still to be discussed, into a community of economically relevant private law.

The two levels of harmonisation of laws

The two levels of harmonisation of laws in the area of private law within the European Community must be viewed against this background. With regard to banking transactions law, these levels are the unification of conflict of laws relevant to banking transactions and the harmonisation of substantive banking transactions.

The first step was the harmonisation of international conflict of laws. The result is that the same national substantive law will be applied regardless of which court in which country is called upon to render a decision in a particular case. This was the goal of the EC Convention on the Law Applicable to Contractual Obligations,[67] as well as the First Protocol on the Interpretation by the Court of Justice of the European Communities of the Convention on the Law Applicable to Contractual Obligations.[68] These documents unified the conflicts rules for contractual debt obligations. Thus, no room was left for different provisions within the Member States concerning international conflict of laws.

In the Convention of Rome, there are no special conflicts rules applicable specifically to banking transactions. Instead, cross-border banking transactions are governed by the relevant general rules. The application of these relevant rules in practice constitutes the conflicts rules for banking transactions.[69]

Efforts to unify international conflicts in law relating to the area of the law of personal property as a whole have been successful only in South America. Attempts to harmonise conflicts of law relating to property within the

---

65. 1997 O.J. (L144) 19.

66. See Hübner, in *Festschrift für Carstens* 139 & n.1, 145 (1984); R. Schmidt, in *Festschrift für Dölle* 485 (1963); Weigel, 1981 *Versicherungswirtschaft* 1165.

67. 1980 O.J. (L 266) 1; see Jayme, *Ein Internationales Privatrecht für Europa* (1991); W. Lorenz, *Praxis des Internationalen Privat- und Verfahrensrechts* 269 (1987); Schnyder, *Wirtschaftskollisionsrecht* (Zürich 1990); Ebke, in *Europäisches Gemeinschaftsrecht und Internationales Privatrecht* 77 (von Bar ed., 1991); Jayme and Kohler, 1988 *Praxis des Internationalen Privat- und Verfahrensrechts (IPRax)* 133; O. Sandrock, 1986 *RIW* 841; Tebbens, "Private International Law and the Single European Market: Coexistence and Cohabitation?", in *Forty Years on the Evolution of Postwar Private International Law in Europe* 49 (Deventer, Neth. 1990).

68. 1989 O.J. (L 48) 1.

69. See e.g., Radicati di Brozolo, *Operazioni Bancarie Internationali e Conflitti di Leggi* (Milan 1984); Jayme, "Kollisionsrecht und Bankgeschäfte mit Auslandsberührung", in *Der europäische Binnenmarkt 1992 Auswirkungen für die deutsche Finanzwirtschaft* 81 (Büschgen and U.H. Schneider eds, 1990); Schütze, in *Der europäische Binnenmarkt 1992 Auswirkungen für die deutsche Finanzwirtschaft*; G.S. Zavvos, "Banking Integration and 1992: Legal Issues and Policy Implications", 31 *Harv. Int'l L.J.* 463, 487 (1990).

framework of the Hague Conference on Private International Law and the European Community have failed.[70]

Neither does the harmonisation of international conflicts in law eliminate the problem that differences remain in substantive law. Therefore, the European Parliament has repeatedly, namely in 1989 and in 1994,[71] stressed the need for a "European Code of Private Law" and the Parliament has asked the Commission to start work on a draft for such a code. And one international but purely private working group, the Commission for European Contract Law, has been working for several years on the formulation of principles for a European law of contracts.[72] The goal has been clearly stated by Professor Lando, the chair of this group: "To unify the substantive law rules . . . is no longer a mere utopia."[73]

One could consider at least a harmonisation of the law of typical commercial contracts. But the Commission of the European Community is presently not even considering a broad harmonisation of contract law. The Commission thinks that a "broad coordination approach" would fail because "it would simply not be possible to reach agreement on this complex area which is so tightly woven together with the entire civil law of the Member States".[74] Regarding the laws governing insurance contracts, this has clearly been stated in the grounds for the proposal for a third Directive concerning direct insurance with the exception of life insurance: "At the present time, it does not appear necessary or appropriate to harmonize the law of contracts."[75]

The result in the area of banking transactions law is a patchwork quilt. Some areas are harmonised or work is being done on them; in other areas, no efforts are being made to achieve harmonisation. The Directive on unfair terms in consumer contracts is gaining importance over the area of banking transactions.[76] The Council Directive of 20 December 1985 regarding consumer protection in the case of contracts made outside places of business has already achieved greater significance than the area of banking transactions.[77]

Among the measures which lie directly in the area of banking transactions law are the following: the Council Directive of 22 December 1986, on consumer credit,[78] a Directive intended to make the actual costs of credit comparable in all

70. See Kreuzer, in *Vorschläge und Gutachten zur Reform des deutschen internationalen Sachen- und Immaterialgüterrechts* 38, 41 (Henrich ed., 1991); see also Jayme and Kohler, *IPRax* 353, 361 (1990).

71. Doc. A3–0329/94; Tilmann, 1995 *ZEuP* 535.

72. Drobnig, in *Festschrift für Steindorff* 1141, 1149 (1990); O. Lando, "European Contract Law", 31 *Am. J. Comp. L.* 653 (1983); O. Lando, "A Contract Law for Europe", 1985 *Int'l. Bus. Law.* 17.

73. O. Lando, "The EEC Convention on the Law Applicable to Contractual Obligations", 24 *Common Mkt. L. Rev.* 159, 161 (1987).

74. Troberg, *supra* n. 2, at 66.

75. Proposal for a Third Council Directive on the Coordination of Laws, Regulations and Administrative Provisions Relating to Direct Insurance other than Life Assurance, 1990 O.J. (C 244) 28. The directive is now adopted.

76. H.E. Brandner and P. Ulmer, "The Community Directive on Unfair Terms in Consumer Contracts: Some Critical Remarks on the Proposal Submitted by the EC Commission", 28 *Common Mkt. L. Rev.* 647 (1991); Wagner-Widuweit, 1988 *Die Bank* 95.

77. 1985 O.J. (L 372) 31.

78. 1987 O.J. (L 42) 48.

the Member States and at the same time contribute to a fair competitive situation among all lenders (these goals are to be achieved by introducing a standard method for calculating the effective annual interest on consumer loans);[79] the Commission recommendation of 8 December 1987 for a code of conduct in the area of electronic funds transfer;[80] the Commission recommendation of 17 November 1988 on payment systems, in particular regarding the relations between credit card holders and issuers;[81] the Directive of the European Parliament and of the Council of 27 January 1997 on cross-border credit transfers;[82] and the Directive of the European Parliament and of the Council of 19 May 1998 on settlement finality in payment and security settlement systems.[83]

Deliberations on the subject of harmonising laws governing mortgage loans and security interests in real property or on introducing a unified European law of real property security interests are still vague. The Commission has so far pointed out that the Amended Proposal for a Council Directive on the Freedom of Establishment and the Supply of Services in the Field of Mortgage Credit[84] recognises and accepts the differing requirements for mortgage credit in the individual Member States. It does not plan a complete harmonisation of these requirements. The present goals instead involve mutual recognition of financing techniques.

THE CONCEPTUAL FRAMEWORK FOR HARMONISATION OF THE LAW OF BANKING TRANSACTIONS

A conceptual approach

Upon examining the individual harmonisation measures relating to banking transactions law, one's first impression is that these measures consist of a disorganised hotchpotch.[85] In some areas every single detail has been included in the harmonisation, while other details have been left out completely or only general basic principles have been listed.

But this first impression is deceptive. The approach thus far used can be explained: first, by the goal of creating an internal market; secondly, by the principle of subsidiarity; thirdly, by the necessary interrelationship of European, international and global harmonisation; fourthly, by the connection of the principle of mutual recognition to the legal approach taken by international

79. 1988 O.J. (C 155) 10–12.
80. 1987 O.J. (L 365) 72.
81. 1988 O.J. (L 317) 55.
82. 1997 O.J. (L 43) 25.
83. 1998 O.J. (L 166) 45.
84. 1987 O.J. (C 161) 4.
85. For a discussion of legal harmonisation in the field of labour law, see Birk, 1 *Europarecht Beiheft* 17, 25 (1990)—"Die Sachbereiche scheinen eher zufällig, die Ergebnisse mager". ["The areas of harmonised law appear coincidental, the results meagre"].

conflicts of law; and fifthly, by the necessity of working on individual parts of harmonisation one at a time.

The creation of an internal market

The need for legal harmonisation to achieve consistent rules for cross-border transactions has already been discussed in general.[86] The process of legal harmonisation also includes those elements which are typical to the law of banking transactions: the formulation of new rules for modern factual situations, such as electronic funds transfer, electronic signatures or electronic money, for which the individual national legal systems have not yet developed codified rules.

It is true that the harmonisation of laws within the European Community has several characteristics. In many cases, the harmonisation of laws relates only to cross-border situations. Likewise, the UN Convention on Contracts for the International Sale of Goods[87] is applicable only when the contracting parties have their places of business in different Member States or when the international conflict of rules in the *lex fori* provide that the law of a Member State shall apply.[88] The range of application of the Unidroit Convention on International Factoring is similar:[89] it applies only when the assigned claims are based on a contract for the sale of goods between a supplier and a debtor which have their places of business in different countries.[90] The consequence of this restricted range of application is that the system of law applicable to domestic transactions differs from that applicable to cross-border transactions.

By contrast, the legal acts undertaken by the European Community are often intended first to govern cross-border and domestic transactions in the same way. Also, legal harmonisation in the area of private law is not limited to commercial law, but instead is comprehensive and can extend to the entire range of civil law to the extent that the specific laws involved are economically relevant. The goal is the creation of a large European internal market without internal borders based on individual responsibility and liability, and this market would be the place to determine the price for goods and services.

The principle of subsidiarity

Within the European Community, a harmonisation of laws is permissible only where it is necessary. Even here the principle of subsidiarity[91] applies. Any call for a comprehensive harmonisation of private law in general or a comprehensive

---

86. See Background Documents, I *YB UN Comm'n Int'l Trade L.* 5–17, UN Doc. A/5728 (1968–70).
87. UN Convention on Contracts, *supra* n. 18.
88. *Ibid.*, Art. 1, 1(b).
89. Convention on Int'l Factoring, reprinted in *The Law of Int'l Trade Finance supra* n. 22, at 667.
90. *Ibid.*, Art. 2.
91. Schelter, 1990 *Zeitschrift für Europäisches Wirtschaftsrecht* 217.

harmonisation of banking transactions law in particular would be improper. Instead, the need for harmonisation of laws must be determined in each individual case.

It is certainly true that in some areas of banking transactions law unified international legal provisions can be dispensed with, because business practice can create these rules, provided that business practice is in fact creating these rules where no additional facilitation of commerce could be expected and where there is no danger to substantive contractual justice. In international underwriting agreements[92] or in international loan agreements with business customers, for example, the competent contracting parties rely on standard contracts which they use regularly. A number of typical contract clauses such as those governing the duties of the agent in an underwriting agreement are standardised. These standards have become established in the market-place. The mere fact that they are stored in word-processing programs, are steadily revised, and are called up in specific cases on personal computers is sufficient to ensure that they will be used regularly. In addition, provision is made that a national system of law with which all the concerned parties are familiar shall apply; often English law is chosen. A harmonisation of laws could not be equivalent to this continual updating of contracts. There is simply no need for such harmonisation, and in some cases the responsible authorities may even lack the specialised knowledge which would be necessary to draft the relevant legal provisions.

Other banking contracts, such as those for project financing, are "tailor-made". They are in fact renegotiated in each individual case. The internationally common contractual practice based on the Anglo-American legal tradition, namely, that each and every issue is stipulated within the contract, likewise makes harmonisation redundant to a great extent.

However, the view that a harmonisation of laws in the area of banking transactions is superfluous is correct only for certain parts of banking business. In other parts, transparency and consistency of law demand harmonisation in the interest of the individual parties involved and in the interest of the safety and soundness of the banking system. There are some areas in which contracts cannot be negotiated in complete detail each time. One example is where contracts are typically made by telephone. Another reason is that even where the banking customers are companies, it cannot be assumed that all of the contracting parties have the necessary specialist knowledge. Not every medium-sized company engaged in exporting is fully familiar with all of the different types of guarantees and the ways in which guarantees are governed by the differing national legal systems. For example, one of the justifications stated for the Ottawa Convention on International Factoring was the need to create a legal framework by means of adopting uniform provisions to facilitate international

92. See Slater, "The Transnational Law of Syndicated Loans—A hopeless cause?", in *The Transnational Law of International Transactions* 329 (Horn and Schmitthoff trans., Antwerp 1982).

factoring and to protect the balance among the interests of the various parties involved in factoring transactions.

In other areas there is no established contract practice. Often, the legal situation is completely unclear. Cross-border transfer of funds is usually carried out by means of a series of contracts: the bank customer gives an order to his domestic financial institution, this institution passes the payment order on to a foreign correspondent bank, and the correspondent bank then issues a payment order to the beneficiary's bank to make the actual payment. In some cases, there may even be four, five, six correspondent banks in different countries which become involved in the transaction. The individual institutions take on substantively differing obligations. In some countries, the contract includes a right of revocation by the originator, but in other countries this right is excluded by law. In the case of delays, the bank customer in some countries may assert direct claims against one of the intermediary banks, but in other countries the bank customer may have rights only against the bank with which he contracts directly. These differences cause legal uncertainty and sometimes lead to unacceptable results when the various national legal systems contain conflicting or mutually exclusive provisions.

Finally, the view that a harmonisation of laws could be unnecessary is certainly not true with regard to cross-border transactions involving consumers. In this area, we must take into consideration that banking contracts contain a large number of special features. In the law of sales, the seller's obligations are nearly identical in the various legal systems. In the case of banking services, however, the specific obligations are determined by the contract and by the applicable national laws, which differ greatly. A loan in one country is not the same as a loan in another country, and a guarantee in one country is not the same as a guarantee in another country.

The interrelationship of global and European harmonisation of laws

Harmonisation of laws is being worked on in many places throughout the world, so appropriate coordination of these efforts is urgently needed. Similar experiences have been made in connection with the law of banking supervision. Legal harmonisation in this area in the European Community is predirected through the standards set up by the Basel Banking Committee or by IOSCO. Similar coordination needs to be arranged between the worldwide harmonisation, for example, through UNCITRAL or Unidroit, and the harmonisation in the emerging "United States of Europe".

It is necessary to determine whether a particular harmonisation should take place on a global level or only within the European Community. Factors to be considered are whether the various initial situations and the differences in legal systems and legal traditions would prevent harmonisation or render it significantly more difficult. But if there is global harmonisation, the regional and national harmonisation must be postponed. The Commission of the European

Community has therefore correctly awaited the conclusion of work by UNCITRAL on a Model Law of International Credit Transfer before deciding whether it would be appropriate to adopt this model law in whole or in part as a Directive in the European Community. The result, of course, would be that a model law by UNCITRAL intended to govern cross-border transfer of funds would or could, by means of its adoption into Community law, also become applicable to govern purely domestic transfer transactions.[93]

A "harmonisation of harmonisation" is also needed. By this, we mean a coordination of provisions at the Community level with the harmonisation measures being carried out by other international institutions. One necessary element is the development of uniform terminology. We should point out here that the International Organisation for Standardisation (ISO) has prepared a uniform vocabulary of banking law terminology.

In addition, coordination of areas of application and substantive rules needs to be achieved in order to prevent harmonisation from creating a new chaos. This danger should not be underestimated.[94] It is problematic but sometimes scarcely avoidable that separate, parallel systems of legal provisions are developed for equivalent factual situations, for example one set of rules for domestic with special consumer protection stipulations and a different set of provisions for cross-border transactions. However, conflicting provisions in legal acts or proposals by various international organisations are not acceptable.

In one recent example, Art. 10 of the UNCITRAL Model Law on International Credit Transfers contained the "same-day rule". A financial institution which accepts a transfer order is obligated to carry out the order on the same day or at the latest on the following day when the payment order is received after the cut-off time for that day. In contrast, Principle Number 4 in the Principles Governing the Transparency of Banking Conditions Relating to Cross-Border Financial Transactions[95] contains a "two-day rule".[96] Such conflicts are not acceptable and damage attempts to achieve legal harmonisation.

---

93. See Directive of 27 January 1997 on cross-border credit transfers, 1997 O.J. (L 43) 25.

94. For an impressive discussion of the situation in international transportation law, see J. Putzeys, "Le Droit Uniforme 'Desuniformisé'?" in *International Uniform Law in Practice* 440 (Unidroit ed., 1988). See generally Trompenaars, *supra* n. 13; Herber, in *Festschrift für Stödter* 55 (1979); Herber, in *Rechtsdogmatik und Rechtspolitik, Hamburger Ringvorlesung* 269 (Karsten Schmidt ed., 1991); Herber, 1987 *Zeitschrift für Gesetzgebung* 17; Kötz, "Rechtsvereinheitlichung—Nutzen, Kosten, Methoden, Ziele", 50 *RabelsZ* 1 (1986); Kropholler, 85 *ZfVR* 143, 156 (1986); F. Majoros, "Konflikte zwischen Staatsverträgen auf dem Gebiete des Privatrechts", 46 *RabelsZ* 84 (1982); Majoros, "Zur Krise der internationalen Kodifikationspolitik", 1973 *Zeitschrift für Rechtspolitik* 63. But see Everling, in *Festschrift für Pescatore* 227, 242 (1987).

95. 1990 O.J. (L 67) 39.

96. The Fourth Principle states: "In the absence of instructions to be [sic] contrary and except in cases of *force majeure*, each intermediary institution should deal with a transfer order within two working days of receipt of the funds specified in the order or should give notification of its refusal to execute the order or of any foreseeable delay to the institution issuing the order and, where, different, to the transferor's institution." 1990 O.J. (L 67) 39, 42.

The connection between the principle of mutual recognition and the principles of international conflict of laws

The first 25 years of the European Community have shown that Article 100 of the Treaty establishing the European Economic Community, which provides for a complete harmonisation of laws, has not been able to achieve complete removal of technical obstacles. In its 1985 White Paper regarding the establishment of an internal market, the Commission proposed a change in strategy.[97] Because the goals of national legislation are substantially equivalent among the various countries, mutual recognition could represent an effective strategy in the creation of a Common Market for commerce. Some have expressed the view that this harmonisation concept developed for removing technical obstacles could further evolve into a principle of mutual recognition of civil law institutions.[98] This recognition would take place "directly", that is, "without a detour through international conflicts rules".[99]

Upon initial examination, a number of provisions in European Community law from most recent times seem to support this view, such as Art. 4 of the Amended Proposal for a Council Directive on the Freedom of Establishment and the Free Supply of Services in the Field of Mortgage Credit.[100] Similar provisions are also found in European insurance law.[101] If this view was correct, it would have unforeseeable consequences for the private law sector.

Before attempting to determine the range of the principle of mutual recognition of financing techniques, one should consider two factors. First, individual banking services, specifically the rights and obligations of the contracting parties, are determined by the law of contracts as well as the law of banking supervision. Behind each individual financial service is also its particular financing technique, which lies in the discretion of the financial institution but which can be subject to mandatory provisions of supervisory or civil law. For example, in accordance with para. 609(a) of the German Civil Code, the debtor's right to terminate a fixed-interest loan secured by a land mortgage can be excluded for a fixed time.[102] If this termination restriction, which is justified by the particular form of financing, were eliminated by European law, the main financing technique used by mortgage banks[103] would

---

97. Completing the Internal Market: White Paper from the Commission to the European Council, COM(85)310 final at 7, margin no. 61, 64.

98. Wolf, 1990 *WM* 1941; Troberg, *supra* n. 2, at 61; Mülbert, 1995 *ZHR* 2.

99. Wolf, *supra* n. 98, at 1942; *contra* U.H. Schneider and Troberg, 1990 *WM* 165, 170.

100. 1987 O.J. (C 161) 4.

101. See, e.g., Art. 25 of the Third Directive, 1990 O.J. (C 244) 28: "The Member State in which the risk is situated shall not prevent the policyholder from concluding a contract conforming with the rules of the home Member State, as long as it does not conflict with legal provisions protecting the general good in the Member State in which the risk is situated." See generally Meyer-Kahlen, *Angleichung des Versicherungsvertragsrechts im Gemeinsamen Markt* (1980); Hübner, 1982 *Zeitschrift für Versicherungswissenschaft* 221; Steindorff, **144** *Zeitschrift für das Gesamte Handels- und Wirtschaftsrecht* 447 (1980).

102. See Goedecke and Kerl, *Die deutschen Hypothekenbanken* 138 (3rd edn 1990).

103. See Fleischmann *et al.*, "Introduction" to *Hypothekenbankgesetz* (3rd edn 1979).

be placed in doubt. Here it becomes clear that a harmonisation of banking supervision law at a European Community level affects banking transactions law and, conversely, a harmonisation of contract law affects banking supervision law.[104]

Secondly, one must distinguish between banking contracts based on the law of obligations and those based on the law of property, and the principle of mutual recognition must be judged in light of these considerations. This principle has become established in Europe in the area of banking supervision law. This means that financing techniques that are governed by supervisory law must be mutually recognised. In civil law, the situation is different. It is true that the Member States' conflict of laws may contain elements of the principle of mutual recognition. However, the issue of which law is applicable to contractual banking obligations remains the basis for these rules; this issue is governed by the EC Treaty on the Law Applicable to Contractual Obligations of 19 June 1980, as discussed above.[105]

In banking contracts involving the law of property, in particular with regard to the recognition of security interests in personal property established in other Member States where the property is later moved to a different country within the European Community, the mere transfer of the principle of mutual recognition is certainly not sufficient. More sophisticated solutions are needed.[106] Factors which must be given due consideration include the intent of the parties, the protection of vested rights, the protection of free commerce, the limited number of rights in real estate and movables in some legal systems, the close relationship between the law of security interests and bankruptcy and social laws, and other factors. It was the intent of the Second EC Banking Directive not only to solve problems of banking supervision law but in addition to end the long-term international discussion regarding the international conflict in the law of property and security interests.[107]

Step-by-step harmonisation

Rightly or wrongly the diverse attempts to achieve harmonisation in the area of private law have repeatedly been strongly attacked. Certainly, a more intensive coordination among the individual harmonisation projects is needed. Questionable, however, is the tendency to restrict the contractual freedom of the

104. See Communication of the Commission: "Freedom to provide services and the interests of the general good in the Second Banking Directive"; and generally Müller-Graff, *supra* n. 4, at 20, 22.
105. See U.H. Schneider and Troberg, *supra* n. 99, at 165.
106. Welter, *Dingliche Sicherheiten zwischen Harmonisierung und gegenseitiger Anerkennung als Prinzipien des europäischen Binnenmarkts* (forthcoming).
107. See, e.g., Martini, *Praxis des Internationalen Privat- und Verfahrensrechts* 168 (1985); Sonnenberger, *Quartalshefte der Girozentrale* bk. IV, vol. 21., at 9, 21, 24 (Vienna 1986); Drobnig, in *Festschrift für Kegel* 141 (1987); Drobnig, 38 RabelsZ 468 (1974); Lüderitz, "Die Beurteilung beweglicher Sachen im Internationalen Privatrecht", in *Gutachten zur Reform des deutschen internationalen Personen- und Sachenrechts* 185 (1972); Schwind, in *Festschrift für Kegel* 599 (1987).

parties and to adopt mandatory provisions where it is not even clear which interests these provisions are intended to protect. There is also a trend towards a general division of contract law into a law of consumer contracts and a separate law for commercial and professional activities. The criticism here is not directed towards the goal of consumer protection but instead against this systematic split and its consequences.

One example is the Council Directive on improper clauses in consumer contracts.[108] As stated by Brandner and Ulmer in their comments on this Directive, the result is that "by means of European harmonisation of laws, the governing principle of socialist contract law would achieve a breakthrough at the same time as the formerly socialist eastern European countries are attempting to introduce market economy structures through orientation toward middle and western European contract law".[109] This view may be a bit exaggerated, but it certainly contains an element of truth. The tendency to use provisions of supervisory law rather than provisions of contract law is also questionable.[110] Still, it must be pointed out that, within the European Community, many legal systems do not distinguish clearly between administrative law, regulatory law, and private law.

The work involved in implementing harmonisation measures into national law is equally important. Many problems are caused by the step-by-step procedure in legal harmonisation, that is, harmonisation of individual types of contracts without developing general legal principles. The danger is the loss of systematic order within a set of laws. If every harmonisation measure is simply adopted into national law "word for word" or by means of a simple translation, one continues to add a number of "satellite laws" to national codifications. If systematic insertion into existing national law does not take place, the great codifications are threatened with collapse.[111] Only if systematic insertion succeeds can the loss of valuable parts of national legal culture be avoided. The goal should be therefore to develop a "European Uniform Code for Banking Contracts" that fits into the systems of national law of the Member States.

CONCLUSION

The object of this chapter was not to give more force to a call for more extensive harmonisation of commercial law in general or the law of banking transactions in particular, whether globally or within the European Community. Instead, the need for legal harmonisation must be examined carefully in each individual case. Against this background, we have attempted to make clear that harmonisation in the area of private law is already taking place worldwide, both on a global

108. 1993 O.J. (L 95) 29.
109. Brandner and Ulmer, 1991 *Der Betriebs-Berater [BB]* 701-2.
110. Bleckmann, *supra* n. 41, at margin no. 504.
111. See also Herber, 1987 *Zeitschrift für Gesetzgebung* 17; Herber, in *Rechtsdogmatik und Rechtspolitik, Hamburger Ringvorlesung* 269 (Karsten Schmidt ed., 1991).

scale and within the European Community. In the long run, a global Uniform Commercial Code for international business transactions may evolve. The European Community is playing a special role in this process, as it is developing into a community of economically relevant private law.

UWE H. SCHNEIDER

CHAPTER 11

THE SINGLE EUROPEAN CURRENCY[1]

.

INTRODUCTION

The introduction of the single European currency—the euro—on 1 January 1999 has far-reaching consequences for European banking law. It affects numerous types of transactions entered into by banks both in the wholesale and retail markets. This chapter examines, from the English law perspective, the legal framework adopted by the European Commission for the introduction of the euro and considers specific legal and practical issues that arise. A timetable for introducing the euro is set out on page 228 and a glossary of terms is set out in Appendix 3.

Eleven Member States adopted the euro on 1 January 1999: Austria, Belgium, Finland, France, Germany, Ireland, Italy, Luxembourg, Netherlands, Portugal and Spain. Denmark and Sweden decided not to participate. Greece is currently ineligible to join. The UK decided not to join the single currency in the first wave of membership. UK government policy is that, in principle, UK membership of a successful single currency would be beneficial if certain economic tests are satisfied. UK businesses are being urged to prepare intensively for the single currency, so that the UK can join, if it wishes to do so, early in the next UK Parliament (due to start not later than May 2002). An outline national changeover plan was published by H.M. Treasury as a consultative document in February 1999.

---

1. The author, Geoffrey Yeowart, is a partner of Lovell White Durrant, London, and Chairman of the Single Currency Working Party of the City of London Law Society, Banking Law Sub-Committee. The views expressed in this chapter are the author's personal views and do not necessarily represent those of his firm or the Sub-Committee. The legal position is stated as at 1 March 1999.

TIMETABLE FOR INTRODUCTION OF THE EURO

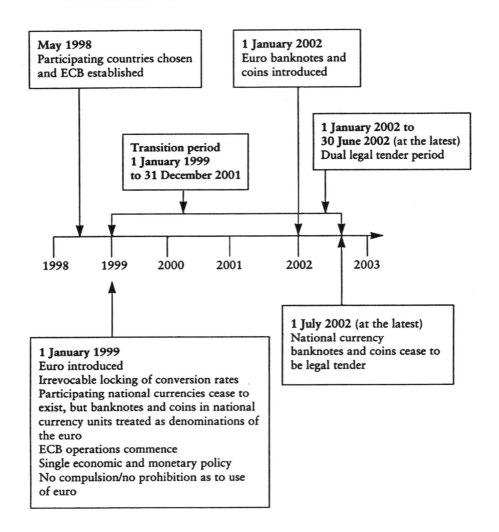

LEGAL FRAMEWORK FOR INTRODUCING THE EURO

Basis of legal framework

The European Commission originally planned to create the legal framework for introducing the euro by a single Council Regulation under Article 109l(4) of the Treaty on European Union, but ran into a timing dilemma. The Article 109l(4) powers could be exercised only after it was known which Member States would be the first to participate. The business sector urged the Commission to legislate much sooner, in order to confirm the substitution of the euro for the European currency unit (ECU) at the 1:1 conversion rate and to ensure continuity of contract.

Consequently, a "building block" approach was used, by adopting three Council Regulations in three stages on different legal bases. The first Regulation was adopted in June 1997 under the fast-track procedure provided by Article 235 of the Treaty.[2] The second Regulation was adopted in May 1998 and the third Regulation was adopted in December 1998, both under Article 109l(4).[3] The text of the Regulations is set out in full in Appendices 4, 5 and 6.

An important difference between the Regulations is that the first Regulation applies to all Member States (both "ins" and "outs"), whilst the second and third Regulations do not apply to the UK (as it has opted "out"), except insofar as monetary provisions are recognised by English courts under the principles of private international law. Each Regulation will be directly applicable in each Member State to which it applies, without the need for national implementing legislation.

First Regulation

The first Regulation deals with three main issues:

(a) substitution of the euro for the existing ECU on 1 January 1999;
(b) contract continuity and freedom of contract;
(c) conversion and rounding rules.

It came into force on 20 June 1997.

Second Regulation

The second Regulation deals with the remaining aspects of the introduction of the euro:

(1) substitution of the euro for participating national currencies;
(2) arrangements which will apply during the transition period from 1 January 1999 to 31 December 2001;

---

2. Council Regulation (EC) No 1103/97 of 17 June 1997.
3. Council Regulation (EC) No 974/98 of 3 May 1998 and Council Regulation (EC) No 2866/98 of 31 December 1998.

(3) redenomination of existing monetary obligations;
(4) introduction of euro banknotes and coins;
(5) provisions which apply at the end of the transition period.

Third Regulation

The Third Regulation irrevocably fixed the conversion rates between the euro and the national currencies of the Member States which adopted the euro.

The second and third Regulations came into force on 1 January 1999. The more important provisions of the Regulations and their legal implications are highlighted below.

ECU denominated obligations

The private ECU was widely used in the financial markets. There was considerable debate on the question of how these private ECU obligations would be affected by the introduction of the euro. The reason is that the ECU was not a currency but a unit of account based on a basket of twelve currencies. The euro was expected to have a different economic value.

The legal position was clarified by the adoption of the first Regulation. Briefly, this states that, from 1 January 1999, every reference in a legal instrument to the ECU (as officially defined) will be replaced by a reference to the euro at the rate of 1 euro to 1 ECU. It also contains a presumption that, where a legal instrument refers to the ECU, without this definition, the parties intended to refer to the official ECU, with the result that the 1:1 conversion rate applies. This presumption is rebuttable if the parties intended otherwise.

Why is this presumption necessary? The reason is that the types of ECU clause used in the financial markets varied. The most common, the "open basket" clause, linked the private ECU with the value and composition of the official ECU from time to time, provided it remained the EC unit of account. In some cases, the definition did not expressly refer to the official ECU but was intended to be used as a parallel unit of account and was treated as such in the markets. In other cases, there was no definition of the ECU at all, as in the case of many ECU deposits.

However, it is only the "specific basket" clause which is expected to fall outside the presumption. In these clauses, the composition of the ECU basket has been specifically frozen at a particular point of time: for instance, before the Spanish Peseta and Portuguese Escudo joined the official ECU basket. It is thought that most bonds using this fixed definition have matured already. It is possible that "fixed basket" clauses might still be found in some older derivatives.

The term "legal instruments" is defined, for the purposes of the first Regulation, to include not only legislative and statutory provisions but also contracts and payments instruments (except banknotes and coins) and other instruments with legal effect.

Continuity and freedom of contract

The first Regulation also deals with the key question of contract continuity. It is important that one party to an existing contract which extends beyond 1 January 1999 should not be able, unilaterally, to terminate or vary his contract merely because the contract currency has been replaced by the euro, unless this right is specifically conferred by the contract itself. The European Commission was urged to create a robust legal framework to ensure continuity of contract, while recognising the freedom of parties to agree such changes to their contracts as they might think appropriate. In response to concern on this issue, Article 3 of the first Regulation expressly states that the introduction of the euro will not:

— have the effect of altering any term of a legal instrument; or
— discharge or excuse performance under a legal instrument; or
— give a party the right unilaterally to alter or terminate a legal instrument;

subject to whatever the parties may have agreed, so preserving freedom of contract.

The parties are free to make whatever changes they choose to the terms of their contract, provided that this is done by mutual agreement. They may even agree to terminate the contract or to redenominate monetary obligations into a different currency such as US dollars. Article 3 will, however, prevent one party unilaterally altering or terminating the contract, unless the power to act unilaterally is conferred by the contract itself.

Article 3 refers only to the "introduction" of the euro. It is unclear to what extent this will be treated as covering commercial and economic consequences flowing from the introduction of the euro. A court will have a discretion as to how widely or otherwise to interpret Article 3. It is hoped that, save in exceptional cases, the courts will give a fairly wide purposive interpretation to the wording of Article 3.

Article 3 is a major step towards achieving legal certainty within the European Union. It forms part of English law, even though the UK has decided not to join in the first wave of membership.

Contracts governed by the law of a state outside the European Union

Article 3 of the first Regulation will not alter domestic contract law in jurisdictions outside the EU. Although international law broadly requires states to recognise the currency of another, there may be areas of uncertainty. The UK Financial Law Panel has investigated the legal position in the main financial centres outside the EU. It has published reports on the position under Japanese law, Swiss law and Singapore law. Independently, legislation has been enacted to clarify the position under the laws of the States of New York, Illinois, California and Singapore.

Force majeure

Force majeure and impossibility clauses are not specifically dealt with by Article 3. There was some concern initially that, because Article 3 is expressed to be subject to anything which the parties may have agreed, a *force majeure* or impossibility clause in an existing contract might override the continuity principle.

A typical *force majeure* clause is intended to excuse one party from liability where performance of his obligations is prevented or delayed by events outside his control. It is unlikely that the introduction of the euro would, of itself, operate to trigger a typical clause, in the absence of other factors. However, as the types of clause in use differ considerably, it is possible that they could give rise to uncertainty in some cases.

A statement has been included in recital 7 of the first Regulation that the principle of continuity should be compatible with anything which "parties might have agreed with reference to the introduction of the euro". Although this recital is not conclusive, it may assist in indicating that the exception to the continuity principle is intended to apply only where parties have turned their minds to the introduction of the euro and agreed a different provision.

Interest rates

If a borrower is paying interest at a fixed rate, the question arises whether he would be entitled to a rate adjustment if market interest rates are generally lower for the euro. The first Regulation states, in its recitals, that the principle of continuity of contracts implies in particular that the introduction of the euro does not alter the nominal interest rate payable by the debtor under a fixed rate instrument. Article 3 goes on to provide that, unless the parties have otherwise agreed, the introduction of the euro will not alter any term of a contract. So, unless a borrower has an express contractual right to prepay his debt or to reset the interest rate, the Regulation will give him no right to do this unilaterally.

The first Regulation does not seek to treat consumers and non-consumers differently in relation to interest payments. Submissions were made to the Commission that this would be inappropriate. Retail and wholesale markets are closely linked, since fixed rate finance offered to retail customers is normally hedged through derivatives in the wholesale market.

Neither Regulation expressly provides for what is to happen when a pricing source used in a contract for calculating a monetary amount disappears because it is linked to a participating national currency (see page 241 below).

Legal status of the euro and participating national currencies

A fundamental point to understand is that the euro is a *substitute* currency from 1 January 1999; it does not co-exist in parallel with national currencies. Instead, participating national currencies have ceased to exist as currencies in their own right. Existing banknotes and coins in those currencies are treated as denominations of the euro. The conversion rate between the euro unit and each participating national currency unit has been irrevocably fixed. So, Deutschemark banknotes and coin continue to be legal tender in Germany, and French Franc banknotes and coin continue to be legal tender in France, but each is treated as a sub-unit of the euro. Where a legal instrument refers to a national currency unit, this is treated as valid as if reference were made to the euro unit at the fixed conversion rate.

Euro banknotes will be introduced on 1 January 2002 and will be the only banknotes which have legal tender status in *all* participating Member States. They will be issued by the European Central Bank and central banks of the participating Member States. Coins in euros and cents will be introduced on the same date by participating Member States and only these coins will have legal tender status in all participating Member States. Except for the issuing authority and persons specifically designated by the national legislation of the issuing Member States, no party will be obliged to accept more than fifty coins in any single payment. Participating Member States are required to ensure adequate sanctions against counterfeiting and falsification of euro banknotes and coins.

National banknotes and coins will cease to be legal tender within their relevant territories by 30 June 2002 at the latest; this dual legal tender period may be shortened by national law and most Member States are expected to do this.

No compulsion, no prohibition principle

The substitution of the euro for the national currency of each participating Member State does not in itself have the effect of altering the denomination of legal instruments existing on the date of substitution.

The basic intention is that, in the transition period from 1 January 1999 to 31 December 2001, there should be no compulsion on a party to pay in euro and no prohibition on his doing so. However, there is an inherent inconsistency between these two principles, since "no prohibition" for one party might lead to "compulsion" for the other party. How are these principles implemented?

Generally, where a contract requires payment in a particular national currency unit, payment will continue to be made in that currency unit during the transition period, unless the parties to the contract otherwise agree or unless the amount is payable by crediting the recipient's account. Equally, where a contract requires payment in the euro unit, payment is to be made in that unit, unless the amount is payable by crediting the recipient's account.

The debtor has an option, under Article 8(3) of the second Regulation, to pay either in euro units or in national currency units where:

— the debt is denominated either in the euro unit or in the national currency unit of a participating Member State;

— the amount is payable within the same Member State by crediting it to an account of the creditor.

The bank receiving the amount is required to make the necessary conversion to credit it to the account in the same currency in which the account is kept, using the fixed conversion rate.

This option clearly applies to domestic payments within a participating Member State. An important question is to what extent it also applies to cross-border payments. The essential factors appear to be that, first, the bank account which receives the credit must be in the "home" Member State of the national currency in which the debt is denominated and, second, payment must be made to the credit of that account either in that national currency unit or in the euro unit. If these conditions are fulfilled, it appears to be irrelevant that the creditor or the debtor (or both of them) is located outside the relevant Member State, or that the transmission of funds is initiated from outside that Member State. So, the Article 8(3) option is exercisable where an amount denominated in French Francs is payable within France by crediting it to the creditor's account, even if one or both of the parties are located outside France. In contrast, the option is not exercisable where an amount denominated in French Francs is payable to the creditor's account with a bank in a different Member State, such as an account in London or Frankfurt.

The second Regulation is silent on the question whether a bank may charge a fee for such a conversion. However, the European Commission has adopted a Recommendation[4] on banking charges for conversion, which Member States are invited to support. Banks were required to implement by 1 January 1999 a standard of good practice on conversion, based on the following.

Practice that the Commission considers to be legally required

— no charges for converting payments from the national currency unit to the euro unit (and vice versa) during the transition period;
— no charges for converting accounts from the national currency unit to the euro unit at the end of the transition period;
— fees for services denominated in the euro unit should be no different from those for identical services denominated in the national currency unit.

Other recommended practice

— no charges for converting outgoing payments from the national currency unit to the euro unit (and vice versa) during the transition period;
— no charges for converting accounts from the national currency unit to the euro unit during the transition period;

4. Commission Recommendation No 98/286/EC of 23 April 1998.

— no charges to customers (i.e. account holders) for exchanging "household amounts" of national banknotes and coin for euro banknotes and coin during the final period ("household amounts" being quantified by volume and frequency in a transparent manner).

Redenomination during the transition period

The second Regulation empowers a Member State on or after 1 January 1999 to take measures in order to redenominate existing government debt issued in its own national currency under its own national law. An issuer of existing debt denominated in the national currency of a participating Member State is also free, unless redenomination is expressly excluded by the terms applicable to it, to redenominate such debt during the transition period if that Member State takes measure to redenominate all or part of its own government debt (Article 8(4) of the second Regulation). This provision is expressed to apply to debt issued by the general government of a Member State, as well as to bonds and other forms of securitised debt negotiable in the capital markets and to money market instruments, issued by other debtors.

A participating Member State may also take measures to enable certain markets to change from a national currency to the euro for operating purposes. These markets include those for the regular exchange, clearing and settlement of specified instruments and systems for the regular exchange, clearing and settlement of payments.

There has been debate as to how far redenomination should go. There are at least three possibilities: simple redenomination (a change in the currency unit in which the nominal value of a debt security is expressed); renominalisation (a change in the minimum nominal amount in which a debt security is held after redenomination in order to achieve a round amount); and reconventioning (a change in the terms applicable to the debt security to reflect different conventions on such matters as calculating interest and frequency of payment). A narrow definition of "redenomination" is used for the purposes of Article 8(4): it involves simply changing the currency unit in which the debt is stated without having the effect of altering any other term of the debt (which is regarded as a matter subject to the relevant national law).

Unless voluntarily redenominated during the transition period, all legal instruments existing at the end of that period will be automatically read as if references to national currency units were to euro units at the fixed conversion rate. The conversion and rounding rules contained in Articles 4 and 5 of the first Regulation will also operate where applicable.

Netting of mutual claims

Netting, set-off and other techniques with similar effect broadly continue to apply during the transition period to monetary obligations, irrespective of whether they are denominated in euro or a participating national currency, where netting, set-off or similar techniques are permitted or imposed by national law of a participating Member State. Conversion is effected at the fixed conversion rates.

Conversion and rounding rules

The conversion rate between the euro and the national currency of each participating Member State was irrevocably locked from 1 January 1999 on the basis that one euro equals:

Austrian Schilling	ATS	13.7603
Belgian Franc	BEF	40.3399
Deutschemark	DEM	1.95583
Finnish Markka	FIM	5.94573
French Franc	FRF	6.55957
Irish Pound	IEP	0.787564
Italian Lira	ITL	1936.27
Luxembourg Franc	LUF	40.3399
Netherlands Guilder	NLG	2.20371
Portuguese Escudo	PTE	200.482
Spanish Peseta	ESP	166.386

The currency code for the euro is "EUR" and it is represented by the "€" symbol. The exchange rate between the euro and non-participating currencies such as sterling will fluctuate from day to day.

The conversion rate may not be truncated or rounded when making conversion: for instance, it may not be shortened to 1.95 Deutschemarks. If the result of conversion is not an exact number, it will be rounded up or down to the nearest sub-unit. If this produces a result exactly half-way, the sum will be rounded up. Inverse rates (e.g. an approximation to the reciprocal of DEM 1.95583, such as 0.511292) are not permitted. They would produce inaccurate results for larger amounts.

Conversion from one participating national currency unit into another during the transition period involves a two-step process:

— the first step is to convert to euro from the first currency at the fixed conversion rate, with the result being rounded to not less than three decimals;
— the second step is to convert the resulting amount in euro to the second currency at the relevant fixed conversion rate.

It is the result, rather than the method itself, which is important. An alternative method of calculation may be used if it produces the same result.

Monetary amounts to be paid or accounted for when a rounding takes place after a conversion into the euro unit is rounded up or down to the nearest cent. Monetary amounts to be paid or accounted for after conversion into a national currency unit are rounded up or down to the nearest sub-unit or, in the absence of a sub-unit, to the nearest unit, or according to national law or practice to a multiple or fraction of the sub-unit or unit of the national currency unit. If the application of the conversion rate gives a result which is exactly half-way, the sum is rounded up.

Dual price display

The Commission has stated that it believes imposing mandatory dual display in European regulations would not be appropriate. Instead, the Commission has adopted a Recommendation[5] on dual price displays which Member States are invited to support. This sets out a standard of good practice. It calls for retailers to indicate clearly whether they will accept payments in euro units in the transition period. Where a dual display of prices or other monetary amounts is provided, the standard also requires that:

— conversion rates must be used for calculating the counter-values in dual displays;
— rounding to the nearest cent must be adhered to as a minimum standard of accuracy for prices or other monetary amounts which have been converted from a national currency unit to the euro unit;
— dual displays of prices and other monetary amounts must be unambiguous, easily identifiable and clearly legible.

In addition, the following basic standards of clarity in dual displays should be observed:

— the unit in which the price is set and in which amounts to be paid are to be calculated is to be distinguished from the counter-value which is displayed for information purposes only;
— dual displays of prices and other monetary amounts should not be overloaded with excessive numbers of figures. As a general rule, dual displays of prices on individual products can be limited to the final price which consumers have to pay. Dual displays on receipts and other financial statements can be limited to the total amount.

Dual displays on benchmark indicators such as bank statements and bills from utility companies should begin early in the transition period.

CONTINUITY OF CONTRACT AND OTHER SPECIFIC LEGAL ISSUES

This section examines some specific legal issues to consider in banking transactions in the light of the legal background outlined in the first part of this chapter.

5. Commission Recommendation No 98/287/EC of 23 April 1998.

Contract continuity

English law recognises that a contract may be discharged on the ground of frustration only where a supervening event occurs which renders it physically or commercially impossible to perform the contract or transforms the obligation to perform into a radically different obligation. The purpose of the doctrine of frustration is to avoid the injustice which would otherwise be caused by insisting on the literal performance of a contract after a significant change of circumstances. However, the doctrine may not be lightly invoked to relieve a contracting party of an imprudent commercial bargain or one which has merely become more difficult or expensive to perform. Nor may it be invoked where the parties have foreseen the effect on their contract of the relevant event and provided for what is to happen if it occurs, whether by means of an express clause or through the pricing. Where risk has been allocated by the parties in the contract, the courts will not normally intervene to re-allocate risk in a different way.

Foreseeability is an important issue in this context. It has been said that, as monetary union has been foreseeable since the Maastricht Treaty on European Union was ratified in November 1993, the risk of frustration being successfully invoked is confined only to contracts entered into before ratification of the Treaty. Indeed, it has been pointed out that monetary union has been foreseeable for even longer—the publication of the Delors Report being cited as one earlier milestone. This is a strong argument, although it is perhaps unwise to assume that frustration is wholly excluded by the fact that monetary union was foreseeable. Three factors are relevant:

— The first is the degree of foreseeability: it appears that the supervening event must be one which the parties could reasonably be expected to have foreseen as a real likelihood. The existence of the UK's right to opt "out" of the third stage of economic and monetary union may be a complicating factor here.
— The second is the extent of foreseeability: it appears that not only must the supervening itself be foreseeable, but its consequences and effect on the contract must also be foreseeable.
— The third is the existence of any other indication that, even though the event was foreseen, it was not the intention of the parties (or one of them) to assume the risk of its occurrence.

For instance, the parties may actually state in the contract that, if the event occurs, they will then decide how it is to affect the contract. By providing that it is to be the subject of further negotiation, the parties have made clear that their original contract is not intended to allocate the risk of its occurrence. So, if it does occur and no agreement is reached, the contract may then be frustrated.

It is equally arguable that, although economic and monetary union might have been foreseeable once the Maastricht Treaty was ratified, the effect of monetary union on many types of contract might not have become reasonably foreseeable to parties to a contract until later. Even after the consequences of economic and monetary union became foreseeable, contracting parties might have decided not to attempt to legislate for this in their contracts until the legal position was clarified by an EU Council Regulation establishing the legal framework for the introduction of the euro, or the market association representing practitioners in the particular market had made recommendations or at least given guidance on the appropriate options to adopt.

There is one possible exception to this general comment. In the case of private ECU denominated instruments, there is a stronger case for arguing that the parties should have foreseen the impact of the single currency on the ECU. Even here, there may have been some doubt as to how the changeover from the ECU to the single currency would be effected, at least prior to the Madrid Summit in December 1995, when it was stated that the conversion rate would be one ECU for one euro.

If a contract were to be frustrated, two legal consequences would flow. First, the contract would be automatically discharged. It would not be left to one or both parties to decide, in their judgement, whether or not to terminate. Second, if a contract were to become impossible of performance or were otherwise frustrated, all sums paid in pursuance of the contract before the time of its discharge would be recoverable from the recipient as money received by him for use of the payer, under section 1(2) of the Law Reform (Frustrated Contracts) Act 1943. There are two exceptions. Section 1(2) does not apply:

— if the contract itself allocates risk of loss resulting from the supervening event;
— if the payee is able to establish to the court that it is proper to sever the part of the contract already performed and for that part to subsist despite the frustration of the remainder.

It has been suggested that, where the original pricing of a derivative transaction has been fixed on the basis of the expected life of the transaction, it may be difficult successfully to claim severance.

The introduction of the euro should not, of itself, be a frustrating event, where the contract is still capable of performance by payment in the successor currency. There was concern that grey areas might exist where, for instance, an existing national currency was itself the subject-matter of the contract (as in the case of a currency or interest rate swap).

The position has been considered in detail by the Financial Law Panel. In its report on continuity of contracts in English law (January 1998), the Panel stated that it had been unable to identify any classes of transaction or forms of contract commonly used in financial and commercial markets, and governed by English law, where the continuity principle is likely to be called into question by economic and monetary union. In the absence of the first Regulation, the Panel considered that disputes as to contract continuity might conceivably have arisen, for instance, where:

— changes occur in the economic value of private ECU obligations upon the ECU being replaced by the euro on 1 January 1999; and
— both currencies in a cross-currency swap are replaced by the euro at the same time, so removing the volatility which it was the purpose of the contract to hedge against and converting the contract effectively into an annuity.

However, the Panel considered that Article 3 of the first Regulation clearly provides for contract continuity in these cases.

As Article 3 does not apply to domestic contract law outside the European Union, the legal position may differ in other jurisdictions. The Financial Law Panel has investigated the legal position in Japan and reported in July 1997 that legal thinking broadly indicates contract continuity is likely to be respected under Japanese law. It also reported in May 1998 that, although market participants which have substantial business in Switzerland will need to take appropriate advice on their individual positions, no serious or unexpected Swiss legal issues are foreseen in the Swiss markets. The Panel further reported in July 1998 on the position under Singapore law and broadly concluded that no major problems were foreseen. The position was not wholly clear in relation to the ECU but there were thought to be few examples of longer-term ECU obligations governed by Singapore law.

It is sensible for banks and borrowers to take local legal advice and, if the position is unclear, to seek to agree a continuity clause, assuming both parties are willing to do so. Care should be taken to avoid a mismatch (page 244).

Use of continuity clauses in contracts

One question that is frequently asked is whether it is sensible to include a continuity clause in a contract. There is no single answer and the question needs to be decided case by case. As the continuity principle is clearly established by Article 3 of the first Regulation, it greatly reduces the need to use a continuity clause where the contract is governed by the law of an EU Member State. Some participants in the derivatives market have chosen to include continuity clauses. The International Swaps and Derivatives Association (ISDA) has produced a specimen continuity clause for use in ISDA Master Agreements if the parties so wish.

A continuity clause typically states that, unless the parties otherwise expressly agree, the occurrence or non-occurrence of an event associated with economic and monetary union will not of itself discharge a contract, or entitle one party unilaterally to vary or terminate it. A continuity clause may minimise the risk of a party attempting to escape from a loss-making contract because of the changeover to the euro. But there could be a risk in committing to continue a contract without at the same time agreeing how any costs and risks resulting from economic and monetary union should be allocated between the parties. Continuity clauses do not normally deal with this latter aspect. If it is used, a continuity clause requires careful drafting and it is sensible to base it on a standard clause such as the ISDA provision. An ill-drafted clause may create more problems that it solves.

The impact on pricing sources used in contracts

Pricing sources such as benchmarks for fixing interest rates may disappear if linked to a national currency which itself is replaced by the euro. It is unlikely that a contract will be treated, at least under English law, as frustrated by reason only of the disappearance of a price source. But this could lead to a dispute as to how much is payable under the contract.

Where a national price source is to be discontinued, a successor price source is expected to be designated in nearly all cases. Several Member States are introducing domestic legislation to designate successor price sources. For instance, legislation in Germany empowers the Federal Government to substitute for Frankfurt Interbank Offered Rate (FIBOR) the interest rate which functionally corresponds most closely to it. France has adopted a similar approach in relation to Paris Interbank Offered Rate (PIBOR). The successor for both these national rates is Euro Interbank Offered Rate (EURIBOR), which is a pan-European rate calculated from a panel initially of 47 banks in the euro zone and up to 10 banks outside it.

There was some concern that the substitution of a euro zone rate for a national rate could produce a different economic result, although the practical risk of this happening appears to have diminished as the relevant rates converged. As such national legislation applies only to contracts governed by the law of the relevant Member State, the position is less clear where the contract is governed by the law of a different jurisdiction.

The UK approach is different. The preferred course is to leave it to practitioners to settle market practice and to avoid the need for the government to intervene. If a contract were to fail to provide a mechanism for identifying a replacement price source, the contract might be unenforceable due to uncertainty. The English courts are expected to lean towards implying a term that the nearest comparable successor rate should be adopted in the absence of a contrary intention of the parties, where there are ground for doing so. However, this may not necessarily be easy to do in all cases. Trade associations in the international markets, particularly the British Bankers' Association (BBA) and ISDA, have done much useful work in identifying affected benchmark rates and liaising with price sponsors and screen service providers to ensure that designated replacement rates are provided. The Financial Law Panel has suggested that the attainment of a consistent market practice in this area is the best way to assist the English courts in their wish to maintain the continuity of contracts.

Banks and their advisers should ensure that existing contracts are adequately worded (or amended) to identify an appropriate successor rate or to include a fall-back provision under which an alternative rate is fixed by one or more reference banks. Many contracts will, if well drafted, already cover the possibility of the price source being replaced.

How changes in market conventions may affect existing contracts

The leading international trade associations have combined to recommend harmonised market conventions for interest calculations, trading and settlement, which apply from 1 January 1999 to new transactions in euros in the financial markets.[6] This initiative to harmonise market conventions has received widespread support, although further work is required to ensure that the recommended conventions are universally used.

Broadly, unless otherwise agreed by the parties or required by national legislation, "legacy" transactions will continue to be subject to existing conventions, even if they are redenominated into euros. This is intended to minimise the legal complications and risk of mismatches which might otherwise arise where existing transactions have been hedged in the derivatives market.

Some consequential changes may be necessary. For instance, both EURIBOR and the BBA's euro LIBOR will be quoted for "spot" value, with settlement being two business days after the trade date. Several national rates are currently based on a different settlement cycle (Sterling uses same-day settlement). Interest will also be calculated using the actual number of days divided by 360 (Sterling, the Belgian Franc and the Escudo currently use a 365-day year). Documentation may need to be amended to reflect this change in market conventions to a "spot" rate and a 360-day year.

A potential issue has also been identified in applying the recommended convention that TARGET operating days should be the basis for defining euro business days. TARGET is the Trans-European Automated Real Time Gross Settlement Express Transfer system. It operates every day, except Saturdays, Sundays, Christmas and New Year's Day, if the national real time gross settlement systems (RTGS) of at least two Member States are open. Care should be taken, when using this business day definition, to check whether existing national legislation affects time of payment when this falls on a local bank holiday. For purely domestic transactions, the parties may prefer to continue to use national business day conventions.

Increased costs

The European Commission has suggested that, although it is a matter of contract, increased cost clauses in finance documents that refer to liquidity, reserve or similar requirements, should not be triggered by reason only of the

6. See the Joint Statement published on 29 May 1997 by the Association Cambiste Internationale, the International Primary Market Association, the International Securities Market Association, the International Swaps and Derivatives Association, the International Paying Agents Association, Cedel Bank and Morgan Guaranty as Operator of the Euroclear System.

introduction of the euro and the change of legal framework. However, if regulatory changes were to occur after the euro is introduced, an increased cost clause could be triggered, depending on its precise wording.

If the monetary policies introduced by the European Central Bank within the euro area after January 1999 result in increased costs for lenders, lenders might well wish to pass these to borrowers to the extent that they are not covered by the contractual interest rate. Modern increased cost clauses are often drafted in wide terms to include reference to any central bank or regulatory authority, but clauses in older loan documents (particularly those involving bilateral loans in domestic currencies) or negotiated clauses may be more narrowly framed. Banks and borrowers may need to evaluate whether increased cost provisions could be triggered and, if so, with what result.

Private ECU denominated contracts

Existing ECU denominated contracts and debt securities which extend beyond 1 January 1999 should be reviewed. It is important to establish what type of ECU definition is used and whether the conversion rate of 1 euro for 1 ECU (which is presumed in the absence of contrary intention) will apply.

ECU bond documentation for outstanding issues should also be checked to see whether it provides that the disappearance of the ECU triggers a mechanism for payments to be made in another currency. Although it is expected that a court would normally treat the bond as converted from ECU to euro in the light of the first Regulation, it is possible that, depending on the wording of the relevant provision, a court might feel constrained to give effect to the trigger mechanism in certain cases. Specific legal advice should be taken on the interpretation of such trigger clauses.

Where loan agreements contain an option to borrow in ECUs, they should be amended to permit borrowings in euros instead after 1 January 1999.

Review of contracts

It is necessary for parties to existing contracts to evaluate whether the changeover to the euro adversely affects contracts which refer to a national currency which is replaced by the euro and which extends beyond 1 January 1999, including derivatives, forward foreign exchange contracts, fixed interest instruments, long-term supply contracts and contracts governed by the law of a non-EU jurisdiction. As indicated above, the disappearance of a currency, interest rate, exchange rate, price source, index or settlement system may affect a contract, unless an appropriate successor rate, source, index or system is identified and agreed.

As to derivatives, ISDA established a Protocol under which parties to ISDA Master Agreements were able to accede on a collective basis to specific contractual amendments on such matters as continuity, replacement price sources, business days, rounding and updated definitions. The amendments are incorporated in Master Agreements where both parties adhered on similar terms to the Protocol. The time limit for adherence was 30 September 1998 and adherence letters were delivered by 1,130 entities before that date (estimated to cover more than 600,000 ISDA Master Agreements). The BBA also established an EMU Protocol to amend the IFEMA, ICOM and FEOMA Master Netting Agreements. This covers similar issues to those in the ISDA Protocol but also deal specifically with barrier options.

If the legal position on contract continuity would be less clear in jurisdictions outside the European Union, it might be sensible to choose the law of a Member State, such as English law, to govern a contract involving a European currency replaced, or expected to be replaced, by the euro, unless a specific clause is included to deal with continuity. Article 3 of the first Regulation gives considerable comfort as to continuity in relation to contracts governed by the law of an EU Member State.

It is important to guard against the risk of mismatches. For instance, where the exposure of a company under a loan or debt security is hedged by a currency or interest rate swap, it is essential that the hedge is not thrown out of synchronisation by the introduction of the euro. This risk could arise particularly where the different transactions are goverened by different laws (e.g. if the loan or bond is goverened by English law and the swap by New York law). Again, care needs to be taken when selecting the governing law.

Settlement of monetary obligations denominated in participating national currencies

Where a contract stipulates a participating national currency for payment, the second Regulation provides that payment will continue to be made in that currency during the transition period, unless the parties otherwise agree or the debtor pays in euros under the Article 8(3) option (see page 233).

So, a debt of 100 Deutschemarks payable in Germany by crediting the creditor's bank account in Frankfurt may be paid under this option either in Deutschemark units or in euro units. If a payment in euros is made, the account is then credited with a corresponding amount in Deutschemark units. But what if the relevant contract is governed by English law? Payment in euros should be recognised by an English court if it is a valid discharge of the debt under the law of the place of performance. In the above example, payment in euros of a debt denominated in Deutschemarks to a bank account in Frankfurt would be valid in Germany because Article 8(3) would apply there. In contrast, Article 8(3) would not permit a debt denominated in Deutschemarks to be satisfied by a payment in euros to an account outside Germany, such as one in Paris.

Payment in euros in the UK after 1 January 1999

While the UK is outside the euro area, Article 8(3) will not permit a sterling debt to be discharged by a payment in euros to an account in London. Payments in euros may, however, be freely made in euros in the UK if mutually agreed by the parties to a contract or if the contract confers on one party the option to pay in euros.

In practice, the euro is expected to become the most widely used foreign currency in the UK for businesses. Although a party to a UK domestic transaction is not obliged to accept a cheque drawn in euros or a participating national currency, it may do so if it wishes. The use of euros in retail transactions is predicted to increase substantially after euro banknotes and coins are introduced on 1 January 2002. Businesses will need to establish clear guidelines on (i) when they are obliged to accept euro payments and (ii) when they are not obliged but may wish to do so. They may also wish to consider whether to include in future contracts an express option enabling them to choose the currency in which payment is to be made or received and the place of payment.

Redenomination of bonds and debt securities into euros

The second Regulation states that an issuer of existing private sector debt securities denominated in the national currency of a participating Member State is free, unless precluded by the terms of the issue, to redenominate them during the transition period if that Member State takes steps to redenominate all or part of its own govenment debt (Article 8(4)). The effect of Article 8(4) on legal instruments governed by the law of the relevant participating Member State seems reasonably clear. Whether Article 8(4) enables redenomination by an issuer of private sector debt securities governed by the law of a different jurisdiction, such as the UK, is less clear.

If issuers decide to redenominate their debt securities, they may also wish to alter the nominal amount to achieve a convenient round figure and also to change the market conventions relating to them. It is prudent to assume that, where a contract is governed by English law, the alteration of any other term can be done only by agreement of all relevant parties, unless the contract itself provides an alternative procedure for doing this. The International Primary Market Association (IPMA) has made available standard language for use by issuers of new debt securities who wish to provide for redenomination, renominalisation and reconventioning.

CONCLUSION

A considerable amount of preparation work for the launch of the euro was carried out in the London financial markets. Although initially certain operational issues arose in using the new euro payment systems, the launch itself went remarkably smoothly. While only time will reveal what contractual issues may emerge, the legal framework established for the euro should go a long way towards providing legal certainty.

GEOFFREY YEOWART*

* This chapter has been written as a general guide only. It should not be taken as legal advice in relation to a particular situation or transaction. It does not obviate the need to take specific legal advice if appropriate.

GENERAL BUSINESS CONDITIONS (GERMANY): BUNDESVERBAND DEUTSCHER BANKEN

* The present translation is furnished for the customer's convenience only. The original German text of the General Business Conditions is binding in all respects. In the event of any divergence between the English and the German texts, constructions, meanings or interpretations, the German text, construction, meaning or interpretation shall govern exclusively.

BASIC RULES GOVERNING THE RELATIONSHIP BETWEEN THE CUSTOMER AND THE BANK

1. Scope of application and amendments of these Business Conditions and the Special Conditions for particular business relations

(1) Scope of application

The General Business Conditions govern the entire business relationship between the customer and the bank's domestic offices (hereinafter referred to as the "Bank"). In addition, particular business relations (such as securities transactions, ec service, use of cheques, savings accounts) are governed by Special Conditions, which contain deviations from, or complements to, these General Business Conditions; they are agreed with the customer when the account is opened or an order is given. If the customer also maintains business relations with foreign offices, the Bank's lien (No. 14 of these Business Conditions) also secures the claims of such foreign offices.

(2) Amendments

Any amendments of these Business Conditions and the Special Conditions will be notified to the customer in writing. They shall be deemed to have been approved unless the customer objects thereto in writing. Upon notification of such amendments, the Bank shall expressly draw the customer's attention to this consequence. The customer's objection must be dispatched to the Bank within one month from the notification of the amendments.

2. Banking secrecy and disclosure of banking affairs

(1) Banking secrecy

The Bank has the duty to maintain secrecy about any customer-related facts and evaluations of which it may have knowledge (banking secrecy). The Bank may only disclose information concerning the customer if it is legally required to do so or if the customer has consented thereto or if the Bank is authorized to disclose banking affairs.

(2) Disclosure of banking affairs

Any disclosure of details of banking affairs comprises statements and comments of a general nature concerning the economic status, the creditworthiness and solvency of the customer; no information will be disclosed as to amounts of balances of accounts, of savings deposits, of securities deposits or of other assets entrusted to the Bank or as to amounts drawn under a credit facility.

(3) Prerequisites for the disclosure of banking affairs

The Bank is entitled to disclose banking affairs concerning legal entities and on businesspersons registered in the Commercial Register, provided that the inquiry relates to their business activities. The Bank does not, however, disclose any information if it has received instructions to the contrary from the customer. Details of banking affairs concerning other persons, in particular private customers and associations, are disclosed by the Bank only if such persons have expressly agreed thereto, either generally or in an individual case. Details of banking affairs are disclosed only if the requesting party has substantiated its justified interest in the information requested and there is no reason to assume that the disclosure of such information would be contrary to the customer's legitimate concerns.

(4) Recipients of disclosed banking affairs

The Bank discloses details of banking affairs only to its own customers as well as to other credit institutions for their own purposes or those of their customers.

3. Liability of the Bank; contributory negligence of the customer

(1) Principles of liability

In performing its obligations, the Bank shall be liable for any negligence on the part of its staff and of those persons whom it may call in for the performance of its obligations. If the Special Conditions for particular business relations or other agreements contain provisions inconsistent herewith such provisions shall prevail. In the event that the customer has contributed to the occurrence of the loss by any own fault (e.g. by violating the duties to cooperate as mentioned in No. 11 of these Business Conditions), the principles of contributory negligence shall determine the extent to which the Bank and the Customer shall have to bear the loss.

(2) Orders passed on to third parties

If the contents of an order are such that the Bank typically entrusts a third party with its further execution, the Bank performs the order by passing it on to the third party in its own name (order passed on to a third party). This applies, for example, to obtaining information on banking affairs from other credit institutions or to the custody and administration of securities in other countries. In such cases, the liability of the Bank shall be limited to the careful selection and instruction of the third party.

(3) Disturbance of business

The Bank shall not be liable for any losses caused by *force majeure*, riot, war or natural events or due to other occurrences for which the Bank is not responsible (e.g. strike, lock-out, traffic hold-ups, administrative acts of domestic or foreign high authorities).

4. Set-off limitations on the part of the customer

The customer may only set off claims against those of the Bank if the customer's claims are undisputed or have been confirmed by a final court decision.

5. Right of disposal upon the death of the customer

Upon the death of the customer, the Bank may, in order to clarify the right of disposal, demand the production of a certificate of inheritance, a certificate of executorship or further documents required for such purpose; any documents in a foreign language must, if the Bank so requests, be submitted in a German translation. The Bank may waive the production of a certificate of inheritance or a certificate of executorship if an official or certified copy of the testamentary disposition (last will or contract of inheritance) together with the relevant record of probate proceedings is presented. The Bank may consider any person designated therein as heir or executor as the entitled person, allow this person to dispose of any assets and, in particular, make payment or delivery to this person, thereby discharging its obligations. This shall not apply if the Bank is aware that the person designated therein is not entitled to dispose (e.g. following challenge or invalidity of the will) or if this has not come to the knowledge of the Bank due to its own negligence.

6. Applicable law and place of jurisdiction for customers who are businesspersons or public-law entities

(1) Applicability of German law

German law shall apply to the business relationship between the customer and the Bank.

(2) Place of jurisdiction for domestic customers

If the customer is a businessperson other than a "Minderkaufmann" (small trader) and if the business relation in dispute is attributable to the conduting of such businessperson's trade, the Bank may sue such customer before the court having jurisdiction for the bank office keeping the account or before any other competent court; the same applies to legal entities under public law and separate funds under public law. The Bank itself may be sued by such customers only before the court having jurisdiction for the bank office keeping the account.

(3) Place of jurisdiction for foreign customers

The agreement upon the place of jurisdiction shall also apply to customers who conduct a comparable trade or business abroad and to foreign institutions which are comparable with domestic legal entities under public law or a domestic separate fund under public law.

KEEPING OF ACCOUNTS

7. Periodic balance statements

(1) Issue of periodic balance statements

Unless otherwise agreed upon, the Bank issues a periodic balance statement for a current account at the end of each calendar quarter, thereby clearing the claims accrued by both parties during this period (including interest and charges imposed by the Bank). The Bank may charge interest on the balance arising therefrom in accordance with No. 12 of these Business Conditions or any other agreements entered into with the customer.

(2) Time allowed for objections; approval by silence

Any objections a customer may have concerning the incorrectness or incompleteness of a periodic balance statement must be raised not later than within one month following its receipt; if the objections are made in writing, it is sufficient to dispatch these within the period of one month. Failure to make objections in due time will be considered approval. When issuing the periodic balance statement, the Bank will expressly draw the customer's attention to this consequence. The customer may demand a correction of the periodic balance statement even after expiry of this period, but must then prove that the account was either wrongly debited or mistakenly not credited.

8. Reverse entries and correction entries made by the Bank

(1) Prior to issuing periodic balance statement

Incorrect credit entries on current accounts (e.g. due to a wrong account number) may be reversed by the Bank through a debit entry prior to the issue of the next periodic balance statement to the extent that the Bank has a repayment claim against the customer; in this case, the customer may not object to the debit entry on the grounds that a disposal of an amount equivalent to the credit entry had already been made (reverse entry).

(2) After issuing a period balance statement

If the Bank ascertains an incorrect credit entry after a periodic balance statement has been issued and if the Bank has a repayment claim against the customer, it will debit the account of the customer with the amount of its claim (correction entry). If the customer objects to the correction entry, the Bank will re-credit the account with the amount in dispute and assert its repayment claim separately.

(3) Notification to the customer; calculation of interest

The Bank will immediately notify the customer of any reverse entries and correction entries made. With respect to the calculation of interest, the Bank shall effect the entries retroactively as of the day on which the incorrect entry was made.

9. Collection orders

(1) Conditional credit entries effected upon presentation of documents

If the Bank credits the countervalue of cheques and direct debits prior to their payment, this is done on condition of payment, even if these items are payable at the Bank itself. If the customer surrenders other items, instructing the Bank to collect an amount due from a debtor (e.g. interest coupons), and if the Bank effects a credit entry for such amount, this is done under the reserve that the Bank will obtain the amount. This reserve shall also apply if the items are payable at the Bank itself. If cheques or direct debits are not paid or if the Bank does not obtain the amount under the collection order, the Bank will cancel the conditonal credit entry regardless of whether or not a periodic balance statement has been issued in the meantime.

(2) Payment of direct debits and of cheques made out by the customer

Direct debits and cheques are paid if the debit entry has not been cancelled prior to the end of the second bank working day after it was made. Cheques payable in cash are deemed to have been paid once their amount has been paid to the presenting party. Cheques are also deemed to have been paid as soon as the Bank dispatches an advice of payment. Direct debits and cheques presented through the clearing office of a "Landeszentralbank" are paid if they are not returned to the clearing office by the time stipulated by the Landeszentralbank.

10. Risks inherent in foreign currency accounts and transactions

(1) Execution of orders relating to foreign currency accounts

Foreign currency accounts of the customer serve to effect the cashless settlement of payments to and disposals by the customer in foreign currency. Disposals of credit balances on foreign currency accounts (e.g. by means of transfer orders to the debit of the foreign currency credit balance) are settled through or by banks in the home country of the currency unless the Bank executes them entirely within its own organisation.

(2) Credit entries for foreign currency transactions with the customer

If the Bank concludes a transaction with the customer (e.g. a forward exchange transaction) under which it owes the provision of an amount in a foreign currency, it will discharge its foreign currency obligation by crediting the account of the customer in the respective currency, unless otherwise agreed upon.

(3) Temporary limitation of performance by the Bank

The Bank's duty to execute a disposal order to the debit of a foreign currency credit balance (paragraph 1) or to discharge a foreign currency obligation (paragraph 2) shall be suspended to the extent that and for as long as the Bank cannot or can only restrictedly dispose of the currency in which the foreign currency credit balance or the obligation is denominated, due to political measures or events in the country of the respective currency. To the extent that and for as long as such measures or events persist, the Bank is not obligated either to perform at some other place outside the country of the respective currency, in some other currency (including Deutsche Mark) or by providing cash. However, the Bank's duty to execute a disposal order to the debit of a foreign currency credit balance shall not be suspended if the Bank can execute it entirely within its own organisation. The right of the customer and of the Bank to set off mutual claims due in the same currency against each other shall not be affected by the above provisions.

DUTIES OF THE CUSTOMER TO COOPERATE

11. Duties of the customer to cooperate

(1) Change in the customer's name, address or powers of representation towards the Bank

A proper settlement of business requires that the customer notify the Bank without delay of any changes in the customer's name and address, as well as the termination of, or amendment to, any powers of representation towards the Bank conferred to any person (in particular, a power of attorney). This notification duty also exists where the powers of representation are recorded in a public register (e.g. the Commercial Register) and any termination thereof or any amendments thereto are entered in that register.

(2) Clarity of orders

Orders of any kind must unequivocally show their contents. Orders that are not clearly worded may lead to queries, which may result in delays. In particular, when giving orders to credit an account (e.g. transfer orders), the customer must ensure the correctness and completeness of the name of the payee, as well as of the account number and the bank code number stated. Amendments, confirmations or repetitions of orders must be designated as such.

(3) Special reference to urgency in connection with the execution of an order

If the customer feels that an order requires particularly prompt execution (e.g. because a money transfer must be credited to the payee's account by a certain date), the customer shall notify the Bank of this fact separately. For orders given on a printed form, this must be done separately from the form.

(4) Examination of, and objection to, notification received from the Bank

The customer must immediately examine statements of account, security transaction statements, statements of securities and of investment income, other statements, advices of execution of orders, as well as information on expected payments and consignments (advices) as to their correctness and completeness and immediately raise any objections relating thereto.

(5) Notice to the Bank in case of non-receipt of statements

The customer must notify the Bank immediately if periodic balance statements and securities statements are not received. The duty to notify the Bank also exists if other advices expected by the customer (e.g. security transaction statements, statements of account after execution of customer orders or payments expected by the customer) are not received.

COST OF BANK SERVICES

12. Interest, charges and out-of-pocket expenses

(1) Interest and charges in private banking

Interest and charges for loans and services customary in private banking are set out in the "Price Display—Standard rates for private banking" (Preisaushang) and, in addition, in the "Price List" (Preisverzeichnis). If a customer makes use of a loan or service listed therein and unless otherwise agreed between the Bank and the customer, the interest and charges stated in the then valid Price Display or Price List are applicable. For any services not stated therein which are provided following the instruction of the customer or which are believed to be in the interests of the customer and which can, in the given circumstances, only be expected to be provided against remuneration, the Bank may at its reasonable discretion determine the charges (Section 315 of the German Civil Cide—Bürgerliches Gesetzbuch).

(2) Interest and charges other than for private banking

The amount of interest and charges other than for private banking shall, in the absence of any other agreement, be determined by the Bank at its reasonable discretion (Section 315 of the German Civil Code).

(3) Changes in interest and charges

In the case of variable interest rate loans, the interest rate will be adjusted in accordance with the terms of the respective loan agreement.

(4) Customer's right of termination in case of changes in interest and charges

Interest adjustment and changes in charges according to paragraph 3 will be notified to the customer by the Bank. If charges are increased, the customer may, unless otherwise agreed, terminate with immediate effect the business relationship affected thereby within one month from the notification of the change. If the customer terminates the business relationship, any such increased interest and charges shall not be applied to the terminated business relationship. The Bank will allow an adequate period of time for the settlement.

(5) Out-of-pocket expenses

The customer shall bear all out-of-pocket expenses which are incurred when the Bank carries out the instructions or acts in the presumed interests of the customer (in particular, telephone costs, postage) or when credit security is furnished, administered, released or realised (in particular, notarial fees, storage charges, cost of guarding items serving as collateral).

(6) Peculiarities relating to consumer loans

The interest and costs (charges, out-of-pocket expenses) for those loan agreements which require the written form pursuant to Section 4 of the Consumer Credit Act (Verbraucherkreditgesetz) are determined by the provisions of such contract documentation. If an interest rate is not stated therein, the legal interest rate shall apply; costs not stated therein are not owed (Section 6 (2) of the Consumer Credit Act). For overdraft credits pursuant to section 5 of the Consumer Credit Act, the interest rate shall be determined by the Price Display and the information provided by the Bank to the customer.

SECURITY FOR THE BANK'S CLAIMS AGAINST THE CUSTOMER

13. Providing or increasing of security

(1) Right of the Bank to request security

The Bank may demand that the customer provide the usual forms of security for any claims that may arise from the banking relationship, even if such claims are conditional (e.g. indemnity for amounts paid under a guarantee issued on behalf of the customer). If the customer has assumed a liability for another customer's obligations towards the Bank (e.g. as a surety), the Bank is, however, not entitled to demand that security be provided or increased for the debt resulting from such liability incurred before the maturity of the debt.

(2) Changes in the risk

If the Bank, upon the creation of claims against the customer, has initially dispensed wholly or partly with demanding that security be provided or increased, it may nonetheless make such a demand at a later time, provided, however, that circumstances occur or become known which justify a higher risk assessment of the claims against the customer. This may, in particular, be the case if

— the economic status of the customer has changed or threatens to change in a negative manner or

— the value of the existing security has deteriorated or threatens to deteriorate.

The Bank has no right to demand security if it has been expressly agreed that the customer either does not have to provide any security or must only provide that security which has been specified. For loans subject to the Consumer Credit Act, the Bank is entitled to demand that security be provided or increased only to the extent that such security is mentioned in the loan agreement; when, however, the net loan amount exceeds DM 100,000,—, the Bank may demand that security be provided or increased even if the loan agreement does not contain any or any exhaustive indications as to security.

(3) Setting a time period for providing or increasing security

The Bank will allow adequate time to provide or increase security. If the Bank intends to make use of its right of termination without notice according to No. 19(3) of these Business Conditions, should the customer fail to comply with the obligation to provide or increase security within such time period, it will draw the customer's attention to this consequence before doing so.

14. Lien in favour of the Bank

(1) Agreement on the lien

The customer and the Bank agree that the Bank acquires a lien on the securities and chattels which, within the scope of banking business, have come or may come into the possession of a domestic office of the Bank. The Bank also acquires a lien on any claims which the customer has or may in future have against the Bank arising from the banking relationship (e.g. credit balances).

(2) Secured claims

The lien serves to secure all existing, future and contingent claims arising from the banking relationship which the Bank with all its domestic and foreign offices is entitled to against the customer. If the customer has assumed a liability for another customer's obligation towards the Bank (e.g. as a surety), the lien shall not secure the debt resulting from the liability incurred before the maturity of the debt.

(3) Exemptions from the lien

If funds or other assets come into the power of disposal of the Bank under the reserve that they may only be used for a specified purpose (e.g. deposit of cash for payment of a bill of exchange), the Bank's lien does not extend to these assets. The same applies to shares issued by the Bank itself (own shares) and to securities which the Bank keeps in safe custody abroad for the customer's account. Moreover, the lien extends neither to the profit-participation rights/profit-participation certificates (Genußrechte/Genußscheine) issued by the Bank itself nor to the Bank's subordinated obligations confirmed by document or unconfirmed.

(4) Interest and dividend coupons

If securities are subject to the Bank's lien, the customer is not entitled to demand the delivery of the interest and dividend coupons pertaining to such securities.

15. Security interests in items for collection and discounted bills of exchange

(1) Transfer of ownership by way of security

The Bank acquires ownership by way of security of any cheques and bills of exchange deposited for collection at the time such items are deposited. The Bank acquires absolute ownership of discounted bills of exchange at the time of the purchase of such items; if it re-debits discounted bills of exchange to the account, it retains the ownership by way of security in such bills of exchange.

(2) Assignment by way of security

The claims underlying the cheques and bills of exchange shall pass to the Bank simultaneously with the acquisition of ownership in the cheques and bills of exchange; the claims also pass to the Bank if other items are deposited for collection (e.g. direct debits, documents of commercial trading).

(3) Special-purpose items for collection

If items for collection are deposited with the Bank under the reserve that their countervalue may only be used for a specified purpose, the transfer or assignment of ownership by way of security does not extend to these items.

(4) Secured claims of the Bank

The ownership transferred or assigned by way of security serves to secure any claims which the Bank may be entitled to against the customer arising from the customer's current account when items are deposited for collection or arising as a consequence of the re-debiting of unpaid items for collection or discounted bills of exchange. Upon request of the customer, the Bank retransfers to the customer the ownership by way of security of such items and of the claims that have passed to it if it does not, at the time of such request, have any claims against the customer that need to be secured or if it does not permit the customer to dispose of the countervalue of such items prior to their final payment.

16. Limitation of the claim to security and obligation to release

(1) Cover limit

The Bank may demand that security be provided or increased until the realisable value of all security corresponds to the total amount of all claims arising from the banking business relationship (cover limit).

(2) Release

If the realisable value of all security exceeds the cover limit on a more than temporary basis, the Bank shall, at the customer's request, release security items as it may choose in the amount exceeding the cover limit; when selecting the security items to be released, the Bank will take into account the legitimate concerns of the customer or of any third party having provided security for the customer's obligations. To this extent, the Bank is also obliged to execute orders of the customer relating to the items subject to the lien (e.g. sale of securities, repayment of savings deposits).

(3) Special argreements

If for a specific security item assessment criteria other than the realisable value, another cover limit or another limit for the release of security have been agreed, these other criteria or limits shall apply.

17. Realisation of security

(1) Option of the Bank

In case of realisation, the Bank may chose between several security items. When realising security and selecting the items to be realised, the Bank will take into account the legitimate concerns of the customer and any third party who may have provided security for the obligations of the customer.

(2) Credit entry for proceeds under turnover tax law

If the transaction of realisation is subject to turnover tax, the bank will provide the customer with a credit entry for the proceeds, such entry being deemed to serve as invoice for the supply of the item given as security and meeting the requirements of turnover tax law (Umsatzsteuerrecht).

TERMINATION

18. Termination rights of the customer

(1) Right of termination at any time

Unless the Bank and the customer have otherwise agreed to a term of a termination provision, the customer may at any time, without notice, terminate the business relationship as a whole or particular business relationships (e.g. the use of cheques).

(2) Termination for reasonable cause

If the Bank and the customer have agreed on a term or a contrary termination provision for a particular business relationship, such relationship may only be terminated without notice if there is reasonable cause therefor which makes it unacceptable to the customer to continue the business relationship, after having given due consideration to the legitimate concerns of the Bank.

19. Termination rights of the Bank

(1) Termination upon notice

Upon observing an adequate notice period, the Bank may at any time terminate the business relationship as a whole or particular relationships for which neither a term nor a diverging termination provision has been agreed (e.g. the chequing agreement authorizing the use of the cheque card and cheque forms). In determining the notice period, the Bank will take into account the legitimate concerns of the customer. The minimum termination notice for the keeping of current accounts and securities accounts is one month.

(2) Termination of loans with no fixed term

Loans and loan commitments for which neither a fixed term nor a diverging termination provision has been agreed may be terminated at any time by the Bank without notice. When exercising this right of termination, the Bank will give due consideration to the legitimate concerns of the customer.

(3) Termination for reasonable cause without notice

Termination of the business relationship as a whole or of particular relationships without notice is permitted if there is reasonable cause which makes it unacceptable to the Bank to continue the business relationship, after having given due consideration to the legitimate concerns of the customer. Such cause is given in particular if the customer has made incorrect statements as to the customer's financial status, provided such statements were of significant importance for the Bank's decision concerning the granting of credit or other operations involving risks for the Bank (e.g. the delivery of the cheque card), or if a substantial deterioration occurs or threatens to occur in the customer's financial status, jeopardizing the discharge of obligations towards the Bank. The Bank may also terminate the business relationship without notice if the customer fails to comply, within the required time period allowed by the Bank, with the obligation to provide or increase security according to No. 13(2) of these Business Conditions or to the provisions of some other agreement.

(4) Termination of consumer loans in the event of default

Where the Consumer Credit Act contains specific provisions for the termination of a consumer loan subsequent to a payment default, the Bank may only terminate the business relationship as provided therein.

(5) Settlement following termination

The bank shall allow the customer a reasonable time period for the settlement, in particular for the repayment of a loan, unless it is necessary to attend immediately thereto (e.g. the return of the cheque forms in the event of termination of a chequing agreement).

PROTECTION OF DEPOSITS

20. Deposit Protection Fund

The Bank is a member of the Deposit Protection Fund of the Association of German Banks (Einlagensicherungsfonds des Bundesverbandes deutscher Banken e.V.) (hereinafter referred to as "Deposit Protection Fund"). To the extent that the Deposit Protection Fund or its mandatory makes payments to a customer, the respective amount of the customer's claims against the Bank is transferred simultaneously to the Deposit Protection Fund. The same applies if in the absence of instructions from the customer the Deposit Protection Fund makes payments into an account which is opened in favour of the customer at another bank. The Bank shall be entitled to disclose to the Deposit Protection Fund or to its mandatory all relevant information and to place necessary documents at their disposal.

THE BANKING CODE (UNITED KINGDOM): 1998 REVISED EDITION

British Bankers' Association, The Building Societies Association, Association for Payment Clearing Services

THE BANKING CODE

This is a voluntary Code followed by banks and building societies in their relations with personal customers in the United Kingdom. It sets standards of good banking practice which are followed as a minimum by banks and building societies subscribing to it. As a voluntary Code, it allows competition and market forces to operate to encourage higher standards for the benefit of customers.

The standards of the Code are encompassed in the 11 key commitments found at the beginning. These commitments apply to the conduct of business for all products and services provided to customers.

Mortgages are covered in more detail in the Council of Mortgage Lenders' Code of Mortgage Lending Practice. Not all subscribers to the Banking Code are members of the Council of Mortgage Lenders.

The Code does not apply to the selling of investments or investment activities as defined by The Financial Services Act 1986.

The Code provides valuable safeguards for customers. It should help them understand how banks and building societies are expected to deal with them. Customers should check who subscribes to it by contacting the Associations shown above.

The Independent Review Body for the Banking and Mortgage Codes monitors compliance by banks and building societies with the Code and also oversees its review from time to time.

Copies of the Code are available from banks and building societies and the Associations shown above.

Within the Code, "you" means the customer and "we" means the bank or building society the customer deals with.

This revised edition is effective from 31 March 1999 unless otherwise indicated.

CONTENTS

1. KEY COMMITMENTS

1.1 We, the subscribers to this Code, promise that we will:
— act fairly and reasonably in all our dealings with you;
— ensure that all services and products comply with this Code, even if they have their own terms and conditions;
— give you information on our services and products in plain language, and offer help if there is any aspect which you do not understand;
— help you to choose a service or product to fit your needs;
— help you to understand the financial implications of:
    — a mortgage;
    — other borrowing;
    — savings and investment products;
    — card products.
— help you to understand how your accounts work;
— have safe, secure and reliable banking and payment systems;
— ensure that the procedures our staff follow reflect the commitments set out in this Code;
— correct errors and handle complaints speedily;
— consider cases of financial difficulty and mortgage arrears sympathetically and positively;
— ensure that all services and products comply with relevant laws and regulations.

2. INFORMATION

Information available

2.1 When you become a customer and at any time you ask, we will give you:

Key features
— clear written information explaining the key features of our main services and products;

Your account

- information on how your account works, including:
  - stopping a cheque or other types of payment;
  - when funds can be withdrawn after a credit has been paid into your account and when funds begin to earn interest;
  - unpaid cheques;
  - out of date cheques;
  - when your account details may be passed to credit reference agencies;

Tariff

- a tariff, covering basic account services. This will also be available in branches;

Interest rates

- information on the interest rates which apply to your account(s), when interest will be deducted or paid to you and, on request, a full explanation of how interest is calculated.
- information on where you can get up-to-date details of the interest rates on savings and investment products we offer, including:
  - the newspapers we usually use to notify interest rate changes. These newspapers will reflect the readership of our customers;
  - telephone number(s); and
  - if we have one, our Internet web site address.

ATM charges

2.2 We will give you details of any charges we make for using Automated Teller Machines (ATMs) when we issue the card.

Overdrafts and fixed term products

2.3 We will tell you of any additional charges and interest you may have to pay if:

- your account becomes overdrawn without agreement;
- you exceed your overdraft limit;
- your loan falls into arrears;
- you change your mind about a fixed term product.

Mortgage tariff

2.4 Before you take out a mortgage and at any time you ask, we will give you a tariff covering the operation and repayment of your mortgage, including charges and additional interest costs payable should you fall into arrears.

Other charges

2.5 We will tell you the charges for any other service or product before or when it is provided or at any time you ask.

Helping you to choose savings and investment accounts

2.6 We will take care to give you clear and appropriate information on the different types of savings and investment accounts available from us to help you to make an informed choice on the product to fit your needs. We will help you understand how your savings and investment accounts work, including any additional charges or loss of interest for withdrawal or cancellation.

2.7 We will give you information on a single savings or investment account if you have already made up your mind.

Cooling-off

2.8 If you are not happy about your choice of savings or investment account(s), (except for a fixed rate account) within 14 days of opening it, we will help you switch accounts or we will give all your money back with interest. We will ignore any notice period and any additional charges.

Terms and conditions

Plain language

2.9 All written terms and conditions will be fair in substance and will set out your rights and responsibilities clearly and in plain language, with legal and technical language used only where necessary.

Joint accounts

2.10 If you have a joint account, we will give you additional information on your rights and responsibilities.

Closure

2.11 Unless there are exceptional circumstances, e.g. fraud, we will not close your account without giving you at least 30 days' notice.

Keeping you informed of changes

Changes to terms and conditions

2.12 Occasionally terms and conditions may have to be changed. We will tell you how you will be notified of these changes. We will always give you at least 30 days' notice before any change takes effect.

2.13 If the change is clearly to your disadvantage, we will:

— notify you personally; and
— ignore any notice period on your account for at least 60 days starting from the date of the notice so that you can, if you wish, switch your account or close it.

You will not have to pay any additional charges or additional interest as a result of this switch or closure during this 60 day period.

2.14 If there have been significant changes in any one year, we will give or send you a copy of the new terms and conditions or a summary of the changes.

Changes to interest rates are specifically covered by section 2.16.

Charges

2.15 If we increase a charge for basic account services, we will give you at least 30 days' notice.

Interest rates

2.16 The interest rates which will apply to your accounts may change from time to time. When we change the interest rates, we will tell you about the changes for:

(A) BRANCH-BASED ACCOUNTS

— within 30 days, by letter, e-mail, or other personal notice; or
— within 3 working days of the change:
— by prominent notices in branches; and
— by placing notices in the newspapers we usually use. To help you compare rates more easily, our notices will state clearly the previous and new interest rates; and
— by having the previous and new interest rates for your accounts available on our telephone help lines and, if we have one, our Internet web site; and
— our staff will always be able to help you.

(B) NON BRANCH-BASED ACCOUNTS

— Within 30 days by letter, e-mail or other personal notice;

(C) AND FOR ALL ACCOUNTS

— To help you compare interest rates on all our savings and investment accounts more easily, we will send you, at least once a year, a summary of these products and the current interest rates unless the account is a passbook account with less than £100 in it. This summary will also include:
— superseded accounts clearly marked;
— the names of the newspapers we usually use to notify interest rate changes;
— our telephone help line numbers; and
— if we have one, our Internet web site address.
In addition, we will also tell you the different interest rates which have applied to the account during the year.

Superseded accounts

2.17 From time to time, we offer new savings and investments accounts. If you have any type of savings and investment account, other than a fixed rate account, which has been "superseded" because:

— new accounts are no longer opened; or
— the account is not actively promoted;

we will either:

(a) keep the interest rate on the superseded account at the same level as an account with similar features from the current range; or
(b) switch the superseded account to an account with similar features from the current range.

Examples of similar features include notice periods, types of withdrawals, numbers of free withdrawals, how deposits and withdrawals from the account are made.

This means that the interest rate on your account will always be at least as good as the interest rate on an account with similar features from the current range.

2.18 Where there is no account with "similar features" we will, within 30 days of your account becoming superseded, contact you to:

— tell you that the account is superseded;

— tell you about our other accounts; and
— help you switch accounts without any notice period and without any additional charges.

Marketing of services

2.19 Occasionally we will bring to your attention additional services and products which may be of benefit to you.

However, when you become a customer, we will give you the opportunity to say that you do not wish to receive this information.

2.20 We will remind you, at least once every three years, that you can ask not to receive this information.

Consent to marketing

2.21 Unless you specifically request it, or give your express consent in writing, we will not pass your name and address to any company, including other companies in our group, for marketing purposes. You will not be asked to give your permission in return for basic banking services.

Host mailing

2.22 We may tell you about another company's services or products and, if you respond positively, you may be contacted directly by that company.

Minors

2.23 We will not send marketing material indiscriminately and, in particular, we will be selective and careful if you are under eighteen years old or where material relates to loans and overdrafts.

Advertising

2.24 We will ensure that all advertising and promotional material is clear, fair, reasonable and not misleading.

Helping you to choose a mortgage

2.25 Choosing a mortgage may be your most important financial commitment. There are three levels of service which may be provided and we will tell you which we offer at the outset. These are:

(a) advice and a recommendation as to which of our mortgages is most suitable for you. When giving advice, we will take care to help you to select a mortgage to fit your needs by asking for relevant information about your circumstances and objectives. Our advice will also depend on your particular needs and requirements and on the market conditions at the time. The reasons for the recommendation will be given to you in writing before you complete your mortgage.
(b) information on the different types of mortgage products we offer so that you can make an informed choice of which to take;
(c) information on a single mortgage product only, if we offer only one mortgage product or if you have already made up your mind.

Before you take out your mortgage, we will confirm, in writing, the level of service given.

2.26 Mortgages are covered in more detail in the Council of Mortgage Lenders' Code of Mortgage Lending Practice.

3. ACCOUNT OPERATIONS

Running your account

Statements

3.1 To help you manage your account and check entries on it, we will give you regular account statements. These are normally provided monthly, quarterly or as a minimum annually, unless this not appropriate for the type of account (for example on a passbook account). You may ask for account statements to be sent more frequently than normally available on your type of account.

3.2 If you have a type of account which is accessible by card, and you have a card, we will introduce systems by 1 July 1999 to send you account statements at least quarterly if there have been any card transactions on that account. This does not apply to passbook accounts.

3.3 If your statement or passbook has an entry which seems to be wrong, you should tell us as soon as possible so that we can resolve matters.

Pre-notification

3.4 If charges and/or debit interest accumulate to your current or savings account during a charging period, you will be given at least 14 days' notice of the amount before it is deducted from your account. The 14 days start from the date of posting the notification.

Cheques

3.5 We will keep original cheques paid from your account or copies for at least six years except where these have already been returned to you.

3.6 If, within a reasonable period after the entry has been made, there is a dispute with us about a cheque paid from your account, we will give you the cheque or a copy as evidence (except where the cheque has already been returned to you). If there is an unreasonable delay we will recredit your account until the matter is resolved.

3.7 If you already have your paid cheques returned, we will continue to return your cheques or copies to you and we will tell you our charges for this service.

3.8 When we need to tell you that one of your cheques or other items has been returned unpaid, we will do this either by letter or by other private and confidential means.

Cards and pins

3.9 We will send you a card only if you request it or to replace one which has already been issued.

3.10 Your PIN (Personal Identification Number) will be advised only to you and will be issued separately from your card.

PIN self-selection

3.11 We will tell you if you can select your own PIN and, if so, you will be encouraged to do so carefully. This should make it easier for you to remember your PIN.

We will have systems in place to allow you to select your own PIN by 1 July 2000.

3.12 You can ask not to be issued with a PIN.

Lending

Financial assessment

3.13 All lending will be subject to our assessment of your ability to repay. This assessment may include:

— taking into account your income and commitments;
— how you have handled your financial affairs in the past;
— information obtained from credit reference agencies and, with your consent, others, for example employers, other lenders and landlords;
— information supplied by you, including verification of your identity and the purpose of the borrowing;
— credit assessment techniques, for example credit scoring;
— your age;
— any security provided.

Guarantees

3.14 If you want us to accept a guarantee or other security from someone for your liabilities, you may be asked to consent to the disclosure, by us, of your confidential financial information to the person giving the guarantee or other security or to their legal adviser. We will also:

— encourage them to take independent legal advice to make sure that they understand their commitment and the potential consequences of their decision. All the documents they will be asked to sign will contain this recommendation as a clear and prominent notice;
— advise them that by giving the guarantee or other security they may become liable instead of or as well as you;
— advise them of what the limit of their liability will be. An unlimited guarantee will not be taken.

Foreign exchange services

3.15 We will give you an explanation of the service, details of the exchange rate and an explanation of the charges which apply to any foreign exchange transactions which you are about to make. Where this is not possible, we will tell you the basis on which these will be worked out.

3.16 If you wish to transfer money abroad, we will tell you how this is done and will give you, at least, the following information:

— a description of the services and how to use them;
— an explanation of when the money you have sent abroad should get there and any reason for potential delays;
— any commission or charges which you will have to pay, including a warning where a foreign bank's charges may also have to be paid by the recipient.

4. PROTECTION

Confidentiality

4.1 We will treat all your personal information as private and confidential (even when you are no longer a customer). Nothing about your accounts nor your name and address will be disclosed to anyone, including other companies in our group, other than in four exceptional cases permitted by law. These are:

— where we are legally compelled to do so;
— where there is a duty to the public to disclose;
— where our interests require disclosure;
   This will not be used as a reason for disclosing information about you or your
   accounts (including you name and address) to anyone else including other
   companies in our group for marketing purposes.
— where disclosure is made at your request or with your consent.

Credit reference agencies

4.2 Information about your personal debts owed to us may be disclosed to credit
reference agencies where:
— you have fallen behind with your payments; and
— the amount owed is not in dispute; and
— you have not made proposals satisfactory to us for repayment of your debt
   following formal demand; and
— you have been given at least 28 days' notice of our intention to disclose.

4.3 We will not give any other information about you to credit reference agencies
without your consent.

Data protection

4.4 We will explain that you have a right of access under Data Protection legislation to
your personal records held on our computer files.

Bankers' references

4.5 We will tell you if we provide bankers' references. If a banker's reference about you
is requested, we will require your written consent before it is given.

Protecting your accounts

Identification

4.6 When you first apply to open an account, we will tell you what identification we
need to prove identity. This is important for your security and is required by law. We will
also tell you what checks we may make with credit reference agencies.

4.7 If we record telephone conversations, out terms and conditions will explain this.

Taking care

4.8 The care of your cheque book, passbook, cards, electronic purse, PINs, passwords
and selected personal information is essential to help prevent fraud and protect your
accounts. Please ensure that you:

— do not keep you cheque book and cards together;
— do not allow anyone else to use your card, PIN and/or password;
— always take reasonable steps to keep you card safe and your PIN, password and
   selected personal information secret at all times;
— never write down or record your PIN on the card or on anything kept with or
   near it;
— never write down or record your PIN, password or selected personal information
   without disguising it, for example, never write down or record your PIN using
   the numbers in the correct order;

— destroy the notification of your PIN and/or password as soon as you receive it.

4.9 It is essential that you tell us as soon as you can if you suspect or discover that:

— your cheque book, passbook, card and/or electronic purse has been lost or stolen;
— someone else knows your PIN, password or your selected personal information.

Loss—what to do

4.10 The fastest method of notifying us is by telephone, using the numbers previously advised or in telephone directories.

4.11 Once you have told us that a cheque book, passbook, card or electronic purse has been lost or solen or that someone else knows your PIN, password or selected personal information, we will take immediate steps to prevent these from being used to access your accounts.

4.12 We will refund you the amount of any transaction together with any interest and charges:

— where you have not received your card and it is misused by someone else;
— for all transactions not authorised by you after you have told us that someone else knows your PIN, password or selected personal information;
— if additional money is transferred from your account to your electronic purse after you have told us of its loss, theft or that someone else knows your PIN;
— where faults have occurred in the ATMs, or associated systems used, which were not obvious or subject to a warning message or notice at the time of use.

Electronic purse

4.13 You should treat your electronic purse like cash in a wallet. You will lose any money left in the electronic purse at the time it is lost or stolen, in just the same way as if you lost your wallet. However, if your electronic purse is credited by unauthorised withdrawals from your account before you tell us of its loss, theft or misuse, your liability for such amounts will be limited to a maximum of £50, unless you have acted fraudulently or with gross negligence.

Cards

4.14 If your card is misused before you tell us of its loss or theft, or that someone else knows your PIN, your liability will be limited to a maximum of £50, unless you have acted fraudulently or with gross negligence.

4.15 Where a card transaction is disputed, we have the burden of proving fraud or gross negligence or that you have received your card.

In such cases we would expect you to cooperate with us and with the police in any investigation.

Fraud and gross negligence

4.16 If you act fraudulently you will be liable for all losses. If you act with gross negligence which has caused losses you may be liable for them. This may apply if you fail to follow the safeguards set out in section 4.8.

5. DIFFICULTIES

Financial difficulties

5.1 We will consider cases of financial difficulty sympathetically and positively. Our first step will be to try to contact you to discuss the matter.

How we can help

5.2 If you find yourself in financial difficulties, you should let us know as soon as possible. We will do all we can to help you overcome your difficulties. The sooner we discuss your problems, the easier it will be for both of us to find a solution. The more you tell us about your full financial circumstances, the more we may be able to help.

5.3 With your cooperation, we will develop a plan with you for dealing with your financial difficulties, consistent with both our interests and yours.

5.4 If you are in difficulties you can also get help and advice from debt counselling organisations. At your request and with your consent, we will liaise, wherever possible, with debt counselling organisations that we recognise, for example:

— Citizens Advice Bureaux; or
— money advice centres: or
— The Consumer Credit Counselling Service.

Complaints

Internal procedures

5.5 We have internal procedures for handling complaints fairly and speedily and we will tell you what these are. These will include establishing a set time for an initial acknowledgement to your complaint. We will tell you how long it might take us to respond more fully.

5.6 If you wish to make a complaint, we will tell you how to do so and what to do if you are not happy about the outcome. Staff will help you with any queries.

Ombudsmen

5.7 Banks and building societies have separate independent ombudsmen or arbitration schemes. The ombudsmen or arbitrators are available to resolve certain complaints made by you if the matter remains unresolved through our internal complaints procedures.

5.8 All building societies must belong to the Building Societies Ombudsman Scheme.

5.9 All banks subscribing to this Code must belong to the Banking Ombudsman Scheme or, where appropriate, to one of the arbitration schemes listed below.

5.10 We will display a notice in a prominent position in all our branches stating which Ombudsman or arbitration scheme we belong to and that copies of the Code are available on request.

5.11 We will give you details about which Ombudsman or arbitration scheme is available to you. You can also get information by contacting the appropriate Ombudsman or arbitration scheme at the addresses listed below:

The Office of the Banking Ombudsman
70 Gray's Inn Road
London WC1X 8NB
Tel: 0171 404 9944
Enquiries only—LO-call Tel: 0345 660902

The Office of the Building Societies Ombudsman
Millbank Tower
Millbank
London SW1P 4XS
Tel: 0171 931 0044

The Finance and Leasing Association Arbitration Scheme
Imperial House, 15-19 Kingsway,
London WC2 6UN
Tel: 0171 836 6511

The Consumer Credit Trade Association Arbitration Scheme
Tennyson House
159/163 Great Portland Street
London W1N 5FD
Tel: 0171 636 7564

Monitoring and compliance

5.12 We will comply with the law and follow relevant codes of practice or similar documents as members of the British Bankers' Association (BBA), The Building Societies Association (BSA) and the Association for Payment Clearing Services (APACS). The main codes include:

— BBA, BSA, FLA Code of Practice on the Advertising of Interest Bearing Accounts;
— BBA Guide to Bankers' References (Status Enquiries);
— BBA Dormant Accounts Procedure;
— BSA Code of Practice on Linking of Services;
— CML Code of Mortgage Lending Practice;
— CML Statement of Practice on Handling Arrears and Possessions;
— CML Statement of Practice on the Transfer of Mortgages;
— Association of British Insurers (ABI) General Business Code of Practice;
— British Codes of Advertising and Sales Promotion;
— ITC (Independent Television Commission) Code of Advertising Practice;
— Guide to Credit Scoring.

5.13 We have a "Code Compliance Officer" and our internal auditing procedures monitor compliance with the Code.

Review body

5.14 The Code is monitored by the Independent Review Body for the Banking and Mortgage Codes comprised of representatives from the banks and building societies and independent consumers. The address is:

Pinners Hall 105–108 Old Broad Street
London EC2N 1EX
Tel: 0171 216 8800

Complaints concerning the general operation of the Code can be made to them.

5.15 We complete a "Statement of Compliance" every year which is signed by our Chief Executive and sent to the Independent Review Body for the Banking and Mortgage Codes.

6. HELP SECTION

Sponsoring associations

Enquiries about the Code and requests for copies of it can be addressed to the British Bankers' Association, The Building Societies Association and the Association for Payment Clearing Services. The addresses and telephone numbers are shown at the front of this booklet.

Copies of the Code

All institutions subscribing to the Code will make copies of it available to customers. Copies of the CML Code of Mortgage Lending Practice are available from the Council of Mortgage Lenders (CML) 3 Savile Row, London W1X 1AF, recorded help line telephone number 0171 440 2255.

Additional information

Additional information on a variety of banking and mortgage matters is available in the form of "Bank Facts" from the BBA, "Fact Sheets" and information leaflets from the BSA and CML and "Pay Points" from APACS. In addition, the Associations operate customer information lines or "help lines".

Websites

Internet sites:

> www.bba.org.uk
> www.cml.org.uk
> www.bsa.org.uk
> www.apacs.org.uk

Useful definitions

These definitions explain the meaning of words and terms used in the Code. They are not precise legal or technical definitions.

ATM (AUTOMATED TELLER MACHINE)

A cash machine or free standing device dispensing cash and providing other information or services to customers who have a card.

BANKER'S REFERENCE

An opinion about a particular customer's ability to enter into or repay a financial commitment.

BASIC BANKING SERVICE

The opening, maintenance and operation of accounts for money transmission by means of cheque and other debit instruments. This would normally be a current account.

CARDS

A general term for any plastic card which may be used to pay for goods and services or to withdraw cash. For the purposes of this Code, it excludes electronic purses.

CREDIT REFERENCE AGENCIES

Organisations, licensed under the Consumer Credit Act 1974, which hold information about individuals which is of relevance to lenders. Banks and building societies may refer to these agencies to assist with various decisions, e.g. whether or not to open an account or provide loans or grant credit. Banks and building societies may give information to or seek information from these agencies.

CREDIT SCORING

A system which banks and building societies use to assist in making decisions about granting consumer credit. Credit scoring uses statistical techniques to measure the likelihood that an application for credit will be a good credit risk.

ELECTRONIC PURSES

Any card or function of a card which contains real value in the form of electronic money which someone has paid for in advance, some of which can be reloaded with further funds and which can be used for a range of purposes.

GUARANTEE

An undertaking given by a person called the guarantor promising to pay the debts of another if that other person fails to do so.

NOTICE PERIOD

Where notice periods are specified, the notice period starts from the date of posting the notification.

OUT OF DATE CHEQUE

A cheque which has not been paid because its date is too old, normally more than six months.

PASSWORD

A word or an access code which the customer has selected to permit them access to a telephone or home banking service and which is also used for identification.

PERSONAL CUSTOMER

A private individual who maintains an account (including a joint account with another private individual or an account held as an executor or trustee, but excluding the accounts of sole traders, partnerships, companies, clubs and societies) or who receives other services from a bank or building society.

PIN (PERSONAL IDENTIFICATION NUMBER)

A number provided on a strictly confidential basis by a bank or building society to a card holder. Use of this number by the customer will allow the card to be used to withdraw cash and access other services from an Automated Teller Machine (ATM).

SECURITY

A word used to describe items of value such as title deeds to houses, share certificates, life policies, etc, which represent assets used as support for a loan. Under a secured loan the lender has the right to sell the security if the loan is not repaid.

SELECTED PERSONAL INFORMATION

A selection of memorable facts and information of a private and personal nature chosen by the customer (the sequence of which is known only to the customer) which can be used for identification and to verify identification when accessing accounts.

TARIFF

A list of charges for services provided by a bank or building society.

UNPAID CHEQUE

This is a term for a cheque which, after being paid into the account of a person to whom it is payable, is subsequently returned "unpaid" ("bounced") by the bank or building society whose customer issued the cheque. This leaves the person to whom the cheque is payable without the money in his/her account.

Third Edition March 1997
Revised Third Edition, September 1998
Published by BBA Enterprises Ltd

GLOSSARY OF TERMS RELATING TO ECONOMIC AND MONETARY UNION (CHAPTER 11)

BBA
British Bankers' Association.

CENT
The denomination of a one hundredth part of a euro.

COMMISSION
European Commission, the Community institution which implements the decisions of the Council, ensures compliance with the Treaty and proposes legislation.

COUNCIL
Council of the European Union, the supreme legislative body of the European Union comprising representatives of the governments of the Member States, normally the ministers responsible for the matters under discussion.

COUNCIL REGULATION
A regulation made by the Council which has direct effect in Member States.

ECB
European Central Bank which, in effect, makes and carries out, in conjunction with participating central banks, the single monetary policy of the monetary union.

ECOFIN
Council of Finance Ministers of the European Union.

ECU
European Currency Unit.

EMU
Economic and Monetary Union.

ESCB
European System of Central Banks, comprising the ECB and all of the national central banks.

EURO
The name of the single European currency, which is divided into 100 cents.

EURIBOR
Euro Inter-Bank Offered Rate (introduced from 4 January 1999).

EUROPEAN UNION OR EU

The European Union as established by the Maastricht Treaty, comprising (i) the European Community as set up by the earlier Treaty of Rome and including its own institutions (e.g. the European Commission); (ii) inter-governmental co-operation for common foreign and security policy; and (iii) inter-governmental co-operation on security and home affairs.

FIBOR

Frankfurt Inter-Bank Offered Rate.

FINANCIAL LAW PANEL

An independent panel which aims to identify areas of uncertainty in English law affecting financial markets and to seek to have them removed or their scope altered.

FIRST REGULATION

Council Regulation (EC) No 1103/97 of 17 June 1997 which came into force on 20 June 1997, giving effect to certain aspects of the legal framework for the introduction of the euro.

IPMA

International Primary Market Association.

ISDA

International Swaps and Derivatives Association, Inc.

LIBOR

London Inter-Bank Offered Rate.

MEMBER STATE

A member state of the European Union.

NCU

The national currency unit of a participating Member State which is to be treated as a denomination of the euro from 1 January 1999 until its withdrawal as legal tender.

OFFICIAL ECU

The unit of account of the EU defined as the aggregate of fixed amounts of each of twelve Member States' national currencies, being the twelve Member States at the time that the basket was fixed.

PIBOR

Paris Inter-Bank Offered Rate.

PRIVATE ECU

The ECU when used in private transactions, such as bank accounts, bond issues and foreign exchange trading; the exchange rate between a national currency and the private ECU could differ from the theoretical rate, based on the composition of the official ECU, due to market forces.

RTGS

Real-Time Gross Settlement, a payment system that settles in real-time as opposed to end-of-day net settlement.

SECOND REGULATION

Council Regulation (EC) No 974/98 of 3 May 1998 on the introduction of the euro which will come into force on 1 January 1999.

TARGET

Trans-European Automated Real-time Gross Settlement Express Transfer system, being the pan-European infrastructure to enable national RTGSs to inter-link with each other, so enabling same-day real-time payments in euro throughout the EU.

THIRD REGULATION

Council Regulation (EC) No 2866/98 of 31 December 1998 on the conversion rates between the euro and the currencies of the Member States adopting the euro.

TRANSITION PERIOD

1 January 1999 to 31 December 2001.

TREATY

The Treaty on European Union signed at Maastricht which specifies, *inter alia*, the framework for EMU.

COUNCIL REGULATION (EC) No 1103/97 OF 17 JUNE 1997 ON CERTAIN PROVISIONS RELATING TO THE INTRODUCTION OF THE EURO

THE COUNCIL OF THE EUROPEAN UNION,

Having regard to the Treaty establishing the European Community, and in particular Article 235 thereof,

Having regard to the proposal of the Commission,[1]

Having regard to the opinion of the European Parliament,[2]

Having regard to the opinion of the European Monetary Institute,[3]

(1) Whereas, at its meeting held in Madrid on 15 and 16 December 1995, the European Council confirmed that the third stage of Economic and Monetary Union will start on 1 January 1999 as laid down in Article 109j(4) of the Treaty; whereas the Member States which will adopt the euro as the single currency in accordance with the Treaty will be defined for the purposes of this Regulation as the "participating Member States";

(2) Whereas, at the meeting of the European Council in Madrid, the decision was taken that the term "ECU" used by the Treaty to refer to the European currency unit is a generic term; whereas the Governments of the fifteen Member States have achieved the common agreement that this decision is the agreed and definitive interpretation of the relevant Treaty provisions; whereas the name given to the European currency shall be the "euro"; whereas the euro as the currency of the participating Member States will be divided into one hundred sub-units with the name "cent"; whereas the European Council furthermore considered that the name of the single currency must be the same in all the official languages of the European Union, taking into account the existence of different alphabets;

(3) Whereas a Regulation on the introduction of the euro will be adopted by the Council on the basis of the third sentence of Article 109l(4) of the Treaty as soon as the participating Member States are known in order to define the legal framework of the euro; whereas the Council, when acting at the starting date of the third stage in accordance with the first sentence of Article 109l(4) of the Treaty, shall adopt the irrevocably fixed conversion rates;

(4) Whereas it is necessary, in the course of the operation of the common market and for the changeover to the single currency, to provide legal certainty for citizens and firms in all Member States on certain provisions relating to the introduction of the euro well before the entry into the third stage; whereas this legal certainty at an early stage will allow preparations by citizens and firms to proceed under good conditions;

(5) Whereas the third sentence of Article 109l(4) of the Treaty, which allows the Council, acting with the unanimity of participating Member States, to take other measures necessary for the rapid introduction of the single currency is available as a legal

1. OJ No C369, 7.12.1996, p. 8.
2. OJ No C 380, 16.12.1996, p. 49.
3. Opinion delivered on 29 November 1996.

basis only when it has been confirmed, in accordance with Article 109j(4) of the Treaty, which Member States fulfil the necessary conditions for the adoption of a single currency; whereas it is therefore necessary to have recourse to Article 235 of the Treaty as a legal basis for those provisions where there is an urgent need for legal certainty; whereas therefore this Regulation and the aforesaid Regulation on the introduction of the euro will together provide the legal framework for the euro, the principles of which legal framework were agreed by the European Council in Madrid; whereas the introduction of the euro concerns day-to-day operations of the whole population in participating Member States; whereas measures other than those in this Regulation and in the Regulation which will be adopted under the third sentence of Article 109l(4) of the Treaty should be examined to ensure a balanced changeover, in particular for consumers;

(6) Whereas the ECU as referred to in Article 109g of the Treaty and as defined in Council Regulation (EC) No 3320/94 of 22 December 1994 on the consolidation of the existing Community legislation on the definition of the ECU following the entry into force of the Treaty on European Union[4] will cease to be defined as a basket of component currencies on 1 January 1999 and the euro will become a currency in its own right; whereas the decision of the Council regarding the adoption of the conversion rates shall not in itself modify the external value of the ECU; whereas this means that one ECU in its composition as a basket of component currencies will become one euro; whereas Regulation (EC) No 3320/94 therefore becomes obsolete and should be repealed; whereas for references in legal instruments to the ECU, parties shall be presumed to have agreed to refer to the ECU as referred to in Article 109g of the Treaty and as defined in the aforesaid Regulation; whereas such presumption should be rebuttable taking into account the intentions of the parties;

(7) Whereas it is a generally accepted principle of law that the continuity of contracts and other legal instruments is not affected by the introduction of a new currency; whereas the principle of freedom of contract has to be respected; whereas the principle of continuity should be compatible with anything which parties might have agreed with reference to the introduction of the euro; whereas, in order to reinforce legal certainty and clarity, it is appropriate explicitly to confirm that the principle of continuity of contracts and other legal instruments shall apply between the former national currencies and the euro and between the ECU as referred to in Article 109g of the Treaty and as defined in Regulation (EC) No 3320/94 and the euro; whereas this implies, in particular, that in the case of fixed interest rate instruments the introduction of the euro does not alter the nominal interest rate payble by the debtor; whereas the provisions on continuity can fulfil their objective to provide legal certainty and transparency to economic agents, in particular for consumers, only if they enter into force as soon as possible;

(8) Whereas the introduction of the euro constitutes a change in the monetary law of each participating Member State; whereas the recognition of the monetary law of a State is a universally accepted principle; whereas the explicit confirmation of the principle of continuity should lead to the recognition of continuity of contracts and other legal instruments in the jurisdictions of third countries;

(9) Whereas the term "contract" used for the definition of legal instruments is meant to include all types of contracts, irrespective of the way in which they are concluded;

(10) Whereas the Council, when acting in accordance with the first sentence of Article 109l(4) of the Treaty, shall define the conversion rates of the euro in terms of each of the national currencies of the participating Member States; whereas these conversion rates should be used for any conversion between the euro and the national currency units or between the national currency units; whereas for any conversion between national currency units, a fixed algorithm should define the result; whereas the use of inverse rates for conversion would imply rounding of rates and could result in significant inaccuracies, notably if large amounts are involved;

4. OJ No L 350, 31.12.1994, p. 27.

(11) Whereas the introduction of the euro requires the rounding of monetary amounts; whereas an early indication of rules for rounding is necessary in the course of the operation of the common market and to allow a timely preparation and a smooth transition to Economic and Monetary Union; whereas these rules do not affect any rounding practice, convention or national provisions providing a higher degree of accuracy for intermediate computations;

(12) Whereas, in order to achieve a high degree of accuracy in conversion operations, the conversion rates should be defined with six significant figures; whereas a rate with six significant figures means a rate which, counted from the left and starting by the first non-zero figure, has six figures,

HAS ADOPTED THIS REGULATION:

Article 1

For the purpose of this Regulation:
- — "legal instruments" shall mean legislative and statutory provisions, acts of administration, judicial decisions, contracts, unilateral legal acts, payment instruments other than banknotes and coins, and other instruments with legal effect,
- — "participating Member States" shall mean those Member States which adopt the single currency in accordance with the Treaty,
- — "conversion rates" shall mean the irrevocably fixed conversion rates which the Council adopts in accordance with the first sentence of Article 109l(4) of the Treaty,
- — "national currency units" shall mean the units of the currencies of participating Member States, as those units are defined on the day before the start of the third stage of Economic and Monetary Union,
- — "euro unit" shall mean the unit of the single currency as defined in the Regulation on the introduction of the euro which will enter into force at the starting date of the third stage of Economic and Monetary Union.

Article 2

1. Every reference in a legal instrument to the ECU, as referred to in Article 109g of the Treaty and as defined in Regulation (EC) No 3320/94, shall be replaced by a reference to the euro at a rate of one euro to one ECU. References in a legal instrument to the ECU without such a definition shall be presumed, such presumption being rebuttable taking into account the intentions of the parties, to be references to the ECU as referred to in Article 109g of the Treaty and as defined in Regulation (EC) No 3320/94.

2. Regulation (EC) No 3320/94 is hereby repealed.

3. This Article shall apply as from 1 January 1999 in accordance with the decision pursuant to Article 109j(4) of the Treaty.

Article 3

The introduction of the euro shall not have the effect of altering any term of a legal instrument or of discharging or excusing performance under any legal instrument, nor give a party the right unilaterally to alter or terminate such an instrument. This provision is subject to anything which parties may have agreed.

Article 4

1. The conversion rates shall be adopted as one euro expressed in terms of each of the national currencies of the participating Member States. They shall be adopted with six significant figures.

2. The conversion rates shall not be rounded or truncated when making conversions.

3. The conversion rates shall be used for conversions either way between the euro unit and the national currency units. Inverse rates derived from the conversion rates shall not be used.

4. Monetary amounts to be converted from one national currency unit into another shall first be converted into a monetary amount expressed in the euro unit, which amount may be rounded to not less than three decimals and shall then be converted into the other national currency unit. No alternative method of calculation may be used unless it produces the same results.

Article 5

Monetary amounts to be paid or accounted for when a rounding takes place after a conversion into the euro unit pursuant to Article 4 shall be rounded up or down to the nearest cent. Monetary amounts to be paid or accounted for which are converted into a national currency unit shall be rounded up or down to the nearest sub-unit or in the absence of a sub-unit to the nearest unit, or according to national law or practice to a multiple or fraction of the sub-unit or unit of the national currency unit. If the application of the conversion rate gives a result which is exactly half-way, the sum shall be rounded up.

Article 6

This Regulation shall enter into force on the day following that of its publication in the *Official Journal of the European Communities*.

This Regulation shall be binding in its entirety and directly applicable in all Member States.

Done at Luxembourg, 17 June 1997.

For the Council
The President
A. JORRITSMA-LEBBINK

COUNCIL REGULATION (EC) No 974/98 OF 3 MAY 1998 ON THE INTRODUCTION OF THE EURO

THE COUNCIL OF THE EUROPEAN UNION,

Having regard to the Treaty establishing the European Community, and in particular Article 109l(4), third sentence thereof,

Having regard to the proposal from the Commission[1],

Having regard to the opinion of the European Monetary Institute[2],

Having regard to the opinion of the European Parliament[3],

(1) Whereas this Regulation defines monetary law provisions of the Member States which have adopted the euro; whereas provisions on continuity of contracts, the replacement of references to the ecu in legal instruments by references to the euro and rounding have already been laid down in Council Regulation (EC) No 1103/97 of 17 June 1997 on certain provisions relating to the introduction of the euro[4]; whereas the introduction of the euro concerns day-to-day operations of the whole population in participating Member States; whereas measures other than those in this Regulation and in Regulation (EC) No 1103/97 should be examined to ensure a balanced changeover, in particular for consumers;

(2) Whereas, at the meeting of the European Council in Madrid on 15 and 16 December 1995, the decision was taken that the term "ecu" used by the Treaty to refer to the European currency unit is a generic term; whereas the Governments of the 15 Member States have reached the common agreement that this decision is the agreed and definitive interpretation of the relevant Treaty provisions; whereas the name given to the European currency shall be the "euro", whereas the euro as the currency of the participating Member States shall be divided into one hundred sub-units with the name "cent", whereas the definition of the name "cent" does not prevent the use of variants of this term in common usage in the Member States; whereas the European Council furthermore considered that the name of the single currency must be the same in all the official languages of the European Union, taking into account the existence of different alphabets;

(3) Whereas the Council when acting in accordance with the third sentence of Article 109l(4) of the Treaty shall take the measures necessary for the rapid introduction of the euro other than the adoption of the conversion rates;

(4) Whereas whenever under Article 109k(2) of the Treaty a Member State becomes a participating Member State, the Council shall according to Article 109l(5) of the Treaty take the other measures necessary for the rapid introduction of the euro as the single currency of this Member State;

1. OJ C 369, 7.12.1996, p. 10.
2. OJ C 205, 5.7.1997, p. 18.
3. OJ C 380, 16.12.1996, p. 50.
4. OJ L 162, 19.6.1997, p. 1.

(5) Whereas according to the first sentence of Article 109l(4) of the Treaty the Council shall at the starting date of the third stage adopt the conversion rates at which the currencies of the participating Member States shall be irrevocably fixed and at which irrevocably fixed rate the euro shall be substituted for these currencies;

(6) Whereas given the absence of exchange rate risk either between the euro unit and the national currency units or between these national currency units, legislative provisions should be interpreted accordingly;

(7) Whereas the term "contract" used for the definition of legal instruments is meant to include all types of contracts, irrespective of the way in which they were concluded;

(8) Whereas in order to prepare a smooth changeover to the euro a transitional period is needed between the substitution of the euro for the currencies of the participating Member States and the introduction of euro banknotes and coins; whereas during this period the national currency units will be defined as sub-divisions of the euro; whereas thereby a legal equivalence is established between the euro unit and the national currency units;

(9) Whereas in accordance with Article 109g of the Treaty and with Regulation (EC) No 1103/97, the euro will replace the ECU as from 1 January 1999 as the unit of account of the institutions of the European Communities; whereas the euro should also be the unit of account of the European Central Bank (ECB) and of the central banks of the participating Member States; whereas, in line with the Madrid conclusions, monetary policy operations will be carried out in the euro unit by the European System of Central Banks (ESCB); whereas this does not prevent national central banks from keeping accounts in their national currency unit during the transitional period, in particular for their staff and for public administrations;

(10) Whereas each participating Member State may allow the full use of the euro unit in its territory during the transitional period;

(11) Whereas during the transitional period contracts, national laws and other legal instruments can be drawn up validly in the euro unit or in the national currency unit; whereas during this period, nothing in this Regulation should affect the validity of any reference to a national currency unit in any legal instrument;

(12) Whereas, unless agreed otherwise, economic agents have to respect the denomination of a legal instrument in the performance of all acts to be carried out under that instrument;

(13) Whereas the euro unit and the national currency units are units of the same currency; whereas it should be ensured that payments inside a participating Member State by crediting an account can be made either in the euro unit or the respective national currency unit; whereas the provisions on payments by crediting an account should also apply to those cross-border payments, which are denominated in the euro unit or the national currency unit of the account of the creditor; whereas it is necessary to ensure the smooth functioning of payment systems by laying down provisions dealing with the crediting of accounts by payment instruments credited through those systems; whereas the provisions on payments by crediting an account should not imply that financial intermediaries are obliged to make available either other payment facilities or products denominated in any particular unit of the euro; whereas the provisions on payments by crediting an account do not prohibit financial intermediaries from coordinating the introduction of payment facilities denominated in the euro unit which rely on a common technical infrastructure during the transitional period;

(14) Whereas in accordance with the conclusions reached by the European Council at its meeting held in Madrid, new tradeable public debt will be issued in the euro unit by the participating Member States as from 1 January 1999; whereas it is desirable to allow issuers of debt to redenominate outstanding debt in the euro unit; whereas the provisions on redenomination should be such that they can also be applied in the jurisdictions of

third countries; whereas issuers should be enabled to redenominate outstanding debt if the debt is denominated in a national currency unit of a Member State which has redenominated part or all of the outstanding debt of its general government; whereas these provisions do not address the introduction of additional measures to amend the terms of outstanding debt to alter, among other things, the nominal amount of outstanding debt, these being matters subject to relevant national law; whereas it is desirable to allow Member States to take appropriate measures for changing the unit of account of the operating procedures of organised markets;

(15) Whereas further action at the Community level may also be necessary to clarify the effect of the introduction of the euro on the application of existing provisions of Community law, in particular concerning netting, set-off and techniques of similar effect;

(16) Whereas any obligation to use the euro unit can only be imposed on the basis of Community legislation; whereas in transactions with the public sector participating Member States may allow the use of the euro unit; whereas in accordance with the reference scenario decided by the European Council at its meeting held in Madrid, the Community legislation laying down the time frame for the generalisation of the use of the euro unit might leave some freedom to individual Member States;

(17) Whereas in accordance with Article 105a of the Treaty the Council may adopt measures to harmonise the denominations and technical specifications of all coins;

(18) Whereas banknotes and coins need adequate protection against counterfeiting;

(19) Whereas banknotes and coins denominated in the national currency units lose their status of legal tender at the latest six months after the end of the transitional period; whereas limitations on payments in notes and coins, established by Member States for public reasons, are not incompatible with the status of legal tender of euro banknotes and coins, provided that other lawful means for the settlement of monetary debts are available;

(20) Whereas as from the end of the transitional period references in legal instruments existing at the end of the transitional period will have to be read as references to the euro unit according to the respective conversion rates; whereas a physical redenomination of existing legal instruments is therefore not necessary to achieve this result; whereas the rounding rules defined in Regulation (EC) No 1103/97 shall also apply to the conversions to be made at the end of the transitional period or after the transitional period; whereas for reasons of clarity it may be desirable that the physical redenomination will take place as soon as appropriate;

(21) Whereas paragraph 2 of Protocol 11 on certain provisions relating to the United Kingdom of Great Britain and Northern Ireland stipulates that, *inter alia*, paragraph 5 of that Protocol shall have effect if the United Kingdom notifies the Council that it does not intend to move to the third stage; whereas the United Kingdom gave notice to the Council on 30 October 1997 that it does not intend to move to the third stage; whereas paragraph 5 stipulates that, *inter alia*, Article 109l(4) of the Treaty shall not apply to the United Kingdom;

(22) Whereas Denmark, referring to paragraph 1 of Protocol 12 on certain provisions relating to Denmark has notified, in the context of the Edinburgh decision of 12 December 1992, that it will not participate in the third stage; whereas, therefore, in accordance with paragraph 2 of the said Protocol, all Articles and provisions of the Treaty and the Statute of the ESCB referring to a derogation shall be applicable to Denmark;

(23) Whereas, in accordance with Article 109l(4) of the Treaty, the single currency will be introduced only in the Member States without a derogation;

(24) Whereas this Regulation, therefore, shall be applicable pursuant to Article 189 of the Treaty, subject to Protocols 11 and 12 and Article 109k(1),

HAS ADOPTED THIS REGULATION:

PART I. DEFINITIONS

Article 1

For the purpose of this Regulation:
— "participating Member States" shall mean Belgium, Germany, Spain, France, Ireland, Italy, Luxembourg, Netherlands, Austria, Portugal and Finland,
— "legal instruments" shall mean legislative and statutory provisions, acts of administration, judicial decisions, contracts, unilateral legal acts, payment instruments other than banknotes and coins, and other instruments with legal effect,
— "conversion rate" shall mean the irrevocably fixed conversion rate adopted for the currency of each participating Member State by the Council according to the first sentence of Article 109l(4) of the Treaty,
— "euro unit" shall mean the currency unit as referred to in the second sentence of Article 2,
— "national currency units" shall mean the units of the currencies of participating Member States, as those units are defined on the day before the start of the third stage of economic and monetary union,
— "transitional period" shall mean the period beginning on 1 January 1999 and ending on 31 December 2001,
— "redenominate" shall mean changing the unit in which the amount of outstanding debt is stated from a national currency unit to the euro unit, as defined in Article 2, but which does not have through the act of redenomination the effect of altering any other term of the debt, this being a matter subject to relevant national law.

PART II. SUBSTITUTION OF THE EURO FOR THE CURRENCIES OF THE PARTICIPATING MEMBER STATES

Article 2

As from 1 January 1999 the currency of the participating Member States shall be the euro. The currency unit shall be one euro. One euro shall be divided into one hundred cent.

Article 3

The euro shall be substituted for the currency of each participating Member State at the conversion rate.

Article 4

The euro shall be the unit of account of the European Central Bank (ECB) and of the central banks of the participating Member States.

PART III. TRANSITIONAL PROVISIONS

Article 5

Articles 6, 7, 8 and 9 shall apply during the transitional period.

Article 6

1. The euro shall also be divided into the national currency units according to the conversion rates. Any subdivision thereof shall be maintained. Subject to the provisions of this Regulation the monetary law of the participating Member States shall continue to apply.

2. Where in a legal instrument reference is made to a national currency unit, this reference shall be as valid as if reference were made to the euro unit according to the conversion rates.

Article 7

The substitution of the euro for the currency of each participating Member State shall not in itself have the effect altering the denomination of legal instruments in existence on the date of substitution.

Article 8

1. Acts to be performed under legal instruments stipulating the use of or denominated in a national currency unit shall be performed in that national currency unit. Acts to be performed under legal instruments stipulating the use of or denominated in the euro unit shall be performed in that unit.

2. The provisions of paragraph 1 are subject to anything which parties may have agreed.

3. Notwithstanding the provisions of paragraph 1, any amount denominated either in the euro unit or in the national currency unit of a given participating Member State and payable within that Member State by crediting an account of the creditor, can be paid by the debtor either in the euro unit or in that national currency unit. The amount shall be credited to the account of the creditor in the denomination of his account, with any conversion being effected at the conversion rates.

4. Notwithstanding the provisions of paragraph 1, each participating Member State may take measures which may be necessary in order to:
   — redenominate in the euro unit outstanding debt issued by that Member State's general government, as defined in the European system of integrated accounts, denominated in its national currency unit and issued under its own law. If a Member State has taken such a measure, issuers may redenominate in the euro unit debt denominated in that Member State's national currency unit unless redenomination is expressly excluded by the terms of the contract; this provision shall apply to debt issued by the general government of a Member State as well as to bonds and other forms of securitised debt negotiable in the capital markets, and to money market instruments, issued by other debtors,
   — enable the change of the unit of account of their operating procedures from a national currency unit to the euro unit by:
      (a) markets for the regular exchange, clearing and settlement of any instrument listed in section B of the Annex to Council Directive 93/22/EEC of 10 May 1993 on investment services in the securities field[5] and of commodities; and
      (b) systems for the regular exchange, clearing and settlement of payments.

5. Provisions other than those of paragraph 4 imposing the use of the euro unit may only be adopted by the participating Member States in accordance with any timeframe laid down by Community legislation.

6. National legal provisions of participating Member States which permit or impose netting, set-off or techniques with similar effects shall apply to monetary obligations,

5. OJ L 141, 11.6.1993, p. 27. Directive as amended by Directive 95/26/EC of the European Parliament and of the Council (OJ L 168, 18.7.1995, p. 7).

irrespective of their currency denomination, if that denomination is in the euro unit or in a national currency unit, with any conversion being effected at the conversion rates.

Article 9

Banknotes and coins denominated in a national currency unit shall retain their status as legal tender within their territorial limits as of the day before the entry into force of this Regulation.

PART IV. EURO BANKNOTES AND COINS

Article 10

As from 1 January 2002, the ECB and the central banks of the participating Member States shall put into circulation banknotes denominated in euro. Without prejudice to Article 15, these banknotes denominated in euro shall be the only banknotes which have the status of legal tender in all these Member States.

Article 11

As from 1 January 2002, the participating Member States shall issue coins denominated in euro or in cent and complying with the denominations and technical specifications which the Council may lay down in accordance with the second sentence of Article 105a(2) of the Treaty. Without prejudice to Article 15, these coins shall be the only coins which have the status of legal tender in all these Member States. Except for the issuing authority and for those persons specifically designated by the national legislation of the issuing Member State, no party shall be obliged to accept more than 50 coins in any single payment.

Article 12

Participating Member States shall ensure adequate sanctions against counterfeiting and falsification of euro banknotes and coins.

PART V. FINAL PROVISIONS

Article 13

Articles 14, 15 and 16 shall apply as from the end of the transitional period.

Article 14

Where in legal instruments existing at the end of the transitional period reference is made to the national currency units, these references shall be read as references to the euro unit according to the respective conversion rates. The rounding rules laid down in Regulation (EC) No 1103/97 shall apply.

Article 15

1. Banknotes and coins denominated in a national currency unit as referred to in Article 6(1) shall remain legal tender within their territorial limits until six months after the end of the transitional period at the latest; this period may be shortened by national law.

2. Each participating Member State may, for a period of up to six months after the end of the transitional period, lay down rules for the use of the banknotes and coins denominated in its national currency unit as referred to in Article 6(1) and take any measures necessary to facilitate their withdrawal.

Article 16

In accordance with the laws or practices of participating Member States, the respective issuers of banknotes and coins shall continue to accept, against euro at the conversion rate, the banknotes and coins previously issued by them.

PART VI. ENTRY INTO FORCE

Article 17

This Regulation shall enter into force on 1 January 1999.

This Regulation shall be binding in its entirety and directly applicable in all Member States, in accordance with the Treaty, subject to Protocols 11 and 12 and Article 109k(1).

Done at Brussels, 3 May 1998.

For the Council
The President
G. BROWN

APPENDIX 6

COUNCIL REGULATION (EC) NO 2866/98 OF 31 DECEMBER 1998 ON THE CONVERSION RATES BETWEEN THE EURO AND THE CURRENCIES OF THE MEMBER STATES ADOPTING THE EURO

THE COUNCIL OF THE EUROPEAN UNION,

Having regard to the Treaty establishing the European Community, and in particular Article 109l(4), first sentence thereof,

Having regard to the proposal from the Commission,

Having regard to the opinion of the European Central Bank[1],

(1) Whereas according to Article 109j(4) of the Treaty, the third stage of Economic and Monetary Union shall start on 1 January 1999; whereas the Council, meeting in the composition of Heads of State or Government, has confirmed on 3 May 1998 that Belgium, Germany, Spain, France, Ireland, Italy, Luxembourg, the Netherlands, Austria, Portugal and Finland fulfil the necessary conditions for the adoption of a single currency on 1 January 1999[2];

(2) Whereas according to Council Regulation (EC) No 974/98 of 3 May 1998 on the introduction of the euro[3], the euro shall be the currency of the Member States which adopt the single currency as from 1 January 1999; whereas the introduction of the euro requires the adoption of the conversion rates at which the euro will be substituted for the national currencies and at which rates the euro will be divided into national currency units; whereas the conversion rates in Article 1 are the conversion rates referred to in the third indent of Article 1 of Regulation (EC) No 974/98;

(3) Whereas according to Council Regulation (EC) No 1103/97 of 17 June 1997 on certain provisions relating to the introduction of the euro[4] every reference to the ECU in a legal instrument shall be replaced by a reference to the euro at a rate of one euro to one ECU; whereas Article 109l(4), second sentence, of the Treaty, provides that the adoption of the conversion rates shall by itself not modify the external value of the ECU; whereas this is ensured by adopting as the conversion rates, the exchange rates against the ECU of the currencies of the Member States adopting the euro, as calculated by the Commission on 31 December 1998 according to the established procedure for the calculation of the daily official ECU rates;

(4) Whereas the Ministers of the Member States adopting the euro as their single currency, the Governors of the Central Banks of these Member States, the Commission and the European Monetary Institute/the European Central Bank, have issued two Communiqués on the determination and on the adoption of the irrevocable conversion rates for the euro dated 3 May 1998[5] and 26 September 1998, respectively;

(5) Whereas Regulation (EC) No 1103/97 stipulates that the conversion rates shall be

---

1. OJ C 412, 31.12.1998, p. 1.
2. Council Decision 98/317/EC of 3 May 1998 in accordance with Article 109j(4) of the Treaty (OJ L 139, 11.5.1998, p. 30).
3. OJ L 139, 11.5.1998, p. 1.
4. OJ L 162, 19.6.1997, p. 1.
5. OJ C 160, 27.5.1998, p. 1.

adopted as one euro expressed in terms of each of the national currencies of the Member States adopting the euro; whereas in order to ensure a high degree of accuracy, these rates will be adopted with six significant figures and no inverse rates nor bilateral rates between the currencies of the Member States adopting the euro will be defined,

HAS ADOPTED THIS REGULATION:

Article 1

The irrevocably fixed conversion rates between the euro and the currencies of the Member States adopting the euro are:

1 euro	=	40,3399	Belgian francs
	=	1,95583	German marks
	=	166,386	Spanish pesetas
	=	6,55957	French francs
	=	0,787564	Irish pounds
	=	1 936,27	Italian lire
	=	40,3399	Luxembourg francs
	=	2,20371	Dutch guilders
	=	13,7603	Austrian schillings
	=	200,482	Portuguese escudos
	=	5,94573	Finnish marks.

Article 2

This Regulation shall enter into force on 1 January 1999.

This Regulation shall be binding in its entirety and directly applicable in all Member States.

Done at Brussels, 31 December 1998.

For the Council
The President
R. EDLINGER

COMMISSION RECOMMENDATION OF 23 APRIL 1998 CONCERNING BANKING CHARGES FOR CONVERSION TO THE EURO (98/286/EC)

THE COMMISSION OF THE EUROPEAN COMMUNITIES,

Having regard to the Treaty establishing the European Community, and in particular Article 155 thereof,

1. Whereas the euro will become the currency of the participating Member States as from 1 January 1999; whereas the euro will be substituted for the national currencies of the participating Member States at the conversion rates; whereas during a transitional period the euro will exist in different denominations; whereas the national currency units will be sub-units of the euro according to the conversion rates; whereas according to Article 4(3) of Council Regulation (EC) No 1103/97 of 17 June 1997 on certain provisions relating to the introduction of the euro,[1] the conversion rates are to be used for conversions either way between the euro unit and the national currency units; whereas the draft Council Regulation on the introduction of the euro[2] imposes certain obligations to convert;

2. Whereas the Commission considers that banks are not legally entitled to charge:

— for the conversion of incoming payments denominated in the euro unit or in the national currency unit during the transitional period,
— for the conversion of accounts from the national currency unit to the euro unit at the end of the transitional period,
— a different fee for services denominated in the euro unit from that charged for otherwise identical services denominated in the national currency unit;

3. Whereas the Commission considers that, in order to facilitate the smooth introduction of the euro, banks should go beyond the minimum required by law by providing without charge the conversion of accounts from the national currency unit to the euro and during the transitional period, by providing without charge the conversion of outgoing payments from the national currency unit to the euro unit and vice versa during the transitional period, and by providing for the exchange without charge to their customers of "household amounts" of the national banknotes and coin for euro banknotes and coin during the final period;

4. Whereas for reasons of clarity and completeness the legal requirements as interpreted by the Commission as well as the recommendations of the Commission should be presented together; whereas the term "standard of good practice" is used to signify both the legally required and the recommended practice;

5. Whereas the standard of good practice should not include conversion without charge of accounts from the euro denomination into the national denomination, as this is not necessary for the introduction of the euro, nor should it include the exchange of

1. OJ L 162, 19.6.1997, p. 1.
2. OJ C 236, 2.8.1997, p. 8.

euro-area national banknotes for other euro-area national banknotes without charge, as the need for such exchange is not affected by the introduction of the euro; whereas the standard of good practice should cover the transparency of any charges for such conversions;

6. Whereas the standard of good practice should not include the exchange of national banknotes and coin other than in household amounts; whereas banks and retailers should negotiate any charges for the withdrawal from retailers of national banknotes and coin and for the delivery to retailers of euro banknotes and coin, taking into account arrangements made by the competent authorities at national level;

7. Whereas for all conversions between any national currency unit and the euro unit and vice versa, and for all exchanges of banknotes and coin of participating Member States, banks should show clearly the application of the conversion rates in accordance with the provisions of Regulation (EC) No 1103/97; whereas the use of the conversion rate and any charges should be transparent; whereas the standard of good practice in so far as it concerns transparency of charges should be implemented by banks in advance of 1 January 1999, wherever possible, in order to reduce the risk that consumers may wrongly attribute already existing charges to the introduction of the euro;

8. Whereas banks which implement the standard of good practice should publicise this, to demonstrate that they comply with the standard, and all banks should in any event inform their customers in advance of 1 January 1999 whether they apply the standard of good practice and, if not, for which conversions they intend to charge;

9. Whereas the Commission intends to monitor the application of the standard of good practice; whereas such monitoring activity is addressed in Recommendation 98/288/EC on dialogue, monitoring and information to facilitate the transition to the euro;[3] whereas the dialogue provided for in that Recommendation may include discussions on the implementation and monitoring of the standard of good practice; whereas the dialogue could also address aspects of charging for conversion which could extend beyond the scope of the standard of good practice as laid down by this Recommendation;

10. Whereas consumers without a bank account may need special consideration in relation to the exchange of banknotes and coin denominated in the national currency for banknotes and coin denominated in euro, during the final period to be determined by local conditions within each Member State;

11. Whereas the issue of charging for conversion to the euro has been discussed at the Round Table in May 1997; whereas an expert group has been established to examine the issue, involving all sectors concerned, and its report has been published;[4] whereas the conclusions of the experts' report have been accepted by the Commission in its Communication 'Update on practical aspects of the introduction of the euro' adopted on 11 February 1998[5] and discussed at the Round Table in February 1998,

HEREBY RECOMMENDS:

Article 1

Definitions

For the purpose of this Recommendation, the following definitions apply:

(a) "Banks" are credit institutions as defined in Council Directive 77/780/EEC,[6] and any other financial institutions as defined in Article 4(1) of Council Regulation (EC) No 3604/93,[7] whose business is to carry out activities related to the

3. See page 29 of this Official Journal.
4. Report of the rexpert group on banking charges for conversion to the euro, Euro Paper No. 14.
5. COM (1998) 61 final.
6. OJ L 322, 17.12.1977, p. 30.
7. OJ L 332, 31.12.1993, p. 4.

conversion of payments and accounts and the exchange of notes and coin, and bureaux de change and post offices;

(b) "national currency unit" is the unit of the currency of a participating Member State, as that unit is defined on the day before the start of the third stage of economic and monetary union; "the national currency unit" in this Recommendation refers to the national currency unit of the Member State where the bank making the conversion is located;

(c) "participating Member States" are those Member States which adopt the single currency in accordance with the Treaty;

(d) "conversion" is the change of denomination of a monetary amount from the national currency unit to the euro unit and vice versa at the conversion rate, in accordance with the provisions of Regulation (EC) No 1103/97;

(e) "euro unit" is the currency unit of the euro as referred to in the second sentence of Article 2 of the draft Council Regulation on the introduction of the euro;

(f) "transitional period" is the period beginning on 1 January 1999 and ending on 31 December 2001;

(g) "final period" is the period beginning on 1 January 2002 and ending on 30 June 2002 at the latest, which period may vary in length according to participating Member State, under the terms of the draft Council Regulation on the introduction of the euro;

(h) "conversion rate" is the irrevocably fixed rate adopted for the currency of each participating Member State by the Council according to the first sentence of Article 109l(4) of the Treaty;

(i) "incoming payments" are payments received for crediting to accounts of beneficiaries;

(j) "outgoing payments" are payments made by debiting accounts of originators;

(k) "accounts" are all types of accounts with banks (as defined in (a)) and include deposit accounts, current accounts, mortgage accounts and securities accounts.

Article 2

Standard of good practice

Banks should implement, in accordance with Article 4, a standard of good practice on conversion without charge, which should include:

(A) PRACTICE THAT THE COMMISSION CONSIDERS TO BE LEGALLY REQUIRED:

(i) the conversion without charge of incoming payments from the national currency unit to the euro unit and vice versa during the transitional period;

(ii) the conversion without charge of accounts from the national currency unit to the euro unit at the end of the transitional period;

(iii) the charging for services denominated in the euro unit at fees no different from those for identical services denominated in the national currency unit.

(B) OTHER RECOMMENDED PRACTICE:

(i) the conversion without charge of outgoing payments from the national currency unit to the euro unit and vice versa during the transitional period;

(ii) the conversion without charge of accounts from the national currency unit to the euro unit during the transitional period;

(iii) the exchange without charge to their customers (namely the account holders) of "household amounts" of the national banknotes and coin for euro banknotes and coin during the final period. Banks should quantify "household amounts" by volume and frequency in a transparent manner.

Article 3

Transparency

1. For all conversions between any national currency unit and the euro unit and vice versa, and for all exchanges of banknotes and coin of participating Member States, banks should show clearly the application of the conversion rates in accordance with the provisions of Regulation (EC) No 1103/97, and should identify separately from the conversion rate any charges for any kind whatever which have been applied.

2. Where banks charge for conversions and exchanges which are not included in Article 2 or where banks do not implement one or more of the provisions of Article 2(b), they should provide clear and transparent information concerning those conversion charges or exchange charges by providing their customers with:

   (a) prior *(ex ante)* written information on any conversion charges or exchange charges which they propose to apply, and

   (b) specific information *(ex post)* on any conversion charges or exchange charges which have been applied, on bank and cardholder statements and any other means used for communicating with the customer. This information should demonstrate clearly to their customers the application of the conversion rates in accordance with the provisions of Regulation (EC) No 1103/97, with any conversion charges or exchange charges being identified separately from the conversion rate and from any other charges of any kind whatever which are applied.

Article 4

Implementation

1. Banks should implement the standard of good practice by 1 January 1999 at the latest, and earlier in the case of Article 3 if this is technically feasible.

2. Banks should inform their customers as soon as possible before 1 January 1999 about whether and to what extent they will implement the standard of good practice.

3. Implementation of the standard of good practice should be publicised by any method which demonstrates that banks comply with the standard, such as:

   (a) professional codes of conduct;

   (b) provisions within a national changeover plan;

   (c) displaying a "conversion symbol" which demonstrates that banks comply with the standard of good practice. A scheme to confer the right to display a conversion symbol should be worked out at national level by the parties concerned, if and when it is considered appropriate.

Article 5

Other recommended measures

The competent authorities of the Member States are invited to consider how best to facilitate the exchange, free of charge, of banknotes and coin denominated in the national currency unit in reasonable amounts and at reasonable frequencies, for banknotes and coin denominated in the euro unit during the final period, in the case of consumers having no bank account.

Article 6

Final provision

Member States are invited to support the implementation of this Recommendation.

Article 7

Addressees

This Recommendation is addressed to the Member States and to banks and their associations.

Done at Brussels, 23 April 1998.

For the Commission
YVES-THIBAULT DE SILGUY
Member of the Commission

INDEX